Asian Economies

History, Institutions, and Structures

Jamus Jerome Lim

Registered Office(s)
John Wiley & Sons, Inc., 111 River Street, Hoboken, NJ 07030, USA
John Wiley & Sons Ltd, The Atrium, Southern Gate, Chichester, West Sussex, PO19 8SQ, UK

Editorial Office
The Atrium, Southern Gate, Chichester, West Sussex, PO19 8SQ, UK

For details of our global editorial offices, customer services, and more information about Wiley products
visit us at www.wiley.com.

Library of Congress Cataloging-in-Publication Data

    Names: Lim, Jamus Jerome, author.
    Title: Asian economies : history, institutions, and structures / Jamus Jerome Lim.
    Description: Hoboken, NJ : Wiley, 2024. | Includes index.
    Identifiers: LCCN 2023050775 (print) | LCCN 2023050776 (ebook) | ISBN 9781119913160 (cloth) |
    ISBN 9781119913184 (adobe pdf) | ISBN 9781119913191 (epub)
    Subjects: LCSH: Economic development—Asia—History—21st century. | Asia—Economic conditions—
    21st century. | Finance—Technological innovations—Asia.
    Classification: LCC HC412 .L565 2024 (print) | LCC HC412 (ebook) | DDC 338.9500905—dc23/eng/20231
    LC record available at https://lccn.loc.gov/2023050775
    LC ebook record available at https://lccn.loc.gov/2023050776

Cover Design: Wiley
Cover Image: © blunameAline/Shutterstock
SKY10066908_021024

A mi bella y paciente esposa, Eneida. Te quiero mucho

Contents

Preface

Introduction

This book's title—*Asian Economies: History, Institutions, and Structures*—was deliberately chosen, to capture the book's emphasis on the enduring legacy of economic history on future prospects, the vast importance of political-economic institutions in shaping this trajectory, and the dramatic way that existing economic structures differ between Asian countries, which in turn condition their approach to economic development.

Also implicit in the title is the comparative nature of each country's development journey, as well as the relationship with the rest of the world, both of which we emphasize. Despite their continental nature—which often afford isolation and inward orientation—the economies of Asia have often been deeply integrated with each other, as well as the world at large. We therefore follow this cue, in our treatment of each country and region.

Motivation and Audience

Why another book on Asian economies? To be candid, there are a host of both more specialized references, such as the excellent books by Naughton (2018) on the Chinese economy, Panagariya (2010) on the Indian economy, and Ito and Hoshi (2020) on the Japanese one—and while they are often far more exhaustive, they are often written from the perspective of the economy in question.[1]

There are also books in this vein that take on a comparative perspective; Bardhan's (2013) comparison of China and India, Vogel's (1993) take on the

---

1 Naughton, B.J., *The Chinese Economy: Adaptation and Growth*, 2nd ed. (Cambridge, MA: MIT Press, 2018); Panagariya, A., *India: The Emerging Giant*, 1st ed. (Oxford: Oxford University Press, 2010); Ito, T. and T. Hoshi, *The Japanese Economy*, 2nd ed. (Cambridge, MA: MIT Press, 2020).

Newly Industrialized Economies (NIEs), and Noland and Pack's (2007) sweeping dissection of the Arab economies come to mind.[2]

There are also collected volumes of essays—handbook-like tomes such as Kaur and Singh (2014)—but these tend to be far less constrained in their scope, and single essays within may be repetitive or incomplete.[3]

Finally, there are books written more for a lay audience, where most recently, the rise of China and India has inspired a cottage industry. Such paperbacks are often featured prominently in airport bookstores, with provocative titles such as *Capitalism with Chinese Characteristics*, *The Argumentative Indian*, and *Vietnam: Rising Dragon*.[4] While wonderful reads, they often represent a particular take, and may not be as heavily referenced as the present book attempts to be.

This book—which emerged from many years of lecturing on Asian Economies at ESSEC Business School—positions itself within the gaps left behind by these other efforts. When I first started teaching the course, I felt bereft of a singular text that captured the breadth and scope of the economies across the world's largest continent. I was left with assigning key chapters within existing texts, but while these did a serviceable job (and exposed students to a wider variety of perspectives), they did not have a coherent narrative nor consistent approach. I wanted a book that would more closely match the needs of my course, which was catered to students who would go on to become practitioners, often in multinational corporations or financial institutions, but who may not have the sort of deep economics background or training that upper-level economics majors or graduate students could be expected to possess.

I wasn't entirely satisfied with the books targeted at a wider audience, either. While these offered important (if idiosyncratic) insights and painted vivid vignettes of contemporary events, they did not deliver in terms of the disciplined theoretical framework that I wanted my students to acquire. I wanted to be able to offer at least some basic analytical tools familiar to practicing economists. Many were in sufficiently steeped in the data for my taste, and I felt that it was important that my students gained a comfort level with essential quantitative knowledge.

---

2 Bardhan, P., *Emerging Giants: Feet of Clay* (Princeton, NJ: Princeton University Press, 2013); Vogel, E.F., *The Four Little Dragons: The Spread of Industrialization in East Asia* (Cambridge, MA: Harvard University Press, 1993); Noland, M. and H. Pack, *The Arab Economies in a Changing World*, 2nd ed. (Washington, DC: Peterson Institute for International Economics, 2007).

3 Kaur, I.N. and N. Singh (Eds.), *The Oxford Handbook of the Economics of the Pacific Rim* (New York: Oxford University Press, 2014).

4 Huang, Y. *Capitalism with Chinese Characteristics: Entrepreneurship and the State* (Cambridge: Cambridge University Press, 2008); Sen, A., *The Argumentative Indian* (London: Allen Lane, 2005); Hayton, B., *Vietnam: Rising Dragon* (New Haven, CT: Yale University Press, 2011).

Approach and Innovations

My hope is that this book fills in the gaps that currently exist in the literature on Asian economies. While it can be profitably deployed as a primary textbook for upper-level undergraduate courses in regional economic studies, or graduate-level classes for non-economics majors—I certainly plan to do so—it can also be used by professionals with less familiarity with this part of the world who seek an in-depth introduction to the region, or by those who already possess some context but want a systematic reference work for diving deeper.

In this vein, this book has several pedagogical innovations that I hope will help with this goal:

- A consistent treatment of each economy or region, with the lens provided by both economic geography and history, before an introduction of the main economic structures and institutions associated with the country/region, which provide essential context. Economic progress is viewed both in a comparative context, as well as set against the country's interactions with the rest of the world. Each chapter then moves on to deal with the latest contemporary developments, before closing with prospects for their future.
- Each chapter is accompanied by a capsule introduction (available online) to a set of analytical tools that is especially relevant to the particular economy at hand. For instance, in trying to understand the growth experience of China, the tools of accounting in the Solow-Swan growth model are extremely useful; similarly, the importance of openness for the export-oriented development of the NIEs is explained via the Ricardian trade model, and fluctuations faced in the Japanese economy by a variation of the Salter-Swan open-economy disequilibrium model.
- As far as possible, each chapter is richly endowed with figures and tables. This serves to cultivate an empirical mindset—so important to the modern observer—as well as build familiarity with essential facts and figures for the economies being discussed.
- Discussion of topics is done in three ways. First, they are used to provide a deeper dive into specific case studies (riffing off the main text), such as the 2016 Indian banknote demonetization or the 1992 Japanese asset bubble. Second, they are used to provide expositional detail for unique structures and institutions, such as Korean *chaebol* or Singapore's band-basket-crawl exchange rate regime. Third, they could offer the intellectual history of ideas that played prominent roles in Asian economies, such as the East Asian export-oriented industrialization model, or the political economy of the West Asian resource curse.
- Creates discussion of political-economy elements—institutions, regimes, and actors—that tend to be de-emphasized by treatments that are more heavily focused on economics. This choice is deliberate: the only way to fully understand the dramatic, heterogenous development trajectories of Asian economies is to recognize that political economy had at least as much to do with their economic evolution, as purely technocratic considerations.

A Note on Nomenclature

This book is, by design, comparative in nature. Hence, it is necessary to represent many quantitative economic statistics—such as gross domestic product (GDP), trade volumes, and financial metrics—in a comparable format and currency.

By and large, these are shown in terms of constant (inflation-adjusted to a single base year) United States dollars (USD), unless the statistic is applied to a contemporaneous measure, in which case, current (nominal) USD is used. On occasion, where justified, such statistics may also be shown in terms of local currency, or in terms of an international dollar.

Why constant USD? Well, for starters, the Greenback (for the moment) remains the global reserve currency, and the U.S. the world's largest economy. It is most familiar to audiences worldwide, and is easily converted into an alternative, preferred currency. The choice of adjusting for inflation is also logical; with diverse rates of inflation—both within a country and between them—it is useful to get a picture of the true—what economists call *real*—macroeconomic picture, undistorted by price differentials.

Some authors and books choose to represent economic statistics, especially for GDP, in terms of a purchasing power parity (PPP)-adjusted "international" dollar (Intl$).[5] We have chosen not to do so, in general, for three reasons. First, the USD is a visceral, widely held, and frequently traded currency, whereas the Intl$ is abstract and not accepted in any given country or territory. Second, in spite of their best efforts, PPP measures capture quality differentials only imperfectly; for instance, even with so-called hedonic adjustments, it is difficult to imagine that even the best-quality healthcare in Sri Lanka might be comparable to that received in South Korea; by the same token, many purchasers would (and did) shun the purchase of a Proton or Perodua (Malaysian), opting instead for a Mazda or Mitsubishi (Japanese). And third, for international business consultants and financial market players—potentially a significant readership for this book—it is generally profits or returns in a globally-accepted currency that matter most. However, in instances where we are thinking either in terms of the cost of living/quality of life (especially expressed in per capita incomes), or when it is the volume of economic activity that matters, we will work with PPP equivalents.

On occasion, we also report Gross National Product (GNP), when such a metric is more illustrative of the situation at hand. In most instances, there is little practical difference between the two metrics, since wealth held abroad tends to be small (GNP measures the value of output of nationals, as opposed

---

5 These are usually termed Geary-Khamis international dollars, a hypothetical monetary unit that accounts for differences in the ability of a given currency to purchase goods and services in different economies at a single point in time. 2000 is typically used as the temporal benchmark.

to GDP, which measures the value of output produced within a nation's borders). In Asia, significant divergences tend to be observed in Japan (which sustains a large positive net international investment position), as well as Lebanon and Turkey (because of their large diasporas).

In most instances, political boundaries for geographic representations are secondary for our purposes. For example, in representing Taiwan as a distinct economy, or Egypt as an economy within Asia, we are not implying any political positions on either the official names of the territories, international recognition (or not) of political status of the location, or even whether these economies should be treated as sovereign states.

By a similar token, we refer to economies by their simple common place-names, as it is their economic boundaries and influence that we are most concerned with. These are usually the ones most identifiable to the average reader, rather than official country names (hence, Korea instead of South Korea or Republic of Korea, or Turkey instead of Türkiye). For the same reason, we also eschew formal naming conventions (Taiwan instead of Republic of China, Iran instead of Islamic Republic of Iran).

Acknowledgments

No scholarly work, even a sole-authored one, is fully attributable to one person. I rest on the shoulders of those I have learned from. These span the fields for which this book covers: macroeconomics (Ken Kletzer, Aart Kraay, Carl Walsh), international (Joshua Aizenman, Phil McCalman), political economy (K.C. Fung, Don Wittman), development (Maureen Lewis, Hans Timmer), and Asian economies (Chua Siow Yue). Anastasia Tsilyk provided amazing research assistance, Olena Kalinina generated many of the beautiful maps and figures, Susan Dunsmore offered valuable copyediting, and Syd Ganaden was the impetus for launching this project.

Abbreviations

ADB: Asian Development Bank, a regional development bank, head-quartered in Manila, the Philippines, that extends development loans and provides economic advisory to member nations in Asia.

AIIB: Asian Infrastructure and Investment Bank, a multilateral development bank with members around the world, headquartered in Beijing, China, that extends infrastructure-related loans.

ASEAN: Association of Southeast Asian Nations, the main regional grouping for Southeast Asian economies, comprising 10 full member countries (Brunei, Cambodia, Indonesia, Laos, Malaysia, Myanmar, the Philippines, Singapore, Thailand, and Vietnam), and 2 observers (Papua and Timor-Leste).

BRI: Belt and Road Initiative, originally known as the "One Belt, One Road" (OBOR) project, is a global infrastructure and trade development strategy initiated by the Chinese government, that now includes around 150 countries and international organizations as participants.

BRICS: An acronym, first coined by Goldman Sachs Investment Research but since adopted by the referent nations themselves, for the major emerging economies of Brazil, Russia, India, and China. The group was formally constituted in 2010 with the inclusion of South Africa, and, in 2024, further enfolds Argentina, Egypt, Ethiopia, Iran, Saudi Arabia, and the United Arab Emirates.

CAREC: Central Asia Regional Economic Cooperation Program, a program established under the auspices of the Asian Development Bank to promote economic cooperation among the economies of Central Asia, South Asia, and the Caucasus.

DM: Developed markets, a category of economies that includes most advanced economies with deep financial markets. While no universal categorization exists, these often include Asian economies such as Hong Kong and Singapore.

EM: Emerging markets, a category of economies that includes most developing economies with reasonably mature financial markets. While no universal categorization exists, these often include Asian economies such as China and India, but also South Korea, Taiwan, and the United Arab Emirates.

EU/EMU: European Union/European Monetary Union, an economic and political union of 27 member states within Europe, of which 19 members utilize a common currency (the euro), and hence are part of the EMU.

FDI: Foreign direct investment, typically the largest and most stable component of international financial flows, and a key component of Asian economies' development strategy of welcoming capital from abroad.

G7/G20: The Group of 7 (20) major economies worldwide that have met regularly to discuss matters of global economic governance. The G7 (G20) comprise Canada, France, Germany, Italy, Japan, the United Kingdom, and the United States (plus Argentina, Australia, Brazil, China, India, Indonesia, Mexico, Russia, Saudi Arabia, South Africa, South Korea, Turkey, and the European Union).

GCC: Gulf Cooperation Council, a common market among a group of hydrocarbon-rich, high-income economies, comprising Bahrain, Kuwait, Oman, Qatar, Saudi Arabia, and the United Arab Emirates.

ICT: Information and communications technology, the hard and soft infrastructure and components that enable modern digital computing, networking, and information exchange.

IMF: International Monetary Fund, an international financial organization that, together with the World Bank, constitute the two original "Bretton Woods" institutions, formed in the aftermath of World War II to govern international financial flows within the global financial system.

N11:   A term coined by Goldman Sachs Investment Research to refer to the "Next 11" economies poised to become the among the largest and most dynamic emerging markets: Bangladesh, Egypt, Indonesia, Iran, Mexico, Nigeria, Pakistan, the Philippines, South Korea, Turkey, and Vietnam.

NIE: Newly Industrialized Economies, sometimes referred to as the Asian Dragons, comprising Hong Kong, Singapore, South Korea, and Taiwan. The next wave of NIEs in Asia, sometimes called the Asian Tigers, include economies such as Malaysia, Indonesia, and Thailand, although there is, as yet, little consensus that these countries have attained NIE status.

OECD: Organisation for Economic Co-operation and Development, a group of industrialized nations often used as a proxy for advanced-economy status.

OPEC: Organization of the Petroleum Exporting Countries, a cartel arrangement of 13 major oil-producing countries, all located in developing economies, with 5 (Iran, Iraq, Kuwait, Saudi Arabia, and the UAE) located in Western Asia. The grouping accounts for about a third of global production and claims almost three-quarters of proven reserves.

OPEC+:   A looser grouping of OPEC nations plus an additional 10 non-OPEC oil-producing economies that may participate in OPEC supply control initiatives, which includes Azerbaijan, Kazakhstan (Central Asia), Bahrain, Oman (Western Asia), Brunei, and Indonesia (Southeast Asia).

SEZ: Special Economic Zone, also sometimes known as Export Processing Zone, which is an area subject to distinct business and trade laws from the rest of the country, and usually subject to no taxes or tariffs, so long as goods produced within the zone are designated for export.

SME: Small and medium-sized enterprises, usually defined as firms that employ less than 200 employees and earning revenue below a certain threshold, although specific thresholds differ.

SOE: State-owned enterprises, usually defined as a firm that is wholly or partially owned by the government, and often directed to fulfill nonmarket objectives.

TFP: Total factor productivity, which is a measure of the contribution of technological progress and efficiency of combining factors of production, after accounting for observable contributors to economic growth, such as physical and human capital accumulation.

UN: United Nations, an umbrella intergovernmental organization, formed in the aftermath of World War II, with the aim of maintaining international peace and security and promoting international cooperation and relations between countries. A host of multilateral agencies, including the Bretton Woods institutions (the IMF and the World Bank), the World Health Organization (WHO), UN Educational, Scientific, and Cultural Organization (UNESCO), and UN Children's Fund (UNICEF), fall within the UN ambit.

USSR: Union of Soviet Socialist Republics, a country that spanned much of Eurasia between 1922 and 1991, including all the modern Central Asian nations.

World Bank: World Bank Group, comprising five subsidiary international financial organizations (the International Bank for Reconstruction and Development, IBRD, the International Development Organization, IDA, the International Finance Corporation, IFC, the Multilateral Investment Guarantee Agency, MIGA, and the International Centre for Settlement of Investment Disputes, ICSID), an international financial organization that, together with the IMF, constitutes the two original "Bretton Woods" institutions, formed in the aftermath of World War II to conduct international development lending within the global financial system.

WTO: World Trade Organization, the successor organization to the General Agreement on Tariffs and Trade (GATT), which is the main multilateral agreement governing international trade between nations.

Introduction: Asia as a Continent in Flux

[T]here is a small group of countries which are quite well off and a much larger group of extremely poor countries . . . countries in the former group are on the whole firmly settled in a pattern of continuing economic development, while in the latter group progress is slower, as many countries are in constant danger of not being able to lift themselves out of stagnation or even of losing ground so far as average income levels are concerned.

—Gunnar Myrdal (1898–1987),
Swedish economist and Nobel Prize-winner

[M]ost of East Asia's extraordinary growth is due to superior accumulation of physical and human capital . . . [i]n this sense there is nothing 'miraculous' about the East Asian economies' success; each has performed these essential functions of growth better than most other economies.

—Lewis Preston (1926–95), American banker and
World Bank President[1]

Introduction

On August 15, 1945, Emperor Hirohito announced Japan's surrender, which brought an end to the hostilities of World War II. Asia lay in ruins. The Empire of Japan had invaded or occupied virtually all of East and Southeast Asia. Western Asia had been part of the European theater, just a few short decades after the previous world war had sparked the final collapse of the six-century-old Ottoman Empire. South and Central Asia, while insulated from the direct ravages of the war, had been indirectly dragged into the conflict; the British

---

1 Birdsall, N., J. Campos, W.M. Corden, C-S. Kim, L. MacDonald, H. Pack, R. Sabor, J. Stiglitz, and M. Uy (Eds.), *The East Asian Miracle: Economic Growth and Public Policy* (Oxford: Oxford University Press, 1993).

Asian Economies: History, Institutions, and Structures, First Edition. Jamus Jerome Lim.
© 2024 John Wiley & Sons Ltd. Published 2024 by John Wiley & Sons Ltd.

Indian Army had been recruited to fight in West and Southeast Asia (along with North Africa), and Central Asia was likewise roped in by the Soviet Union to host refugees and deportees after the German invasion.

Amidst this destruction, Asia began to rebuild. It was starting from a very low base. China hosted coastal cities (such as Guangzhou and Shanghai) that had, over the course of their history, enjoyed significant prosperity. But by the end of the Qing dynasty, the Middle Kingdom had fallen far behind its European counterparts. India, for centuries the world's richest country, had likewise seen deindustrialization and stagnation after close to two hundred years of British dominion.

Despite millennia of being a key player in the global economy, it became increasingly difficult for contemporary observers to see Asia as anything but a relative backwater, doomed to obscurity in global economic and political affairs. The action was all in the West, in Western Europe as well as North America. Even Latin America, which had received significant migrant and capital inflows from the West, was often perceived as having more potential to succeed.

But developments over the course of the subsequent half-century turned these expectations and predictions on their head. Japan—the first industrialized economy in Asia—had been devastated by the ravages of war, and few expected the nation to rebound as quickly as it did after a humiliating military defeat. The oil age was only in its infancy, and the very modest discoveries in Western Asia gave little indication that black gold would subsequently be a central driver for the rise of hitherto peripheral economies, such as Saudi Arabia and the United Arab Emirates, making them among the highest-income nations in the world.

Today, cities across the Asian continent, from Dubai in the west, to Tokyo in the far east, to Singapore at the southeastern tip, are gleaming metropolises, often surpassing the wealth (and often opulence) of the richest cities in the West and, indeed, the rest of the world. Many Asian economies did so with idiosyncratic development formulae, albeit with common themes: robust accumulation of factors of production, such as labor, capital, and education, relatively open trading regimes, and the rapid importation of technological ideas from the developed world. It managed to do so with agility and aplomb, catapulting its constituents at an accelerated rate into the league of major economies.

This book will trace the rise (or, perhaps, re-emergence) of Asian economies. It will do so from the perspective of not just its businesses, workers, and macroeconomic environments, but also draw in the key features of its labor markets, educational frameworks, market structure, and political-economy institutions. We will embark on our explorations with a mindset that does not treat these idiosyncratic institutions as aberrations from Western-style capitalism, but rather as alternative modes of modern economic organization.

We will take both geographical features and historical evolution seriously. Asian nations encompass virtually every possible geographic configuration, and these varied landscapes and natural endowments have shaped the course of their development over centuries. Their histories are equally rich, and in cases such as in China, India, Egypt, and Mesopotamia, were the basis of whole civilizations that stretch back thousands of years.

And we will use these insights from the past not just as a lens to the present, but as a means to possibly peer into their future. The legacy of the past has resulted in these modern economies' structures and institutions, of course, but they will likely also direct the manner by which their subsequent development plays out. Many today may wonder whether Asia's rise will be sustained, and if the region will become ever-more important in the future global economy. Our answer is unequivocally yes, but this does not mean that we should take this rise for granted. Challenges abound, and only by confronting and resolving these constraints to growth will the region achieve its full potential.

The Diversity of Asian Economies

Asian Economies Include Rich and Poor

Asian economies are incredibly heterogeneous. Asia hosts some of the world's richest countries: from the world's second-richest large economy (Japan, after the United States), to one of its richest small economies (Singapore), along with economies that have only become remarkably wealthy within a generation (Brunei, Qatar, and the United Arab Emirates).

But Asia is also home to incredibly poor nations: North Korea is possibly the world's poorest economy, and Afghanistan, East Timor, Myanmar, and Tajikistan all number among the world's least wealthy. Even India—now the second-largest emerging economy, after China—remains the country with the world's largest number of poor people.

And in between, one finds the entire range of possible outcomes; from the economies that are belatedly finding a footing in their development journey and enjoying a growth spurt (such as Bangladesh, the Philippines, Turkmenistan, and Vietnam), to those that enjoyed their phase of accelerated growth, but are now confronting the classic middle-income trap (one thinks of economies such as those of Iran, Lebanon, or Malaysia), to those that appear locked into prolonged periods of anemic growth (Nepal and Yemen come to mind). A map of the world, weighted by per capita incomes, reveals an Asia that is both less prominent than might be suggested by its geographic footprint, but also featuring economies that are more important than they may seem based on physical size alone (Figure 0.1).

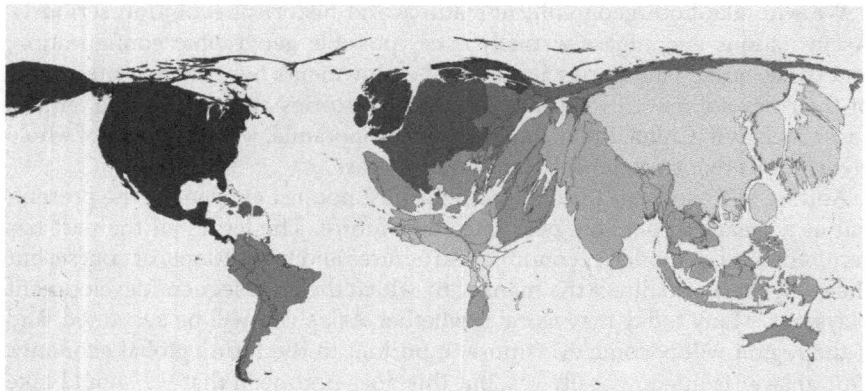

Figure 0.1 A map of the world in terms of per capita GDP becomes almost unrecognizable, as the economic footprint of each country is reshaped in a manner disproportionate to its geographic one.

Variations in Income Differences Stem from Political-Economic Distinctions

Behind these stark outcomes are economic, political, and institutional differences that have led to such outcomes. Many economic structures unique to the region—the mega-conglomerates (such as Japan's *keiretsu* or South Korea's *chaebol*), the prevalence of state-owned or government-linked firms (certainly in China, but also in highly capitalistic economies such as Singapore or the UAE), or the overall dependence on large banks for financial intermediation—were in turn born out of political, policy, and institutional histories.

Much of Asia has, like the rest of the non-Western world, borne the burden of colonization (or, at least, had more than a passing brush with it). India was the jewel in the crown of the British Empire, which also had a presence in Western and Southeast Asia. The Russian Empire dramatically altered Central Asia, both before and during the Cold War. Vestiges of French influence remain in Indochina and Lebanon, as well as in concession territories (such as Shanghai). The Dutch, the Portuguese, and the United States all had forays in Asia, and even the Japanese—belated entrants to the game—held colonies in Asia.

These colonial histories then shaped the sort of political-economic institutions that we find in Asian economies even today. The choice of central planning as opposed to the free market—or some middle-ground *dirigisme*—is the most obvious, but also in terms of the choice of import-substituting relative to export-oriented industrialization strategies, socialist versus capitalist ownership structures, and autocratic or democratic political regimes.

Common Features of Asia's Development Experience

Despite these nontrivial differences, there are also significant commonalities in the development experience, especially on the macroeconomic front.

A Reliance on Factor Accumulation as a Growth Engine

Principal among these is a reliance on factor accumulation as a primary engine for rapid, sustained growth. Riding on a steady pickup in the birthrate following World War II—a phenomenon sometimes referred to as the post-war Baby Boom—Asian economies (along with many others worldwide) enjoyed the fruits of a demographic tailwind that enlarged their working-age laborforce, providing a key input into economies that had hitherto remained mostly poor and backward.

Most Asian economies then channeled their relatively low-skilled workforces toward industrial processes, taking advantage of the lower wages afforded by surplus agricultural workers in the rural economy.[2] Soon, "Made in Asia" became virtually synonymous with low-end manufactured goods, from processed food to clothing and textiles to low-cost consumer electronics.

Labor is only a third of the story, of course. Many of these young populations exhibited the (perhaps stereotypical) trait of high-saving Asian cultures, which provided much of the necessary grist to the mill of capital accumulation, and proved complementary to labor inputs.[3] Asian households and firms simply saved more, on average, and this was an important growth factor, given the strong relationship between investment rates and saving patterns.[4] Where domestic saving fell short, many were able to tap into the global pool of foreign saving and welcome foreign investment via financial inflows.

The stress on capital accumulation has led the leading industrial nations in Asia to become among the most capital-intensive nations in the world. The share of capital stock (as a share of output) in economies such as China, Japan, and South Korea now clearly outstrips that of Western industrialized nations, even those commonly regarded as capital-rich (such as the United States). Asia boasts the highest density of industrial robots—accounting for two-thirds of all installed capacity worldwide—and perhaps more poignantly, is expected to continue to increase these investments, even as other regions pare back (Figure 0.2).

2 Lewis, A. "Economic Development with Unlimited Supplies of Labor," *Manchester School* 22(2) (1954): 139–191.
3 Horioka, C. and A. Terada-Hagiwara, "The Determinants and Long-Term Projections of Saving Rates in Developing Asia," *Japan and the World Economy* 24(2) (2012): 128–137.
4 Feldstein, M. and C. Horioka, "Domestic Saving and International Capital Flows," *Economic Journal* 90(358) (1980): 314–329.

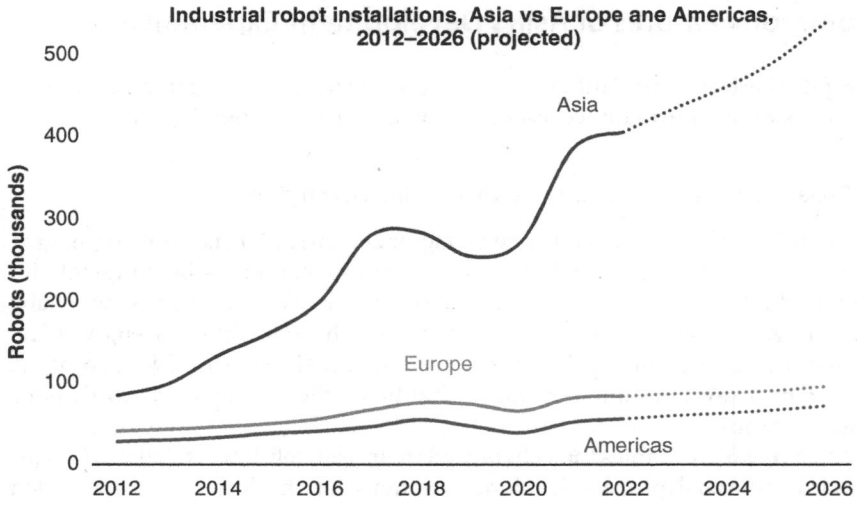

Figure 0.2 Today, Asia has the highest density of industrial robot deployment worldwide, accounting for two-thirds of all installed capacity (with China, at around half of this share, being the largest). Asia has also steadily invested more—and is projected to continue to do so—relative to other regions.

The final third of the story was the rapid increase in educational attainment among Asian economies. This was born of the explicit recognition that raw labor, alone, would be insufficient to drive growth over the long run. Rather, appropriate learning and training would provide the additional skills necessary to ensure a productive workforce. Accordingly, Asian economies ramped up their schooling efforts.

In the 1950s, Asian economies mostly started off behind other developing regions, such as Eastern Europe, Sub-Saharan Africa, and Latin America (Figure 0.3). However, by 2010, the average years of schooling in East, South, and Western Asia had caught up and—in the case of East Asia—largely exceeded those of other developing areas, except when compared to Eastern Europe. These remarkable gains offset the slowing of population expansion—which has unrelentingly begun to work its way to parts of East and Southeast Asia—as improved human capital quality made up for reduced quantity.

Together with increases in these so-called proximate drivers of growth—labor, physical, and human capital—was an emphasis on specialization in production, often as part of a disintegrated production chain,[5] where each country would produce only specific components of a larger product. Hence, a car may

---

5 Feenstra, R., "Integration of Trade and Disintegration of Production in the Global Economy," *Journal of Economic Perspectives* 12(4) (1998): 31–50.

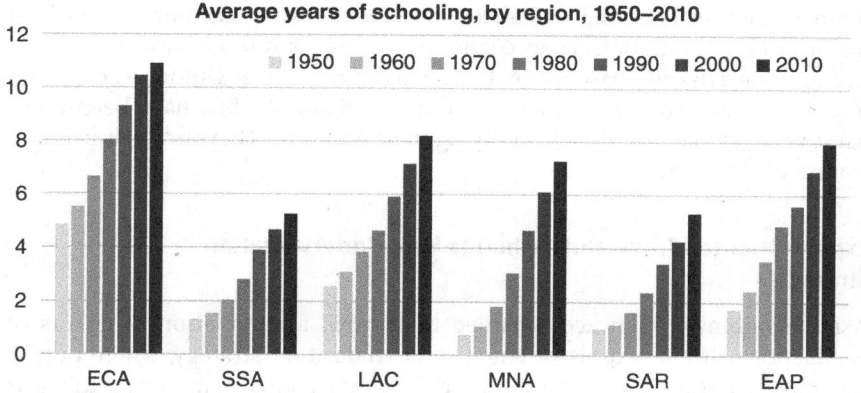

Figure 0.3 Eastern Europe (ECA), Sub-Saharan Africa (SSA), and Latin America (LAC) started off mostly ahead of in terms of educational attainment relative to Asian developing regions, such as Western (MNA), South (SAR), and East (EAP) Asia. However, by 2010, schooling in many Asian regions had caught up or exceeded those of the rest of the developing world.

be designed in Japan, use circuit boards and semiconductors manufactured in South Korea and Taiwan, paired with tires from Indonesia, a brake system from Indonesia, a chassis from Thailand, and fuel pipes from Vietnam. The final assembly and redistribution back to developed markets may occur in China, with marketing provided by a Singaporean firm and after-sales support by call centers in the Philippines.

Eventually, however, "graduating" Asian economies began to climb up the value-added ladder into services—while gradually scaling back on manufacturing production—to become post-industrial economies. In essence, most Asian economies followed a tried-and-tested script for development; indeed, some would argue that the move from primary to secondary to tertiary-dominated economies is the very *definition* of development.

This approach was followed, with notable success, by the Newly Industrialized Economies (NIEs)—Hong Kong, Korea, Singapore, and Taiwan—but has been replicated by many others across the continent, from those in the Far East (China) and Southeast Asia (the Asian Tigers of Indonesia, Malaysia, and Thailand), to Central Asia (Turkmenistan) and its western edges (Iran). South Asia has, somewhat belatedly, also made a foray into decentralized supply chains, with India and Pakistan following the lead set by Bangladesh.[6]

There are notable exceptions to this development pattern. India and the Philippines have experienced premature deindustrialization, with services in

---

6 Wignaraja, G., "The Great Supply Chain Shift from China to South Asia?", *Indian Council on Global Relations*, Essay Paper 34 (Mumbai: Gateway House, 2023).

these economies booming well ahead of manufacturing reaching any point of maturity or saturation. Certain economies—such as Kazakhstan—had inherited an industrialized base while it was part of the Soviet Union. And certain resource-reliant countries, such as Brunei or Saudi Arabia, have been comparatively less successful in diversifying their economies beyond their primary commodity export.

Export-Oriented Trade and Exchange Rate Undervaluation Strategies

Asian economies often accompanied their rapid accumulation of factors of production with an export-oriented industrialization strategy, where output was targeted at a global, rather than a local, market. In some ways, this was necessitated by the disintegrated value-chain approach, given how the routine import and export of parts and components are essential to the model.

But this choice was not a given. At the time of independence, many Asian governments had a choice for their industrialization strategy: export orientation, or (what had seemed to be) the equally compelling option of import substitution. Import substitution—where trade protection would be offered to domestic firms as a reliable outlet for their production, while they were still discovering their manufacturing chops—was chosen by many a regional policymaker, but when the limitations of the model became increasingly evident by the 1980s, most pivoted toward export orientation, even as they maintained certain aspects of protectionism (Figure 0.4).[7] Asia embraced globalization way before globalization became sexy.

It is important to stress, however, that little within the paradigm of export orientation requires completely unfettered trade or unvarnished free-market capitalism.[8] Indeed, Korea and Taiwan are two countries that—even as they moved away from a developmental state—deployed industrial policy (production subsidies for favored sectors) and commercial policy (import tariffs to allow infant industries to grow), especially during the earlier development phase. Others, especially India, have remained markedly recalcitrant in offering market access, especially in agriculture.

The omnipresent state did not limit itself to international trade. International finance, as practiced in Asia, includes significant elements of state interventionism as well. This is most pronounced in exchange rate policy, where

---

7 Stubbs, R., "War and Economic Development: Export-Oriented Industrialization in East and Southeast Asia," *Comparative Politics* 31(3) (1999): 337–355.
8 Chang, H-J., *The East Asian Development Experience: The Miracle, the Crisis and the Future* (London: Zed Books, 2006).

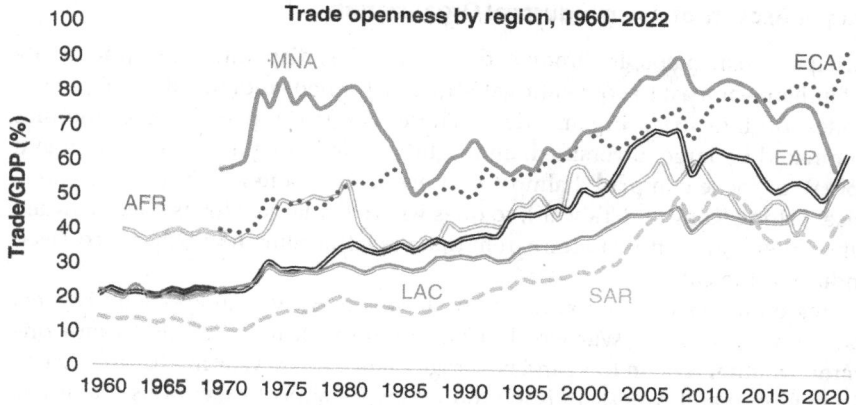

Figure 0.4 By the late 1980s, the limits of import-substituting industrialization had become evident, and most Asian economies that did not initially adopt export orientation pivoted toward the strategy. This resulted in a belated catch-up of trade openness in the region to global norms.

undervalued exchange rates—usually effected with some form of financial repression or outright capital controls—served as an invaluable complement to export-led growth.[9]

The upshot of such interventions to suppress the natural movements of the exchange rate has resulted in, on one hand, the need for institutions to manage the massive reserve build-up (which results from greater-than-normal purchases of the local currency), and, on the other, a sensitivity of policymakers to the ever-present possibility of currency and balance of payments crises (which is the outcome of unexpected sales of domestic currency). This explains, in no small part, the ubiquity of sovereign wealth funds in Asian states, as well as the recurrent financial crises in others, including the two major financial shocks experienced in recent decades: the Asian financial crisis of 1997/1998, and the global financial crisis of 2007/2008.

Distinct Elements of Asian Economic Organization

To the extent that one is able to draw finer distinctions between Asian economies, it is in their industrial organization, as well as other elements of microeconomic structure.

---

9 Dooley, M., D. Folkerts-Landau, and P. Garber, "The Revived Bretton Woods System," *International Journal of Finance and Economics* 9 (2004): 307–313.

Unique Aspects of Asian Industrial Organization

Perhaps most palpable among these are the disparate and potentially unfamiliar—at least to conventional Western-trained students of economics—modes of industrial organization. These designs range from economies dominated by large, diversified, and tightly-linked conglomerates (Japan and Korea), to those comprised almost entirely of small and medium-sized enterprises (Hong Kong and Taiwan), to ones where the largest firms have crowded out smaller competitors to the extent that the latter remain mostly micro-sized (India and the UAE).

Conglomerates can be found on Western shores, of course—think Diageo, Fiat, LVMH, or Time Warner—but these tend to lean primarily toward one sector, whether it be in food and beverages, autos, luxury, or media (the British Virgin Group and American Koch Industries are almost exceptions that prove the rule). But Asian conglomerates frequently span the gamut of sectors, and for Japanese *keiretsus*, even embed within the group a full-scale financial institution.

Similarly, some Western economies—notably Italy with its *distretti industriali*, or Germany with its *Mittelstand*—include a preponderance of smaller firms. But these segments of the economy tend to function both efficiently and relatively independently of one another, rather than being bound in symbiotic networks and overlapping corporate relationships, both informal and formal, which are common in China (where it is known as *guanxi*), Japan (the *kyōryoku kai* and *kinō-teki shudan*), Singapore (industrial parks), Taiwan (*chanye juluo*), and Vietnam (*khu công nghiệp*).[10]

This has led some observers to even brand distinctions drawn along market structure lines as "varieties of capitalism."[11] But the line is often drawn mainly between liberal market economies (such as the Anglo-Saxon economies) and coordinated market economies (those on mainland Europe). Yet this characterization—while useful insofar as it also emphasizes the unique approaches Europe employs for industrial relations between employers and employees—papers over some significant differences in how companies operate in the Asian context.[12]

This is especially so because the state often plays a much greater role in Asian economies, both during the developmental phase, as well as on an ongoing

---

10 The exception here may be Italy, which has the largest number of small and medium-sized enterprises (SMEs), and has among the lowest average enterprise size within the EU. Italian SMEs retain competitiveness by banding together in clusters, not unlike those in industrial parks and special economic zones across East Asia.

11 Hall, P. and D. Soskice, *Varieties of Capitalism: The Institutional Foundations of Comparative Advantage* (Oxford: Oxford University Press, 2001).

12 Hundt, D. and J. Uttam, *Varieties of Capitalism in Asia: Beyond the Developmental State* (London: Palgrave Macmillan. 2017).

basis. This is sometimes referred to with a broad brush as "state capitalism,"[13] but again this term obscures the wide range of ways that the state intrudes into economic relationships in Asian economies, which go beyond regulation and enforcement, to also include more collaborative interventions such as subsidies and tax breaks for favored sectors, or government control of key inputs to production (such as land or energy), or even direct involvement via state-owned enterprises or government-linked firms.

But it goes beyond the state. Asian firms—even those that are clear competitors—frequently recognize the benefits of exploiting economies of scale from supplier networks, and cooperate with each other (as well as the state) to ensure these remain viable. But just as many seek to sign exclusive distribution rights with Western firms for their home countries, and adopt a trader or franchisee mindset, with little desire for additional innovation or value creation of their own (beyond expanding the size of the market). Others exploit cozy connections with the political elite, so much so that influential business groups end up routinely offering campaign or personal contributions, creating jobs in politically important districts, or creating comfortable internships or sinecures for the political class.[14]

The Lesser Importance of Trade Unions for Labor and Greater Use of Banks for Capital

Labor market institutions, such as trade unions, stakeholder management, and other forms of social protection (for example, unemployment insurance or defined-benefit pension systems), also tend to feature less in Asia. Rather, institutions of this nature tend to be less influential, with the state often willing to apply a greater check on the power of labor organizations during collective bargaining. Even Korea—once the bastion of combative labor unions—has mellowed, with union membership now about half that of its heyday in the 1980s.[15] As a consequence, the sort of protections secured by trade unions also tend to be more modest, at least relative to those of the West.

Capital markets are also less developed, on average, in Asian economies. Much like in Europe, where banks are the primary intermediary for financing, as opposed to capital markets[16]—Asian economies rely much more on the banking system (especially large national banks) to channel capital. Many

---

13 Kurlantzick, J., *State Capitalism: How the Return of Statism Is Transforming the World* (New York: Oxford University Press, 2016).
14 Commander, S. and S. Estrin, *The Connections World: The Future of Asian Capitalism* (Cambridge: Cambridge University Press, 2022).
15 To be fair, union membership has likewise declined worldwide, especially in Anglo-Saxon economies.
16 Allen, F. and D. Gale, *Comparing Financial Systems* (Cambridge, MA: MIT Press, 2001).

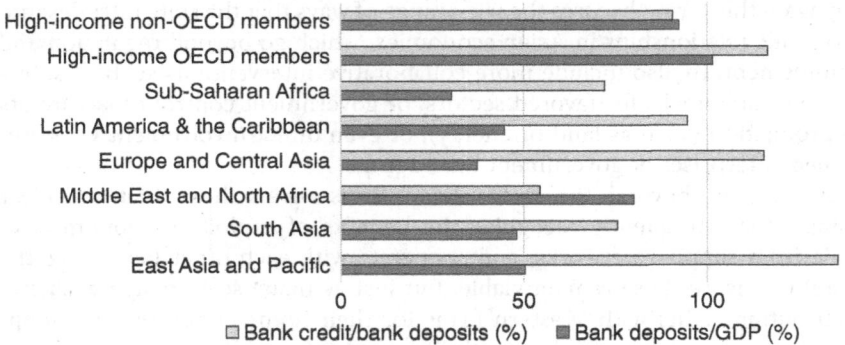

Banking-sector credit relative to deposits, by region, 2011

☐ Bank credit/bank deposits (%)   ■ Bank deposits/GDP (%)

Figure 0.5 The ratio of bank credit to deposits, symptomatic of how reliant a financial system is on banks as intermediaries, is greatest in East Asia, but when the size of deposits are taken into account, both South and Central Asia also appear to be unduly reliant on bank credit.

Asian banks are now among the largest in the world: the largest four banks, by total assets, are in China,[17] and half of the top 20 globally hail from Asia.[18] The dominance of banks is evident beyond raw size. The difference between credit extended by the banking system relative to deposits (as a share of output) is starkest in East Asia (Figure 0.5), and when set against the size of deposits to GDP, regions such as South and Central Asia also appear to be heavily reliant on banks as intermediaries.

For the parts of Asia that rely less on banks, sovereign wealth funds become more critical for channeling finance. The economies of Western and Central Asia are (in)famous for hosting large sovereign wealth funds, such as those in Kazakhstan, Qatar, Saudi Arabia, and the UAE—funded from excess natural resource revenues. But East Asia has a host of such funds, too; these include those based in China, Korea, and Singapore.

Such institutions do not explicitly invest in their own economies—indeed, basic principles of portfolio diversification would suggest doing otherwise—but certain entities, such as Singapore's Temasek and the UAE's Mubadala, do carry development and nation-building mandates, which results in domestic exposures in key infrastructural and strategic assets.

Natural Resources Are Important in Asia, but in Idiosyncratic Ways

Like elsewhere in the world, natural resources are key to economic activity in the region. But due to endowment differences, the role that natural resources play differ.

---

17 These are the Industrial and Commercial Bank of China, China Construction Bank, Agricultural Bank of China, and Bank of China.
18 The rest are from either China or Japan, although anticipated mergers in the Indian banking industry suggest that more banks from the subcontinent will feature in the future, too.

In certain economies in Central Asia (most countries, in one form or another), Southeast Asia (Brunei, Malaysia, Indonesia), and Western Asia (the Gulf States, along with Iran and Iraq), natural resources feature prominently in their export baskets. This could be in terms of energy (coal, oil, and gas), or other commodities, some of which—such as green technology minerals like cobalt, lithium, nickel—are becoming increasingly important in the future global economy.

As a result, their terms of trade and, frequently, the volatility of their output tend to fluctuate according to global commodity cycles. This often means that policymakers in those countries need to manage their economies with an eye toward smoothing out boom-bust cycles, while keeping in mind that their business cycles are likely to be affected in the opposite direction from that of commodity-importing nations.

At the other end of the spectrum are commodity and energy importers, such as China, India, and the NIEs. This aligns their economic cycles more with those of the industrialized nations, albeit their export orientation and overall economic openness often amplify shocks that originate in the West. China, in particular, had the world's highest energy use per unit of GDP between the early 1960s and late 1990s, and even through it has scaled back on being the workshop for the world since the mid-2010s, it retains a natural resource-intensive production profile.

The "Paradox" of Institutional Governance

One important insight that has become relatively well established is the centrality of institutions as a fundamental driver for longer-term economic performance.[19] By and large, this applies to with equal force to Asia. But here Asia presents some potential paradoxes.

For one, Asian economies, while not in prepossession of any claim to superior governance standards than elsewhere, nevertheless appear to have outperformed other regions, at least insofar as growth is concerned. This is in spite of otherwise middling metrics, such as control of corruption, democratic development, or the rule of law.[20] Put another way, improved incomes due to growth appear to have more than offset the negative drag that derives from inadequate institutional quality on incomes,[21] at least in Asia.

Where the constraint from low institutional quality appears to be binding, however, is manifest in those economies in developing Asia being unable

---

19 Acemoğlu, D., S. Johnson, and J. Robinson, "Institutions as a Fundamental Cause of Long-Run Economic Growth," in P. Aghion and S. Durlauf (Eds.), *Handbook of Economic Growth* (Amsterdam: Elsevier, 2005), pp. 385–472.
20 Kaufmann, D., A. Kraay, and M. Mastruzzi, "The Worldwide Governance Indicators: Methodology and Analytical Issues," *Hague Journal of the Rule of Law* 3(2) (2011): 220–246.
21 Kaufmann, D. and A. Kraay, "Growth without Governance," *Economía* 3(1) (2002): 169–229.

to evade the middle-income trap. Countries like Kazakhstan, Malaysia, the Maldives, and Turkey (and the 800-pound gorilla in the room, China) appear tantalizingly close to surmounting the threshold that would break them into high-income status, but governance failures have repeatedly held them back. Without adequately implementing enduring institutional reform, it is likely that these economies will slide back into middle-income territory at the first instance of a major shock, even if they were to become high-income.

But the most pernicious factor that could severely undermine long-run growth has to do with the absence of political stability. This has been especially the case for South Asian economies, from Afghanistan to Pakistan to Sri Lanka. Indeed, it is almost illustrative that Bangladesh—arguably the region's best example of an economic success story—was the country that has enjoyed the most extended period of social peace, with its most recent civil conflict events (a series of coup attempts in the mid-1970s and early 1980s), dating back to four decades prior.

Restoring Asia to Its Place in the Global Economic Hierarchy

Asian Economies Will Become Large and Important

While the rise of Asian economies may appear, to contemporary observers, as an epochal shift, in reality, it is not so much a rise, but perhaps more a return: of the region to its pole position in the global economy, one that it had held for much of its history.

In the 1st century, the two Asian giants were China, under the Western Han Dynasty, and the remnant kingdoms on the Indian subcontinent that had previously been part of the Mauryan Empire (Figure 0.6). Together with Yayoi-era Japan, which was still a fledgling economy at the time, these Asian economies comprised a little more than three-fifths of the world economy. By way of contrast, the mighty Roman Empire—often viewed as one of the major contemporary powers—accounted for less than a tenth.

Indeed, China and India retained their relative dominance of global economic activity at least until the advent of the Industrial Revolution, and remained important for at least a century thereafter. But the much faster speed at which Western economies grew, beginning in the early 19th century, resulted in not just a catch-up, but an absolute overtaking of these formerly influential powers. By the turn of the 20th century, the largest economies globally were overwhelmingly Western, a position that they have retained through modern times.

But once the necessary ingredients for catch-up growth became apparent to Asian economies, most went about systematically implementing policies (described in the earlier section) to belatedly jazz up their economic performance. It is generally a far easier proposition to implement tried-and-tested

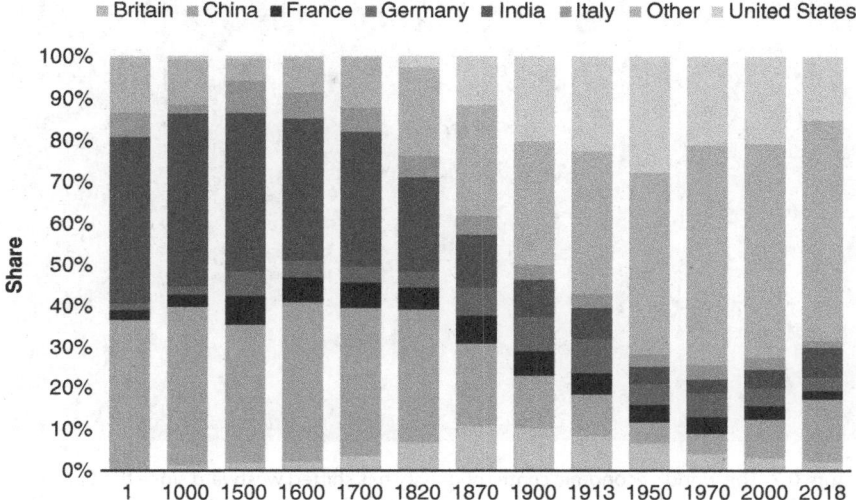

Shares of global economic activity, by major power, 1–2018

Figure 0.6 In the 1st century, China, India, and Japan accounted for three-fifths of global output, and both the Han Dynasty and post-Mauryan Indian kingdoms were several times larger in economic terms than the Roman Empire.

recipes—as nontrivial as successfully *executing* these policies might be—than to be pushing the boundaries of production possibilities when one is already on the frontier. Accordingly, these efforts have translated into a recapturing, by Asian economies, of an ever-larger share of the global economic pie.

Another way to visualize this is to treat each country's GDP as its economic "mass," represent on a two-dimensional map of the Earth what would otherwise rest on the surface of a three-dimensional globe, and proceed to compute the "economic" center of gravity as a weighted average of these projections (Figure 0.7).[22] Doing so reveals that this center remained, for much of the past two millennia, in Central Asia, before shifting westward starting in the 1500s. By the 20th century, it had moved to Europe, before further coming to a rest in the mid-Atlantic at the height of the Cold War.

Since then, however, it has begun an inexorable march eastward, further accelerating since 2000. By 2050, it is expected to come to rest smack between China and India, a reprise of the position it used to be for thousands of years.

But Asian Economies Will Remain Behind in Per Capita Terms

At some level, this should be unsurprising—and perhaps even welcome—given the spatial distribution of human populations worldwide. It has been said that

22 Quah, D., "The Global Economy's Shifting Centre of Gravity," *Global Policy* 2(1) (2011): 3–9.

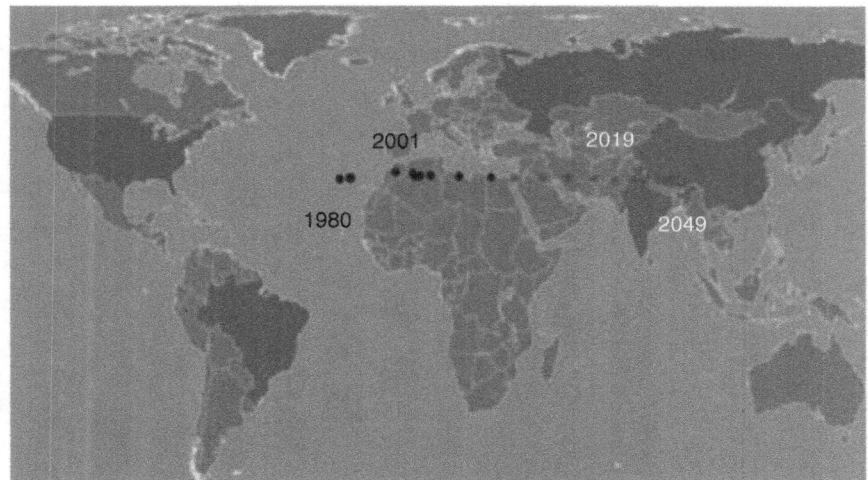

Figure 0.7 The world's economic center of gravity has shifted westward since the first millennium, accelerating especially after the Industrial Revolution. At the height of the Cold War, it rested in the mid-Atlantic, reflecting the dominance of the economies of the United States and the Soviet Union. Since 2000, this center has rapidly shifted back east, and is expected to remain anchored in Central Asia by the middle of this century.

if the entire world were a democracy, all decisions of global significance would be made in the so-called Valeriepieris circle, a 3,400-kilometer-radius region of the world, centered around Myanmar, that encompasses half of the world's population.[23] If so, an acceptance of how economic power would likewise reside close to these population centers makes eminent sense.

Still, it is important to keep in mind that even after these countries grow to become economically consequential, their per capita incomes remain a fraction of that of advanced economies. Even today, with China's and India's economy about a third and a fifth that of the United States, respectively, the gap widens much further in per capita terms: Americans are almost 6 and 30 times richer, respectively.[24] Even within Asia, Japan's capita income is about 3 and 17 times greater than that of China and India, and Indonesia—the third-most populous Asian nation—is about 9 times poorer. There is a distinction between absolute size and relative wealth, and most of the Asian giants have a long way to go.

---

23 Quah, D., "The World's Tightest Circle of People," *Global Policy Opinion*, April 2016, p. 26.
24 The multiple is less dramatic when measured in purchasing power parity (PPP) terms, but at about 3.5 and 9 times, respectively, the difference remains substantial. The relative improvement of incomes of developing countries, when measured in PPP terms, is not unusual, and results from the Penn effect. There are multiple reasons for this, not least because of greater differences in productivity in the tradable versus nontradable sectors in advanced economies (known as the Harrod-Balassa-Samuelson effect). See Feenstra, R., R. Inklaar, and M. Timmer, "The Next Generation of the Penn World Table," *American Economic Review* 105(10) (2015): 3150–3182.

Asia's Close Ties to the World Economy

Asian Economies Are Highly Integrated in Terms of Trade, Especially with Each Other

With few exceptions,[25] Asian economies are incredibly open (Figure 0.8). This is expected for commodity-forward regions, such as Central and Western Asia,

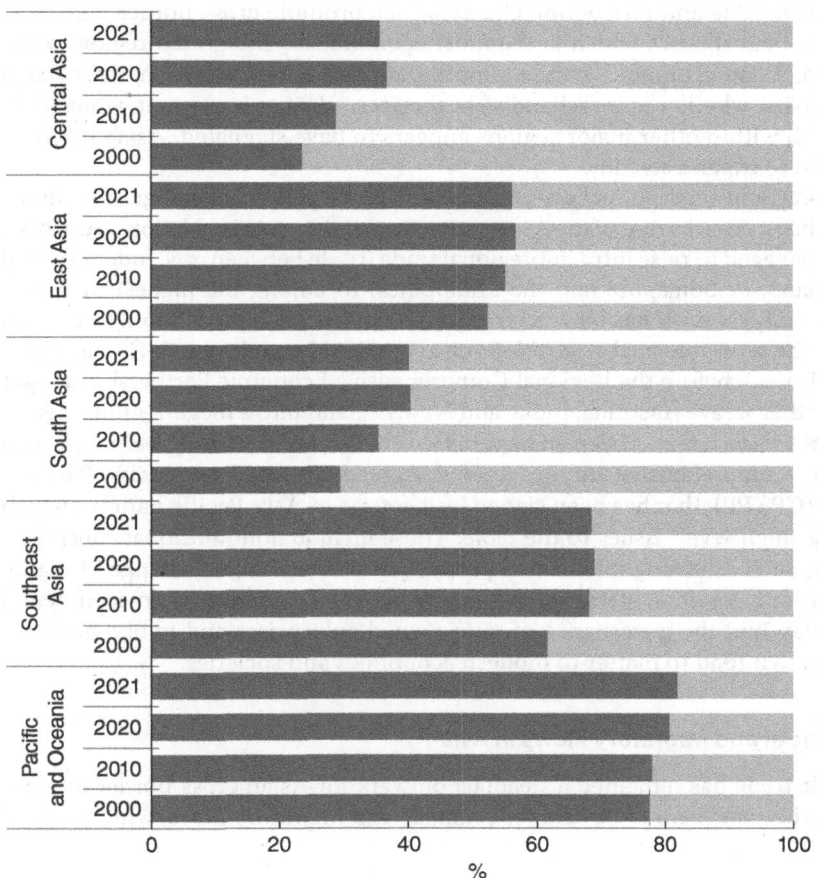

Figure 0.8 Asian economies are not only highly open, but trade a great deal with each other. Even the lagging regions of Central and South Asia have increased their intraregional trade shares in recent times.

---

25 One notable exception is India, which followed an import-substituting industrialization strategy and maintained a trade licensing regime under socialism, at least through the 1980s. Hermit kingdoms, such as Afghanistan or North Korea, also exhibit low trade penetration.

where trade often amounts to between 70–80% of GDP. But it is also the case for East Asia—where trade is about two-thirds of output—and, belatedly, for South Asia (where it is approaching half). This stands in contrast to less than a third in North America, and about half for both Africa and Latin America.

The main reason for this is the sheer fact that distance is a major determinant of trade volumes, and hence neighboring economies have a greater tendency to trade with each other.[26] But much of this is also attributable to the presence of regional value and production chains, which promote cross-border exchange. Other than the EU, which is the most economically integrated region in the world, Asian economies conduct more than half their trade with other Asian countries, whether in merchandise or services.[27] Just as important, while trade growth within other major regions appears to have stagnated, Asia's has continued to expand steadily.

Policy and institutional arrangements have helped usher integration along. Southeast Asia, by dint of the Association for Southeast Asian Nations (ASEAN), has managed to raise intra-subregional trade (trade between, say, Indonesia and Thailand, or Singapore and the Philippines) to among the highest in Asia.[28] Even ASEAN itself has been a force for enhanced trade promotion; this began with the semi-informal ASEAN+3 set-up (ASEAN together with China, Japan, and Korea), before the Regional Comprehensive Economic Partnership sought to further weave Australia, India, and New Zealand into a mega-regional deal.[29]

The region has also been an impetus to other styles of trade agreements, such as the Comprehensive and Progressive Agreement for Trans-Pacific Partnership (CPTPP), that has been signed by a coterie of Asia-Pacific nations, which bring "high-level" issues to the table. These include nontraditional considerations, such as strong intellectual property protection, the exchange of digital goods and services, attention to sustainable development and environmental policies, and the governance of state-owned enterprises and public procurement, that tend to matter to modern economies and societies.

Financial and Migratory Flows in Asia

While trade has remained a steadfast bulwark for Asian cross-border integration, the same cannot be said for financial and migratory flows, which remain

---

26 Anderson, J., "The Gravity Model," *Annual Review of Economics* 3 (2011): 133–160.

27 The equivalent for the EU is about 60%, and North America about 40%.

28 ASEAN is exceeded only by Northeast Asia, but this is somewhat artificial, since that region is comprised of only four countries, which also trade more in general due to their economic size (other than distance, size is the other major determinant of trade volumes).

29 The Regional comprehensive economic partnership (RCEP) entered into force in 2022 for 10 of the original parties, with additional nations ratifying the agreement over the course of the subsequent two years. Notably, however, India withdrew from RCEP negotiations in 2019, and to date has not acceded to the agreement.

nascent. To be fair, the former tends to lag behind goods exchange worldwide, and the latter even more so, given political-economic constraints.

To the extent that a pattern may be discerned from regional cross-border financing, it is that outflows, as evidenced by asset holdings, tend to be more-or-less equally distributed among bank loans, fixed income, foreign direct investment (FDI), and portfolio equity. In contrast, inflows tend to be directed heavily toward FDI, amounting to close to half of regional liabilities.[30] Indeed, over the past two decades, Asia has accounted for between a third and half of all FDI inflows globally.

Still, the region remains heavily influenced by global financial developments, including interest rate policy set by the U.S. Federal Reserve, as well as the relative strength of the US dollar. This, again, is not unique to Asia—the global financial and dollar cycle buffets much of the rest of the world, even relatively large economies such as China, or advanced ones such as Japan[31]—but countries in the region had been part of a so-called "dollar bloc" that had tied their local currencies to the US dollar for decades, and their central banks continue to operate monetary policy in a manner that takes into consideration domestic interest rates vis-à-vis that of the United States.

People flows in Asia have always been more important in terms of temporary migration (tourism) as opposed to permanent ones (emigration), but the latter has enjoyed a boost from both institutional arrangements—such as economic partnerships and customs union agreements—along with income differentials between regional economies, which tends to increase economic incentives for sending and receiving migrant workers.

Like elsewhere, the region was hit hard by the COVID-19 pandemic. This decimated tourism, but also resulted in the relocation of a significant number of workers back to their home countries. While the reopening of borders has seen a resumption of migratory flows, developments that resulted from the episode—such as the increased use of work-from-home schedules and digital meeting and collaboration tools, which has eroded business travel, and a greater sensitivity to political pressure from nativist sentiment, which has weakened the demand for skilled expatriates—may lead to a derailment of what had been hitherto a steady rate of cross-border labor integration in the region.

---

30 Asian Development Bank, *Asian Economic Integration Report 2023: Trade, Investment, and Climate* (Manila: Asian Development Bank, 2023).

31 Obstfeld, M. and H. Zhou, "The Global Dollar Cycle," *Brookings Papers on Economic Activity* 56 (2022): 361–447; Rey, H., "Dilemma Not Trilemma: The Global Cycle and Monetary Policy Independence," *Proceedings of the Economic Policy Symposium* (Kansas City: Federal Reserve Bank of Kansas City, 2013), pp. 285–333.

The Future of Asian Economies

The Shadow of Demographics on Economic Outcomes

Inasmuch as demographic changes were an important contributor to Asia's post-war rise, the self-same pressures will come back to bite many Asian economies over the course of the coming decades. As Asian nations age and their reduced fertility rates play out as population realities, it will become more and more difficult to sustain growth amid shrinking workforces. A demographic reversal is at hand.[32]

Demographic changes are already a factor in play for high-income countries, including those in Asia (such as the NIEs). The peak in the share of working-to-nonworking population (sometimes referred to as the inverse dependency ratio) occurred around 2010, after which the burden of supporting the nonproductive population will only continue to compound in the decades to come. The rest of developing East Asia has likewise seen its peak, since the year 2020 (Figure 0.9), and both the higher peak in the ratio for this region, along with a more rapid decline, will mean a shorter and more challenging transition phase to a post-aged

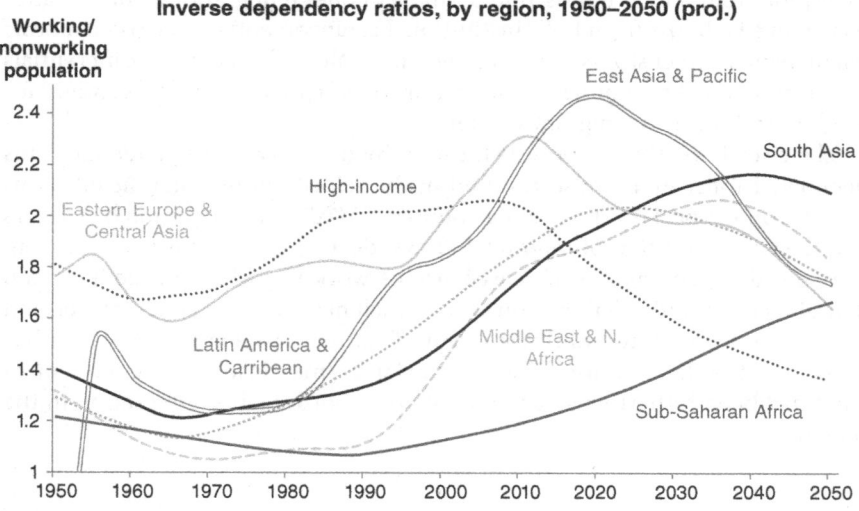

Figure 0.9 There is a difference in the way that demographic pressures will play out in each of the Asian regions—as evidenced by the differential timing and height of the peak in the inverse dependency ratio, as well as the slope of the curves relative to said peak—but for all of Asia, such pressures will come into play some time before 2050.

---

32 Goodhart, C. and M. Pradhan, *The Great Demographic Reversal: Ageing Societies, Waning Inequality, and an Inflation Revival* (London: Palgrave Macmillan, 2020).

society. South and Western Asia have yet to reach their respective turning points in terms of dependency, but these are due to play out in a few decades, after which these regions will need to manage their own demographic shifts.

Demographic shifts will have not only first-order effects—on the size of the labor force, and the costs of supporting youth and retirees—but also second-order ones: a reduction in financing available for capital investment (due to an elderly population drawing down on their retirement savings, or from a "sandwich" generation forced to support both elderly parents and young children), or a diminution of the capacity for advances in total factor productivity (TFP), as a smaller talent pool may imply more limited opportunities for innovative ideas to emerge. Set against this will be a wealthier population that, because they are bearing fewer children, may be willing to invest more in human capital, although there are natural limits to how much this could play an offsetting function, since educational attainment is already relatively high across much of Asia.

The Importance of Productivity Shocks in Conditioning Economic Futures

It is important to stress that demographics, in and of itself, is not destiny. While it will matter immensely, there is one remaining hope: that economy-wide TFP will enjoy a revival, either for Asian emerging economies that have yet to pick the (lower-hanging) fruit of efficiency enhancements that derive from importing known technology, policy, and institutions,[33] or from general-purpose technologies that hold the promise for sustained productivity gains over the long run.[34] This is the great hope that boosters[35] of generative artificial intelligence and general-purpose robotics hold out, as a panacea for what had been close to two decades of disappointing productivity growth, following the global financial crisis.

There is a strong likelihood that this will become the main source of differentiation between Asian economies in the 21st century; it will determine those poised to succeed, versus others that are relegated to languish in economic underperformance and unfulfilled potential. While the factors that drive TFP are often mysterious, in this book, we hope to reveal that—at least when set against the context of history—the strategic policy choices that shape political-economic structures and institutions have an important role to play.

---

33 Comin, D. and M. Mestieri, "Technology Diffusion: Measurement, Causes, and Consequences," in P. Aghion and S. Durlauf (Eds.), *Handbook of Economic Growth* (Amsterdam: Elsevier, 2014), pp. 565–622; Hsieh, C-T. and P. Klenow, "Misallocation and Manufacturing TFP in China and India," *Quarterly Journal of Economics* 124(4) (2009): 1403–1448.

34 Jovanovic, B. and P. Rousseau, "General Purpose Technologies," in P. Aghion and S. Durlauf (Eds.), *Handbook of Economic Growth* (Amsterdam: Elsevier, 2005), pp. 1181–1224.

35 Crafts, N., "Artificial Intelligence as a General-Purpose Technology: An Historical Perspective," *Oxford Review of Economic Policy* 37(3) (2021): 521–536.

What's Politics Got to Do With It?

Even though this book is primarily about Asian economies, political factors will inevitably creep into the discussion. This is not only because the choices over policies and institutions are almost always ultimately taken, shaped, and evolve according to the political environment. It is also because political developments and regimes infuse so much of what we observe in Asian countries today. And they will continue to do so in the future.

One only has to pick up a newspaper to see how such geopolitical concerns have mattered immensely in recent times. Since 2013, Xi Jinping has increasingly taken on the mantle of Mao, culminating, most recently, with a deviation from recent precedent as he installed himself as China's president for a third term. In India, Narendra Modi has likewise taken steps to undermine the country's long-standing democratic traditions, charging his chief political rival (and former secretary-general of the country's main opposition party) with defamation, and winning a two-year jail sentence for this rival.

Such authoritarian tactics have not been limited to the largest countries in Asia. Among smaller economies, a suite of authoritarian parties have either seized or consolidated power in recent decades. This has occurred, for example, in Cambodia (where Hun Manet, the eldest son of dictator Hun Sen, has been appointed the prime minister-designate), Kazakhstan (where Nursultan Nazarbayev stubbornly held onto the reins of power for close to three decades), Myanmar (where General Min Aung Hlaing installed himself as prime minister in 2021), and Thailand (where Prayut Chan-o-cha, another general, seized power via a military coup in 2014).

Even countries where some stirrings of democratic progress seemed possible have now seen a retreat in political rights and civil liberties. The Arab Spring that began in the early 2010s has since fizzled out, and authoritarian leaders either returned to the fore across the region, such as in Afghanistan (where the Taliban's victory over the West led to the assumption of Hibatullah Akhundzada as supreme leader), Egypt (where Abdel Fattah el-Sisi has been president since 2014), Palestine (where Mahmoud Abbas extended his term as president indefinitely in 2009), and Turkey (where Recep Tayyip Erdoğan has repeatedly defied reformists by successfully retaining the presidency), or simply remained in power (Bashar al-Assad in Syria, and the monarchies in the GCC countries and Jordan).

Ultimately, this book is about understanding the forces and factors that have shaped the past and influence the present evolution of Asian economies. These include major macroeconomic drivers such as labor, capital, and productivity; microeconomic conditions such as geographic features, industrial structure, and economic openness; as well as legacies deriving from political-economic institutions and regimes. Only with a keen understanding of these varied elements—and their interrelationships—will we be able to peer into how the future of Asia is likely to unfold.

1

China: The Dragon Awakens, But Will It Roar?

Let China sleep, for when she awakes, she will shake the world.
—Napoleon Bonaparte (1769–1821),
French military leader and emperor

China, by her resources and her population, is capable of being the great-
est Power in the world after the United States.
—Bertrand Russell (1872–1970), Welsh academic

The Chinese people have shown the world that the Chinese nation has
achieved tremendous transformation from standing up, and growing pros-
perous to becoming strong, and that China's national rejuvenation has
become a historical inevitability.
—Xi Jinping (1953–), Chinese president[1]

Introduction

Disembark at any of the major points of entry into China for the first time—
air, rail, or sea—and you will immediately notice that *everything is bigger in
China* (some say this about Chicago, but the Windy City has got nothing on the
Middle Kingdom). Of course, the sheer scale that engulfs you is not merely by
coincidence. Such accommodations are necessary to deal with the sort of volumes expected for a country of 1.4 billion souls, an economy of $17.7 trillion,
exports that gobble up around 15% of global trade (almost twice that of the next-
largest trader),[2] and stock markets—whose capitalization at $14.7 trillion—are

---

1 Xi Jinping. Speech at a ceremony marking the Centenary of the CPC (Beijing: Xinhua, 2021).
2 Nicita, A. and C. Razo, "China: The Rise of a Trade Titan," *UNCTAD News*, April 27, 2021.

Asian Economies: History, Institutions, and Structures, First Edition. Jamus Jerome Lim.

second only to that of the world's deepest and most sophisticated ones in the United States.[3]

By a similar token, China is also incredibly rich. In 2020, the net worth of Chinese citizens breached $120 trillion, comfortably surpassing that of U.S. households.[4] China now routinely tussles with the U.S. for the most number of billionaires; in 2023, the count stood at 495 in the former, versus 735 in the latter.[5] Chinese cities such as Beijing, Hangzhou, Shenzhen, and Shanghai now host comparable numbers of such ultra-high net worth families as the usual suspects such as New York, London, and Moscow.[6]

China's size also means that it now holds the enviable title of being the second-largest economy in the world, and (by a long shot) the largest economy in Asia. Perhaps more impressively, the country has done so in a remarkably short period of time. As recently as 40 years ago, China barely scraped into the top 10 among largest economies globally, lagging behind far smaller European countries, such as France and Italy, and even other developing nations, such as Brazil and Mexico.

Today, China stands almost three times as large as Japan—having only surpassed its neighbor just a decade or so ago—and is rapidly closing in on the United States, which some predict will relinquish its hold as the world's largest economy by the end of this decade. Indeed, in terms of purchasing power parity—which captures output more in terms of the quantities of goods and services that can be procured in a country, rather than their prices (even after conversion to a common currency)—China already holds the title of the largest economy globally.

For those with a sufficiently long view of history, this state of affairs merely marks the (re)ascendance of the Chinese economy to a position that it held

---

3 Ali, A., "The World's 10 Largest Stock Markets," *Visual Capitalist*, October 29, 2020. Recent internationalization efforts, such as the Qualified Foreign Institutional Investor (QFII) programs, Stock Connect program for direct access to Chinese equity markets via Hong Kong, and the incremental inclusion of Chinese stocks into the Morgan Stanley Capital International (MSCI) EM index have further accelerated this process. See Cortina, J., M. Martinez Peria, S. Schmukler, and J. Xiao, "The Internationalization of China's Equity Markets," *IMF Economic Review*, forthcoming.
4 Since wealth is measured in terms of asset prices, such numbers can (and do) fluctuate over time, and 2020 marked a high-water mark in property valuations in the country. Nevertheless, it is reasonable to concede that national wealth in the country will only continue to grow and surpass that of other countries in the years ahead, for much the same reasons that its economy is expected to dominate. See Woetzel, J., J. Mischke, A. Madgavkar, E. Windhagen, S. Smit, M. Birshan, S. Kemeny, and R.J. Anderson, *The Rise and Rise of the Global Balance Sheet* (Washington, DC: McKinsey Global Institute, 2021).
5 Peterson-Withorn, C. "Forbes' 37th Annual World's Billionaires List: Facts and Figures 2023," *Forbes*, April 4, 2023.
6 Hyatt, J., " Beijing Overtakes New York City as City with Most Billionaires: Forbes 2021 List," *Forbes*, April 6, 2021.

through much of recorded human history. In 1820—just as the Industrial Revolution was starting to take hold across the economies of the Western World—China was the world's largest economy, accounting for close to a third of all global output. And while it had, by then, relinquished being the wealthiest, it remained a prosperous nation by most standards.

Yet this enviable position of the Chinese economy and wealthy Chinese individuals belies the fact that, by many rudimentary metrics, the country remains behind that of even some of the laggards in the industrialized West. The flip side of China's giant population base is that all its headline figures must to be scaled by this very base, if one is to have a reasonable sense of the nation's true progress.

In per capita terms, China's GDP—amounting to around $12,648 per head in 2022—is just a smidgen below the threshold of about $13,845 to qualify as high income, meaning that its middle-income status will soon be a thing of the past. But its GDP per capita is a sixth that of the United States, and still below that of relatively less-developed European countries, such as Greece, Hungary, and Poland. Poverty remains a challenge, especially in rural, inland counties, despite the remarkable progress that has been made over the past half-century. And with such vast wealth in certain cities, it is unsurprising that income and wealth inequality in China remains yawning.

Notwithstanding China's remarkable economic achievements over the past half-century, it is perhaps natural to ask ourselves whether this state of affairs is, ultimately, sustainable. But a better understanding of this can only be attained through a keener exploration of the country's rich geo-economic diversity and dense economic history, alongside the evolution of a sociopolitical backdrop that remains one of the most befuddling and complicated national developments of the 20th century.

Economic Geography of China

China's Geography Has Shaped Its Economic Activity

Geographically, China is the second-largest country in the world. At 9.4 million square kilometers (6.3% of the world's landmass), it is slightly ahead of both the United States and Canada (both around 9.1 million km^2), albeit significantly smaller than Russia (16.4 million). However, this large global share belies the reality that much of inner China comprises challenging terrain: desert and high plains in the northwest, and plateau and mountains in the southwest. It is therefore unsurprising that the eastern provinces—closer to the coast—are the most densely populated and economically advanced.

At risk of simplification, China's economic geography is characterized by two imaginary lines: a north-south water availability line—which traverses from around Aihui, a district located in the Northern province of Heilongjiang, to Tengchong, a city in western Yunnan Province—and an east-west monsoon line, which is roughly traced by the Yangtze river.

The north-south bisection divides the country into where access to rainfall and water sources are more (or less) abundant. Of course, access to water resources, in turn, allows for larger settlements, and for economic activities to take place at scale. Consequently, there are few major cities inland, and most industry has historically hugged the eastern seaboard.

The east-west line has historically delineated where the staple food would be rice (below the line), versus wheat (above it). Of course, even in the distant past, it would not be unusual for Southern Chinese to consume wheat noodles or bread, and the Northern would likewise have steady access to rice and rice-based produce. But the fact that the South has always been the rice bowl (and hence rewarded lucratively for it) for the country still stands.

The borders of what we consider modern China have not always been so. Rather, what constitutes the boundaries of the Chinese nation has evolved over time. For instance, at the height of its territorial expansion during the Tang dynasty (around 700 CE), China proper included parts of central Asia (Turkestan, which includes parts of modern-day eastern Uzbekistan, Tajikistan, and southern Kazakhstan and Kyrgyzstan), while segments of southwestern and northeastern China today were parts of other empires. Similarly, Mongol conquests during the Yuan dynasty (around the 13th century) weaved in parts of what is, today, eastern Russia.

That said, the present borders of the People's Republic are undeniably among the broadest that China has ever seen. Even so, "core" China—the provinces along the central and eastern coastline—have remained since the founding of Chinese civilization, and hence it is unsurprising that these are also among the most vibrant economic centers of the nation today.

Chinese Concentrations of Commerce Along the Rivers and Coastlines

China comprises 34 administrative divisions. 23 are provinces (similar to states), 5 are autonomous regions (similar to provinces, but granted more rights of self-government),[7] 4 are directly-administered municipalities (similar to capital territories in many countries),[8] and 2 are special administrative regions (granted even more autonomy than the autonomous regions).[9]

---

7 These are located in the periphery, include large populations of ethnic minorities, and were, unsurprisingly, mostly not part of "core" China through the millennia. They are Guanxi, Tibet (Xizang), Xinjiang, Inner Mongolia, and Ningxia.
8 There used to be 14 of these, before 11 were redesignated as provincial capitals, leaving Beijing, Chongqing, Shanghai, and Tianjin.
9 These are the former colonies of Hong Kong (held by the British) and Macau (held by the Portuguese).

Figure 1.1 Chinese economic geography indicates that development is mostly concentrated along the eastern seaboard, although there are notable inland clusters along the middle and upper Yangtze, including the Szechuan region, sometimes referred to as China's "Midwest."

Three major rivers flow through China, from west to east, before emptying out into the Pacific Ocean. In the north, there is the Yellow River (or *Huanghe*); in the center, the Yangtze River (or *Changjiang*), and in the south, the Pearl River (or *Zhujiang*).[10] Unsurprisingly, given the historical importance of rivers for economical transport, most major clusters of industry occur along these rivers (Figure 1.1).

The Yangtze, in particular, has agglomerations at the upper (where Chongqing and Chengdu are located), the middle (major cities include Wuhan

---

10 There are three terms used to refer to such bodies of water (河. *hé*), 江 (*jiāng*), and 水 (*shuǐ*), the last being the least common (it literally translates as "water," but certain rivers, such as the Han River, do take on this moniker. The term *he* is more commonly applied in the north, *jiang* in the south, and *shui* in the center, although no hard and fast rules exist.

and Changsha), and the lower (Shanghai, Nanjing) stretches.[11] While some of these are not as well known to the rest of the world, such cities can be huge. Changsha, for instance, has a population of 8.2 million, comparable to Switzerland (8.7 million); Wuhan—previously an obscure city until the advent of COVID-19—is a little more populous than the Czech Republic. The cities of the Upper Yangtze have also been economically vibrant, of late; growth rates in the late 2010s, for example, were several percentage points higher than the rest of the country. Some have even tagged this region as China's "Industrial Midwest," after the industrial engine that once powered the rise of the American economy.

Chinese civilization actually began along the Ordos Bulge, a bend in the Yellow River in the province of Inner Mongolia today. The site—like many riverine valleys of the past—was rich in fertile soil, and allowed settlements to develop with sedentary agriculture. Today, however, the core industrial area lies much closer to the delta, and the broader North China Plain region includes major cities such as Beijing, Tianjin, and Qingdao.

To the far south, the Pearl River is the most distributed of the three, with major tributaries to the east, north, and west (perhaps unimaginatively named *Dong, Bei,* and *Xi,* which literally translate to East, North, and West). Along with this dense distribution is an extensive watershed that embeds important cities, such as Guangzhou and Shenzhen, as well as Hong Kong and Macau. Taking the cue once again from recognizable U.S. regions, this area has recently been branded the "Greater Bay Area" (after its better-known namesake in Northern California). But make no mistake: cities in this region are thriving and wealthy, even if they are less known outside of China. The manufacturing hub of Dongguan, for example, hosts a population similar to Chicago, and exports $65 billion a year in shipments. Huizhou, a global manufacturing hub for electronics and machinery exports, is the size of Toronto.

Other less-concentrated corridors of economic activity exist beyond the three river systems. These include the cities along the southeastern coast (across from Taiwan), and those in the northeastern rust belt.

Major Cities in China Are Often Classified into Tiers

Although there is no single officially sanctioned designation for what would define a "Tier 1" city (or, rather, there are too many alternative definitions, official and otherwise),[12] most observers of modern China would recognize four such cities: Guangzhou and Shenzhen to the south, Shanghai in the east

---

11 Naughton, B., *The Chinese Economy: Adaptation and Growth,* 2nd ed. (Cambridge, MA: MIT Press, 2018).
12 Such cities may be classified, as in the *Yicai* taxonomy, according to commercial vibrancy, urban residential vitality, lifestyle diversity, and dynamism. The *South China Morning Post* employs a simplest rating metric based on population size, gross product, and administrative hierarchy.

Table 1.1 A classification of Chinese cities into tiers

Tier	Cities	Total
1	Beijing, Chongqing*, Guangzhou, Shanghai, Shenzhen, Tianjin†	6
2	Changsha, Chengdu, Hangzhou, Nanjing, Ningbo, Qingdao, Shenyang, Wuhan, Zhengzhou	9
3	Changchun, Dalian, Dongguan, Fuzhou, Harbin, Hefei, Ningbo, Shantou, Shijiazhuang, Xi'an, Xiamen	30

Source: Author's compilation, from *Yicai* Global (2020) and *South China Morning Post* (2016).
Notes: Cities marked by * are not included in the *Yicai* list, and those marked by † are not included in SCMP list. Cities listed in the "new Tier 1" of the *Yicai* list are classified here as Tier 2 cities, and only those satisfying all categories at Tier 2 level of the SCMP list are classified as such; what is counted above are the overlap in both lists. Only a selected number of cities in Tiers 2 and 3 are reported, for illustrative purposes.

(and the *de facto* financial capital of the country), and Beijing, the political capital, in the north. Two other cities—the western city of Chongqing, and the northern port-of-entry Tianjin—have also occasionally been featured as Tier 1 cities. Including the greater metropolitan region, these cities host populations of between 17 and 34 million.

Tier 1 cities are generally regarded as the largest and among most dynamic agglomerations of economic life in the country (Table 1.1). They house the most sophisticated middle-class (and upper-class) consumers, the most bustling factories and workshops (albeit usually in the outer suburbs), and host the most important governmental and political functions. Visit any of these in person, and one would be hard-pressed to draw distinctions between the quality of life there, and in any number of selected cities in the rich industrialized world.

But since the status has taken on such outsized importance in the minds of both Chinese urban aspirations as well as foreign investor interest, conferring the rank of "Tier 1" to a city has become somewhat of a badge of honor, and one subject to both celebration and criticism. Admirers see it as an affirmation of the globally competitive nature of Chinese cities, while detractors rue the missed opportunities of those that just fail to make the cut. Moreover, given how China's population tends to be much more widely dispersed than in many other countries, lower-tier cities collectively account for the majority of economic activity and the housing stock—over 60% of GDP, and 50% of housing, by one estimate.[13] Economic centers are

---

13 Rogoff, K. and Y. Yang, "A Tale of Tier 3 Cities," NBER Working Paper 30519, (Cambridge, MA: National Bureau of Economic Research, 2022). Rogoff and Yang's classification differs from the one here, in that as many as 31 cities are regarded as Tier 2, hence Tier 3 cities number as many as 263. Hence, the accounting of their contribution is likely to be an underestimate.

not limited to cities alone. As in other parts of the world, China has special economic zones (SEZs)—areas where business and trade laws may differ from the rest of the country, usually via tax exemptions and tariff relief—but have taken them to the next level, allowing large, interconnected regions to take on the SEZ designation. These include provincial-level SEZs, such as Hainan (the entire island is a free trade port),[14] coastal cities that are open to foreign investment (these include giants such as Shanghai and Guangzhou, but also others such as Qingdao and Ningbo), to megalopolises such as the Jing-Jin-Ji (京津冀) region (which embodies an area about twice the size of South Korea, and having the GDP of Spain).[15] As of 2010, there were 1,600 SEZs in China, at both national and provincial levels, oriented toward goals such as technological development, export-orientation, or catering to border regions.

China Has Resources, But They Are Insufficient

China is not bereft of natural resources. It has extensive deposits of coal, oil,[16] and natural gas, despite being the world's largest oil and gas importer; this is a function of the fact that its production processes are resource-intensive—one does not assume the title of the "world's workshop" without also guzzling vast amounts of energy—although the country's energy use per unit of GDP is falling over time, as it moves up the value chain (Figure 1.2).

The country also leads the world in mining a host of other natural resources, such as gold, iron, zinc, and phosphate. But its dominance in the production of rare earths—metallic elements, bearing exotic names such as praseodymium, scandium, yttrium, that are essential for many green and advanced technologies—has garnered opprobrium among some quarters (by some estimates, China provides more than 85% of the world's rare earths). Some have argued, for instance, that it is a geostrategic vulnerability to have important economic inputs tied to a non-democratic nation, and even more so when the country's policymakers appear

---

14 In addition to free trade status for goods manufacturing, there is an effort to center this development on tourism, especially with duty-free sales. The medium-term objective is to weave it into an integral part of the Southeast Asia-oriented regions in the Greater Bay Area, complementary to Hong Kong and Guangdong.

15 The name is a portmanteau of Beijing, Tianjin, and the ancient name for Hebei province, Jizhou.

16 Data from 2023 indicate that oil production is around 4.3 million barrels a day, making the country the world's fourth-largest oil producer, and more than what most OPEC and OPEC+ nations pump daily.

Energy use per unit of GDP, selected major economies, 1820–2030 (projected)

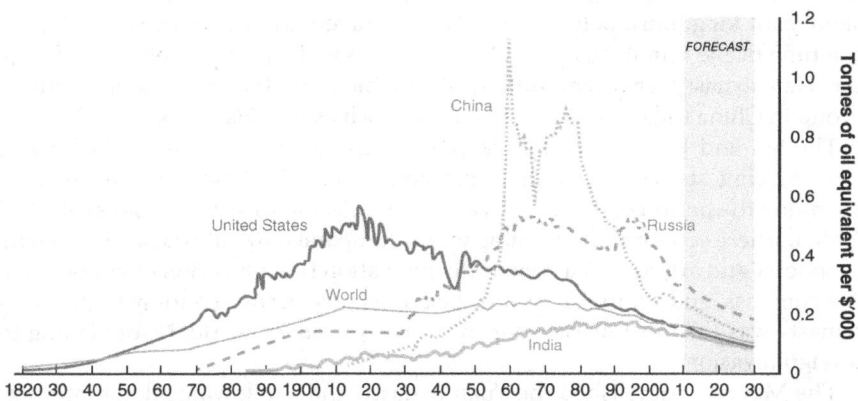

Figure 1.2 Chinese energy utilization was intensive during its fast-growth phase, consistent with its role as the world's workshop, and far exceeded that of other large developing economies such as Russia and India.

willing to weaponize such trade with export restrictions.[17] The counterargument often offered is that it is simply a policy choice; China has demonstrated a willingness to absorb the environmental costs associated with their extraction, while other nations with such deposits have not.[18]

Economic History of China

From Imperialism to Communism: A Capsule History of the Middle Kingdom

It is impossible to encapsulate almost four millennia of Chinese history into a few paragraphs. Nevertheless, it will be useful to briefly touch on the major highlights of this several thousand-year history, to better grasp the key elements of China's sociocultural development, along with the Chinese worldview, insofar as these inform our understanding of its economic history.

---

17 A systematic study of trade data on rare earths concludes, however, that there is little evidence to support the assertion that China has systematically curtailed such exports to specific countries. See Evenett, S. and J. Fritz, "The Scramble for Critical Raw Materials: Time to Take Stock?," *Global Trade Alert Report* 31 (London: CEPR Press, 2023).

18 Other countries, such as Australia and the United States, possess significant deposits of rare earths. However, the toxicity and environmental hazards posed from their mining have led to a reluctance in expanding production.

The earliest verifiable record of China's long history traces back to 1600 BCE,[19] with two successive dynasties—the Shang and Zhou—that were more akin to significant kingdoms, before unification occurred around an imperial state at the time of the Qin dynasty in 221 BCE. This saw further consolidation under the Han dynasty, an event sufficiently momentous that the majority ethnic group in China today continues to refer to itself as the "Han people."

The Sui and Jin—two comparatively undistinguished dynasties—followed, before being succeeded by the Tang and Song. The latter two dynasties—spanning the period 618–1279 CE, are often referred to as the "Golden Age" of China, where economic flourishing was accompanied by cultural achievements (in poetry and art) as well as scientific innovation (the invention of gunpowder, the compass, and printing). At the apex of its power, the economy of the Song dynasty was the most prosperous in the early modern world, before falling to foreign invasion.

The Mongols established the Yuan dynasty, and—following a long interregnum of a return to Han rule under the Ming—China again fell to northern conquerors. Their antagonist this time was the Manchus, who founded the Qing. The Qing, who ruled for close to three centuries, were the last imperial dynasty; China subsequently flirted briefly with a republican state, before communism took over. The regime of the People's Republic of China remains in power till this day.

But don't let the seeming continuity of the historical narrative fool you. For a civilization that has endured for several thousand years, it would not surprise anyone to know that the neat successions discussed above were also interspersed with periods of incredible tumult. The end of the Zhou was followed by rising dissent, during the Spring and Autumn period, before outright conflict, during the Warring States period. Similarly, the collapse of the Han saw sixty years of division, where China was partitioned into Three Kingdoms that frequently were at war with one another.

Still, the philosophy of circularity and continuity—entirely consistent with the cosmologies of Buddhism and Taoism, two of the three dominant religions in Chinese history[20]—imbues the Chinese worldview. It is the basis for the legitimacy of rule; the cyclical conferral and withdrawal of the "Mandate of Heaven" (天命, *tiānmìng*) explain the rise and fall of dynasties.

---

19 There is another dynasty, the legendary Xia (夏), recorded in traditional Chinese historiography, that is believed to have existed between 2205 and 1766 BCE. Archeological corroboration has been comparatively limited, however, with the Erlitou culture—a Bronze Age urban society—as the most likely candidate for the Xia dynasty. Our account here adopts the more standard modern position, which traces the civilization to the Shang.

20 Together with Confucianism, these are known as the "three teachings" (三教, *sān jiào*), and are regarded as entirely consistent with one other, and are often referred to in aggregate.

As opposed to Western notions of history as a linear, progressive process, the ability to view events and developments as variations on a theme has helped China endure the vicissitudes that often accompany an extended history. It has also allowed the country to remain remarkably insular through much of its past and perceive itself largely through a domestic lens, a fact reflected in its name (中国, *zhōngguó*, literally "Middle Kingdom").

A Strong State and Agricultural Success Brought Prosperity But Not Industrialization

Unification under the Qin marks what most economic historians would consider a turning point in state organization of the economy. Much like in other parts of the world, ancient China operated on a feudal system, with competing states, a coarse hierarchy in society—of emperors, nobles, and commoners—and occupational classifications.[21]

Post-unification, there was a pivot toward empire building. The imperial state coordinated development, with a bureaucracy geared toward fostering fiscal and military state capacity, operating alongside a vast agricultural economy. The rural economy became increasingly commercialized, and centers of economic activity naturally rose up; these were, principally, along the major rivers.

By the time of the Song dynasty (circa 1127), China's economy was already a highly productive agricultural behemoth.[22] Agricultural innovations abounded; farmers deployed extensive irrigation systems—some still in use today—and the "dragon backbone pump" (龙骨车, *lónggǔchē*) enabled the efficient transfer of water from rivers to nearby fields (Figure 1.3). Farmers were also given strong incentives to expand production, with leasehold and freehold contracts granted on farmland. It was this efficiency in food production that enabled rapid population growth: between the start of the 15th century through the 19th, there was a quintupling of population, such that China accounted for around a third of the global population by 1820.

The imperial structure also meant that the traditional economy was supported by a number of fairly sophisticated institutional arrangements. Paper money facilitated commercial trade across an extensive empire, and emerged

---

21 These were the so-called "four occupations" (士农工商, *shì nóng gōng shāng*), literally the warrior (who evolved into scholar-officials under the Qin), the farmer, the artisan or craftsman, and the merchant or trader.

22 In addition to the adaptations of imported agricultural varieties (such as early-ripening rice from Southeast Asia), there was also intensive application of labor, and technological progress, via irrigation and soil renewal techniques. China underwent a total of three "green revolutions": during the Western Han (206 BCE to 24 CE), when iron plows were aggressively introduced by the state; during the Northern Song (960–1127) with early-ripening rice; and during late-Ming through mid-Qing (1644–1796), with the spread of New World crops, such as corn and sweet potato.

A Chinese Chain Pump with their singular method of working it.

Figure 1.3 The "dragon backbone pump" method of irrigation, among others, allowed for large agricultural surpluses to develop in China, and enabled the growth of a large population.

during the Tang dynasty as private promissory notes; the Song emperor subsequently took direct control of the system, and issued the world's first government-backed paper money. With the support of the state, the innovation spread quickly. By 1820, a third of all currency in circulation in China was accounted for by paper money.

Markets were competitive, both for outputs and inputs. The economy developed advanced procedures to facilitate commerce and trade. Written contracts were ubiquitous across the empire,[23] regulating relationships in the exchange of land, loans and leases, production, and even employment. The banking system was also sufficiently sophisticated to allow for nationwide money transfer (which is a nontrivial process for a large land mass). Alongside such formal institutions, clan associations[24]—social organizations that offered networking

---

23 While contracts that protected property and regulated trade predate the Chinese empire, the Song saw substantial innovations in different types of contracts, and the mass adoption of contract laws was unprecedented at the time.

24 These associations are often referred to as "companies" (公司, *gōngsī*), a term that taken on its modern meaning, although such organizations date back to much earlier in Chinese history. Clan associations also came to be known as "guilds" (会馆, *huìguǎn*), especially in the diaspora context.

opportunities for those from the same lineage—provided informal socioeconomic support beyond the formal state apparatus.

The (in)famous imperial examination system began in 605 CE (the Chinese have been taking exams for a long, long time!)—while criticized for its inflexibility to innovation by the late Qing—nevertheless allowed a meritocratic system for human capital to develop, at least if one was willing to subject oneself to the rigors of the process. The bureaucrat-scholar—sometimes referred to as a "mandarin" to those outside the realm—became an aspirational position.

The combination of a strong state and agrarian success meant that the economy of the Middle Kingdom had, by the time of the last dynasty in the early 20th century, become a vast, bottom-heavy economy, with efficient, small-scale agricultural production complemented by artisanal output—such as silk, porcelain, and tea—that was widely desired around the world. But in spite of all its successes and wealth, China never made the transition into the next stage of development, and the Industrial Revolution would end up occurring elsewhere.

Falling Behind the West

By the late Qing, old-school technologies were beginning to experience diminishing returns. What was worse, celebrated aspects of the Chinese system also began to erode. For example, military expansionism imposed a greater and greater draw on the public purse, and to meet rising fiscal needs, civil service positions—once the domain of only successful scholars—began to be (horror of horrors) sold, to raise revenue. This was antithetical to the principles of meritocracy upon which the high-functioning bureaucracy was founded, and with the corruption of this once-venerated institution, it was little surprise that it was abandoned in 1905.

The decline of the civil service was but symptomatic of a much broader decline of Chinese civilization around this time. The period between 1839 and 1939—a period known as the "century of humiliation"—saw the end of the dynastic system, the subjugation of the last dynasty (the Qing) to both Japanese and Western powers (Figure 1.4), and a failed effort to modernize the country under republican principles, culminating in a civil war. This narrative plays a central role in the worldview and identity of the Chinese, even today.

Far from a simple story of being overtaken by industrialized powers, the Chinese saw two interconnected factors that led to its travails. The first was domestic weakness, fed by internal disorder (内乱, *nèiluàn*). One such disruption was the Taiping Rebellion—fought between the Qing Empire and the Taiping Heavenly Kingdom, a Christian cult that had also managed to corral a standing militia of half a million soldiers, while also laying claim to half of China—which drained resources from the central administration, and the protracted civil conflict only took a decisive turn after a brutal siege of Anqing, the stronghold of the rebels.

Figure 1.4 Losses in military and civilian conflicts induced a scramble for territorial concessions by external powers, prompting fears of a carving up of the Middle Kingdom. *Source:* National library of france / Wikimedia Commans / Public Domain.

Similarly, the Boxer Uprising—an anti-foreigner movement started by martial arts-practicing peasants (hence the term, "boxer") against colonial oppression—eventually morphed into full-on unrest, lasting for almost two years, eventually engulfing eight different colonial powers along with the imperial government.

Internal challenges of this nature compromised the ability of the Qing to respond to external threats (外患, *wàihuàn*). The inability of the Chinese nation to muster credible responses severely weakened the perception of what had hitherto been viewed as one of the world's great empires, and this was the second key dimension behind the hundred years of humiliation.

The Boxer Uprising, for instance, provided the premise for external powers to demand territorial concessions from the Qing. These were essentially thinly-veiled colonization efforts—albeit somewhat milder, since they did not generally entail wholesale revamps of the prevailing political-economic system (which would have been practically impossible anyway, given China's history, size, and population)—and left a mark on the development of the Chinese economy. Foreign powers brought with them technology and capital, especially in light manufacturing, which the local Chinese business community eagerly lapped up. Concessions have left a mark, even till today; the former French concession in Shanghai hosts a range of high-end European restaurants, while

Qingdao—home to China's second-largest brewery, Tsingtao—reflects the legacy of the German concession there.

This was an unusual position for the Chinese economy. The country had historically been at the forefront of innovation, and, by dint of its superior manufacturing capabilities, this meant that China exported more than it imported. This led to large silver inflows from the rest of the world, and large trade surpluses. At the height of Qing power, the Qianlong Emperor was famously unimpressed by tributes of British manufactures, claiming that he placed no value on "objects strange or ingenious," and that China had no use for them.

China's erstwhile trade surpluses began to reverse, however, when Great Britain discovered a good that would prove irresistible to the Chinese: opium. Grown in British India, usage of the narcotic spread like wildfire across the Chinese population, prompting a crackdown on its sale. Objection by the British—in the name of free trade—then sparked the first of two wars, and the signing of unequal treaties that saw concessions in ports such as Shanghai, Fuzhou (Foochow), Guangzhou (Canton), and Xiamen (Amoy). It also, (in)famously, led to the then-permanent loss of Hong Kong.

But Western powers were not the only ones that shocked the Chinese empire. Japan had begun its modernization process in the late 1860s, and by 1915—having already wrested Korea as a tributary state from China—it was in a position to expand its territorial claims, and promptly did so in Manchuria (in northeast China). Insult was added to injury by the subsequent installation of a puppet emperor, Puyi, who would turn out to be the final emperor of not just the Qing, but the entire dynastic system.

A Brief Flirtation with Republican Government, Before the Communist Takeover

The collapse of the Qing was followed by a Republican period, proclaimed in 1912, and lasting through 1949, when the Communists seized power. The Nationalist Party (*Kuomintang*) ushered in industrialization, supported (perhaps paradoxically) by the influx of ideas and technologies that had entered China through Japanese and Western incursions the century before.

Be that as it may, the Chinese proved to be willing and able learners and imitators. Production capability in light and semi-processed consumer goods was quickly attained, especially around the Shanghai delta region, with forward and backward linkages along the value chain contributing to steady progress in industrialization. In Manchuria, the Japanese combined natural resource extraction with heavy industry, and while the objective was primarily to serve Japanese military interests, the region nevertheless gained a leg up in its industrial development, which would persist beyond the occupation.

The period was punctuated by two wars: the second Sino-Japanese war—occurring in the wings of World War II—and the Chinese Civil War, between the *Kuomintang* and the Chinese Communist Party (CCP). Both wars served to ravage not just the country but also its economy, with efforts to finance the war particularly pernicious for inflation (as is typically the case) and growth, with resources diverted toward wartime production. Ultimately, the CCP prevailed to became the next dynasty to rule the Middle Kingdom, and its Chairman, Mao Zedong, went from scrappy revolutionary to supreme leader.

Stops and Starts under the Communist Regime

While the start of the Republican period saw important moves toward the modernization of the Chinese economy, it was the slow pace of progress that ultimately set the stage for the subsequent Communist takeover.

After all, sentiment had already been ripe for change, as the country's experience with foreign aggression left it suspicious of Western institutions, technology, and worldviews—the very things that were being slowly infused into the Chinese system by the *Kuomintang*. Wartime resource mobilization further primed the economy for central planning, under a socialist industrialization strategy. And the neglect of much of the underdeveloped rural economy—in favor of pockets of promise in the wealthier coastal regions—excluded the vast majority of the Chinese economy from development.[25]

Despite entering the period with great promise—recall, this was a heady time for communist ideals, before experience revealed the system to be fundamentally flawed—and the launch of the great experiment started well enough. Adopting a "big push" industrialization strategy—where large, sustained increases in investment, led by command-and-control planning, were rapidly rolled out across the still-agriculture-heavy economy—the Communist leadership sought to drag the Chinese economy into the 20th century. The focus was on heavy industry. These were the "commanding heights" of steel, heavy chemical, energy, and machinery manufacture,[26] which were widely believed to benefit from state control and direction. Investment rates soared, almost doubling from 26 to 44% of GDP (albeit in a volatile fashion).

Amidst the enthusiasm, however, lay a practical reality: top-down production meant the need to coordinate optimal resource allocation in a large, complex economy without the benefit of detailed data (it was the 1950s, after all, well before the advent of the Internet or even spreadsheets). In decentralized

---

25 Unlike in the West and Latin America, which had already begun on the road to industrialization at the height of the Cold War, Mao could not center China's revolution on the proletariat. He chose the peasants instead, which also made China's communist struggle fundamentally distinct from of other contemporary revolutionaries.

26 The phrase may be traced back to political philosophy, especially Marxist economics, but was popularized by a PBS documentary series of the same name. See Yergin, D., *The Commanding Heights: The Battle for the World Economy* (New York: Free Press, 1988).

capitalist economies, the price system played the essential role of signaling resource needs; in the planned economies of the time, rudimentary input-output tables had to do the job. They proved inadequate for the task.

The excesses of the era came to a head in the Great Leap Forward, which was launched in 1958 and ended four years thereafter. In the run-up to the campaign, there had been a brief spell where liberal ideas were allowed to be expressed—the spirit was captured by the now-popular saying "let a hundred flowers bloom"—but this stance was (unfortunately) quickly reversed, as the CCP subsequently began persecuting perceived dissidents. This crackdown cleared the way for Mao to barrel forward with an ill-advised plan to modernize the Chinese economy by restructuring the agrarian sector around small industrial communes. The most (in)famous of these efforts was the proliferation of backyard smelters, ostensibly to manufacture industrial-grade steel, by melting down household objects such as pots, pans, and utensils. As one might imagine, such amateur efforts were doomed to fail. These communes were also encouraged to pursue controversial agricultural practices, such as close cropping and deep plowing. These untested innovations resulted in unintended declines in primary production. More perniciously, the terrible inefficiency associated with the relocation of workers from farming into makeshift factories, reduction of land dedicated to crops, and diminution of seed stocks (as grain was channeled to cities to feed urban workers) eventually culminated in widespread famine. The Great Chinese Famine resulted in an estimated death toll of perhaps 30 million excess deaths, and tens of millions more in postponed births and malnutrition (Figure 1.5).

As devastating (if somewhat ironic) as the Great Leap Forward was for China's development trajectory, it was nevertheless a program that sought to transform the traditional economy into a modern one. This cannot be said for the subsequent campaign, the Cultural Revolution (Figure 1.6). The decade-long movement was sparked by Mao's insecurity about adherence to communist ideology, and sought to purge the remnants of capitalist and antiquated elements from the economy (while reinstating Mao's central position as leader in the state). Power seizures spread across the country, supported by bands of students known as the "Red Guards," along with the military. This was eventually followed by the formation of revolutionary committees that revamped the curriculum toward ideology rather than knowledge.

The persecution by these groups was hard and fast. In addition to stereotypical class-based discrimination (landlords and the wealthy), academics and other intellectuals were also singled out.[27] Many were pulled from their classrooms—often by their very own students and sometimes even

---

27 There were nine "black" categories that faced discrimination during the Cultural Revolution: landlords, wealthy farmers, right-wingers, traitors, spies, bourgeois sympathizers (which Mao termed "capitalist roaders"), intellectuals, and, of course, antirevolutionaries, and bad influencers.

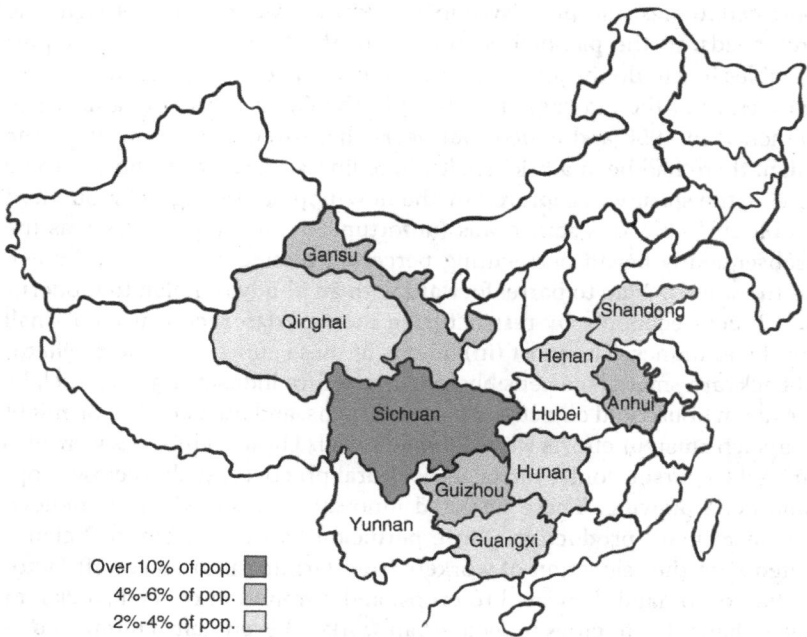

Figure 1.5 The Chinese famine, which occurred between 1959 and 1961, is the largest famine in recorded history, and was concentrated in the inland provinces.

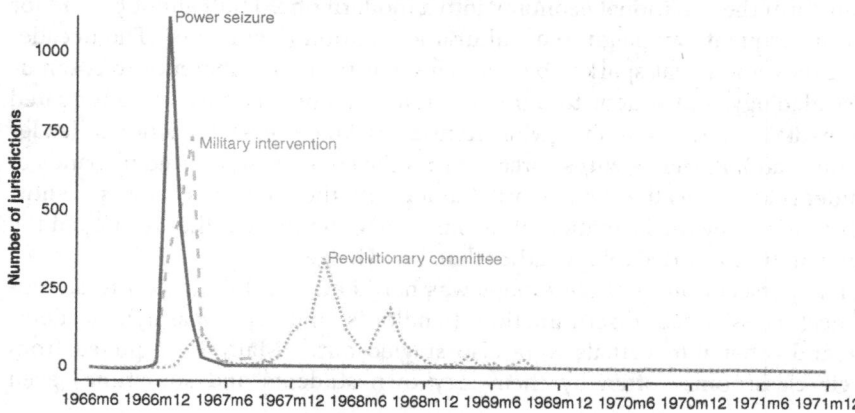

Figure 1.6 The early stages of the Cultural Revolution saw widespread power seizures and military interventions to quell the unrest; this was followed by a second stage where revolutionary committees seized power and induced civil government collapse.

children—denounced and humiliated, forced into public apologies, and in the most egregious instances, maimed and killed. Most were relegated to "rustication" programs where educated youths and teachers were sent to the country-side for reeducation. The Cultural Revolution only ended following the death of Mao, a decade after it began. By that time, hundreds of thousands of China's most talented human capital had been lost, illiteracy had spiked, and a whole generation of students had forgone years of education.

The Modern Chinese Economy

The Road to Reform and Transition of the Chinese Economy

Definitive economic reform—followed by the enduring ascendance of China's economy into the number two in the world—would only occur after Mao's passing. Mao's successor, Deng Xiaoping, had held positions of responsibility within the CCP, but had been sidelined in the years coming up to the Cultural Revolution. After assuming power, Deng reformed socialist ideology toward pragmatism, with the goal of adapting socialism to economic realities.[28] This mindset was perhaps best exemplified by his claim that "it doesn't matter if a cat is black or white, if it can catch mice, it is a good cat." In practice, this generally meant top-down direction, combined with bottom-up autonomy—a combination that enabled China to wriggle free from the institutional trappings of communist economic organization.[29]

To be entirely fair, the communist years were not uniformly detrimental to human and economic development. The ideology of equality saw the expansion in economic and educational opportunities to previously neglected groups, especially women; by the 1980s, despite being only a low-income economy, it boasted a female labor force participation rate well in excess of advanced countries (84% versus 61% in the OECD).[30] Similarly, while the dark years of the Cultural Revolution saw destruction in the *stock* of accumulated human capital, the *flow* of education and healthcare coverage did increase, as the CCP sought to expand such services across the country.

Nevertheless, the Chinese economy remained relatively backward, and required a shot in the arm. Fittingly, the catalyst for this did not derive from

---

28 As is common to many "Great Man" accounts of history, the credit accorded to Deng for China's transformation and subsequent takeoff is probably overwrought; other younger, behind-the-scenes officials—such as Hu Yaobang (a future Secretary-General of the CCP) and Zhao Ziyang (the Premier in the pre-Tiananmen period)—were instrumental in the execution of the new economic vision.
29 Ang, Y.Y., *How China Escaped the Poverty Trap* (Ithaca, NY: Cornell University Press, 2016).
30 This was accompanied by a narrower gender wage gap, estimated to be between 16–22%, in contrast to between 36–38% in the United States during the same period. See Wang, L. and J. Klugman, "How Women Have Fared in the Labour Market with China's Rise as a Global Economic Power," *Asia and the Pacific Policy Studies* 7(1) (2020): 43–64.

the top; rather, the genesis for change was a Chinese village called Xiaogang, located in Anhui, an eastern province. There, a small group of courageous farmers gathered to sign a contract that would assign property rights to each family, so that each household was able to farm and keep excess production.[31]

What is the big deal behind such an arrangement? Well, farming in China then was a *collective* effort; hence, all output produced on the farm belonged to the collective. As one might imagine, this system wasn't particularly endearing for fostering either effort or innovation. Production would often stall once quotas were hit, but—more often than not—they were *not* met, resulting in chronic shortages of food.

The brave farmers who signed the contract committed to not only respecting private property, but to also take care of the children of those that were caught or executed, at least until they turned 18. The contract was signed and hidden in the bamboo slats on the roof of one of the farmers' houses. The signatories then went back to their farming duties, as before.

As simple as this act was, the implications were profound. Secret competition in production ensued, and just by changing the rules, the harvest that season turned out to be greater than the previous five years combined. The farmers were discovered, of course. But because Deng was looking for a new approach, the Chinese leadership would hold up the autonomy demonstrated by Xiaogang as a positive example, branding the new model the "Household Responsibility System."

Success in agricultural production even spread beyond farming, as the model inspired town and village enterprises (TVEs), which were firms established under the purview of the local government, tasked with producing goods and services with an eye toward market competition. The transition away from communist stagnation had begun.

China's evolution into a socialist market economy may be broadly divided into two stages. The first phase, starting around the end of the 1970s and lasting through till the mid-1990s, involved the gradual introduction of market forces into the hitherto command economy. As the central administration loosened its control over the economy, the enormous distortions from prior decades were incrementally wrung out of the system, and market signals took on an ever-more important role in resource allocation.

This process was best exemplified by the dual-track pricing system (双轨制, *shuāngguǐzhì*), which simultaneously required firms to meet government-mandated allocations with sales at state-controlled prices, while also allowing them to sell off excess production in the marketplace. Starting from the

---

31 This fascinating story is recounted in Kestenbaum, D. and J. Goldstein, "The Secret Document That Transformed China," *Planet Money*, January 20, 2012, Washington, DC: National Public Radio.

mid-1980s, these allocations were steadily wound down, which permitted ever-more enterprise output to be offloaded at market prices.

The process was rudely interrupted, however, by the events of Tiananmen Square. Although most observers remember the event more as a failed pro-democracy protest, within China, the conditions that led up to the crackdown were symptomatic of how the first phase of reform was beginning to run into difficulties. As the decade ended, inflation had spiked up, peaking at almost 20% per annum. This ate into real incomes, and—alongside anger about corruption and arbitrary privilege—expectations rose for regime change.

Tiananmen derailed reform for two years, and Beijing sought to consolidate control over various arms of the state, especially over fiscal and monetary policy. But eventually, Deng embarked on his famous "Southern Tour" in 1992, where he visited a number of SEZs, and was able (almost singlehandedly) to revitalize the effort, with a renewed emphasis on the privatization of state-owned enterprises (SOEs) and ending the dual economy system. SEZs subsequently transformed entire economic regions—including much of southeastern China and the Pearl River Greater Bay Area—and remain a key economic engine of China. Thus began the second phase of China's transition, which is ongoing until today.

Perhaps it is unsurprising that the rousing success of the first phase of reform would eventually run into roadblocks. With the pervasive misallocation from the Communist period, allowing efficiency to return to the economy through rudimentary reform was low-hanging fruit; there were virtually no losers. By the second phase, continued restructuring would begin to displace entrenched actors; it was hence inevitable that this would result in more fervent resistance from these potential losers.

Through these tumultuous decades, it is difficult to overstate the influence that Deng had on ensuring that China's transition away from communism did not share the same fate as that of Eastern Europe. By the time the Southern Tour was conducted, the man was already in his late eighties, was officially retired as the paramount leader. Yet he retained his influence over economic and development policy, despite his sole official title being the Honorary President of the All-China Bridge Association.

Socialism with Chinese Characteristics

In a number of ways, the current challenges faced by China's economy stem from the combination of the economy's incomplete transition from a top-down, command-and-control economy, coupled with its aspirations—declared in its Five-Year Plan released in 2020—to break into high-income status by 2025, while doubling its output a decade thereafter. China is attempting to do so by charting its own, unique path; this is the premise for "socialism with Chinese characteristics."

To be clear, China's growth experience between the 1980s through 2010 was unique among large developing economies. The economy expanded at an average rate of 9% per annum for around three decades, and while this was indeed preceded by the success of the Newly Industrialized Economies (NIEs) of Asia, the sustained growth path remains unmatched by any large developing country, for so long. Regardless of what one thinks of China's future prospects, its record for the past thirty years is already undeniably impressive.

There have been detractors of this record, of course. Some have suggested that, because provincial bureaucrats are rewarded based on growth outperformance, official numbers may overstate GDP. Others have pointed to how alternative indicators—such as rail freight volumes or loan disbursements[32]—sometimes paint a conflicting picture of how the economy is doing. Yet others claim that it is impossible to accurately represent GDP in a command economy such as China's, since the growth target is an input, whose fulfillment depends only on the willingness of authorities to dedicate resources and incur debt to achieve the requisite amount of activity.

Even so, there are reasons to believe that China's GDP is reasonably accurate, at least on average. For starters, it is difficult to manipulate economic statistics on a wide scale, for an economy as large as China's.[33] Careful statistical analysis—using satellite data of nighttime lights as a proxy for actual activity—even point to the possibility that China's growth is *understated*.[34] What is most likely is that Chinese GDP data are *smoothed*; hence, the occasional exaggeration is as likely as an understatement.[35]

One lens through which to view the progress of China's development is to consider how its total factor productivity (TFP)—that is, the underlying productivity of the economy, after accounting for contributions from observable factors of production such as labor and capital—evolved during the half-century after reform began.[36]

During the Communist period, the whirlwind of misguided policies meant that China's TFP fluctuated wildly, achieving absurd highs—such as during

---

32 The most famous of these is the so-called Li Keqiang index, a composite of three indicators—railway freight volume, electricity consumption, and bank loan disbursements—that were purportedly deemed by the premier to be more accurate measures of economic activity.

33 What *may* be possible, some contend, is to manipulate the GDP deflator, which—as a blunt instrument—automatically adjusts real growth in a manner consistent with the target that one desires.

34 Clark, H., M. Pinkovsky, and X. Sala-i-Martin, "China's GDP Growth May Be Understated," *China Economic Review* 62 (2020): 101243.

35 Data releases since the COVID-19 pandemic, however, have become increasingly suspect, with unexplained delays in the release of routine economic data, and increasing divergence between proxies and officially-reported numbers.

36 The specific decomposition adopted here is not the only possibility, although most approaches yield comparable qualitative conclusions; for an alternative, see Zhu, X, "Understanding China's Growth: Past, Present, and Future," *Journal of Economic Perspectives* 26(4) (2012): 103–124.

the initial stages of the Great Leap Forward—but also plumbing lows, such as during the Cultural Revolution. After reform was launched in the mid-1970s, TFP growth enjoyed a cycle where there was enormous gains in TFP, as inefficiencies were easily wrung out of the system, and reform occurred almost in the absence of losers. Gains were driven by nonstate actors, such as TVEs, and the economy—which operated in the interior of its production possibilities—rapidly moved to the frontier.

After these gains were exhausted, tradeoffs in the reform process became more evident. Less-efficient SOEs had to make choices between maintaining high levels of employment, versus attaining efficiency in production. Nevertheless, there was a general move toward enhancing the economy's allocation of resources to exploit China's comparative advantages—cheap and abundant labor, along with its centuries-old artisanal tradition that enabled rapid advances in manufacturing capabilities—and this meant that TFP underwent another upcycle, before dipping at the turn of the millennium.

At the 15th Party's Congress in 1997, the privatization of SOEs was legitimized. This—along with China's entry into the WTO in 2001, which prompted further trade and investment liberalization—supercharged another cycle of TFP advancement (Figure 1.7). This time, China's exposure to the global marketplace—coupled with its ability to adopt technologies from abroad and adapt their production processes to Chinese innovation advantages—saw China being able to push its economy to the global production frontier in many sectors of the economy.

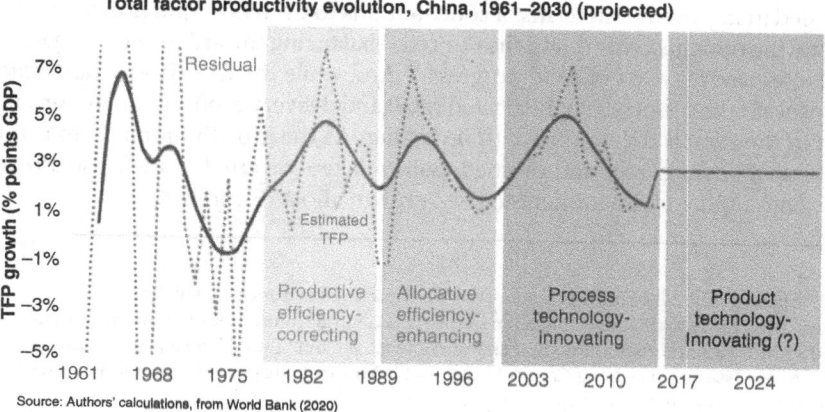

Source: Authors' calculations, from World Bank (2020)

Figure 1.7 Prior to reform, China's TFP was all over the place, fluctuating between absurd highs and lows. Post-reform, TFP first underwent a strong cycle of productive efficiency-enhancing growth, followed by one of improvements in allocative efficiency. As the economy continued to advance, China was able to adopt technologies from abroad and adapt them in their production processes. Whether China will be able to now develop new products of its own and advance the global production frontier will determine its economic success in the future.

This brings us to today. Whether China will be able to now develop new products of its own—while advancing the global production frontier—will determine the path of its TFP, which will bring with it the necessary economic dynamism for the economy to succeed in the decades ahead.

TFP growth, of course, is but one lens through which to view the continuing evolution of China's economy. Another angle is to consider how the economy has shifted away from primary agricultural production, toward secondary industry, and finally expanding the tertiary services. This program—to finally attain high-income status by transitioning away from being the workshop of the world toward advanced manufacturing (via the "Made in China 2025" initiative), and fostering the development of the domestic services sector—has been the overriding focus of Chinese policymakers since around 2015.

Concomitantly, China sought to move away from an investment-heavy, export-oriented growth strategy, to one that emphasized consumption and the domestic market. This so-called "Dual Circulation" approach,[37] championed by the Xi administration, is meant to entrench a more sustainable growth path, going forward. Concomitantly, China has embarked on a "Common Prosperity" (共同富裕, *gòngtóng fùyù*) policy that seeks to promote greater inclusivity in its growth—a challenge for an economy that has seen income inequality rise to levels that are among the highest in the world—by imposing reforms that overhaul excess profits in a range of sectors, including private tuition, video gaming, and technology.[38]

The success of these efforts remains unclear. While agriculture has indeed whittled in importance in terms of contributions to China's output growth, manufacturing remains central, and the desired rebalancing toward services began to stall after several years of solid progress.[39] And while the COVID-19 pandemic did provide the country's sophisticated retail and delivery economy an important shot in the arm, it did not prove to be lasting. As the growth momentum from the post-reopening rebound receded, policymakers reverted to their usual reliance on ramping up investment to keep growth afloat (Figure 1.8).

---

37 The principles underlying this model were first described in a speech, which was subsequently formalized after publication in the CPC Central Committee's bimonthly journal, together with various other follow-up Party documents, including the 14th Five-Year Plan. See Xi, J., "Major Issues Concerning China's Strategies for Mid-to-Long-Term Economic and Social Development," *Qiushi* 21, April 10, 2020.

38 Officially, the goal is to shave China's Gini coefficient—currently at 0.47—to closer to 0.4 by 2025 and 0.35 by 2035.

39 The importance of rebalancing was recognized prior to Xi, with Premier Wen Jiabao, who oversaw economic policy under Hu Jintao, characterizing how there was a risk of the economy being "unbalanced, uncoordinated, and unstable" as early as March 2007. This would prompt an effort to shift from export-oriented, investment-led to inward-oriented, consumer-led growth, manufacturing to services, and surplus saving to saving absorption via a wider social safety net, and reliance on foreign technology to indigenous innovation.

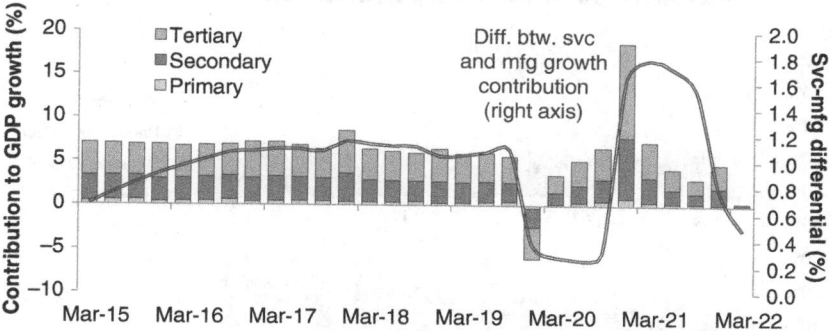

Figure 1.8 The rebalancing of the economy toward services stalled after 2017, and in the period immediately following the COVID-19 pandemic, China's services experienced a shot in the arm, before the economy fell back to the tried-and-tested approach of relying on investment to sustain growth.

A Complicated Dance Between the Public and the Private Sectors

The relationship between public and private enterprises in China is a complicated one. For starters, China has a large number of state-owned enterprises; by one count, there are 144,700 state-owned enterprises (SOEs) in China. These firms span the gamut of industries, and often reach into virtually every aspect of economic life in the country.

SOEs operate along multiple objectives; these could run from the standard profit maximization/cost minimization targets, to maximizing employment opportunities, to promoting social targets. Often, however, larger SOEs are called on to provide indirect welfare through work; accordingly, state firms tend to exhibit lower returns as compared to private ones. While unsurprising, this points to the relative importance of the private sector as a key driver of economic activity.

Between 1980 and 2012, investment by the private sector (relative to the state) fell from more than four-fifths, to a third. Led by the rise of Internet firms and electronic commerce platforms such as Baidu, Alibaba, and Tencent (the so-called BATs), the rate of private investment even overtook public investment in 2010, and persisted through the decade. This peaked in the middle of that decade—where the private investment rate topped 50%—before retreating dramatically thereafter. By 2022, public investment was growing by around one order of magnitude faster than the private sector (Figure 1.9).

The growing importance of the private sector as a dynamo for China's economic vibrancy may, as some have argued, be summed up with five ratios: 50/60/70/80/90.[40] Private firms contribute more than 50% of tax revenue,

---

40 The latter four ratios were documented in Cunningham, E., "What Is the Future of China's Private Sector?" *HKS Perspectives on China* (Cambridge, MA: Harvard Kennedy School, 2022).

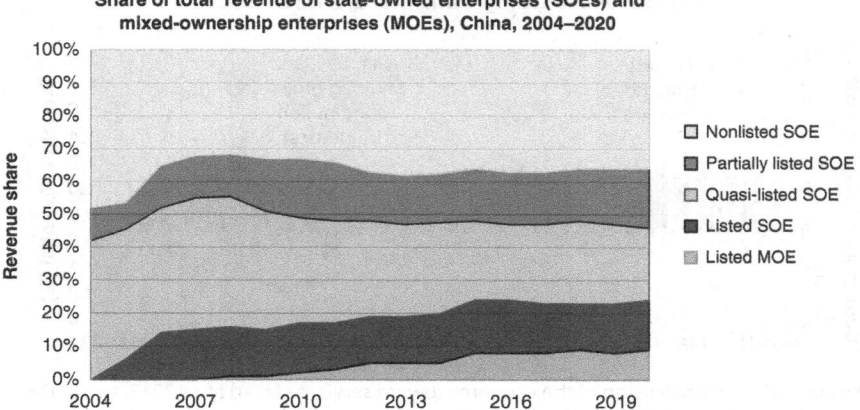

Figure 1.9 China's modern economy is no longer accounted for mainly by state-owned enterprises, which once dominated the landscape, but even after listing, many corporations nevertheless involve significant state ownership.

60% of China's output, 70% of its innovative capacity, 80% of its urban employment, and 90% of its new jobs. Even so, the sector is often shunted aside in the eyes of the CCP, and the manner by which the private sector operates in China differs from the way most observers, accustomed to Western-style capitalism, may be used to (or comfortable with). Importantly, entrepreneurship was not limited to urban China—which has historically been more state-controlled—but thrived in rural areas.[41]

One gnawing aspect of this is the centrality of *guanxi* (关系). While sometimes denigrated as cronyism, *guanxi* is more akin to a relationship-centric (as opposed to institution-specific) approach to doing business. While the preponderance of such ties can give rise to charges of unfairness in service access, violation of bureaucratic neutrality, or corporate corruption, it can also serve as a means of vetting client credibility in a weakly institutionalized environment, and an efficient means of vetting counterparties when informational asymmetries are widespread.

Regardless, the rising importance of the private sector—which is a net positive for growth—is inconsistent with China as a socialist market economy.[42]

41 Huang, Y., *Capitalism with Chinese Characteristics: Entrepreneurship and the State* (Cambridge: Cambridge University Press, 2008).
42 Deng Xiaoping even went as far as to affirm, back in 1980, that "whatever the proportion of the private investment will be, this will cover only a small percentage of the Chinese economy" and that it would "not affect the socialist public ownership of the means of production." That said, he also predicted (in the same interview) the "inevitability of a third world war," which we have yet to see. See Fallaci, O., "Deng: A Third World War is Inevitable," *Washington Post*, September 1, 1980.

More recently, the Xi government has sought to reassert the prominence of the state in the economy by taking ownership control of vertical business groups, with assets fully owned by the State-Owned Assets Supervision and Administration Commission, or other state investment entities. Beijing also imposed a wave of regulatory restrictions that constrained the business operations of a wide swathe of sectors, from Internet finance to private tuition. Such developments have prompted some to declare the end of economic reform in China.[43]

The dominance of such Chinese state capitalism extends beyond the borders of the Middle Kingdom. Across the world, China is now exporting this model of state-led development elsewhere. This is most evident in the Belt and Road Initiative (BRI)—which started life as the "One Belt, One Road" (一带一路, *yīdàiyīlù*) plan[44]—which exports excess Chinese saving to finance infrastructure development in other countries, and has evolved into a major plank of the Xi administration's foreign policy.

The Enduring Pernicious Legacy of the Population Policy

China's demography has always been a significant influence on its development. Through much of its history, China has relied on its agricultural productivity to sustain a growing population. Between the 15th and the early 19th centuries, the number of people quintupled, and by 1820, the country accounted for a third of the global population.

This rapid growth of the population brought concerns of its own. As incomes stagnated in the 19th century in the absence of any shift to modern economic growth, the potential risks from unmitigated population expansion was brought to the fore. Chinese demographers warned of overpopulation, and national policy began to reflect this concern. Officials began to champion the merits of having children later, waiting longer between births, and having fewer children (晚 稀 少, *wǎnxīshǎo*) in the 1970s, and when fears remained, this eventually morphed into the infamous one-child policy.

This approach toward family planning was, on balance, fairly uncompromising. Between 1980 and 2005, families were generally required to limit themselves to one child. This was sometimes enforced with forced sterilizations and abortions, as well as the mandatory insertion of intrauterine devices.

There were variations as to how the rules were effected, of course. Non-Han groups were not expected to adhere to the strictures, to avoid charges of discrimination. In some rural areas, there was also the possibility of having a second child, if the first-born turned out to be a girl.

---

43 Lardy, N., *The State Strikes Back: The End of Economic Reform in China?* (Washington, DC: Peterson Institute for International Economics, 2019).
44 The original nomenclature sounded too simplistic to capture the multifaceted initiative, which prompted its renaming as the BRI. The reference in Chinese, however, remains unaltered.

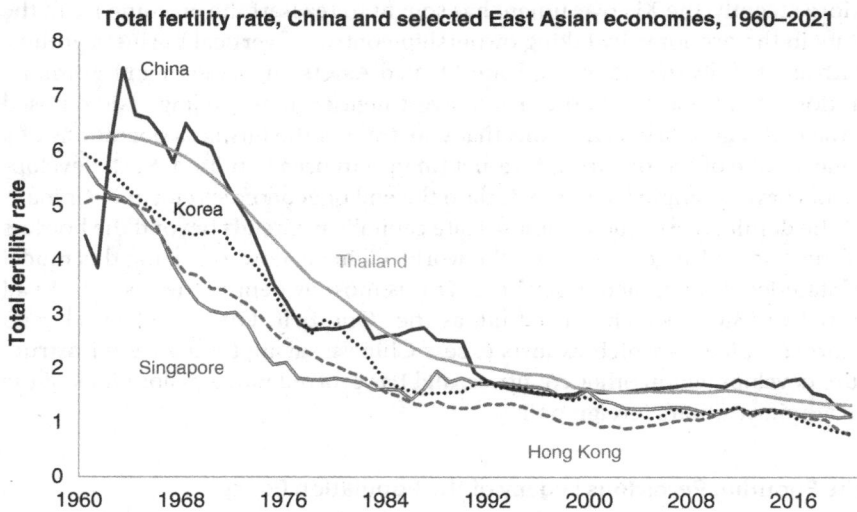

Figure 1.10 Although the total fertility rate declined in China throughout the period that the one-child policy was in place, this was also the case for virtually every other East Asian economy, bringing the actual efficacy of the harsh restrictions in doubt.

Still, the policy was applicable to an overwhelmingly large segment of the population, and fertility rates began to retreat, falling from about 6 in 1970 to less than 2 today. On its face, this might suggest that the strategy was an overwhelming success. But this would be misleading. Even before the official commencement of the policy, China's fertility rates had already begun to decline rapidly—by more than half—between 1970 and 1979 (Figure 1.10). Moreover, even a casual inspection of fertility rates for neighboring countries will reveal that the decrease was far from unique; fertility dropped across East Asia, even though those countries did not pursue anything similar to China's one-child policy.

What was more likely was that all these economies were undergoing demographic transitions—the process where rising incomes, education, and development lead to declines in the number of children born to women—which would have led to fertility reductions, even in the absence of such a draconian policy. If anything, the policy may have precipitated a greater collapse in fertility than desired, and introduced imbalances in the gender ratio, due to a cultural bias toward males, along with the potential practice of sex-selective abortions.[45]

Whether one is persuaded by the effectiveness of the one-child policy for controlling China's population growth, the sharp reversal of fertility to

---

45 The gender ratio currently stands at 105 males per 100 females, and is even more pronounced for age cohorts that were born at the time the policy was in effect. In addition to the inhumanity of sex-selective abortions, another upshot of this imbalance is increased risks of social instability, as many restless young men are unable to settle down in stable marriages.

below-replacement rates[46] has led to a scramble by policymakers to roll back this tumble. Keenly aware of the challenges of managing an aging population before the country became wealthy, policymakers acceded to a two-child limit in 2015. When this revised stance failed to move the needle much on births—beyond a short-lived boost the year after the policy was implemented—a new three-child policy was announced in 2021.

Dividends from Rural-Urban Migration Are Exhausted

Every month, 2 million rural residents are absorbed into Chinese cities. This has created enormous pressure on urban infrastructure, which has meant the need to not only support the ongoing movement of people, but it has also underscored the need to get ahead of impending needs with preemptive construction.

In some instances, this has led to the emergence of so-called "ghost" cities, where Chinese authorities are accused of overbuilding to keep the growth engine humming. The discovery of widespread financial difficulties faced by the country's largest real estate firms in the early 2020s—from private outfits such as Evergrande and Country Garden, but also afflicting state-owned developers such as Central China and Sino-Ocean—has lent further fuel to such charges.

Not all construction in China has resulted in futile white elephants.[47] Some of the most notorious examples of ghost cities—such as *Kongbashi*, a new development district in the Inner Mongolian city of Ordos—have gradually been populated,[48] fed by a shift of municipal buildings, office complexes (and hence jobs), and commercial and recreational amenities to the district, which induces the movement of residents from other parts of the city. Migration of the young from secondary towns does the rest.

Of course, such internal movements of workers from the rural to urban sector—and correspondingly from agriculture into manufacturing—is unsurprising from a development perspective (some would even go as far as to claim that this is the *definition* of development). This process will persist until all surplus labor, moving from the countryside in pursuit of higher wages, is exhausted.[49]

---

46 The replacement fertility rate is generally taken to be 2.1 children per woman in most advanced economies (with the additional 0.1 to account for child mortality), although in certain developing nations this can be as high as 3.5.

47 This point is made in Glaeser et al. (2017), while Rogoff and Yang (2022) contend that Tier 3 cities are facing the greatest difficulties. See Glaeser, E., W. Huang, Y. Ma, and A. Shleifer, "A Real Estate Boom with Chinese Characteristics," *Journal of Economic Perspectives* 31(1) (2017): 93–116.

48 Even the notion that *Kongbashi* and other new city centers remain underpopulated could arise from an inadequate understanding of China's urban development model, which entails the construction of a new center to replace the historical core in rapidly-expanding cities. For example, Shanghai developed *Pudong*, Guangzhou *Zhujiang*, Tianjin *Binhai*, Chengdu *Tianfu*, and so on.

49 This model was developed by Nobel Prize-winner Arthur Lewis, and is known as the dual-sector model: rural-urban migration dynamics are led by capital accumulation in the modern (urban) sector, while the flow of surplus labor from the subsistence (rural) sector keeps wages down, until all the worker surplus is exhausted (this situation is known as the Lewis turning point). See Lewis, A., "Economic Development with Unlimited Supplies of Labor," *Manchester School* 22(2) (1954): 139–191.

China has managed the speed of such unmitigated migration by the household registration system (户口, *hùkǒu*). The modern iteration of the system was implemented in 1958, as a means of tying farmers to the land on which they worked; this in turn ensured a supply of low-cost food to factories in urban areas.[50] Today, the system provides key public services—such as education, healthcare, and public pensions—only to residents registered with a particular town. The *hukou* system favors urban residents—since migrant workers from rural areas are constrained in their access to welfare and social protection—which has resulted in it becoming a *de facto* caste system.

For a long time, this process of inter-provincial and intra-provincial migration—managed by the *hukou* system—kept wages competitive. But China has since passed the turning point where wages remain suppressed due to the presence of excess labor (a constraint it did not face in the 2010s). The lure of urban jobs has thus eroded, with smaller cities struggling to attract internal migrants. With a widening gap between the large coastal cities and others, China embarked on *hukou* reform in 2020. The revised system now offers local officials in smaller cities the right to grant *hukou*, so long as migrants contribute to the local economy—with investment in a business, buying a home, securing a degree, or holding a qualified job—in some way.

Getting to grips with the real estate sector will be an ongoing challenge for policymakers in the years ahead, and the fragility of the construction and property sector (especially overbuilding in Tier 3 cities) is turning out to be one of the key concerns for the Chinese growth model, in its effort to sustain growth into the future. While the earlier round of excesses was rescued by a still-unfolding demographic boom and rapid urbanization—both of which provided the necessary demand to absorb excess supply of housing—it is difficult to argue that the same tailwinds exist today.

Human Capital as a Means to Offset a Shrinking Labor Force

With the labor force not only getting more expensive but also shrinking in size, China has searched for other means to derive a contribution from workers to its growth engine. Like other East Asian economies, it has leaned on developing human capital, through ramping up schooling efforts.

As discussed earlier, the Cultural Revolution had set back the educational endeavors of an entire generation. This is evident in the slower rate of schooling expansion throughout the 1980s—a reflection of the effects of forgone education by those who were students during the time of the Revolution. Perhaps more troubling is the fact that this interrupted education left a pernicious

---

50 The system can be traced as far back as the pre-dynastic era, and was used mainly for conscription and taxation, along with regulating migration.

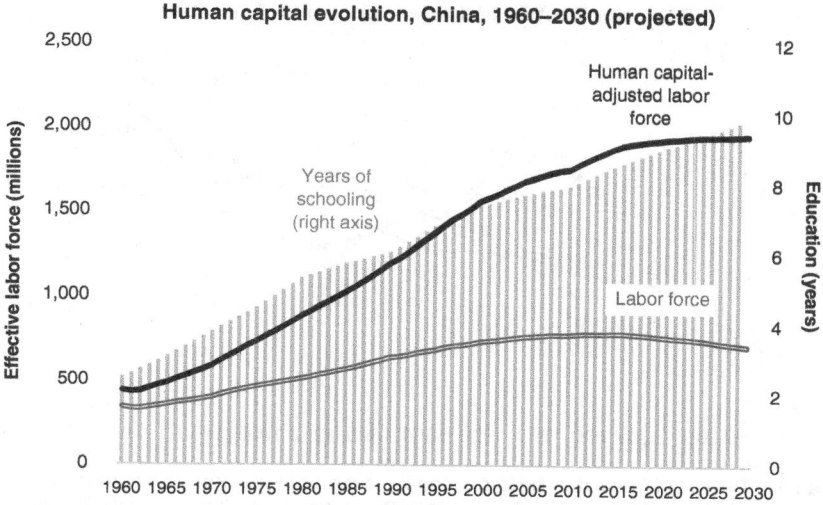

Human capital evolution, China, 1960–2030 (projected)

Figure 1.11 Between the 1990s through till the mid-2010s, China had been able to offset the effects of a slowdown in the labor force that resulted from its one-child policy, but as educational attainment begins to hit diminishing returns, the contribution of human capital will fade into the future.

legacy of lower *subsequent* educational attainment, long after the events of the 1960s and 1970s had passed.[51]

However, between 1990 through till around 2015, educational attainment began to accelerate again, and the labor force—adjusted for human capital formation—continued to grow strongly, even though the raw labor force had already begun to pare back (Figure 1.11). This allowed China to postpone the inevitable effects of a shrinking work force (which resulted from its old-child policy), although even this strategy appears to be approaching its limits.

China's Development in Comparative Perspective

A Return to Historical Dominance

Although China's rise may be perceived as such, in a number of ways, it is not so much a rise as a *return* to the country's historical dominance in the global economy (Figure 1.12). It is clear that, at the time when the historical Jesus walked the Earth, he did so within the context of a Roman empire—the most

---

51 See, for example, Meng, X. and R.G. Gregory, "The Impact of Interrupted Education on Subsequent Educational Attainment: A Cost of the Chinese Cultural Revolution," *Economic Development and Cultural Change* 50(4) (2002): 935–959. The evidence also suggests that the Revolution also left an imprint on other socioeconomic indicators, such as health and income.

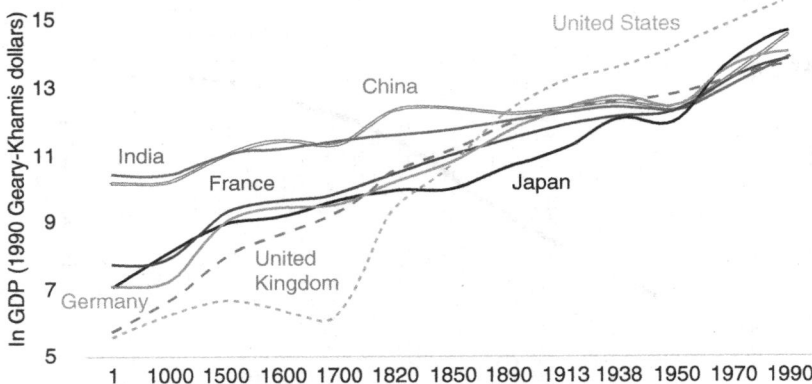

GDP, major Western and Asian economies, 1–1990

Figure 1.12 The rise of China may be understood as a return of the economy to its historical position of global prominence, after the Industrial Revolution led to it being overtaken by Western nations.

prominent empire in Europe at the time—that was dwarfed by its Chinese and Indian counterparts.[52]

Moreover, the Malthusian trap—the inability of pre-industrialized economies to generate enough (agricultural) output to break free from resource constraints that result in a natural ceiling on their population expansion—meant that most economies prior to the mid-17th century grew at broadly comparable rates. It took till the so-called Second Agricultural Revolution—which some have credited as a key precondition for the accompanying Industrial Revolution—before the takeoff of Western economies was achieved.[53]

The return of China to prominence after three centuries of lagging behind the West naturally prompts questions of why the Industrial Revolution did not occur in the two Asian giants of the time (nor in Japan, which did experience

---

52 Notice that the vertical axis is represented in logarithms—useful for cross-country development comparisons where each unit on upward or downward are equivalent in terms of growth rates—but this means that the actual size of the Chinese and Indian economies would be much larger if represented in absolute terms.

53 The First Agricultural Revolution, sometimes referred to as the Neolithic Agricultural Revolution, occurred around 12 millennia ago, and entailed the transition of roaming hunter-and-gatherer societies into sedentary settled ones, domesticating plants into crops and animals for husbandry. Some cite the Arab Agricultural Revolution, where agricultural techniques from the Islamic world were transmitted to Europe, as another important milestone, although this process was more a diffusion than a genuine revolution. The British Agricultural Revolution, which entailed innovative farming techniques (such as crop rotation) and new crops (such as the potato, due to the Columbian exchange), is more reasonably viewed as a genuine revolution, which justifies our adoption of the "second" nomenclature.

its own Revolution during the Meiji Restoration, but notably because of its willingness to import ideas and innovations from the West). This has puzzled economic historians, who have called this period the "Great Divergence."[54]

Scholars have pondered over the reason why it was Britain and the Netherlands that ended up experiencing the Industrial Revolution, even though China's Yangtze Delta region—along with India's Bengal region and eastern Japan—were comparably prosperous, and had many of the preconditions for takeoff.

While the myriad reasons for the Great Divergence fall beyond the scope of our discussion here, it is enough to note, for our purposes, that mid-17th-century Britain had certain advantages—such as easy access to coal reserves (which enabled inventions such as the steam engine), colonialism (that pushed for the deindustrialization of proto-industrial economies), slavery (where access to free labor enabled wealth build-up), marriage patterns (where later marriage permitted a focus on human capital to complement physical capital), and certain institutional innovations (such as property rights and the Industrious Revolution, a period starting in 1600, where rising education and an increase in demand for consumer goods fed longer hours and factory production) all likely played a role.[55]

Beyond the Great Divergence, there was a concurrent "Little Divergence" that was occurring in Asia, as Japan began to blaze ahead of historical leaders China and India in the 19th century. And even in contemporary times, divergences persist, emanating from the fast-growing NIEs, and even between China and India.

---

54 The term was first coined by political scientist Samuel Huntington, but popularized by historian Kenneth Pomeranz in his book of the same name. This view, which posits that any appreciable divergence only emerged in the 19th century, much later than originally suggested by authors such as David Landes and Angus Maddison who operate according to the Europeanist tradition, has come to be known as the "California School" (because many of its proponents are based in universities in that state). See Pomeranz, K., *The Great Divergence: China, Europe, and the Making of the Modern World Economy* (Princeton, NJ: Princeton University Press, 2000).
55 The case for coal is central to Pomeranz (2000), although this is disputed by, among others, Clark, G. and D. Jacks, "Coal and the Industrial Revolution, 1700–1869," *European Review of Economic History* 11(1) (2007): 39–72. The complex interplay between colonialism and industrial development is discussed in Ward, J.R., "The Industrial Revolution and British Imperialism, 1750–1850," *Economic History Review* 47(1) (1994): 44–65. The role of European marriage patterns is described in van Zanden, J., *The Long Road to the Industrial Revolution: The European Economy in a Global Perspective, 1000–1800* (Leiden: Brill Academic, 2009). On slavery, see Heblich, S., S. Redding, and H.-J. Voth, "Slavery and the British Industrial Revolution," NBER Working Paper 30451 (Cambridge, MA: National Bureau of Economic Research, 2022). The industrious revolution was described in de Vries, J., "The Industrial Revolution and the Industrious Revolution," *Journal of Economic History* 54(2) (1994): 249–270; while property rights are emphasized by Landes, D., *The Unbound Prometheus: Technological Change and Industrial Development in Europe from 1970 to Present* (New York: Cambridge University Press, 1969).

One possible explanation for China missing the Industrial Revolution boat may have little to do with other countries, but itself: a veering away from a highly competent state, which had been the mainstay in the Chinese development story and one of the Middle Kingdom's traditional strengths.[56] State capacity began to fray in the late Qing. The sale of mandarin positions weakened the credibility of the state apparatus. The Taiping Rebellion further eroded internal cohesion, and concessions to foreign powers further compromised fiscal balances in an already-overstretched empire. Centuries of remaining largely closed to the external world had fostered technological complacency. It was a retreat from a strong state that ultimately doomed China not only to miss out on the Revolution, but also not even to be in a position to embrace it as a late industrializer.

After all, as recently as the 1950s, per capita incomes were marginally higher in India, and industrial output between the two giants were broadly comparable (and in some instances, superior in India) (Table 1.2). India was even substantially ahead in some elements of infrastructure; in part because of the British colonial legacy, there was more than three times as much railway track laid in the Subcontinental giant. As late as 1990, GDP per capita in India was $1,200 in PPP terms, a hair above China's at $981.

Yet today, incomes in China are three times higher than India, and its GDP about six times larger. China has clearly managed to transform its economy at

Table 1.2 A comparison of China and India in the mid-20th century

Metric	China	India
GDP per capita (PPP $)	799	987
Industrial output per capita		
Coal (kg)	96	97
Steel (kg)	2	4
Electricity (kW)	0.005	0.04
Cotton spindles	0.01	0.02
Railroads (km)	20,746	72,000
Population	546,815	359,000

Source: Author's compilation, from Naughton (2007) and Bolt and van Zanden (2020).
Notes: For industrial output, data for China correspond to 1952, while that for India are for 1950. Railroad data are from 1936.

---

56 There is increasing recognition that, over and above institutional quality, state capacity can make a big difference to development outcomes, especially in managing conflict and promoting economic growth. See Besley, T. and T. Persson, "State Capacity, Conflict, and Development," *Econometrica* 78(1) (2010): 1–34. A comprehensive treatment is available in Dincecco, M., *State Capacity and Economic Development: Present and Past* (Cambridge: Cambridge University Press, 2017).

a faster pace than India's, in part by its earlier and more decisive embrace of liberalization in the economic sphere.

Climbing the Value-Added Ladder

Even China's transition—from communism to state capitalism—is itself a study in contrasts. China chose a distinct route toward liberalization: instead of the "shock therapy" transition favored by many Eastern European countries—where reforms were all enacted at once, and typically involved the rapid privatization of state-owned assets (often to the detriment of the citizenry and leading to the rise of an oligarchic class)—China chose a more gradualist approach. This was, in Deng's words, "crossing the river by feeling the stones," an exploratory process of regime transformation involving the slow but steady reallocation of resources and factors of production. This alternative strategy—of measured reform under the existing rules, without prematurely dismantling price controls before the economy was ready to absorb the full shock—arguably saved the system from a complete implosion.[57]

Today, China has embarked on its deindustrialization process, in its pursuit of high-income status by 2025. The process is ongoing, albeit limited at best. Employment and value-added shares remain significantly above those of upper-middle-income countries, let alone high-income economies (Figure 1.13).

Part of the reason for this tentative progress is due to the fact that it is attempting this shift away from industrial production at an unprecedented pace. Policymakers have also not completely given up on industry, with the stated goal of being a global leader in advanced manufacturing. Perhaps more critically, the start-stop process has been exacerbated by the repeated return to cranking up investment during times of economic slowdown—even in the face of diminishing returns on physical capital[58]—which has delayed the painful resource reallocations that would be necessary for a durable transition. Still, it would be premature to count China out, simply because it is an economy that has repeatedly confounded those who have doubted what concerted central planning is able to accomplish.

Some emerging evidence suggests that China is now actively competing in the most sophisticated industries, and actively innovating at the global technology frontier. Indigenous Chinese firms have entered fields such as artificial intelligence (AI), robotics, and the Internet of Things (IoT).[59] These aren't your

---

57 Weber, I., *How China Escaped Shock Therapy: The Market Reform Debate* (New York: Routledge, 2021).

58 There are good reasons to believe that Chinese investment is far less efficient today than it was in earlier decades. This can be seen by either by estimates of the marginal product of capital or the (inverse of the) incremental capital-output ratio (ICOR), both of which have fallen over time (by some estimates, ICOR is as poor as it has been for several decades).

59 *The Economist*, "Xi Jinping's Bold Plan for China's Next Phase of Innovation," *The Economist*, April 16, 2022.

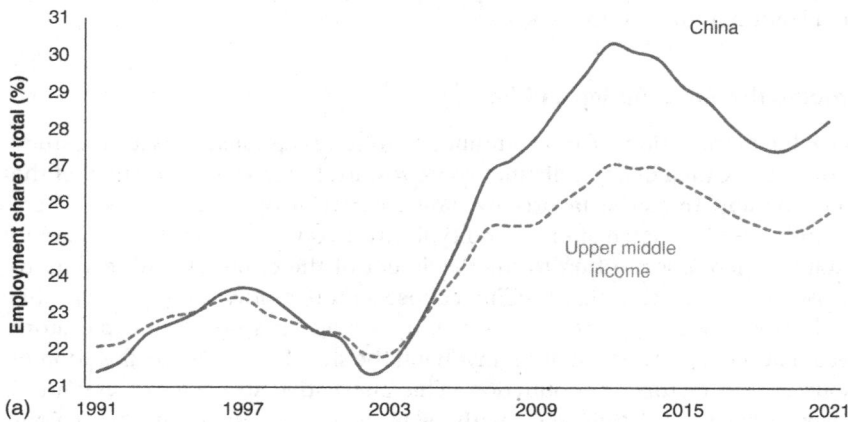

Figure title: **Employment in industry, China and global middle income, 1991–2022**

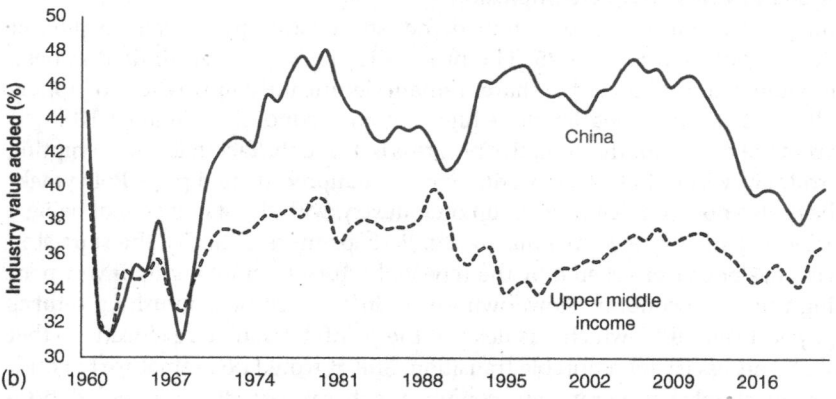

Figure title: **Value-added of industrial sector, China and global middle income, 1960–2022**

Figure 1.13 China is deindustrializing but it has not even reached (a) industrial value added or (b) employment shares consistent with other upper-middle income economies, much less those of high-income countries.

run-of-the-mill manufacturing plants. Revealingly, data on new company registrations show that such economic activity is no longer concentrated in the usual technology corridors; between 2016–21, growth in AI, robotics, and IoT has been highest in Hefei, Wuhu, and Chengdu, cities whose names are not commonly recognized outside of China. Such economic geography suggests that China's advances on this front are on a wider scale than commonly appreciated. And the data speak for themselves; China's manufacturing value-added is already the same as that of the Euro Area and United States, *combined.*

Just as critically, this climb up the value chain has also meant *de facto* control over critical global supply chains, in ways that are often even more thorough than commonly recognized.

Take green energy, for example. Many observers have lamented how China's global dominance in rare earth mining has given it a leg-up in many green technologies, such as electric car batteries and magnets for wind turbines, where such inputs are critical. But China is also often a controlling shareholder of mineral supply chains in third countries. While Australia accounts for a small majority of world lithium production, Chinese shareholders hold a stake of around a third of all global producers. A similar argument could be made about information technology, with China already having established its presence in electronics and computer design and assembly, and is now making a concerted drive into semiconductors and integrated circuits. More generally, China stands today as the largest exporter of intermediate goods worldwide, and in spite of the pandemic and the trend toward reshoring, most manufacturing chains still rely on Chinese components. Taken together, there is a possibility that the economy stands poised to dominate the production of the next-generation goods of the future.

Saving and Capital Accumulation as a Development Strategy

Not all of China's development experience is *sui generis*. Notably, China has followed one tried-and-tested recipe for rapid growth, common among the NIEs of East Asia that preceded its own takeoff: capital accumulation, funded by high domestic saving.

Up until the end of the Cultural Revolution, capital accumulation had been the predominant source of growth, even as TFP growth languished. As discussed earlier, growth since then has benefited from increases in TFP, but the expansion of physical capital remains a prominent driver. In 1980, gross fixed capital formation grew from about 30% of GDP to a peak of 45% in 2013. Today, China's investment rate remains routinely above 40%. For most intents and purposes, such sustained postponement of consumption is unsustainable, and it is entirely reasonable to expect some reversion in the economy's investment toward rates more commonly found in large, fast-growing countries (of around a third of output).

What is perhaps even more impressive is that through much of this period, China ran a current account surplus, implying that the economy was, on net, facing financial *outflows*. What this means, then, is that given its investment rate and current account balance, Chinese households, businesses, and government were collectively setting aside around half of all income as saving, for more than a decade.

Also taking the cue from other NIEs, this pace of capital accumulation was funded from high domestic saving. Of course, in an open economy with unfettered financial flows, leakages abroad would naturally constrain the amounts that could be deployed locally. However, there is a well-recognized propensity for savings to remain within borders,[60] due to reasons of behavior or transactions costs. In addition, China has deployed various other strategies to keep savings at home, notably via capital and foreign exchange controls.

While many might attribute China's remarkable saving rates solely to its frugal consumers, China's household saving rate—which, at around a quarter of GDP, is undeniably high, especially compared to the global average—is not unheard of in other emerging economies (India's household saving rate, for example, has been comparable in the 1990s and 2000s). China's national saving is boosted by high corporate saving, as well as the consistent tendency of its government to run fiscal surpluses (Figure 1.14).

There are solid reasons why China's household saving tends to be so high. These range from demographics (a hitherto young population tends to save more in anticipation for future dissaving when they reach retirement age), a limited social safety net (which necessitates setting aside one's own saving instead of relying on a public pension), financial repression (restrictions on cross-border capital flows, and a limited array of assets into which one may invest), and even gender imbalances (the one-child policy has not only placed the burden of supporting two elderly parents on a sole income earner, the cultural preference for sons has resulted in competitive signaling for marriage, by demonstrating sufficient savings).

In contrast, corporate saving tends to be elevated for different reasons. Principally, firms—especially small and medium enterprises (SMEs)—have had limited access to financing from large state banks. This is especially when compared to state-owned enterprises (SOEs), who enjoy preferential low interest rates due to their perceived safety, and thus comprise the majority of loan volume and up to 90% of corporate bond issuance (despite contributing less than a third to GDP).[61] Hence, Chinese SMEs have relied more frequently on retained earnings compared to SOEs, and this likely accounts for the higher corporate saving rate.

China's fiscal surpluses are less unique, at least from an East Asian perspective, where governments have typically limited welfare payouts, kept budgets

60 This observation—that domestic saving and investment are highly correlated—was first documented by the economists Martin Feldstein and Charles Horioka, in 1980. This is one of the major puzzles in international macroeconomics and finance, and while explanations for why this puzzle exists fall beyond the scope of this book, the reality is that this phenomenon continues to be observed, even today. See Feldstein, M. and C. Horioka, "Domestic Saving and International Capital Flows," *Economic Journal* 90(358) (1980): 314–329.
61 Liu, Z.Z., "China's Village Bank Collapses Could Cause Dangerous Contagion," *Foreign Policy*, July 27, 2022.

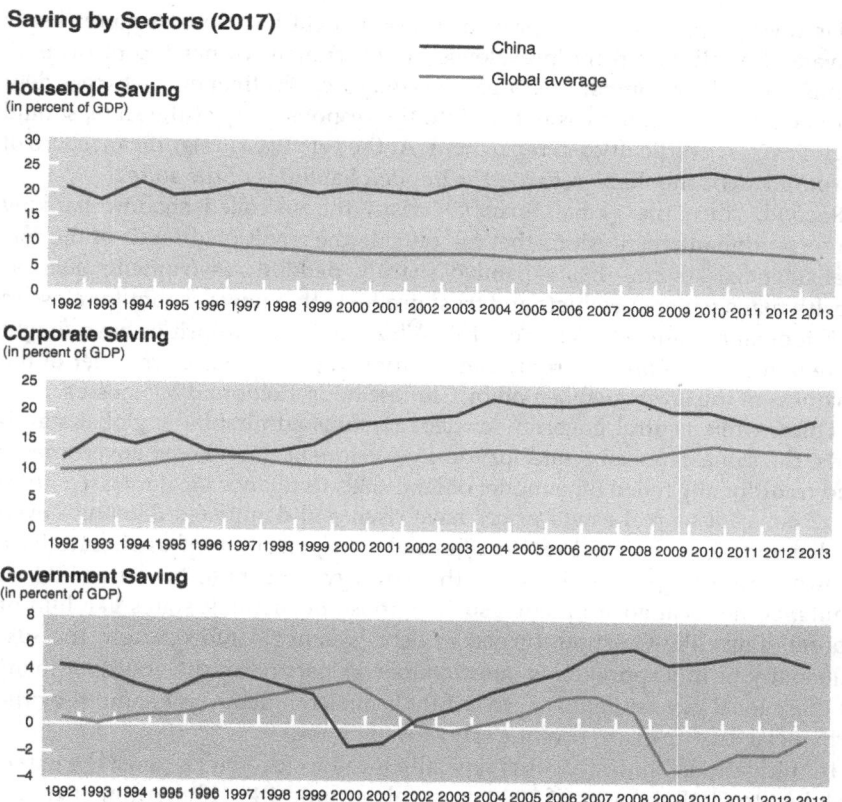

Saving by Sectors (2017)

— China
— Global average

Household Saving
(in percent of GDP)

Corporate Saving
(in percent of GDP)

Government Saving
(in percent of GDP)

Figure 1.14 China's surplus saving has been boosted mainly by high household saving rates, although both corporate and government saving tends to be positive as well.

lean, and enjoyed the upshot from financial repression. Notably, the government has been willing to run deficits where needed to support the economy; it did so in the wake of the Asian financial crisis in 1997–98, and again ran massive budget deficits—estimates place it at more than 3% of GDP for 2020–21— as the government again pulled the fiscal lever to offset the slowdown arising from the pandemic.

Even though China's history of sound government saving has meant a relatively low public debt burden—between 1995 and 2020, the average was only around a third of GDP, and even in the aftermath of the pandemic, debt is still a manageable two-thirds of income—there are three potential vulnerabilities that Chinese policymakers will need to contend with.

First, what appears to be a private corporate debt burden isn't quite clearly private after all. Given the prevalence of government ownership of firms in China—and their comparatively easy access to cheap financing—excess debt taken on by SOEs could easily turn into the responsibility of the state, should such firms face difficulties in repayment. At the very least, a significant share of corporate debt should be regarded as implicit liabilities of the state.

Second, since the global financial crisis, the so-called shadow banking sector—nonbank institutions that fall outside the traditional remit of the formal financial system—has expanded sharply, peddling instruments such as wealth management products and trust products that now account for close to a fifth of all private debt (Figure 1.15). While Chinese authorities have sought to rein in excesses on this front, their continued presence is a reminder of the riskiness of the leverage taken on by Chinese households and businesses.

Third, while central government debt remains admirable by global standards, the same cannot be said for local government debt. Local governments had traditionally relied on a model of land sales to finance local infrastructure provision, but as real estate prices have risen and dampened demand—even as demands for municipal services beyond transportation infrastructure have grown with a larger middle class—this strategy appears to have run into its limits. Some local governments, such as those in rust-belt states like Jilin or poorer states like Guizhou, turned to debt issuance. Unfortunately, the sustainability of this approach is questionable; in particular, the ability of many of these local governments to pay off their incurred debt—as captured by the provincial debt-to-fiscal revenue ratio—is in doubt.

In mitigation, Chinese debt is typically owed to its own citizens; the external debt to GDP ratio, as of 2022, was only around 14%. If anything, the rest of the world owes China more than it owes them, with outstanding claims amounting to more than 5% of global income.[62] Domestic saving rates remain among the highest in the world, and even as this has come down from the peak of around half of GDP, it still hovers comfortably around 45%. And perhaps most critically, policy levers remain in place to cushion against any sudden transition. In particular, Beijing has retained strict rules on financial outflows by citizens and noncitizens alike; such capital controls, while inhibiting the internationalization of the *renminbi*, supports higher debt levels than otherwise.[63]

---

62 Horn, S., C. Reinhart, and C. Trebesch, "How Much Money Does the World Owe China?," *Harvard Business Review*, February 26, 2020.
63 Wang, T., *Making Sense of China's Economy* (New York: Routledge, 2023).

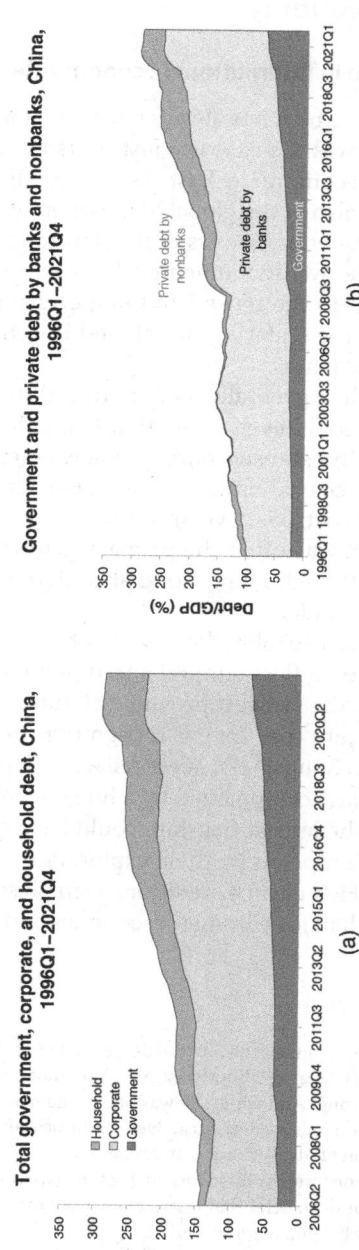

Figure 1.15 (a) Although public debt in China in low by global standards, private debt is high, especially in the corporate sector, which includes many state-linked firms. (b) Moreover, the lightly-regulated shadow banking sector has grown in importance since the global financial crisis, lending a further source of vulnerability.

China and the World Economy

Ancient China's Ambivalence in International Economic Relations

Over the long span of history, China has always been a major influence on the international economy. This was the case not just in its immediate neighborhood, where, as the largest economy in East Asia, it predictably dominated commercial relations. It was also at the global level, where it maintained trading relations with various economic powers of the day, ranging from dealings along the Silk Roads,[64] to the well-documented travels of explorers such as Marco Polo and Ibn Battuta, to the tense late-Qing exchanges with colonial European powers, especially the seafaring British and Dutch. This was by virtue of the country's economic mass.

By and large, the country had generally looked inward insofar as trade ties were concerned, and some would even argue that China has a distinct aversion to international trade.[65] Its extensive port system was geared mainly in the service of connecting major coastal cities (via an extensive canal network[66]) or inland provinces to the coast (via rivers), rather than the world at large. Guangzhou, in the far south, was often the primary gateway between China and the rest of the world, although Hong Kong also played a secondary role, especially vis-à-vis European trade.

This inward orientation was probably the reason why the voyages of Zheng He (also known as Cheng Ho), a fleet admiral and diplomat, were so notable. Zheng He, a Muslim born in the far west province of Yunnan, led seven expeditions during the Ming empire that sought recognition from kingdoms and principalities Southeast Asia, South Asia, West Asia, and East Africa.

Records indicate that he was accompanied by a huge fleet—both in size and number—for each voyage. The largest flagship would have been several times larger than those used by Europeans in their exploration of the New World (Figure 1.16). While Zheng He's naval expeditions were designed to elicit awe and extract tribute—rather than for commerce, conquest, and colonization—it

---

64 Although often referred to in the singular, the Silk Roads were a network of land and maritime routes that connected East Asia with Southeast Asia, the Indian subcontinent, Central and West Asia, East Africa, and beyond. And while silk was one of the main (and most lucrative) commodities that was traded, other goods included tea, dyes, perfumes, and porcelain, and the routes were a source of transmission of ideas, disease, and religion.

65 Such a position that would be bolstered by incidents such as the *haijin* (海禁, literally, "sea ban"), which was a series of isolationist policies that restricted private maritime trade and coastal settlement during the Ming and early Qing empires.

66 The most famous of these was the Grand Canal, for which construction commenced during the Sui Dynasty (581–618 CE), and is the longest artificial river in the world. The Grand Canal runs between Beijing (and the Yellow River) in the north and Hangzhou (and the Yangtze River) in the south, and played an important role in unifying northern and southern China.

Figure 1.16 Chinese historical records suggest that the largest of Zheng He's ships, so-called "Treasure Ships," measured in excess of 120 meters in length. This would have dwarfed the *Santa Maria*—the largest of the three ships used by Columbus to sail across the Atlantic to the New World.
Source: Mary Harrsch / Flickr / CC BY-NC-SA 2.0

is not difficult to imagine how the fleet would have impressed each port of call, and extended Chinese influence all over Asia at that time. Some have even argued that had Zheng He not stopped at Africa and had continued on to round the Cape of Good Hope on to Europe, global history would have evolved very differently. While speculative, it is probably fair to say that, in spite of the country's ambivalent views on international economic relations, it neverthe- less exerted a pull, both positive and negative, on other economies in Asia.

This traditional dominance, of course, quickly reversed during China's cen- tury of humiliation. Like in many other parts of the world, China was forced to open up to Western trade in the 19th century, the result being Treaty Ports where foreign influence increasingly held sway. But the effects of such ports on Chinese development were not uniformly negative. For example, Shanghai and Tianjin (as well as Hong Kong, which was a concession rather than a Treaty Port) became even more prominent commercial centers due to their status, and the transfer of technology in light industry led to proto-industrialization during the Republican period.

Contemporary China's Deep Integration with the Global Economy

Yet China's return to global economic prominence has relied heavily on inter- national connections. Trade went from a single-digit share of output—similar to the United States at the time—to a peak of around two-thirds prior to the global financial crisis, before retreating to about two-fifths in 2020. While the Chinese economy is undoubtedly more inward-looking today than it was in the past, it retains a level of trade integration that is closer to that of small open economies (such as Canada, Mexico, or South Korea), as opposed to the United States, which is quintessentially cited as a closed economy.

Furthermore, China remains a critical node in the East Asian production network. Its role has evolved over time, of course. When the economy first reopened in the 1980s, it enjoyed high levels of foreign direct investment (FDI) into its SEZs, principally from the large ethnic Chinese diaspora located in Hong Kong, Singapore, and Taiwan, and (to a lesser extent) those residing in Malaysia and Indonesia. It was such FDI from Hong Kong investors into Shenzhen that led to its meteoric rise (Figure 1.17).

China became so integrated into the global economic system that some have argued that China and the United States constituted a "revived Bretton Woods" system, with China as a peripheral economy benefitting from a relatively undervalued exchange rate to drive its export-led economic model.[67] This,

---

67 The original Bretton Woods system had the United States as the center economy, and the system of fixed rates to the U.S. dollar meant that European economies with relative weaker exchange rates during the 1944–1971 period often experienced rapid, export-led economic growth that accelerated their post-war recoveries. This international monetary system was abandoned in the 1970s after the U.S. suspended the convertibility of the dollar to gold, and major economies adopted floating exchange rate regimes. The revived system relies on exchange rate policy aimed at actively maintaining an undervalued rate vis-à-vis the dollar as a strategy for development. See Dooley, M.P., D. Folkerts-Landau, and P.M. Garber, "The Revived Bretton Woods System," *International Journal of Finance and Economics* 9 (2004): 307–313.

Figure 1.17 From its humble beginnings as sleepy coastal town, Shenzhen has rapidly developed to become China's premier tech city. This meteoric rise began with the designation of China's first SEZ, which absorbed foreign direct investment and (especially) manufacturing business from nearby Hong Kong, as it deindustrialized.
Source: (a) Chris / Flickr / CC BY-NC 2.0, (b) Charlie fong / Wikimedia Commans / CC BY-SA 4.0

understandably, prompted not a small amount of protestation from the United States—facing yawning bilateral trade deficits with China that amounted to a whopping $268 billion in 2008 (or 1.8% of GDP)—that the Middle Kingdom was engaged in unfair economic competition.

These sizable bilateral surpluses were not incurred vis-à-vis the U.S. alone; China also did so relative to many other emerging markets, as well as most economies within the Euro Area. In many cases, China has even usurped the U.S. as the principal trading partner with these economies; such nations include not just Asian nations, such as Indonesia, South Korea, and Saudi Arabia, but also further afield, with economies such as Brazil and Russia. With China's surpluses, at its peak, accounting for almost 1% of world GDP, there was a sense that such giant surpluses could become a source of global instability.[68]

---

68 Ultimately, the global financial crisis was less of a result of China's large trade surpluses, *per se*, as much as poorly-deployed financial inflows received by the United States and other Western nations, such as Spain and the United Kingdom.

Furthermore, it is generally inappropriate to attribute observed current account imbalances to China's export prowess alone. As the final assembler in the East Asian production chain, the entire final price of a product is attributed to China as an export. Yet, typically, only a fraction (and sometimes a tiny fraction) of the actual product value accrues to Chinese nationals.

Nowhere is this illustrated more vividly than when looking at the iPhone. Apple's flagship mobile device is famously assembled in China, by the precision contract manufacturer Foxconn (which, incidentally, is a Taiwanese corporation). Since the final product is shipped from China, the full value of the phone is attributed to China, as part of its export basket. Yet a careful decomposition of the major components and costs of the iPhone reveals that only a small fraction—around 4% in 2009—is China's contribution, even as the iPhone-specific trade surplus is recorded at around 73%.[69]

The upshot of China's current account surpluses is that the country has simultaneously had to endure a substantial financial outflow.[70] Much of China's foreign asset holdings, especially by the official sector, is destined for low-yielding U.S. Treasuries. While Chinese policymakers have scaled back their exposure to such securities, the amounts remain astronomical, and remain just a little shy of $1 trillion.

This translates into a significant, low-interest loan from Chinese savers to American consumers. Unsurprisingly, this unwitting lending has not endeared itself to the Chinese, even among the policymakers who recognize that this outcome is the consequence of its own pursuit of currency undervaluation. Cognizant of the long-run political economic implications of this development strategy, China has begun a process seeking to internationalize the *renminbi*. This approach has been most advanced in terms of the push by Chinese authorities to invoice cross-border trade in its domestic currency, as well as encouraging its use offshore as a vehicle for exchanges it is not directly involved in.

But even as policymakers have encouraged the *private* sector to evolve away from the greenback, the public sector has been far less reticent in pursuing the same; China still officially pegs the *renminbi* to a basket of currencies

---

69 This was the case for the iPhone 3, where China's assembly costs were only $6.50, in contrast to a total bill of materials amounting to $172.46. See Xing, Y. and N. Deter, "How the iPhone Widens the United States Trade Deficit with the People's Republic of China," *Aussenwirtschaft* 66 (2011): 339–350. This has changed as China has climbed the value ladder, albeit trade statistics continue to exaggerate the Chinese surplus; for the iPhone X, Chinese inputs amounted to about a quarter of value-added. See Xing, Y., "How the iPhone Widens the U.S. Trade Deficit with China: The Case of the iPhone X," *Frontiers of Economics in China* 4 (2020): 642–658.

70 This is the consequence of the current account identity, which states that the current account (CA), financial account (FA), and capital account (KA) must sum to zero. For virtually all economies, the capital account (international capital transfers, which are mainly comprised of debt forgiveness or gift and inheritance taxes) is negligible, and so CA =−FA, that is, a current account surplus must result in financial outflows.

dominated by the U.S. dollar, and its reserves are still overwhelmingly denominated in dollars (although it has steadily sold its holdings since 2020).[71] Just as important, it has held back from allowing full convertibility of the *renminbi*, which means that full internationalization remains impossible.

Some have suggested that, with rising wages, China will inevitably become less attractive as a global manufacturing hub. The day of reckoning—when Chinese factories are no longer internationally competitive—may well be in the offing, but this may still be a half-decade or so away. After all, rising productivity has gone some way to offset the cost disadvantage. And costs should be viewed holistically; beyond low wages, China possesses an entire manufacturing ecosystem of upstream and downstream components suppliers, often collocated in the same SEZ or industrial park, that is not easily found elsewhere.

The Xi government's recent turn toward greater self-reliance[72] (自力更生, *zì lì gēng shēng*), and the related dual circulation strategy, should therefore be understood in the context of China's inescapable ties to the world economy. No matter how much policymakers may seek to reorient the economy inward, China is far from autarky, and is unlikely to head that way anytime in the near future. All that said, it remains a reality that China's export share of output—which peaked at 36% in 2006—has hovered closer to 20% since 2016, which speaks to its inward turn over time.

The All-Encompassing Belt and Road Initiative (BRI)

With the BRI, China has sought to revive the notion of 21st-century Silk Roads, to foster international trade and infrastructure networks, both by land and sea. The effort has two main thrusts: a so-called Silk Road Economic Belt—a transcontinental passage that links Central, South, and Southeast Asia, Russia, and Europe—and a Maritime Silk Road, which connects China's coastal regions to South, Southeast, and West Asia, the South Pacific, and Eastern Africa.

To lend support to the initiative, China recycled a good amount of its domestic excess savings into related financing vehicles. The flagship lending institution for the BRI is the Asian Infrastructure Investment Bank (AIIB), which, as the name implies, focuses on infrastructure projects (although the "Asian" is somewhat of a misnomer, since it comprises more than a hundred members from all inhabited continents). China also created a separate Silk Road Fund,

---

71 Basic economic theory tells us that money fulfills three functions: a medium of transaction, a unit of account, and a store of value. The private (public) function of a currency in these dimensions are as a vehicle (intervention) currency, an invoicing (anchoring) currency, and as an investment (reserve) currency.

72 The term recalls a Mao-era slogan, which emphasized how China would revive its economic fortunes through its own, independent efforts, by embracing Communist principles.

devoted to investing in businesses. The AIIB was initially capitalized at $100 billion, and the Fund at $40 billion. Their sheer size—the AIIB has about half the capital of the World Bank, and two-thirds that of the Asian Development Bank—is a testament to how seriously China treats the BRI.

The sometimes ill-defined (or perhaps all-encompassing) nature of the initiative has meant that just about any trade, financial, infrastructure, or policy program that China has embarked on in recent years ends up being classified as a BRI project. Still, the sheer amounts of cash involved, along with the extensive geographic reach, has meant that the BRI has been a mainstay in global development conversations since 2013.

Although many mainstream news sources (and even certain Western-centric policy shops) have hyperventilated over the risks posed by Chinese debt diplomacy and economic expansionism via the BRI, the reality is somewhat more complicated, and a middle-ground approach—where the effects should neither be overestimated nor dismissed—is probably justified.[73]

To be clear, the initiative has seen bilateral debt owed to China rise in a significant way, especially in the developing world. Chinese construction projects and manufacturing complexes dot the landscape of many an African or Southeast Asian nation. But the track record of these projects is typically mixed, as one might expect for investments in emerging markets, with a nontrivial number failing to pay off economically.

Moreover, a more careful examination of lending relationships such as the dreaded "debt trap"—where Chinese creditors have been accused on making loans to finance strategic assets around the world, and forcibly taking such facilities over when indebted countries fail to repay—reveals more nuance than commonly assumed. The poster child for such Chinese neocolonialism is the Sri Lanka port of Hambantota, which saw the majority-owner China Merchants Port Holdings take over operations in 2017, after the Sri Lanka government signed a concession lease agreement. Contrary to the popular narrative, this agreement did not result from loan default by Sri Lanka, followed by a debt-for-equity swap. Instead, Hambantota was leased to the Chinese conglomerate to turn around profitability at the ailing port.[74]

73 Two such examples, corresponding to the effects of the BRI in Asia and Africa/Latin America, respectively, are Gong, X., "The Belt and Road Initiative and China's Influence in Southeast Asia," *Pacific Review* 32(4) (2019): 635–665; and Bräutigam, D. and K. Gallagher, "Bartering Globalization: China's Commodity-Backed Finance in Africa and Latin America," *Global Policy* 5(3) (2014): 346–352.
74 There is, however, a separate question of whether the funds received for the stake in the port were appropriately deployed thereafter. The money was not directed toward repayment of the loan for financing the port's construction, but to cover the balance of payments difficulties for the country. Similarly, the issue of whether it was commercially viable to build the port in the first place—or whether the port was simply a glaring example of political corruption—remains open. See Moramudali, U., "The Hambantota Port Deal: Myths and Realities," *The Diplomat*, January 1, 2020.

BELT AND ROAD INITIATIVE

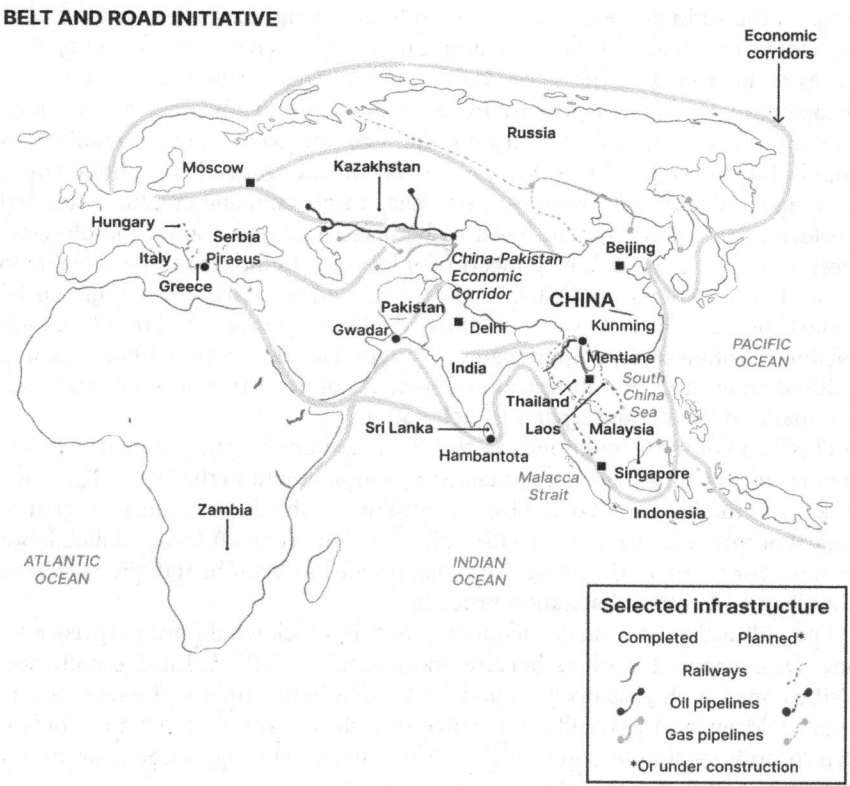

Figure 1.18 While unarguably ambitious, the track record for the Belt and Road Initiative is mixed. A nontrivial number of projects have been completed under the scheme, and while returns on some projects, such as Sri Lanka's Hambantota, have been disappointing, others, such as the revitalization of Greece's Piraeus, have found greater success.

Overall, the track record for the initiative remains mixed (Figure 1.18). Exaggerated claims aside—China claims the creation of 420,000 jobs and 40 million lifted out of poverty as a result of BRI-related stimulus—a substantial number of projects, ranging from energy to real estate to transport, have nevertheless been financed under the auspices of the scheme, and a nontrivial number have been completed. And for every project with lukewarm returns (such as Hambantota), there have also been others that have enjoyed better returns (such as the revitalization of the Greek port of Piraeus).

The China Shock and the Sino-U.S. Trade War

China's membership in the World Trade Organization (WTO) had profound effects not just within China, but also on the rest of the world. After all, it entailed the sudden injection of a 735 million-strong labor force into a global workforce that was only around four times larger; given the prevailing low wages of the average Chinese worker at the time, this meant a sudden influx of cheap competition for, especially, lower-skilled labor in advanced economies.

Economic theory offers sharp predictions for what trade liberalization implies for the welfare of workers, especially for the relatively less-skilled ones residing in advanced economies.[75] As cheap imports, made in China, flooded world markets, workers who used to be able to access a solid, middle-class lifestyle on just a high school education or less now found themselves unable to do so. Entire regions—industrial towns that used to churn out manufactured goods—began to be hollowed out, and even those who managed to retain their livelihoods often saw a drop in their real wages. Hence, even as China's opening uplifted an entire generation from the ravages of poverty, it also left an indelible mark on their counterparts in rich nations.

This has come to be known as the "China shock":[76] the effect that rising exports from China has on manufacturing employment in the West. The trade shock was further exacerbated by a technological shock; the nature of technological progress favored those with skills,[77] which often left lower-skilled labor behind. For many in the West, this adjustment has been brutal, giving rise to populism and anti-globalization protests.

The political economic consequences of this shock would not surprise anyone. Disenchanted workers became increasingly disaffected and embittered, disillusioned with globalization and hopes of a better life for themselves and their children, and yearned for a return to a closed world. Nativist politicians that promised simple solutions, such as simply closing borders or taxing imports, appealed to this class of voters.

---

75 The standard approach relies on the so-called 2×2×2 Heckscher-Ohlin model, which postulates that in a two-country world with two factors (say, labor and capital) and two goods, each country will tend to export the good that uses intensively the factor in which it is more abundantly endowed (that is, a labor-abundant economy such as China will tend to export goods that use labor more intensively in its manufacture), and import the other good. One of the key implications of this model has to do with returns to factors; trade will lead to increases (decreases) in the relative price of goods that are produced with the abundant (scarce) factor, and more than proportionate increases (decreases) in returns to the abundant (scarce) factor (this result is known as the Stolper-Samuelson theorem). Hence, for China, the price of capital-intensive goods will tend to decline, accompanied by a disproportionately greater contraction in returns to capital. Conversely, in advanced economies such as the United States, the price of labor-intensive goods will drop, while wages will fall even more. An analogous argument can be made for high versus low-skilled workers.

76 Autor, D., D. Dorn, and G. Hanson, "The China Shock: Learning from Labor Market Adjustment to Large Changes in Trade," *Annual Review of Economics* 8(1) (2016): 205–240.

77 This is the case not only for those with high levels of human capital able to deliver skilled services, but even within industry, advanced manufacturing techniques increasingly require extensive training to operate and execute sophisticated equipment and processes.

The result of this has been a shift toward more protectionist trade policies in recent decades. Nowhere is this more evident than in the United States. Following the election of Donald Trump as the 45th president, the U.S. commenced a trade war with China.

In January 2018, the Trump administration announced the first of a wide slate of tariffs on Chinese manufactured goods.[78] Over several phases, tariffs were ratcheted up, from an average of 3.1% to 19.3%, and the coverage of goods subject to tariffs went from nothing to around two-thirds of all Chinese exports. Unsurprisingly, China retaliated with tariffs of its own, which it strategically imposed on mainly agricultural goods produced in states most supportive of Trump (in comparison, tariffs on Chinese goods were more wide-ranging).

Consistent with the mindset at the time—exemplified by Trump's infamous tweet that "trade wars are good, and easy to win"—the back-and-forth of tariff escalations occupied economic headlines for the better part of two years. Along the way, other economies, including Europe, were dragged into the fray, and faced commercial policy aggressions of their own. A grudging agreement was eventually reached in December 2019 (this was known as "Phase One"), where China agreed to purchase commitments for U.S. exports. However, over the course of 2020, it became clear that actual purchases fell far short of commitments.[79] Small wonder that even after the Biden administration took over in 2021, there was little hurry to repeal the tariffs.

The trade war also, perhaps unsurprisingly, prompted China to turn inward in ensuring the resilience of its industrial production. For instance, the Huawei Mate 20 Pro, a 4G smartphone, had only a quarter of its components made in China, with around three-quarters of its parts sourced from Northeast Asia. In contrast, the Huawei Mate 30, its 5G equivalent, boasted analogous shares of 40% and 90%, respectively.

This inward turn has not always resulted appropriate choices. In response to the COVID-19 pandemic—which, of course, originated in a Chinese city, Wuhan—China has steadfastly refused to import Western vaccines, despite their higher efficacy. As a result of this stubborn insistence on domestic drugs—coupled with a zero-COVID policy that steadfastly refused to treat the disease as endemic—the country has had to endure repeated lockdowns, which has become a millstone holding down the economy in the post-pandemic period.

---

78 These tariffs were first imposed on solar panels and washing machines, but more and more items were added over time. At the peak, fully 66% of Chinese exports were subject to tariffs (on the Chinese side, the coverage was 58%).

79 The purchase commitments were to amount to around $159 billion of U.S exports in 2020. Actual purchases amounted to $94 billion, which fell short of even pre-trade war purchases of $95 billion (in 2017).

Conclusion

Scenarios for China's Long-Term Growth

China's baseline rate of long-term growth, into the next decade or so, will likely be between 5 and 6%. Such a forecast is based on reasonable projections of the country's labor force evolution, educational attainment, physical capital accumulation, and TFP.

Crucially, this path stands in contrast to either China boosters that believe that China still has decades of close to 10% growth left in the tank, or China detractors who believe that the best days are behind it, and growth is now consigned to a growth rate—around 2% or so—that is typical in advanced economies. Notwithstanding this caveat, it is useful to document the underlying premises behind why such a growth trajectory is the most reasonable one, going forward.

The undeniable reality of China's impending demographic change is that it will be the result of the years when the one-child policy was in place. Despite the backtracking that has occurred since 2015, demographic transformations, virtually by definition, take time to play out, and that is assuming the success of the two (and now three) child policy in actually boosting fertility. As such, the China's active labor force, which peaked in 2019, will begin a gradual process of inexorable decline, which may at best be ameliorated—but never reversed—by any potential increases in labor force participation, the employment rate, or hours worked.[80] What's worse, the legacy of the one-child policy will continue to bite as the population ages; many of China's younger workers fret about the so-called 4-2-1 problem, of a single child needing to support two parents and four grandparents.

This has led to youth unemployment[81] of one in five for those under 25 years, a rate four times higher than the national rate (of around 5%). Structural labor market mismatches—those working in menial or blue-collar jobs tend to earn a hefty premium over white-collar graduates, even though university education is still perceived as more prestigious—have led to disillusionment among the young. Even those who are employed have pushed back, with many embracing the counterculture "lying flat" movement (躺平, *tǎng píng*), where adherents choose to reject societal pressures to overwork.

But as this chapter has made clear, over the course of the next decade or so, China's still-lagging levels of educational attainment will provide some backstop to labor force decline. This will translate into a contribution of human capital that nets out at essentially zero, instead of taking a point or two off GDP growth (which would be the case if it were no longer possible to eke out gains from additional expansion in human development).

---

80 Minzner, C., "China's Doomed Fight Against Demographic Decline," *Foreign Affairs*, May 3, 2022.

81 Youths are defined as those aged between 16 and 24 years old.

The challenges of a shrinking workforce due to demographics could perhaps be rapidly overcome by manpower policy, such as a decision to raise the retirement age—which currently ranges between 50 to 60—to the more common norm in developed economies, of around 65. But the efficacy of such changes assume that behavioral norms, built over an extended period of time, will adapt to policy diktat. Unless Chinese policymakers *mandate* that workers continue to work into their sixties and seventies, the marginal increases in the labor force accruing to those willing to postpone retirement may well be insufficient to counter the tsunami of exits from those who decide to call it quits at, say, 55 years.

By a similar token, China's incredible rate of investment does not appear to be sustainable for another decade or two. Recall, investment is postponed consumption, and the standard pattern exhibited by an aging population is to *dissave.* And even among the younger demographic, escalating housing prices mean that, in contrast to earlier generations, mortgage debt is now higher than ever before (around 62% of GDP, compared to 28% a decade prior).

Hence, it appears far more likely that—even if we allow for cultural differences in bequest motives, a predilection for housing as a savings vehicle, and weak social safety nets, all of which encourage higher-than-expected rates of saving— the rate of physical capital accumulation will slow. This will hold the economy-wide capital-output ratio at the current level—which, at around 3.0, is already among the most capital-intensive globally—rather than at rates that average above 40%. This is especially so given the government's recognition that corporate borrowing for continued investment is already at unsustainable levels, and it has even strongly encouraged corporations into rolling out debt-for-equity swaps.

Irrespective of one's assumptions, there are precious few instances where China's economy will not displace that of the United States at some point over the course of the next decade or two (in purchasing power parity (PPP) terms, it already has done so, around 2015) (Figure 1.19). It is often on this basis that casual observers believe that China is the most powerful economy in the world.

However, it should be stressed that widespread prosperity has not yet been achieved, and even in the best-case scenario, per capita incomes for the average Chinese citizen will remain less than half that of their American counterparts. It will be many decades yet before Chinese households catch up with living standards in the U.S., although its more modest aspiration of becoming a high-income country—China's estimated income is around $12,562 in 2021, and the threshold established by the World Bank for that year is $12,695—is almost certain to occur before 2025.

Political Economy Risks for China's Economic Prospects

Recent events have presented material risks to this baseline. In October 2022, Xi Jinping ascended into an unprecedented (in the post-Mao regime) third five-year term as the leader of the Chinese Communist Party. This overturned the existing norm of each paramount leader serving only two terms.

China's GDP and GDP per head

Percentage difference to US GDP at current dollars and PPP dollars

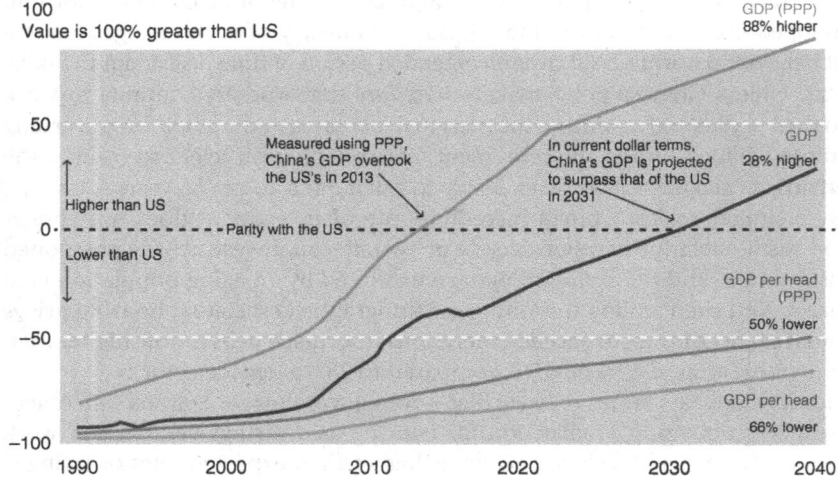

Figure 1.19 In terms of economic size, China will very likely overtake the United States as the world's largest economy sometime in the next two centuries (it already has when measured in purchasing power parity terms), but it continues to lag significantly behind in terms of individual prosperity, and even under the most optimistic projections, per capita incomes will remain less than half that of its U.S. counterparts.

While there is no *a priori* reason why the concentration of political power should necessarily result in a derailment of China's development—it has, after all, successfully pulled off a half-century of accelerated development under a one-party state—there is evidence that the quality of institutions associated with democracies tends to drive long-run growth, and such institutions tend to thrive best in democratic societies.[82]

In what is perhaps an uncomfortable echo of China's century of humiliation, its current political economy challenges are not limited to domestic concerns, but also entail an international dimension. As China has grown in size and

---

82 The empirical evidence tends to be fairly clear that high-quality *institutions* are important for long-run growth, the evidence in favor of *democracy* driving growth is more mixed, with some authors finding strong evidence in favor of democracy, while others presenting a more nuanced picture. See Acemoğlu, D., S. Johnson, and J. Robinson, "Institutions as a Fundamental Cause of Long-Run Economic Growth," in P. Aghion and S. Durlauf (Eds.), *Handbook of Economic Growth*, vol. 1 (Amsterdam: Elsevier, 2005), pp. 385–472; Acemoğlu, D., S. Naidu, P. Restrepo, and J. Robinson, "Democracy Does Cause Growth," *Journal of Political Economy* 127 (2019): 47–100; and Persson, T. and G. Tabellini, "Democracy and Development: The Devil in the Details," *American Economic Review* 96 (2006): 319–324.

power, it has prompted fears of a Thucydides Trap:[83] the notion that war may be inevitable when a rising global power confronts an incumbent. This spirit of suspicion and insecurity has not been confined to the political arena, as the Sino-American trade war and U.S.-led efforts to counter the BRI via the Build Back Better World (B3W) initiative have demonstrated.

It is foolhardy to bet against China, especially in light of its track record. Nevertheless, it is important to recognize that the economy is sailing into unfamiliar waters, one that has not been tested since 1976. More than ever before, the direction taken by its political regime—both internally and in foreign relations—will shape its economic future in the decades to come.

---

83 The reference is due to American political scientist Graham Allison, who observed that of the 16 past cases when a rising global power contended with an incumbent ruling one, war has resulted in 12 of them. See Allison, G., *Destined for War: Can America and China Escape Thucydides's Trap?* (Boston, MA: Houghton Mifflin Harcourt, 2017).

2

Japan: Asian Standard-Bearer or Has-Been?

To strive for the common prosperity and happiness of all nations, as well as the security and wellbeing of our subjects, is the solemn obligation which has been handed down by our imperial ancestors.
—*Michinomiya Hirohito (1901–89), 124th Emperor of Japan*

The [bursting of] the bubble of the 1980s . . . was just about the largest loss of wealth in human history in peacetime.
—*Richard Koo (1954–), Chief Economist, Nomura Securities*[1]

Introduction

Most first-time visitors to Japan would, on arrival, marvel at the wide-ranging signs of prosperity: the gleaming buildings, the immaculately dressed office crowd, the stark orderliness of traffic coupled with the cleanliness of the streets, the effusive civility of the service staff. The infrastructure is modern and efficient, the food is high-quality and delicious, and the people are educated and polite. It would be near incomprehensible to imagine that this was an economy in the doldrums, and anything less than a testimony to the remarkable success of Japanese-style capitalism.

Yet take a gander at business and finance publications and you will be confronted with a much more distressing picture: an economy that has grown, on average, at only 0.7% annually over the past three decades, where prices have fallen in half in those last 30 years, and commentators who routinely proclaim the economy as a has-been or, worse, one destined for inexorable decline.

Whence the source of this dissonance? The reality is that, since the eve of World War II, through the boom years in the 1980s, till the largely postindustrial

---

1 Koo, R., "Putting Japan's Lost Decade in Perspective," *NPR Morning Edition*, Washington, DC: National Public Radio, 2009.

Asian Economies: History, Institutions, and Structures, First Edition. Jamus Jerome Lim.
© 2024 John Wiley & Sons Ltd. Published 2024 by John Wiley & Sons Ltd.

economy of today, Japan has remained among the most advanced and sophisticated economies in the world. While it no longer is growing as it did in the postwar period, it is still remarkably wealthy. Japanese per capita incomes are among the highest in Asia, and the highest for a large economy. In nominal terms, Japan's GDP is within the top-5 worldwide.

Japan was not always among the pole economies in Asia. Throughout much of its history, Japan was a distinctive economic backwater, drawing ideas, knowledge, and technology from the dominant power of the East, i.e. China. Yet Japan became the first Asian economy to industrialize. Starting in 1880, Japan began a relentless march toward industrialization, and sustained this remarkable economic progress for close to a century.

But Japan did so—to abuse an old Frank Sinatra trope—in its own way. While it drew liberally from the lessons of the West in informing its industrialization journey, it also adapted many of its historical institutions and practices in ways that repurposed—rather than replaced—these idiosyncratic pieces. It is in part this rethinking that allows us to see that capitalism can take on many different forms and yet be successful.

These past successes notwithstanding, the country must still chart its way into the future. Today's Japan is the oldest society in the world, with more than 36 million (or 29% of the population) over the age of 65, and 19 million (over 15%) older than 75. Such a superaged society presents unique economic challenges, not least being the fact that the working-age population will have to bear an ever-greater burden of elderly dependent support.

Japan is a fascinating textbook case study of how to grow an economy quickly—and break into high-income status—while retaining many features of one's culture and society. To fully grasp this phenomenon, it is necessary to understand the fundamental geographic constraints to its economic development, and how its feudal history—which echoes those of Western Europe somewhat more than commonly acknowledged—may have played a role in shaping its 20th-century ambitions.

Economic Geography of Japan

Japan as an Island Economy

Japan is an island nation. Four larger islands—Hokkaido in the north, the "mainland" of Honshu in the middle, and Shikoku and Kyushu in the south—which, together with the much-smaller Okinawa in the far south, constitute what most consider the main islands of Japan.

These islands—together with the 6,800 or so other islands that constitute the Japanese archipelago—were formed as a result of volcanic activity 15 million years ago, and today, mountains cover more than two-thirds of the geography of the islands, limiting inhabitable areas to only about a quarter of the land.

Yet Japan has made the very most with that limited amount of land. Today, each of the five main islands boasts an economy that is comparable to entire nations. Kyushu and Shikoku produce the same amount as Norway and New Zealand, respectively, and Hokkaido has a similar GDP to that of the Ukraine. Even tiny Okinawa has economic activity similar to that of Guatemala.

The production of the different regions on the mainland, which together contribute around 80% of Japan's total output, may likewise even be compared to different economies, and together amount to about the combined GDP of France and Canada.

This impressive economic size notwithstanding, the mountainous interior makes much of Japan ill-suited for agriculture, with arable land making up only around 16% of all land available. Even so, this has not stopped Japan from its pursuit of rice production (of indigenous short-grain varieties), along with a smattering of other grains, such as wheat and barley, along with fruit. Much of Japan's agricultural production occurs on the northernmost island of Hokkaido—sometimes referred to as the breadbasket of Japan—which also boasts the cultivation of livestock and animal products.

Although agriculture can hardly be regarded as a source of comparative advantage for an island chain bereft of much flat cultivable land, the Japanese have nevertheless made it work. Japan is fully self-sufficient in rice, which is a source of national pride. The government has supported agriculture, via subsidies, to the tune of an estimated $62 trillion a year (or 1.3% of GDP); this amounts to around 56 cents for every dollar of agricultural output, and is more than twice the OECD average.[2] And price support is only part of the picture: import tariffs on agricultural produce can be as high as 800%. Small wonder, then, that Japanese rice, while undeniably of high quality, is also the most expensive globally.

Japan's island characteristics—the country has one of the longest coastlines in the world—has also meant a penchant for seafood, translating into a fishing industry $14 billion in size, with two-thirds consumed domestically. The population's almost insatiable demand for seafood has led its commercial fleet far beyond territorial waters, including crossing into the Southern Ocean (and other nations' sanctuary waters) in pursuit of whales.

Beyond agriculture, however, Japan's primary production is severely limited by an absence of endowments in natural resources. While the country does have some limited deposits of minerals (such as coal and copper), these are too miniscule to be economically significant.[3] Indeed, the paucity of natural resources is often cited as a justification for Japanese expansion into

---

2 Troutman, K., "Will Japan Bet the Farm on Agricultural Protectionism?", *Realtime Economics* (Washington, DC: Peterson Institute for International Economics, 2014).
3 However, Japan may have significant deposits of offshore rare earths, albeit accessible only via deep-sea mining. It is unclear whether government policy will move decisively toward developing this resource, however, with current regulations limiting overall access.

Manchuria—and subsequently the rest of Southeast Asia—in the period preceding World War II.

Industrial Concentrations on the Japanese Mainland

Japan has three major industrial agglomerations, all located on the mainland: the megalopolis of Tokyo-Yokohama, the port city of Osaka, and the (significantly smaller) city of Nagoya. These three cities, along with the settlements within the Pacific Industrial Belt (or *Taiheiyō* belt)—an urbanized, industrial corridor in the southwestern end of Honshu, akin to the Northeast megalopolis of the United States between Boston and Washington, DC—house the majority of the population and economic prowess of Japan (Table 2.1).

Tokyo anchors the eastern end of the Pacific Industrial Belt, with Nagoya and Osaka constituting major cities in the central segment (Figure 2.1). Fukuoka—Japan's second-largest port city, and the only economic zone specifically dedicated to startups—anchors the western end. Virtually all manufacturing that constitutes Japan's $5 trillion GDP is found within this zone. The concentration of manufacturing activity within this narrow corridor has given rise to powerful economies of scale, as the fixed costs of supplying energy, raw materials, and transportation infrastructure are limited to a relatively small geographical area.

Of the three major cities, the Greater Tokyo area—with a population of around 37 million[4]—remains the densest, most diversified, and most sophisticated.

Table 2.1 Major Japanese cities along the Pacific Industrial Belt

Region	City	Population (million)	Output ($ billion)
Kanto	Greater Tokyo	37.3	1,800
Chubu	Greater Nagoya	9.6	256
Kansai	Greater Kyoto	2.8	115
Kansai	Greater Osaka	12.1	516
Chugoku	Greater Hiroshima	2.1	61
Kyushu	Greater Fukuoka	5.5	101

Source: Author's compilation.
Notes: Only a selected number of metropolitan areas with output above $100 billion or population above 2 million are reported, and areas include constituent cities. Regions are listed from east to west; other regions within the belt include Shikoku. Estimates of population and output may be computed from differing definitions of city limits, and may not correspond perfectly.

---

4 The more limited definition of just the Tokyo-Yokohama region houses about 13 million, with 8.9 million in Tokyo and 3.7 million in Yokohama.

Figure 2.1 Japanese economic geography indicates that development mostly occurs along the coastal regions, owing to Japan's mountainous topography. Concentrations of activity can be seen around the cities of Tokyo-Yokohama, Osaka, and Nagoya, as well as cities along the Pacific Industrial Belt in the southwest.

It encapsulates the two major cities of Tokyo and Yokohama, along with the industrial area of Kawasaki sandwiched in-between. It serves as the political and economic capital, and—as an urban economy *par excellence*—it is the world's second largest (after New York).

The agglomeration of urban activity into these major extended metropolitan areas occurred during the first wave of Japanese industrialization, which began in the mid-19th century. These then-emergent regions have proved to be remarkably resilient. In the final stages of World War II, the Japanese mainland suffered extensively from Allied bombing activity. This was not limited to just the two (in)famous nuclear bombs dropped on Hiroshima and Nagasaki; incendiary bombs were just as devastating, and leveled about half of all structures in the 66 targeted cities. Yet in the wake of the destruction, most cities were rebuilt, and over the course of the next two decades, returned to their relative position in the distribution of city sizes prior to the war.[5]

Tokyo as the Central Growth Pole

Tokyo was not always the preeminent growth pole for the economy. In the Middle Ages, Osaka was considered Japan's primary economic hub, and also briefly served as the imperial capital. Another historical capital—Kyoto—is today the cultural anchor, but nevertheless houses major information technology and electronics firms, such as Kyocera, Nintendo, and Shimadzu. And Nagoya is driven (literally and figuratively) by automotive sector, with powerhouses such as Mitsubishi and Toyota running major industrial divisions in the city.

Be that as it may, Tokyo—the "Eastern Capital"—continues to define Japan, Inc. Indeed, as the world's largest metropolitan economy, one could make the case that it is a driver of not just the growth dynamic within Japan, but also across East Asia.

Economic History of Japan

Japan's Feudal History Left an Economic Legacy

Although Japan's existence as an independent civilization dates back to at least 300 BCE,[6] much of this period was relatively undistinguished from an economic perspective. Between the 3rd and 12th centuries, there was some degree of political centralization, but the houses of the various emperors that assumed power, while venerated, were not especially powerful. Much of the cultural practices and political-economic organization took their cue from the regional hegemon—China—and interclan conflict was rife.

The country descended into a feudalistic period from the end of the 12th century until 1602. During that time, local warlords, known as *daimyōs*, exerted power over their respective domains (藩, or *hans*). Although security was tenuous, such divisions—much like analogous developments in medieval Europe—meant that governmental functions became decentralized, which permitted their independent development.

---

5 This speaks to how economic geography likely respects a mix of location fundamentals, amplified by increasing returns. See Davis, D. and D. Weinstein, "Bones, Bombs, and Break Points: The Geography of Economic Activity," *American Economic Review* 92(5) (2002): 1269–1289.

6 This was known as the Yayoi period, where the country had transitioned to a settled agricultural society, although archeological evidence suggests that the culture may have settled earlier, as far back as between 800 and 1000 BCE.

Also similar to Europe was the emergence of knights and nobles, a warrior class known in Japan as the *samurai*. The samurai operated as well-paid retainers of the *daimyō*; however, they assumed not only military and security functions, but also those of administration, tax collection, and public goods provision. Active economic competition between *hans* attracted artisans and merchants, which in turn contributed toward economic vibrancy. For their part, wealthy samurai households also stimulated consumption, not only of daily necessities but also of luxuries, such as porcelain and silk.

Japan underwent a period of repeated civil war and social unrest between the mid-15th and early 17th centuries, before Tokugawa Ieyasu, a powerful warlord emerging from Southwestern Honshu, united Japan through conquest and established a military dynasty, or shogunate. Ieyasu proceeded to move the capital from Kyoto to a harbor city to its east, Edo (modern-day Tokyo). There, the Tokugawa shogunate ruled Japan for more than a quarter of a century.

The Edo period was distinguished by stable, if unremarkable, economic development. Urbanization increased, as did road networks. An expansion of irrigation technologies enabled significant expansion in rice cultivation, and a number of proto-industrial activities emerged, such as craft production in the major cities.

The Tokugawa shogunate did impose a number of broad changes to policy. One of these was an isolationist approach to foreign interactions (*sakoku*), where relations with other countries were severely curtailed. Another was the creation of a caste social structure (*shinō-kōshō*), topped by a small number of *daimyō* lords, and comprising the *samurai*, farming peasants, artisans, and merchants. Finally, the *shōgun* also imposed a tribute system, requiring "alternate attendance" (*sankin-kōtai*) of the *daimyō* lords in the capital every other year. These policies would go on to become the foundation of much of Japan's later industrial takeoff, and shape its political economy thereafter.

Sakoku severely restricted trade to just four gateways,[7] which was essentially a mercantilist approach to commercial contact. This history was likely the basis of the subsequent comfort with the neomercantilist mindset pursued during Japan's rapid growth phase.[8]

The legacy of *sakoku* is also reflected in Japan's contemporary immigration policies, which remain among the most xenophobic among modern economies. For a large, otherwise economically open economy, the nation's resident

---

7 Japan traded with the Chinese as well as the Dutch East India Company at Nagasaki, with the indigenous Ainu people in Hokkaido, with the Koreans at Tsushima, and the Ryūkyū Kingdom at Satsuma (modern-day Kagoshima).

8 Japanese neomercantilism was not restricted to the trade domain, but also enfolded industrial and financial policies, all of which together explain a good part of how the Japanese capitalist model diverged from those pursued in the West. See Nester, W., *Japan's Growing Power over East Asia and the World Economy* (London: Palgrave Macmillan, 1990).

foreign population amounts to only a little more than 2% of the total. In contrast, South Korea absorbs more than 3% foreign-born, while France, Germany, and Italy clock in at around 13%, 19%, and 11%. While Chinese students now comprise the largest bloc of English-language learners in the world, many Japanese still struggle with conversational English.

However, *sakoku* permitted controlled exposure to Western ideas. Known as *rangaku* (literally, "Dutch learning")—a term owing to the fact that Dutch traders were the only foreigners tolerated in the country (and hence the source of such information transfer)—the policy allowed Japan to remain abreast of European technology and knowledge during the crucial post-Renaissance and Scientific Revolution phases of Western civilization.

Shinō-kōshō meant the need to develop local state capacity for the purposes of tax collection: *daimyōs* outsourced tax collection to the *samurai*, whose stipends were in turn dependent on what was collected from farmers. Although such attempts were not uniformly successful—excessive taxation would occasionally prompt demonstrations and uprisings by the local peasant population—the tenancy system was an important reason why bottom-up development was viable, once the economy was freed from its feudal constraints.

The pursuit of *shinō-kōshō* also set the stage for a number of subsequent organizational features of Japanese society. The original Japanese industrial conglomerates—the *zaibatsu*—evolved from the most successful merchant houses. Perhaps more importantly, disenfranchised *samurai* formed the core of the professional management class hired by the *zaibatsu*, as their ample human resources were redirected away from militaristic and into economic endeavors.

Japanese urban development was also profoundly influenced by *sankin-kōtai*. The system was instituted to undermine the possibility of the *daimyōs* seizing the *de facto* throne, after amassing enough power within their own domains. But the need to cater to large, wealthy families in Edo led to its development as a consumption center, whereas the transportation of taxed grains from the western *hans* to be redistributed and shipped onward resulted in the growth of Osaka as a city, functioning as a domestic entrepôt.

At the same time, key commercial institutions necessary for effective capitalism, such as fractional reserve banking, commodity futures markets, and wholesale/retail linkages, likewise arose in response to the need to serve a distributed network of commercial interests, due to *sankin-kōtai*.

The Meiji Restoration and Industrialization

In 1853, American Commodore Matthew Perry's "black ships" sailed into Tokyo Bay (Figure 2.2). This marked the end of Japanese seclusion, as the Tokugawa shogunate acquiesced to a series of trading agreements, first with the United States, then with other Western nations. But make no mistake: this was a forced opening, in exchange for peace.

Figure 2.2 The arrival of Commodore Perry's black ships was not only symbolic of the relative superiority of seafaring technology in the West vis-à-vis Asia, it also marked the beginning of Japan's opening to the West, which would ultimately result in its earlier industrialization relative to the rest of Asia.

The uncontrolled trade liberalization led to the collapse of many Japanese businesses, as domestically-made goods were unable to outcompete the lower prices and higher productivity of those made in the post-Industrial Revolution West. Unable to assure the Japanese people of their security, the Tokugawa shogunate rapidly lost legitimacy, which was further undermined by a coalition of *daimyōs* that switched allegiance back to then-15-year-old emperor.

In some ways, this forced opening—with its Treaty Ports and internal civil conflict—was not dissimilar to what played out in China, during the Opium Wars. The samurai—whose stipends had become a severe drag on state finances, despite their relatively small (and evidently ineffectual) presence—began to see the gradual erosion of their privileges.[9] This culminated, unsurprisingly, in

---

9 This process began in 1871, when the *danpatsurei* (lit., "Cropped Hair Edict") was rolled out, which encouraged the samurai to cut their distinctive top-knot, and two years later, the *chouheirei* (lit., "Conscription Edict") replaced the samurai as the sole armed force, with a Western-style conscripted army. The process culminated with the *haitōrei* (lit., "Sword Abolition Edict"), issued in 1876, which prohibited the carrying of weapons in public, except by *daimyōs*, military, and law enforcement officials. That same year saw the *chitsuroku-shobun* (lit., "Stipend Measure"), which permanently suspended government stipends to the samurai.

revolts, but these were handily suppressed by the newly conscripted imperial army, armed with Western military technology.[10]

Thus began the Meiji Restoration—the return to political power of the Meiji Imperial House—which was much more consequential than just a political regime change. The restoration could perhaps be better described as a revolution, ushering in unprecedented changes in policy. From 1868, Japan began to rapidly modernize, to become the first industrialized nation in the East.

The far-reaching reforms of the Meiji era began with a series of monetary and financial reforms. The dispossession of the samurai, who had accounted for a little less than a third of fiscal expenditures, despite comprising just 7% of the population, placed public finances on a much more sustainable footing. Revenue was further complemented by the sale of land to pay down debt.

Along with changes to the public fisc, there were changes to monetary policy. The Bank of Japan (BoJ) was established in 1882 to manage a new common currency, the *yen*, which replaced the messy array of incompatible monies issued by the *hans*.

Land taxes were also altered. The decentralized tax authority granted to the *daimyōs* was reconsolidated under the national government, and existing rice and crop taxes were replaced with a uniform land tax calculated on the basis of potential, rather than actual, yield. This encouraged increased effort toward production. Coupled with imported Western agricultural techniques, agricultural productivity rose sharply as a result.

Beyond public finance, the Meiji government began a relentless process of reforming other sectors in the economy along Western lines. Education became nationalized, with compulsory primary education extended to the masses, and elite university education aligned toward scientific and technological subjects.

The abolition of the feudal caste system enabled greater vertical mobility than before, with talented individuals now having an opportunity to secure lucrative jobs. Migration from rural areas to bustling cities was encouraged by extensive railroad construction. Such horizontal mobility provided a steady flow of labor for the factories, necessary for full-scale industrialization.

The ethos behind the industrialization drive was very much led by private enterprise from the beginning. Policymakers would assist with infrastructure and guidance (and the occasional subsidy), but the inclination was toward providing an environment favorable for businesses to succeed. Pro-business policies allowed a strong merchant class to develop, and their entrepreneurship led to the formation of manufacturing and industrial conglomerates, the *zaibatsu*.

---

10 The setting was the basis for the Oscar-nominated film *The Last Samurai*, which in turn was historical fiction, with the lead (played by Tom Cruise) based on an actual Frenchman, Jules Brunet, rather than an American. Brunet was a decorated officer—a *Légion d'honneur* recipient—who went on to fight on the side of the shogunate. Prior to his passing, he was rehabilitated, and retired with the rank of general.

Japan's Emergence as the First Asian Industrial Power

The *zaibatsus* all started off in a specialized business: Mitsubishi in shipping and shipbuilding, Mitsui in textiles and trade, Sumitomo in mining, Yasuda in banking and finance. There were two types of *zaibatsu* families: those who had already seized business opportunities and achieved prominence during the Edo period (Mitsui, Sumitomo), and newer merchant families that only came onto the scene in the Meiji era (Mitsubishi, Yasuda, Asano, Furukawa).[11]

Regardless of origins, their *modi operandi* were similar. *Zaibatsus* were vertically-integrated monopolies, with a holding company atop; the group would comprise a wholly-owned banking subsidiary that provided financing, along with several industrial subsidiaries which, in turn, would oversee additional subsidiaries in related, downstream businesses. For example, an iron mining operation would sell its ore solely to an iron refiner within the group, which in turn would offload its production to a steel manufacturer.

After establishing commercial eminence in a given sector and market, *zaibatsu* would expand into others, which resulted in horizontal diversification. This resulted in conglomerates with overlapping interests, including banking and finance, trade, mining and industrial metals, textiles, and electrical machinery. Even after achieving significant size, however, capital funds and management would remain tightly controlled by the founding family, and stockholding was generally closed to the rest of society.

The *zaibatsu* led the charge—figuratively as well as literally—of Japan's expansion into the rest of the region. Indigenous Japanese industrialists would allow Japan the wherewithal to push out the foreign merchant operations that had, to their credit, also ushered in knowledge and technology transfer through trade. But Japan's relative scarcity of natural resources meant that it had to look abroad for the raw materials necessary to keep its industrial engine humming. These conglomerates eventually outcompeted the British and American trading companies in nearby markets, and began to be recognized as an economic power in its own right.

Pre-War Militarism Enabled by Economic Strength

As it turns out, Japan was not satisfied with merely economic dominance. Backed by its industrial prowess, Japan began its militaristic expansion into the region. This was not merely by accident; the Meiji government had, early on, committed to the twin policies of "prosperous country, strong military" (富国強兵, *fukoku kyōhei*), in its desire to catch up with the West.

---

11 The so-called Big Four (四大財閥, *yondai zaibatsu*), in order of their founding, were Sumitomo, Mitsui, Mitsubishi, and Yasuda.

Perhaps not ironically, Japan's imitation of the West extended to include the acquisition of colonies. The nation's first foray was into Taiwan, which became a dependency in 1895, and it was quickly followed by others, including Southern Sakhalin (1905), Korea (in 1910), and Manchuria (in 1931). These territories, in turn, spawned new *zaibatsus*, such as Nissan and Nakajima, that produced military hardware that furthered Japan's expansionist ambitions.

At the same time, Japan's political economy was reorganizing in furtherance of its military objectives. What had been a messy evolution toward parliamentary democracy—albeit one where the Meiji oligarchs still controlled the main levers of power—gradually consolidated toward a top-down, centrally-planned state. The Great Depression was comparatively mild in Japan, but it prompted the passage of a number of laws, each of which brought increasing parts of the Japanese economy under national control.[12]

Real military spending steadily ramped up over the course of the 1930s, and after 1936, such spending even took priority over civilian spending, peaking just after the height of Japanese territorial expansion, in 1942.[13] The year after, Japanese GNP was roughly equally distributed between the metaphorical "guns" and "butter."

Postwar Rebuilding and the Japanese Economic Miracle

Japan was defeated in World War II. But the loss didn't just stop with the end of Japan's ability to extract resources from East and Southeast Asia. Mainland Japan was devastated by bombing expeditions (Figure 2.3), and the rehabilitation of the economy had to occur—according to the terms of surrender listed in the Potsdam Declaration—under the supervisory oversight of the Allied powers (which principally meant the United States). In practice, these terms included a dissolution of the *zaibatsu*—which were perceived, not without cause, as integral to the Japanese war effort[14]—alongside land and labor market reforms[15] meant to promote greater democratization of the economic system. The economy rebounded, for sure, but quickly overheated, with hyperinflation posing a threat to its continued recovery.

Not wanting an unstable Japan just as the Cold War was starting to take shape, Allied policies shifted toward a series of contractionary financial and monetary policies known as the Dodge Line (after its architect, American economist Joseph Dodge). These included programs aimed at balancing the budget to reduce inflation, plans to improve the efficiency of tax collection, and

---

12 These began with the Major Industrial Control Law (1931) through to the National Mobilization Law (1938).
13 Flath, D., *The Japanese Economy*, 4th ed. (New York: Oxford University Press, 2022).
14 Bisson, T.A., "Increase of Zaibatsu Predominance in Wartime Japan," *Pacific Affairs* 18(1) (1945): 55–61.
15 Land reforms were designed to remove the burden of landlordism, and created incentives for the expansion of rice cultivation. Labor market reforms enabled collective bargaining, and improved worker representation by granting additional legal rights to trade unions.

Figure 2.3 The bombing of Tokyo was symptomatic of the extent of shock to the Japanese economy that followed World War II. Although the destruction wrought on Hiroshima and Nagasaki due to nuclear bombs is better known, firebombs were often even more destructive, given the widespread use of wood in building construction at the time. Incredibly, rebuilding occurred at the same sites where the devastation occurred.
Source: US military / Wikimedia Commans / Public Domain.

a decrease in the scope of government intervention, with the goal of enfolding Japan back firmly into the free world's global economic system.

The return of price stability, combined with deregulation and generous foreign aid—Japan borrowed extensively from the World Bank, with funds used to launch power plants, modernize factories, and construct key transportation networks such as the country's famous *Shinkansen* bullet trains—proved to be a potent mix. Without military priorities, the nation's energies were channeled into a harnessing the dynamics of economic performance, ushering in a high-growth period averaging 10% per annum, between 1950 and 1973.

This Japanese Miracle was led by factors of production that were firing on all cylinders. Like many economies, Japan experienced a postwar baby boom, with the three years between 1947 and 1949 marking the high point of births for the entire 20th century.[16] These children entered the workforce in the 1960s, and were a major tailwind behind Japan's incredible growth during the period.

---

16 Excess births during this period were significant: in excess of 2.6 million each year, and markedly higher than prior highs of between 2.2 and 2.3 million. This was the first baby boom generation (団塊の世代, *dankai no sedai*). Japan also experienced a second boom—its echo boom generation—between 1971 and 1974.

The relative youthfulness of the working-age population also contributed to growth. Younger workforces tend to save more, either for life cycle or consumption-smoothing reasons.[17] This, in turn, provided a steady flow of financing for postwar rebuilding, and resulted in a surge in investment that contributed to Japan becoming a capital-intensive economy.

Postwar education in Japan also underwent renewed reform, which sought to impose standards of education more common to democratic societies, such as coeducational schools and a modernization of the curriculum. This expanded educational program—emphasizing science and technology, as well as vocational training—was the foundation for the industrious Japanese work-force during the miracle years.

Finally, the contribution of total factor productivity (TFP) was significant during this phase. The ability of Japanese industry to continue to absorb frontier technology from the West, while expanding its indigenous innovative capacity—especially in the production of automobiles, electronics, and machinery—meant that that TFP contributions accounted for as much as half or more of total output. Process innovations—including just-in-time inventory management, lean manufacturing, and automated quality control—all emerged during this period, and set Japan apart as a rising leader in global industry.

Japan's rapid rebuilding and entry into the ranks of fully-fledged advanced industrial economies occurred amid extensive public and private sector involvement in the economy. The *zaibatsu* (財閥, "financial clique") firm structure, although officially eliminated, did not disappear after the war. Instead, comparable industrial conglomerates—rebranded as *keiretsu* (系列, "enterprise group")—rose to take their place.

The powerful Ministry of International Trade and Industry (MITI) led the public-sector effort with unabashed industrial policy.[18] Such interventions have included production subsidies, commercial and industrial loans extended on generous terms by the Development Bank of Japan and the Bank of Japan, technological intelligence and licensing, and support for export orientation, coupled with import protection. While industrial policy has received criticism

---

17 The life-cycle theory of saving, due mainly to Franco Modigliani, suggests that the young would dissave in their youth and retirement years, but save much more during their prime working years, peaking in the high-earning years prior to retirement. Models of saving based on consumption smoothing rely on Milton Friedman's permanent income hypothesis, which posit very similar implications for peak saving during the middle years of the life cycle. In Japan's context, the reduction of saving due to the war would have also suggested an increased propensity to save in the postwar years. For more on the life-cycle model, see Browning, M. and T. Crossley, "The Life-Cycle Model of Consumption and Saving," *Journal of Economic Perspectives* 15(3) (2001): 3–22.

18 Johnson, C., *MITI and the Japanese Miracle: The Growth of Industrial Policy, 1925–1975* (Palo Alto, CA: Stanford University Press, 1982). MITI has since been superseded by the Ministry of Economy, Trade, and Industry.

from certain quarters, its central role in driving 20th-century Japanese economic development is undeniable.[19]

Japan's Development in Comparative Perspective

Japan's Takeoff as Its First Growth Miracle

While Japan's miracle years may strike many as unprecedented in modern economic history (at least until the advent of the NIEs), Japan's initial industrialization phase was itself a remarkable growth episode. Japan's takeoff ranks among the longest in duration, fastest in per capita output growth, and all occurring from among the lowest in initial per capita income.[20] This is, needless to say, an impressive feat, and one that, up till that point, had not been seen among the economies of Asia.

Japanese industrialization occurred relatively late; the earliest estimates indicate that it began at around 1870, which aligns with second-wave industrializers, such as Australia, Italy, and the Netherlands, and many of the Scandinavian economies. In a sense, it benefited from being able to import technology from industrial pioneers, such as France and Great Britain, and hence its growth may be reasonably viewed as more a catching-up to the global frontier, than pushing it forward. However, not all late industrializers were able to capitalize on this fact to leapfrog those that preceded them, and so Japan's ability to exploit its later arrival remains a testament to the nation's economic acumen.

Besides starting from a relatively poorer level of per capita incomes, Japan's other initial conditions were also comparatively less favorable for growth. Adult literacy in the 1890s only encompassed around half of the population, and the island nation was significantly less urbanized than most of the late industrializers.

Industrialization eventually catapulted Japan into the ranks of the larger economies in the world. Owing to its population size—at the point of takeoff, it boasted more than 34 million souls—it is unsurprising that, following an extended period of sustained, rapid growth, it would also grow to become one of the larger economies at the global level (Table 2.2).

The Rise and Fall of Japanese Saving, and Its Capital Legacy

A major contributor to Japan's growth performance was its rabid accumulation of capital. This was no accident. U.S. aid flows helped pump up national saving

19 Shinohara, M., *Industrial Growth, Trade, and Dynamic Patterns in the Japanese Economy* (Tokyo: University of Tokyo Press, 1982).
20 Ito, T. and T. Hoshi, *The Japanese Economy*, 2nd ed. (Cambridge, MA: MIT Press, 2020).

Table 2.2 Japan and comparable economies in their takeoff phase

Country	Years	At takeoff		Growth rate	
		GDP	GDP per capita	GDP	GDP per capita
United Kingdom	1780–1830	51,877	3,049	1.3	0.3
Belgium	1825–1880	8,699	2,424	3.8	1.8
France	1818–1860	55,645	1,804	2.3	1.5
Germany	1850–1900	76,806	2,276	4.7	2.2
the Netherlands	1870–1914	8,928	2,133	4.4	4.0
Italy	1861–1913	67,133	2,558	2.4	1.1
United States	1840–1890	57,904	3,319	12.6	2.0
Canada	1850–1900	5,268	2,120	7.6	2.4
Sweden	1850–1890	5,937	1,715	2.7	1.3
Denmark	1870–1915	6,028	3,193	4.6	2.0
Norway	1843–1890	1,956	1,521	3.7	1.8
Australia	1861–1811	6,166	4,544	10.0	1.6
Japan	**1870–1930**	**54,410**	**1,580**	**4.9**	**1.9**

Source: Author's compilation, from Bolt, J. and J.L. van Zanden (2020) *Maddison Project Database, Version 2020*, Groningen: Groningen Growth and Development Centre.
Notes: Takeoff periods are estimates based on the available literature, and may differ from other authors. Per capita GDP are measured in 2011 Geary-Khamis international dollars, while GDP levels are in millions of the same metric. If actual data are unavailable, estimates based on interpolations of GDP per capita and population, based on nearest years available, are provided. Growth rates, in%, are simple average annual rates over the relevant period.

in the immediate aftermath of the war. Thereafter, saving rates gradually picked up to just shy of a third of national income, among the thriftiest in the world at the time, and substantially greater than rates typical in European nations.

Private saving rates were elevated not just because of a young post-boom workforce, which was (by far) the most important driver.[21] Japan's government also sought to actively encourage—to a point of propaganda—increased saving as a means of achieving economic independence after the war.[22] This policy was further supported by public institutions geared toward the promoting saving. Such institutions include a postal banking system—where post offices,

---

21 There are at least 30 competing explanations for high Japanese saving, which are too many to dive into here. However, demographic, reconstruction, and policy factors, emphasized here, are probably the most encompassing and most widely accepted justifications. See Hatashi, F., "Why Is Japan's Saving Rate So Apparently High?" *NBER Macroeconomics Annual* 1 (1986): 147–210.
22 Garon, S., "Postwar Japan's National Salvation," *Asia-Pacific Journal* 9(50) (2011): 3660.

which tend to have significant geographical reach, are concomitantly roped in to provide banking services[23]—and reformed national pension systems, which aimed at expanding saving not just for public employees, but also those not well covered by their private-sector employers.[24]

Such active promotion of household saving has since evolved into memes about the metaphorical Mrs Watanabe—a personification of the Japanese housewife, who controlled household finances and was often actively involved, especially in the 2000s, in speculative investment and foreign exchange trading—as the central force behind Japanese household saving behavior. Regardless of the relative importance of specific factors behind Japan's high saving in the four-decade period between 1945 and 1985, these drivers have since receded, and the country's household saving rate has, accordingly, collapsed. From its position as one of the highest savers among the OECD—household saving was second only to Italy in 1985—Japan is now firmly ensconced among the lowest savers, such as Australia, Denmark, Finland, and the United States (Figure 2.4).

The leading cause of this decline would not surprise anyone: it is an aging society—its over-65-year-olds' share of the population, at 29%, is the highest in

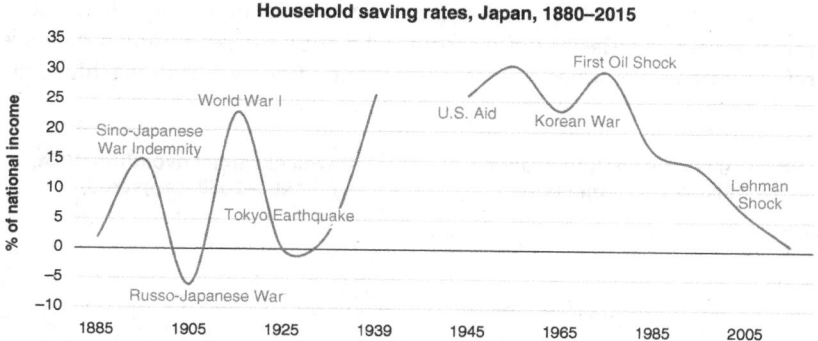

Figure 2.4 Saving rates were boosted by foreign aid in the immediate aftermath of the war, then rose steadily to a peak of almost a third of income in the mid-1970s. Since then, however, the saving rate has steady declined, and is now close to the very low rates seen in low-saving nations like the United States.

---

23 The postal savings system intermediates an estimated 10–20% of deposits, and is subsequently invested by entities such as the Export-Import Bank and Japan Development Bank. The system has been undergoing reform since 2002, however, to further improve efficiency through quasi-privatization.

24 Anderson, S., "The Political Economy of Japanese Saving: How Postal Savings and Public Pensions Support High Rates of Household Saving in Japan," *Journal of Japanese Studies* 16(1) (1990): 61–92.

the world—and an elderly population has a tendency to dissave. The patterns of saving led by demographic trends is essentially the same as what occurred in Japan's high-saving phase, albeit acting in reverse.

The saving grace (no pun intended) has been Japan's ability to continue to draw on its positive net international investment position, which has meant the continued repatriation of factor income from assets held abroad. To some extent, this countenances the country's current low saving. But there has been another offsetting factor, which is corporate Japan's inability to expend retained earnings, which has resulted in sustained high rates of corporate saving—averaging around 5% annually since 2015. Taken together, gross domestic saving remains fairly elevated, at around mid-20%.

The legacy of Japan's high-saving years can be seen in the economy's capital intensity today. Japan's capital-output ratio—a measure of the country's stock of capital available for production, adjusted by the size of its economy—is among one of the most capital-intensive economies worldwide. Indeed, while many would consider a country such as the United States as an archetypal example of a capital-intensive, capital-exporting economy, Japan's utilization of capital—at four times GDP, almost twice as much as the U.S.—puts this impression to shame (Figure 2.5).

This capital intensity is tangible not just in its deployment in manufacturing—Japan's industrial robot-led automobile factories are the mainstay of movies—but its ubiquity elsewhere in Japanese life is evident to any visitor to the country. Japanese cities are often fronted by entire stores in downtown areas bereft of human customer service. Instead, one finds vending machines lined

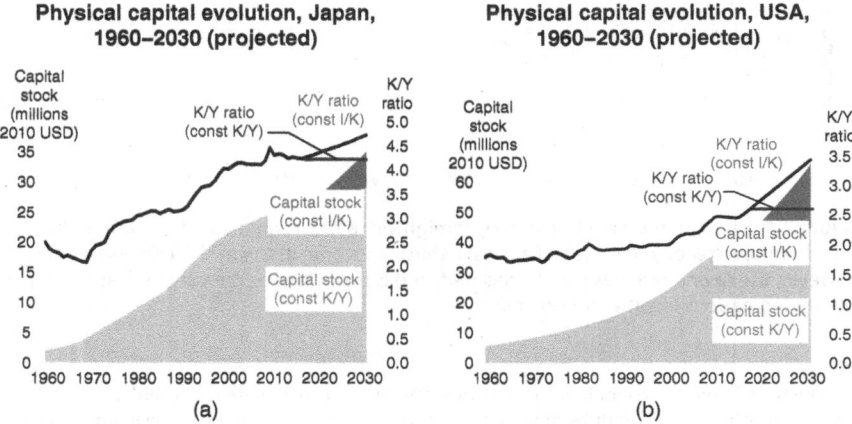

Figure 2.5 (a) After postwar rebuilding, Japan steadily increased its capital stock, to a point where it is, today, among the most capital-intensive nations in the world. (b) In contrast, the United States—often held up as an example of a capital-exporting economy—is only a little more than half as capital-intensive as Japan. This difference will likely remain, going forward, regardless of whether one assumes a constant investment rate (I/K) or capital output ratio (K/Y).

Figure 2.6 It is common to see entire stores in downtown areas of major cities occupied only by vending machines, which is emblematic of the country's substitution of labor for capital, even in typically service-oriented functions, such as retail.
Source: Jim Jetson / Flickr / CC BY 2.0.

end-to-end (Figure 2.6), a phenomenon emblematic of the substitution of capital for labor. Robots are also pervasive in other areas of Japanese life, from nursing homes—where care robots offer comfort to terminally-ill patients in their final moments—to actual homes, where robots execute a whole range of domestic functions, from cleaning chores to guard duties to child play.

Alliance Capitalism and Japan, Inc.

Japan's industrial conglomerates—whether the original *zaibatsu*, or its successor *keiretsu*—are an undeniably unique style of industrial organization, especially in contrast to the standard forms of business structures common in other parts of the world. It is idiosyncratic structures like this (along with features such as Japan's neomercantilist approach to trade and its high-saving, bank-centric financial system) that have led to the development of the Japan-specific form of capitalism.[25] *Keiretsu*, and business groups more generally, can

---

25 A thorough exposition of the unique industrial organization of Japanese firms will go beyond the scope of this chapter. A detailed discussion of the strengths and weaknesses of this approach to capitalism is provided in Aoki, M. and R. Dore (Eds.), *The Japanese Firm: Sources of Competitive Strength* (Oxford: Oxford University Press, 1994).

also exert an influence on the emergence of greater product variety, especially impacting international trade potential.[26]

The most distinctive feature of the *keiretsu* is their vertical integration: within a *keiretsu*, there are firms upstream and downstream in the production process, or distribution network, or financial flow.[27] For example, Toyota would rely solely on Totoda Gosei (a resin and rubber manufacturer) for steering wheels, JTEKT (an automotive components supplier) for bearings and drivetrains, Toyota Tsusho (a trading company) for distribution and operational support, and Toyota Central (an R&D outfit) for fundamental and applied research.

The structure also includes extensive horizontal integration; top-level businesses that compete in different sectors, but are nevertheless tightly linked to one another with cross-shareholdings of equity.[28] The Mitsubishi group, for instance, includes Mitsubishi UFJ (a financial group), Mitsubishi Heavy Industry (an engineering, electronics, and electrical corporation), Mitsubishi Shoji (a trading company), along with Mitsubishi Motors (an automobile manufacturer), Mitsubishi Chemical (a chemicals and pharmaceuticals business), Nippon Yusen (a shipping firm), and Kirin (a beverage producer), among others.[29] The group would revolve around the financial services firm, which would also provide banking services to other members of the *keiretsu*.

Supporting the horizontal and vertical *keiretsu* structures are more loosely-affiliated small supplier associations (*kyōryoku kai*), which would share best practices and collaborate to reduce costs by increasing communication along the supply chain, as well as *ad hoc* strategic alliances (*kinō-teki shudan*) that would form to pursue joint ventures or participate in project consortia (Figure 2.7).

Although the *keiretsu* maintained a number of features common to the *zaibatsu*—notably, they retained many of the vertical and horizontal integration features common to their predecessors—they were also distinct in a number of ways.[30] For starters, *keiretsu* are seldom owned by a single family, and shareholding tends to be widely distributed among individuals and firms. Moreover, the cross-shareholding structure was nowhere near as extensive in the *zaibatsu*, nor were financial services arms at the center of the group.

---

26 Feenstra, R., T.-H. Yang, and G. Hamilton, "Business Groups and Product Variety in Trade: Evidence from South Korea, Taiwan, and Japan," *Journal of International Economics* 48(1) (1999): 71–100.

27 These are sometimes referred to as the *sangyo* (production), *ryutsu* (distribution), and *shihon* (capital) *keiretsu*. See Gerlach, M., *Alliance Capitalism: The Social Organization of Japanese Business* (Berkeley, CA: University of California Press, 1992).

28 Kikkawa, T., "*Kigyo Shudan*: The Formation and Functions of Enterprise Groups," *Business History* 37(2) (1995): 44–53.

29 The first three—MUFJ, Mitsubishi Heavy Industry, and Mitsubishi Shoji—are viewed as the core "Three Great Houses," while the others are part of the 10 "major" group companies.

30 Yamamura, K., "Zaibatsu, Prewar and Zaibatsu, Postwar," *Journal of Asian Studies* 23(4) (1964): 539–554.

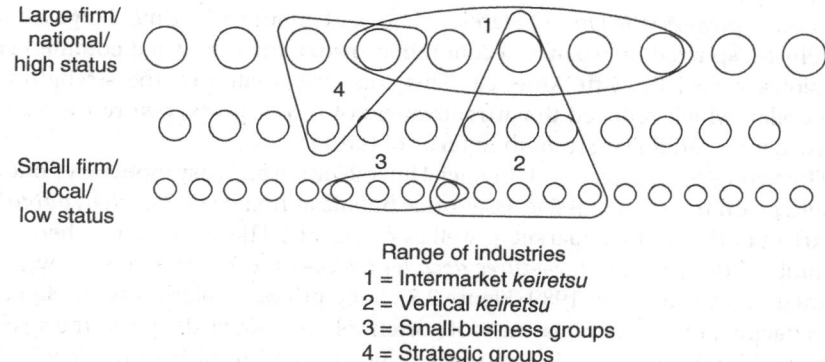

Range of industries
1 = Intermarket *keiretsu*
2 = Vertical *keiretsu*
3 = Small-business groups
4 = Strategic groups

Figure 2.7 The *keiretsu* structure comprises both vertical (up and downstream within the same industry) and horizontal (diversified businesses within the same group) components, along with more loosely-affiliated small-business groups known as *kyōryoku kai*, and ad hoc strategic alliances called *kinō-teki shudan*.

While some less-charitable characterizations refer to the structure as a cartel, they may be better understood as a unique business practice, distinct from Western-style capitalism.[31]

Since the 1990s, however, the formerly closed relationships between *keiretsu* companies have relaxed. For example, Aisin and Denso, two large auto parts manufacturers within the conglomerate, now supply transmission systems and climate control systems to clients beyond the Toyota Group. Even the extent of cross-shareholding has fallen; for TOPIX-listed firms, cross-shareholdings amount to less than 10%, from highs of more than a third in the 1980s.

The Modern Japanese Economy

The Lost Decades

It took two back-to-back global oil shocks—the first from the Yom Kippur war in 1973, and the second from the Iranian Revolution in 1979—to knock Japanese growth off its miracle trajectory. Like virtually all energy-importing economies worldwide, these multiple shocks led to a downshifting of growth, while simultaneously igniting inflation.

In toto, the Japanese economy powered through these shocks admirably, and by the 1980s, it was beginning to seriously challenge the two other major

---

31 Cutts, R., "Capitalism in Japan: Cartels and *Keiretsu*," *Harvard Business Review*, July–Aug. (1992).

economic powers (the United States and Soviet Union) of the time. Large trade surpluses, spurred by Japanese economic prowess, further fueled commercial tensions, especially with America. This was exacerbated by the strength of the dollar, which reduced the attractiveness of U.S. exports, before the Plaza Accord reversed dollar strength in favor of the yen.

The strong yen, coupled with financial liberalization and easy monetary policy, would go on to feed a massive asset price bubble at home (バブル景気, *baburu keiki*), in both the stock market as well as real estate. The stock market became so inflated that, even today—*three decades hence*—indexes have not recovered to their highs attained in 1989 (Figure 2.8). Land prices, similarly, rose to ridiculous heights; the (in)famous anecdote often told is how, at the peak, the space occupied by the Imperial Palace (about the size of Central Park in New York City) was estimated to be worth more than the entire state of California.[32]

By 1991, the bubble had begun to deflate, and the collapse in real estate and equity prices pulled prices, more generally, downward as well. Deflation, in turn, gave rise to a fall in real GDP, and the decade that followed quickly became known as the "Lost Decade" (失われた十年, *ushinawareta jūnen*). As the economy stumbled along in the 2000s, analysts were quick to christen the

Figure 2.8 The stock market, as measured by the Nikkei 225 index, became so inflated during the asset price bubble of the 1980s that it has yet to recover to the highs that were attained at the end of 1989 (the TOPIX index reveals a similar picture). A similar overvaluation of land assets occurred during the time.

---

32 The palace was, of course, never for sale; this estimate was based on comparable land valuations in locations close to the palace in Tokyo, then multiplied accordingly. The account is discussed in Werner, R., *Princes of the Yen* (New York: Routledge, 2003).

lost 20 or 30 years. Japan thus became entrenched in the minds of many as a cautionary tale of a post-industrial, underperforming economy.

It is often tempting to be lulled into thinking that such a diagnosis is genuinely reflective of the realities of the Japanese economy. To disabuse oneself of this pathology, it is only necessary to adjust for both population size as well as inflation. Once we recognize that Japan has, in contrast to other advanced economies, faced a more steadily shrinking population as well as faced extended periods of deflation and disinflation, it becomes amply clear that adjustments to GDP per head would place Japan in a much more advantageous position than first meets the eye. Indeed, after normalizing per capita incomes to the same level starting in 1999, Japan ends up beating almost all the other advanced industrialized G7 economies, along with Spain (Figure 2.9).

Post-Bubble Deflation and Disinflation

The relatively impressive per capita growth performance of Japan should not obscure the fact that the post-deflation years have, regardless, presented a number of unique challenges, especially from a macroeconomic perspective.

As corporations unwound from the ravages of the post-bubble collapse, nonperforming loans began to pile up on the banking sector's balance sheets. Yet banks would engage in sham loan restructurings, and thereby keep credit flowing to such insolvent firms. Rather than shedding workers and losing market share,

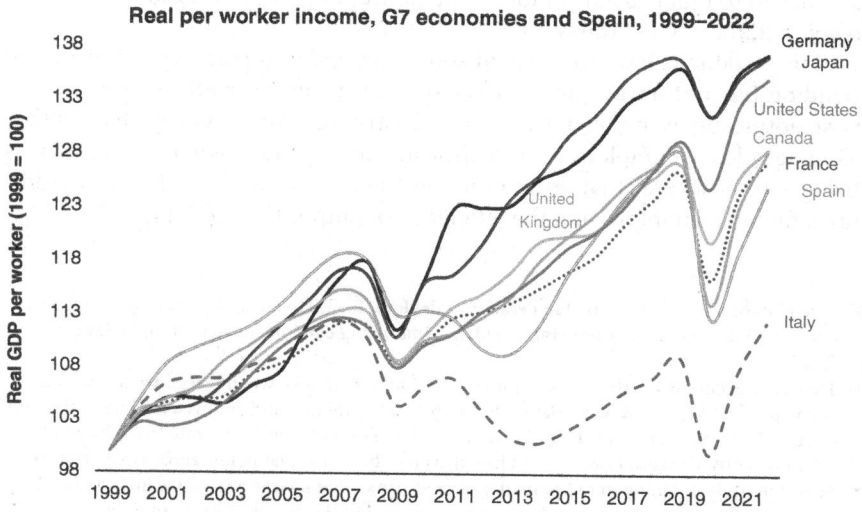

Figure 2.9 Once both relative inflation and workforce differentials are taken into account, Japan's real GDP per worker over the past two decades has outperformed that of virtually all other G7 economies, as well as that of Spain.

these firms would instead limp on, as "zombie" companies, which have in turn sapped Japanese corporate vitality.[33] To add to the challenges, consumers have often held back on spending in the face of persistent deflation and disinflation,[34] preferring instead to defer (especially large-scale) purchases to a later time.

These are the classic signs of a liquidity trap: where the necessary interest rate to stimulate activity falls below the so-called "zero lower bound"—the threshold for which most central banks are able to reduce the target policy rate[35]—and so aggregate demand is held in thrall of collapsing prices.

To revive the economic vigor that the private sector seemed intent on relinquishing, Japanese government policymakers have pursued an aggressive mix of fiscal and monetary policies designed to provide stimulus to the otherwise moribund macroeconomy.

On the monetary side, the BoJ has pursued some form of unconventional monetary policy over the past two decades, with little interruption. In 1999, the institution adopted a zero interest-rate policy (ZIRP), where it provided ample funds to meet short-term credit demand, thereby pushing the short-term interest rate to zero. Since this policy rate is nevertheless constrained by the zero lower bound, the BoJ eventually accompanied ZIRP with quantitative easing (QE) in 2001 (Figure 2.10). The goal of QE is to lower the *long-term* interest rate, via large-scale purchases of financial assets.[36]

To lend further support to the economy, the Ministry of Finance also pursued massive government expenditure programs. Since 1992, the Japanese government has never recorded a fiscal surplus. As a result, Japan's national debt began to build steadily, more than quintupling, from around 40% of GDP to about 225% of GDP today.

All those deficits have to be spent somehow, and unfortunately, government spending has not always been directed toward the most effective uses. The most notorious examples have been infrastructure projects that have either taken decades to complete, or have little apparent productive purpose, such as "bridges to nowhere" that seem more destined for channeling fiscal expenditures, rather than improving the efficiency of output (Figure 2.11).

---

33 The phenomenon is described in detail in Caballero, R., T. Hoshi, and A. Kashyap, "Zombie Lending and Depressed Restructuring in Japan," *American Economic Review* 98(5) (2008): 1943–1977.

34 Deflation occurs when there is a negative inflation rate; that is, when prices are decreasing from one period to the next. Disinflation is comparatively milder, and entails a decline in the rate of inflation from one period to the next, such as a decrease in the inflation rate from 2% to 1%.

35 More recently, the zero lower bound has proven to be somewhat below zero, as savers have revealed themselves willing to maintain deposits in banks that charge a negative interest rate. Nevertheless, economists (and logic) generally suggest that this negative rate can only be of a fairly limited magnitude, and maintained for only so long, before savers will choose to exit the financial system altogether, rather than see their savings erode.

36 The yield on a bond is generally inversely proportionate to its price. Hence, steady purchases that increase demand on such bonds will increase its price, and thereby lower the interest rate.

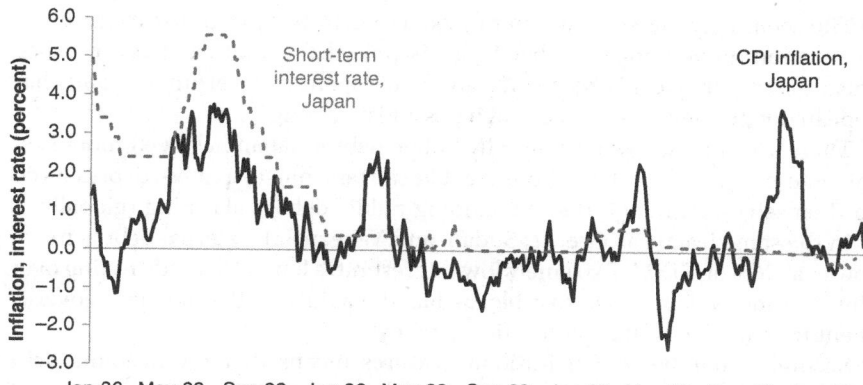

Figure 2.10 In the face of either deflation or disinflation, Japan has pursued a zero interest rate policy for the short-term interest rate over the past few decades, with very few deviations. The BoJ has also expanded ZIRP to include quantitative easing, which seeks to suppress the long-term interest rate.

Figure 2.11 Japan's pursuit of government-led fiscal pump priming, amid a liquidity trap, has resulted in less-than-desirable public projects, including notorious "bridges to nowhere," such as this unfinished bridge that terminates at the side of a mountain.
Source: Nkns / Wikimedia Commans / CC-BY-SA 3.0.

The seemingly massive burden of Japanese debt has prompted much prognostication among analysts that Japan is poised for another massive crisis, this time in public debt. Yet the durability of Japanese government bonds has repeatedly (for decades) proven such pessimists wrong.

There are at least five reasons why public debt in Japan has been more sustainable than might first meet the eye. For starters, most Japanese debt is owed to themselves. Although the outstanding public debt is alarming (globally, it is in the same league as Greece, Sudan, and Venezuela), external debt is much lower, at 96% of GDP.[37] Extremely low interest rates have also made rolling over this enormous debt stock possible, as has the ability of the Japanese government to issue bonds in its domestic currency.

Second, a number of institutional features means that the headline debt figure may be misleading. After two decades of quantitative easing, the BoJ holds a good deal of debt on its balance sheet, and it does so for stabilization, and not financing, objectives. Third, owing to widespread cross-agency debt holding—a direct public-sector analogue to the cross-shareholding practices of the *keiretsu*—gross public debt is likely overstated, with *net* debt smaller than reported. Fourth, despite such large liabilities, the country as a whole maintains even larger assets, such that its net international investment position (NIIP)—the difference in its external financial assets and liabilities—is significantly positive.[38] And, finally (and perhaps most crucially), risk-averse investors continue to regard Japanese debt as "safe," which is almost a self-fulfilling prophecy that validates such continued debt issuance.

The Paradox of Technology in Modern Japan

While its long-held dominance in the sector has receded in recent years, it is undeniable that Japan was historically a global leader in the production of advanced technological goods, especially in modern consumer electronics and components (especially semiconductors).

This is coupled with world-class research and development (R&D). Japan ranks just after China and the United States in terms of international patent applications, and maintains a substantial lead over the next global contenders.[39] Fascinatingly, Japanese R&D is led by the private sector: of the 3.3% of GDP spent nationwide, less than a quarter originates from the government or higher

---

37 Unfortunately, this ratio has increased substantially over the past decade. In 2012, this share was 52% of output, out of a total public debt burden of 229%, which was less than a quarter. Today, the ratio is much closer to two-fifths.

38 For 2021, Japan's reported NIIP was $3.4 trillion (or 63% of GDP).

39 In 2020, the top three countries in terms of patent applications to the World Intellectual Property Organization were China (72,349), the United States (56,114), and Japan (49,537). The next three countries in the list are the European Patent Office (39,052), South Korea (19,766), and the international bureau (13,508). See WIPO, *Patent Cooperation Treaty Yearly Review: The International Patent System* (Geneva: World Intellectual Property Organization, 2021).

Type-1: Corporate Seal   Type-2: Banking Seal   Type-3: Identification Seal

Figure 2.12 Registered corporate (*daihyō-in*) and banking (*ginkō-in*) seals are still frequently used to authenticate documents needed for commercial contracts, and their ubiquity in corporate Japan has been implicated as a hurdle to more widespread adoption of electronic recordkeeping and digital communications.

education sector.[40] Such a reliance on private initiative even puts free market-oriented Anglo-Saxon economies—such as the United States or the United Kingdom, which sustain higher proportions of public R&D—to shame. In this sense, then, Japanese R&D has a tendency to stress commercial objectives; more "development" than "research."

The prominence of such high-tech goods in Japan's manufacturing profile has led many to conceive of Japan as a quintessentially technologically sophisticated economy. In spite of this reputation, however, the operation of the economy is, in certain ways, remarkably low-tech.

Take, for example, the process of verifying business documents. Japan has obstinately clung on to the need to authenticate documents with official corporate seals (Figure 2.12). It took the COVID-19 pandemic—and its attendant limitations on physical interactions for months—to lead to the recognition that such practices inhibit a transition to a more efficient system of electronic recordkeeping and digital communications.

More generally, Japan's ability to break free from the currently very limited contribution of TFP to its growth—and hence create the conditions for sustained future growth, even as other factors such as the labor force and capital accumulation become drags on potential growth—may well hinge on how it is not only able to exploit the promises of the information and communications technology (ICT) and digital revolutions fully into its relatively unproductive services sector, but also to alter the qualitative direction of its R&D efforts, toward more basic research.[41]

---

40 See OECD, *Research and Development Statistics* (Paris: Organisation for Economic Co-operation and Development, 2020).

41 To its credit, the Japanese government appears to be aware of this deficiency, and has sought to generously fund basic research initiatives at universities. However, in spite of its continued impressive rate of patent registrations, these awards are seldom concentrated in new economy areas such as ICT and biopharmaceuticals.

Japanese Employment Trends and Its Silver Economy

The Japanese workplace often conveys the impression of rigid hierarchy, long hours (including semi-mandatory after-work "leisure" involving karaoke and drinking), and lifetime employment. Such a characteristic "salaryman" (サラリーマン, *sararīman*) is now in retreat, but it remains true that unemployment rates are very low and are stable by global standards. Between 1953 and 2022, the average was 2.5%, and record lows and highs were 1.0 and 5.5%, respectively—rates that high-unemployment European nations can only fantasize about (globally, unemployment hovers between 5% and 6%).

Not only is the unemployment rate low, job turnover tends to be very low. Employees stay in a job, on average, for around 12 years, almost three times that in the United States, and longer than in almost all European countries (save a few on the periphery, such as Greece, Italy, and Portugal). The turnover rate—the percentage of employees leaving a firm over time—is about 7%, a fraction that of the rest of Asia, and especially fast-growing Asian economies like China.[42] The typical salaryman would only hold five jobs over the entire lifetime, as opposed to twice as many in many other advanced economies.

Employers in Japan tend to discourage quits, even during recessions dismissals are avoided in favor of keeping workers in their positions—even when such retention often means having employees sit at their desks reading newspapers during downturns—but the upshot of such labor market stability and implicit insurance is that average wages tend to be on the lower end among advanced economies (and more akin to countries with far lower per capita incomes).

The possibly more insidious tradeoff such practices entail is that younger workers often find it difficult to break into the workforce. The youth unemployment rate is often a few percentage points higher than the rest of the working-age population, and female labor force participation correspondingly lower (more akin to Southern European countries than Asia, although this has picked up noticeably in recent years). The practice of lifetime employment has therefore inadvertently given rise to a dual labor market: one for the elderly, and another for youth, as non-regular employees.

Elevated unemployment of this nature also does not bode well for an otherwise well-qualified junior workforce. Since the modernization of education during the Meiji period, Japanese educational standards have consistently been very high, with an emphasis on science and technology in education, inspired by similar models in Northern European countries. Average years of schooling in Japan amount to around 13.5 years, comparable to the most educated nations in the West, even if Asian standards tend to emphasize different aspects of learning.

---

42 Watanabe, M. and H. Miyadera, "Moving Past Japan's Archaic Employment Practices," *BRINK*, October 10, 2017.

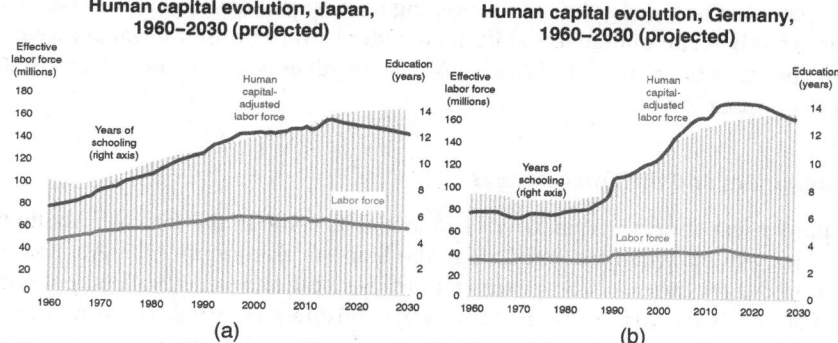

Figure 2.13 (a) Japan will face significant shrinkages in its labor force in the future due to its aging population, but will have little room to expand educational attainment, being already one of the most educated workforces worldwide. (b) While not as severe as countries such as Germany, diminishing returns to human capital will be a challenge to Japan's growth in the decade to come.

The future workforce will also have to contend with the fact that Japanese human capital will have to be built on a shrinking working-age population, while concurrently having little additional room to increase attainment; at 14 years, Japan is already among the most educated societies worldwide, and every other person in the workforce already possesses a tertiary education (second highest among OECD countries). While the coming drag from shrinking human capital will not be as severe as some European nations (Germany, in particular, will experience a greater drag from contracting human capital), it is clear that diminishing returns to human capital will plague Japan's growth prospects in the decade ahead (Figure 2.13).

Despite such strong headwinds to economic competitiveness, Japan remains stubbornly resistant to the most straightforward way of plugging the gap in its labor market: accepting more migrants. As recently as 2012, there were only 682,000 foreign workers, out of a labor force of 65.3 million. In recent years, this has more than doubled, albeit from a low base; as of 2021, Japan entertained 1.7 million foreigners among its 68.2 million workers. Still, at 2.5% of the total labor force, this representation is miniscule.

Undoubtedly, this modest increase has been motivated, in part, by the clear need for trained labor to undertake functions that cannot easily be replaced by substitution via capital. We typically think of these as services, especially in healthcare—after all, most of us would rather interact with a human doctor or nurse—but Japan has shown itself to be willing to accept robotic interventions even in such settings (palliative-care robots, which offer companionship and comfort to those in hospitals, nursing homes, and hospices).[43] On balance, there has been an undeniable shift in attitudes toward immigration, in no small part because of an increased desire to cater to silver economy needs amidst an aging population.

Abenomics and the Three Arrows

Japan's latest effort to revitalize its economy has come in the form of "Abenomics," a three-part plan launched after Abe Shinzō's election in 2012. Abenomics featured three "arrows," comprising monetary, fiscal, and structural components.

The first two parts were, in some ways, business as usual; Japan had been pursuing policies to eliminate deflation and increase demand through government spending for the better part of two decades prior. Yet in other ways it is different, as even the first two arrows now received the explicit endorsement of the government as a coordinated national strategy, drawing parallels to the *fukoku kyōhei* program during the Meiji era. Abenomics was also different in one marked way: compared to the efforts before, it was actually modestly successful.

The monetary arrow tasked the BoJ with reaching an inflation target of 2% (from the original 1%). To do so, the BoJ expanded its strategy for QE in 2013, to include not just quantitative but also *qualitative* changes to its balance sheet (essentially, with the inclusion of riskier assets into the slate of approved securities subject to QE). Three years thereafter, the central bank revealed an even more expansive "yield curve control" approach, which targets not just the usual 10-year rate, but the entire suite of longer-term rates along the yield curve.[44] Together, these efforts did elevate headline inflation and—while still averaging closer to 1% over the period—the uptick has been viewed positively by most observers.

Fiscal policies were a little more stop-and-go, especially since the deficit-financed nature of this particular arrow also prompted calls for increases to the consumption tax. This tax saw two hikes during the tenure of Abe: one in 2014, and again in 2019.[45] While such a move probably prevented the budget balance

---

43 Matei, A., "Robots and the Future of Dying," *Nuvo*, July 26, 2018.

44 The yield curve is the plot of yields for bonds with different maturity dates. Typically, the yield curve is constructed from a range of 3 months through either 10- or 30-year maturities. A yield curve typically slopes upward—longer maturities yield more—but "inversion" occurs when the long-term rate falls below the short-term rate (and this is usually regarded as a leading indicator of an impending recession).

45 To be clear, the first hike—from 5% to 8% in April 2014—was proposed by the administration of Yoshihiko Noda. The second hike, from 8% to 10%, was led by the Abe administration, but was postponed twice; the hikes were originally scheduled for October 2015 and April 2017, before finally being implemented in October 2019. Abe was also the Prime Minister for two periods, between 2006–2007, and 2012–2020, although the latter tenure has been regarded as far more distinguished.

from going too far out of whack, it also moderated the expansionary effects of other government spending, since tax policy was operating in a different direction from expenditure policy. The net effect of fiscal stimulus for GDP has likewise been positive, with GDP growth moving into a slightly higher gear through the second half of the 2010s.

Although postmortems often grade the first two arrows as the more successful of the three, it is the final arrow that has always been the most ambitious, and—almost by definition—the most enduring. Successful structural changes are difficult to effect anywhere, but a number of proxy indicators suggest that the Abe administration did manage to kickstart a process of reform that may last well beyond the decade that Abenomics was in place.

The most notable structural reform that Abenomics prompted was an effort to increase the contribution of women in the labor force, embodied in the political rallying cry "active participation of women" (女性 の 活躍, *josei no katsuyaku*). Here, the results are unequivocal: in 2012, Japan's female labor force participation rate was 48%, but by 2020, it had risen to 53%. This places Japan in a similar ballpark to Korea (54%) and the United States (56%), and far above that of laggard Southern European countries (Greece and Italy have rates in the low 40s), albeit behind leading East Asian countries (like China and Singapore, where rates are in the mid-60s). Still, a full 5 percentage-point increase in participation, supported by a generous expansion in the quantity and quality of childcare services, is nothing to sniff at.

During the period, Japan saw a stabilization in its fertility rate, at around 1.3. While some may regard this as an indictment of Abenomics' goal of raising fertility, it should be set against the continued decline and even more dismal rates common in high-income East Asian economies, where fertility hovers around 1. Employment, in general, may also have been better than in the absence of Abenomics; one estimate suggests a counterfactual of a decline in employment by close to 3 percentage points due to demographic changes, when the reality was an increase of around 1 percentage point.[46]

Japan and the World Economy

Japan's Export-Oriented Economy

Japan's legacy of *sakoku* was reflected primarily via its neomercantilist approach that emphasized export-orientated growth and foreign asset acquisition. That said, despite this particular trade and investment strategy, its approach has been comparatively mild, especially compared to other countries at a similar

---

46 Kawaguchi, D., K. Kawata, and T. Toriyabe, "An Assessment of Abenomics from the Labor Market Perspective," *Asian Economic Policy Review* 16(2) (2021): 247–278.

stage of development. For example, Japan's average annual tariff rates were systematically lower than that of the U.S. between 1870 until the 1960s, when they converged to similar levels. Similarly, even though inward foreign direct investment (FDI) has been very limited in Japan, this has been more due to difficulties in foreign corporations succeeding in the country's idiosyncratic business environment, than explicit restrictions on foreign investment.

Even so, as the economy rose in power and influence over the course of the 20th century, other countries (predictably) began to push back at its dominance in international economic exchange.

This opposition was most visceral in the United States. The success of the Japanese export machine—particularly in affordable, fuel-efficient cars (which were especially attractive in the aftermath of the 1970s oil price shocks)—led to calls by Big Three American automakers (Ford, GM, and Chrysler) for protection from unmitigated exports from the Land of the Rising Sun. American policymakers responded, and in 1981, "Voluntary" Export Restraints (VERs)— where, under pressure from the importing country, the exporting nation applies quotas to its quantity of exports—were applied to the export of Japanese automobiles Stateside.

However, VERs did not end up improving the imbalance. Japanese car manufacturers responded with a mix of transplanting final assembly plants to the Southern U.S. states (where weaker union laws kept wages suppressed) as well as going up the value chain. It was around this time that Japan's Big Three (Honda, Nissan, and Toyota) began introducing larger, more expensive models to the U.S. market, along with luxury divisions (Acura, Infiniti, and Lexus). Together, these moves allowed profits to remain elevated, even as the actual number of cars were scaled back, in accordance with the VERs.

Japan's global economic footprint was further bolstered by a stronger yen. By 1985, the U.S. dollar has become widely perceived as overvalued. This led to an agreement among the major economic powers of the time to jointly intervene in currency markets to weaken the greenback. This Plaza Accord ultimately delivered a rapid depreciation of the dollar, which conversely meant a substantial appreciation of the yen.[47]

The strong yen would spark a global buying spree by Japanese investors, especially in the United States. At one point, it seemed like every other major Japanese corporation was acquiring American assets, such as New York hotels, Hollywood studios, and Detroit auto shops. That many of these seeming bargains were not necessarily sound was secondary; the sense of being bought out predictably led to a political backlash, with the U.S. Congress responding to this "economic Pearl Harbor" with further trade restrictions.

---

47 The Plaza Accord was in fact so successful in depreciating the dollar that another agreement, the Louvre Accord, was eventually signed just two years later to halt the continued decline of the dollar and stabilize foreign exchange markets.

The Flying Geese Model

Not every country was opposed to the export of Japanese financial flows. Japan has famously promulgated the so-called "flying geese" (雁行形態論, *gankō keitai-ron*) paradigm of technological adoption and development, where underdeveloped nations in the region would benefit from successively aligning themselves behind Japan's relative economic leadership and financial muscle, and eventually develop themselves, even as the lead nation gradually sheds its least competitive industries.

After this first round, the second-tier economies, such as the NIEs, would be in a position to take the lead in disseminating their accumulated surpluses and capital. The next tiers of ASEAN and East Asian economies—for example, Thailand and Malaysia—would then benefit from the NIEs investments in them, similar to how geese fly in formation.[48]

East Asian economies have certainly benefitted from this flow of financial investment into their economies, and the reality of the past half-century is that many less-developed economies in the region appear to have steadily evolved their dynamic comparative advantage. They have moved up the value chain of production, after they benefit from the initial injection of capital from Japan, in a manner similar to this model.

Today, outward FDI from Japan to the rest of Asia remains a mainstay. Japanese FDI flows into Southeast Asia, for example, are not only large and stable—the typical characteristic of FDI versus portfolio flows, more generally—but also extremely diversified, going into sectors as distinct as natural resources, real estate, electronics and electrical manufacturing, automotives, and financial services (Figure 2.14). This has undeniably made a significant difference to the growth trajectory of many such regional economies, and has unsurprisingly garnered a vastly different reaction from host governments, vis-à-vis advanced Western economies.

Conclusion

Japan's Long-Term Growth Prospects

Some analysts have looked at Japan's lost decade or two and concluded that Japan will never dig itself out of its growth depression. Others have studied the country's impending demographic crunch, and claim that any country that boasts more than 90,000 centenarians—while remaining overwhelmingly closed to foreign immigrant labor—can never secure a future with vibrant

---

48 Akamatsu, K., "A Historical Pattern of Economic Growth in Developing Countries," *The Developing Economies* 1 (1962): 3–25.

Greenfield FDI into south-east Asia
2003-2017, $bn

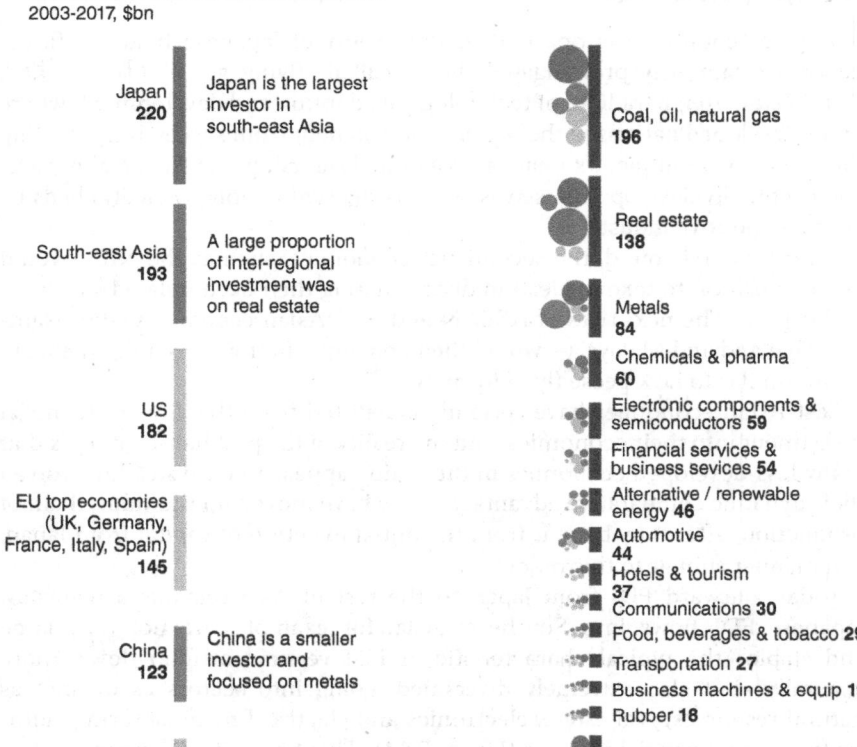

Japan **220**	Japan is the largest investor in south-east Asia
South-east Asia **193**	A large proportion of inter-regional investment was on real estate
US **182**	
EU top economies (UK, Germany, France, Italy, Spain) **145**	
China **123**	China is a smaller investor and focused on metals
South Korea **98**	

Coal, oil, natural gas **196**
Real estate **138**
Metals **84**
Chemicals & pharma **60**
Electronic components & semiconductors **59**
Financial services & business sevices **54**
Alternative / renewable energy **46**
Automotive **44**
Hotels & tourism **37**
Communications **30**
Food, beverages & tobacco **29**
Transportation **27**
Business machines & equip **19**
Rubber **18**
Others **119**

Figure 2.14 Outward FDI from Japan to Southeast Asia, besides being large and stable, is also extremely diversified, with flows to a wide range of economic sectors. Japan is also one of the oldest investors in the Asia, having followed the flying geese model since at least the end of World War II.

growth prospects. Yet others point to the gradual slide of Japanese universities from global rankings—the University of Tokyo, once the top-ranking tertiary institution in Asia, is now routinely displaced by schools in China and the NIEs—and believe that the Japanese economy's retreat is inevitable.

While a shrinking labor force, an expanding (and dissaving) elderly population, and diminished returns to education are all undeniably drags on growth potential, this chapter has also argued that there are important mitigating factors.

Japan has belatedly become more open to immigration as a means of supplementing its aging workforce. In downtown Tokyo, the ubiquity of vending machines has been gradually replaced by convenience stores staffed with

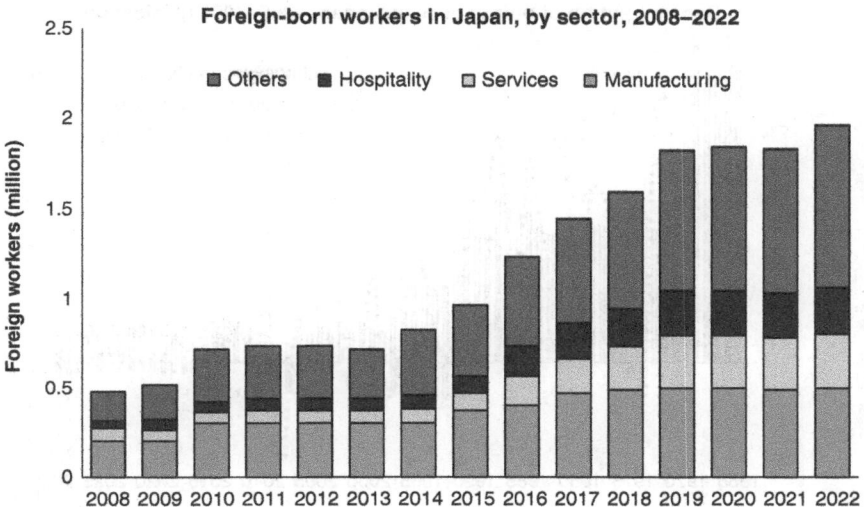

Figure 2.15 The total number of foreign workers has increased by close to fourfold over the past decade and a half, from 486,000 to 1.8 million. The majority are from China and Vietnam, and are deployed in areas ranging from manufacturing to services to hospitality to healthcare.

foreign-born (albeit Japanese-speaking) workers. Between 2008 and 2022, the total number of foreign workers increased by close to fourfold. The greatest numbers hail from China and Vietnam, followed by the Philippines (Figure 2.15). Importantly, domestic attitudes are starting to shift; in a survey conducted in 2020, a supermajority of respondents agreed or somewhat agreed with the need for more immigrants.[49]

While saving rates have plunged as the population has aged, capital accumulation may well remain afloat, if Japan chooses to repatriate returns from its enormous holdings of assets abroad. And even if such net international factor income is not deployed toward domestic investment, the inflows will support consumption for its population.

More fundamentally, Japanese innovation—at least as exemplified by patent activity—remains globally competitive, which will act as a boost for productivity. There are also other, low-hanging fruit on this front, as well; if Japan is able to better incorporate the bounty of the ICT revolution into its economic processes, for instance, it could reap some (admittedly modest) gains from a tried-and-tested contributor to TFP growth (Figure 2.16).

---

49 Some 26% agreed and 44% somewhat agreed to the question of whether more foreigners were needed in the country, and even when asked pointedly about whether more foreigners were needed *in their own resident area*, 57% agreed or somewhat agreed with the proposition.

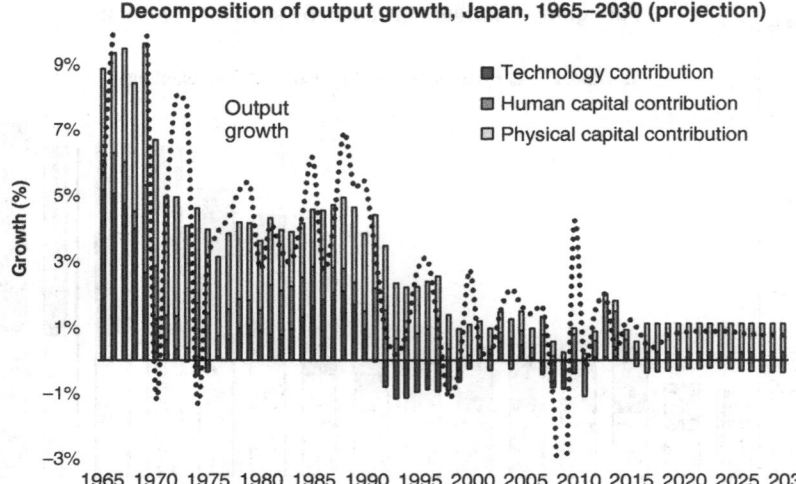

Figure 2.16 Although human capital will undoubtedly be a drag on Japan's future potential growth, it may be more than offset by capital accumulation from repatriated financial flows from the country's substantial foreign asset holdings, as well as some modest TFP contribution.

The legacy of Abenomics—an experiment that lasted close to a decade—has hinted at two possibilities: that the short-term performance of the Japanese economy may be amenable to well-designed policies aimed at managing its unique business cycle, while its longer-term outcomes could likewise be conditioned (even if not completely altered) by policies aimed at effecting structural change.

All these, together, suggest that Japan's baseline long-term growth could well hover just below one, instead of fully going into negative territory. Regardless, it will almost certainly be the case that Japan will still influence the region economically, even as its citizens continue to thrive domestically.

3

India: Emerging Giant or Slumbering Elephant?

I dream of India becoming a great economic superpower.
—Dhirubhai Ambani (1932–2002), co-founder, Reliance Industries

I do not want India to be an economic superpower. I want India to be a happy country.
—J.R.D. Tata (1904–93), former Chairman, Tata Group

Introduction

With a little less than 1.4 billion people inhabiting a land mass of around 3.3 million square kilometers—almost three times smaller than China, despite a comparable population—it is little surprise that one of the first impressions one has on arriving in India is how colorful but *crowded* the nation is.

Crowded as it may be, the Subcontinent—as India is often referred to by its own people, together with the alternative Hindu name Bhārat—is indeed also enormously colorful. This is captured, visually, by the bright *saris* and *cholis* that adorn the womenfolk, the vibrant tones imparted by turmeric and chilies into the nation's varied cuisine, and the dyes that mark the statues and paintings of the Hindu deistic pantheon. But it is also captured metaphorically by the variety of languages, religions, and peoples that call themselves Indian, along with the rich history of a civilization that has spanned several millennia.

India today is, indeed, a story of contrasts and contradictions, woven into a tapestry of ideas and ideologies that have served its people for well over thousands of years. But add to this deep history an institutional layer of democracy—India is the largest (if still imperfect) democracy in the world—and one gets a sense of how adaptive and complex its political economy must be, to serve its diverse constituents.

Asian Economies: History, Institutions, and Structures, First Edition. Jamus Jerome Lim.
© 2024 John Wiley & Sons Ltd. Published 2024 by John Wiley & Sons Ltd.

India's heterogeneity extends beyond sociocultural and political elements. India is on track to displace Germany as the world's fourth-largest economy sometime in the middle of this decade, and when measured in PPP terms, it is already definitively the world's third-largest.

But this distinction itself hints at India's principal economic challenge: in spite of its absolute size, it remains one of the poorest economies globally. In per capita GDP terms, India's was $2,277 in 2021 dollars, and even in more flattering purchasing power terms, it was only $7,242 that year. This places India firmly among lower-middle-income countries, and in the same ballpark as nations like Côte d'Ivoire, Zimbabwe, Laos, or Nicaragua.[1]

What is even more stark is how certain regions of India are *even poorer*, with large swathes of the population still living in significant poverty, and exhibiting dramatically different levels of health and education consonant with their varied incomes. Yet so long as certain states continue to severely underprovide essential public services (and, even when provided, reveal woeful levels of service quality), it is likely that such within-country income disparities will persist.

Alas, such economic disparities are not limited to households. The Indian corporate landscape is currently dominated by so-called "large business houses" (LBHs), groups that concentrate commercial activity even more than is usual in Asia. Such LBHs—many of which, like Tata or Reliance, may be recognized of even outside of India—often crowd out smaller upstarts in many sectors of the Indian economy, eroding competition and limiting options available to the consumer.

The trifecta of large economic size, low per capita incomes, and wide-ranging inequalities makes India unique on the modern global economic stage, and to understand the current state that the Subcontinent finds itself in requires a clear grasp of the country's rich history, varied geography, and idiosyncratic economic structure.

Economic Geography of India

North Versus South India, and East Versus West

The traditional separation often drawn when thinking about India is one between the North and South.

North India was traditionally known as Āryāvarta (आर्यावर्त, literally the "Land of the Aryans"), and occupies the greater part of the country. The

---

1 The former two are comparator economies in nominal GDP per capita, while the latter two are in GDP per capita measured via PPP.

country's three major rivers—the Brahmaputra, the Ganges, and the Indus—flow through northern Indo-Gangetic plains.[2] South India has been referred to as Dakṣiṇāpatha (दक्षिणपथ, literally "Southern Road"). The south is mostly comprised of the Deccan plateau, but includes coastal regions of the peninsula. It constitutes only around a fifth of the territory.

Most contemporary observers, including many Indians, subscribe to such a north-south difference between the peoples as well, that of northern Aryans vis-à-vis southern Dravidians. Recent research has suggested that this distinction is somewhat exaggerated.[3] Both populations find their roots in South Asian hunter-gatherers and Iranian agriculturalists; ancestral North Indians merely have additional genes injected from Southeastern steppe pastoralists. Regardless, both groups have experienced extensive admixture, due to complex patterns of human migration that date back thousands of years.

And like many civilizations extending into millennia, the borders of India have waxed and waned. Importantly, India had been—even until the 20th century—somewhat more expansive than it currently is. Hence, while the north-south distinction is often applied by observers of the Subcontinent, there is at least another important geographical distinction: an east-west one.

At the far eastern end of modern India lie the so-called "Seven Sister" states,[4] a region that has historically included a number of nominally independent kingdoms, before falling under British influence as Burma, and being thereafter incorporated into modern India. In contrast, what was since ancient times the eastern half of Bengal is, today, the independent nation of Bangladesh.[5]

To India's northwest is Pakistan, a Muslim-majority region that had been a part of India, but was partitioned out following Britain's exit. There have even been times in India's long history—such as at the height of the Mauryan Empire, around 265 BCE—when parts of what is modern-day Afghanistan were enfolded into Indian territory.

---

2 The South has three major rivers as well—the Godavari, Kaveri, and Narmada—but these systems are shorter, and hence their drainage basins tend to be less important for the country as a whole (while of course being very important to the states in which the rivers traverse). That said, the Godavari does traverse five states and has a significant influence on economic activity therein, and hence is often referred to as the "Ganges of the South" (*Dakshina Ganga*).
3 Narasimhan, V. et al., "The Formation of Human Populations in South and Central Asia," *Science* 365(6457) (2019): eaat7487.
4 Officially, together with the state of Sikkim, this is known as the Northeast Region. The Seven Sisters were inaugurated as new states in 1972.
5 The province of East Bengal was itself meant to be the exclave of East Pakistan, but following a war of independence in 1971, the province seceded into modern Bangladesh.

India's Economic Centers Are Scattered Across the Land Mass

India is a federal union, constituted of 28 states,[6] along with a scattering of 8 union territories (which fall, in whole or part, under the administrative jurisdiction of the central government).[7] The union government takes the federalist model seriously; power is heavily devolved to the states, almost to the detriment of greater economic direction and guidance from the center.

India's principal cities are distributed akin to points on a compass: New Delhi in the north, Mumbai in the west, Kolkata in the east, Chennai in the south, and Bengaluru around the middle (although technically the city is located in Karnataka, a southern state). These five boast populations above 10 million, and are officially regarded as "megacities."[8] Like many major economies, the country maintains distinct political (Delhi) and economic (Mumbai) capitals.

Surrounding each of these cities are broader regions that concentrate economic activity.[9] The traditional industrial powerhouses of Maharashtra and Gujarat produce much of India's electronics and processed food (along with automobiles), while West Bengal has a long history of textile production that dates back centuries (Figure 3.1). Services, in contrast, are more heavily represented around (predictably) the capital, as well as in southern states, such as Karnataka—where Bengaluru's legendary reputation in outsourced services is now accepted worldwide—along with neighboring Tamil Nadu, which likewise excels in software and other high-skilled services.

This mapping of the formal economy belies the much wider distribution of industry and services performed by the *un*organized sector. India has a massive number of informal businesses—smaller establishments that are either not registered, or employ only a handful of workers—and a geographic accounting of unorganized services reveals significant agglomerations across almost the entire landmass, save the northeast.

Lest one is given the impression that India's economy is a story of industrial and service clusters, it is important to stress that agriculture and other primary sectors remain a large part of the economy. The country is the second-largest

---

6 Due to its political history, Indian states have been constituted and reconstituted fairly frequently, with the latest (Telangana) having attained statehood as recently as 2014 (it was carved out of Andhra Pradesh).

7 Most of these are comparatively small regions that are either contested or formed from former colonies; notably, however, Delhi—the federal territory on which the capital occupies—is a union territory.

8 The 2011 Indian census classified the Greater Delhi (then 16.3 million, but 31.2 million as of 2021), Mumbai (18.4/20.7 million), and Kolkata (14.1/15.0 million) urban areas as megacities—technically, those with populations above 10 million—while the 2021 census added Chennai (11.2 million) and Bengaluru (12.8 million) to the list. By 2030, Ahmedabad and Hyderabad are expected to cross the threshold to qualify as megacities.

9 Ghani, E., W. Kerr, and S. O'Connell, "Spatial Determinants of Entrepreneurship in India," *Regional Studies* 48(6) (2014): 1071–1089.

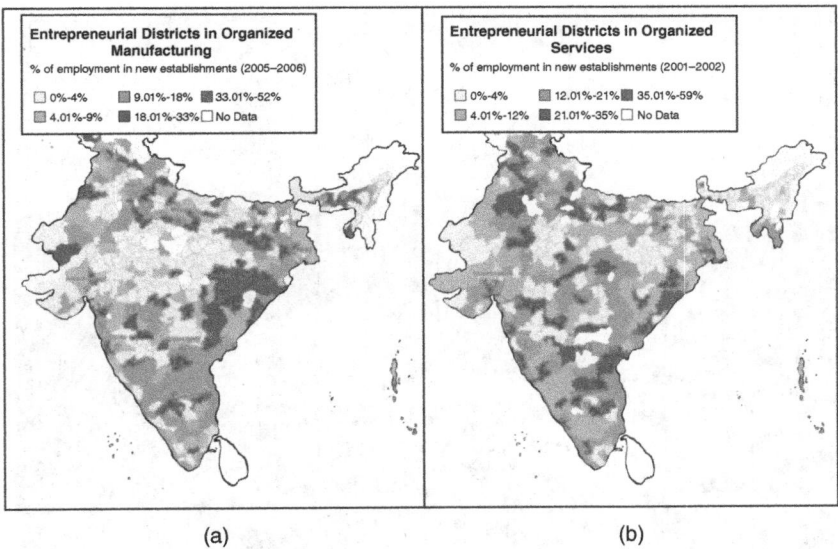

Figure 3.1 (a) Organized Indian manufacturing tends to concentrate around the western and eastern hubs of Maharashtra-Gujarat and West Bengal, respectively, while (b) services are found closer to the northern and southern hubs of Delhi and Tamil Nadu-Karnataka, respectively.

global producer of wheat and rice, two major staples. It is also a major producer of buffalo and cow milk, and the world's most productive country in the former. India exports tons of tea and coffee every year.

Agrarian activity can be found in every state. Agriculture is so pervasive that states that lead in the secondary and tertiary sectors—such as Gujarat, Uttar Pradesh, and West Bengal—are also among the largest crop-producing states.

Pockets of agricultural excellence exist. Assam, a verdant, subtropical state nestled within the Seven Sisters, is responsible for half of all Indian tea production, for which India (as a whole) is the fourth largest exporter worldwide. Jute, a key input for West Bengali textile manufacturing, is also produced mainly in that state.

Primary production provides a little shy of half of all employment, despite only contributing a fifth to value added; the dominance of agricultural work in the labor force—and especially among the poorer classes—is the main driver for Indian recalcitrance in international trade negotiations involving liberalization of the sector.

India's Poverty Map

It is well recognized that India still has a vast number of people living in poverty, and its eradication will be one of the principal challenges the nation will

Figure 3.2 The slums in downtown Mumbai stand in stark contrast against adjacent modern housing, and are a reminder of how inequality can rise sharply in fast-growing countries, before they are addressed by redistributive policy.
Source: Sthitaprajna / Flickr / CC BY SA 2.0.

have to confront as it develops. But if there is an underappreciated aspect of India's economic geography, it is how much of the relative impoverishment can be found in the country's northeast.

There are pockets of poverty across just about every district of the Subcontinent,[10] of course, and the major cities all have their share of slum dwellings (Dharavi, in Mumbai, is widely regarded as one of the largest, densest slums worldwide, albeit one that has an active informal economy estimated at $1 billion in turnover). On occasion, these massive slums stand in uncomfortable contrast against modern developments (Figure 3.2).

But like other parts of the world, poverty tends to be more common in rural areas, where outward signs of immiseration may not be as evident. Still, the country's woeful road network often means long trips by village women just to secure water, or piles of uncleared trash littering the edges of rural settlements. It is also evident from the practice of open defecation (Figure 3.3).

---

10 Of all districts, only Kottayam, a southern Kerala district, has registered zero on the multidimensional poverty index. NITI Aayog, *India National Multidimensional Poverty Index: Baseline Report* (New Delhi: Government of India, 2021).

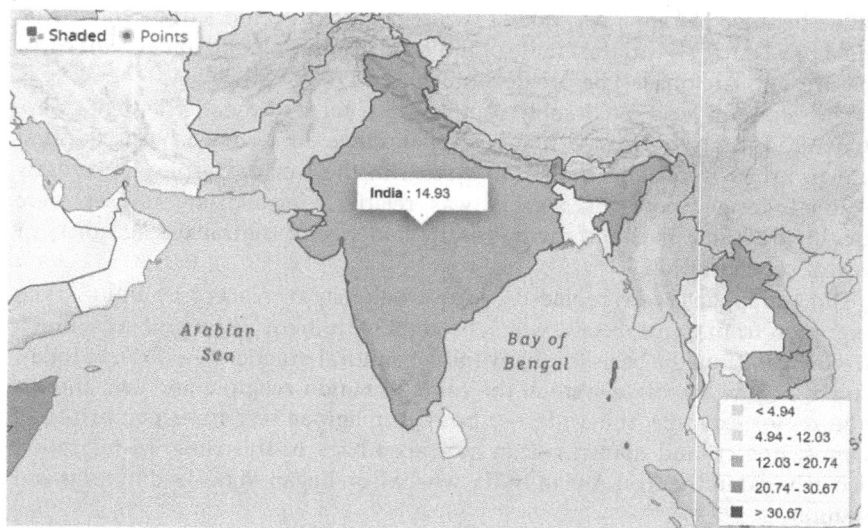

Figure 3.3 Defecation in the open is symptomatic of both a failure of public infrastructure services as well as the incidence of poverty. While the proportion of the population practicing open defecation has steadily fallen since 2011 (where data from the national census were available), the problem remains pervasive.

In reality, statistics of this nature tend to reflect not only low levels of income, but also the systemic underprovision of public infrastructure and services (which in turn helps perpetuate the cycle of poverty). Even so, such realities are more prevalent in the northeastern part of the country—Assam, Bihar, Chhattisgarh, Jharkand, Odisha, and Uttar Pradesh, for instance—and while there has been some improvement in dealing with this public policy failure over time, the issue remains a chronic challenge for subnational governments in those states. It is perhaps no surprise that Mother Teresa—the Albanian-born nun and winner of the Nobel Prize for Peace who ministered to the poor in India—chose to focus her ministry to the poor in Kolkata, located in the country's northeast.

Economic History of India

From Harappan to Republic: Bhārata Born and Reborn

Like China, India is one of the world's oldest continuing civilizations, with archeological evidence pointing to the emergence of an advanced society in the Indus River valley region around 3300 BCE. Harappan civilization—so called because Harappa was one of two major urban centers (the other being Mehenjo-Daro[11])—was the cradle of Indian civilization,[12] and underwent early, mature, and late phases, before declining circa 1700 BCE.

The economy was remarkably sophisticated for its time. Settlements were structured in a grid format, and Harappan cities developed what is the first known urban water and sanitation system in the world. Despite the orderly planned design, however, society was relatively egalitarian; houses were roughly the same size, and there is scant evidence of centralized authority or wealth concentration.

The Harappans were replaced (some would say displaced) by Indo-Aryan migration from Central Asia, which brought with them Vedic practices, much of which became the basis for many Indian cultural practices we observe today. These include the caste system, the roots of Hindu religion, and arts and literature; for example, the Vedas—a body of religious scriptures comprised of hymns, poetry, and mantras—can be traced back to this time. In-migration also ushered in the Iron Age in India, where iron began to be used in tools and weapons.

The early Iron Age was followed by a period known as the *Mahājanapadas* (sometimes translated as "Great Realm"), characterized by a series of oligarchic kingdoms,[13] before a unification of sorts occurred under the Mauryan Empire, in 322 BCE. Although founded by Chandragupta Maurya (from which the dynastic name derives), the Mauryans are probably best known for their greatest emperor, Ashoka. At its height, the empire's boundaries stretched across virtually the entire Subcontinent, with only the southernmost tip of the peninsula remaining nominally independent.

The Mauryans ruled for close to a century and a half, before their decline. Several minor dynasties followed, before culminating in the Gupta Empire. Founded by Sri Gupta in the middle of the 3rd century, the imperium found its zenith between 319–467 CE, a period frequently invoked as the "Golden Age" of India. Like the Mauryans before them, the Guptas oversaw control over most of Bhārat, but, following their loss of control over western India in the middle of the 5th century, began a gradual decline.

The host of successor powers did not much distinguish themselves, nor did they control as much territory. It took an external force—Islam—to regain

---

11 Both Harappa and Mehenjo-Daro are located in modern-day Pakistan; the former in Punjab province, and the latter in Sindh. Both sites likely had populations of between 30,000 to 60,000. Other major urban centers include Ganeriwala, Dholavira (in the south), and Rakhigarhi (in the east). See Coningham, R. and R. Young, *The Archeology of South Asia: From the Indus to Asoka, c. 6500 BCE–200 CE* (Cambridge: Cambridge University Press, 2015), and Dyson, T., *A Population History of India from the First Modern People to the Present Day* (Oxford: Oxford University Press, 2018).
12 Genetic evidence suggests that, despite being located in the north of the country, Harappan civilization was comprised of mainly ancestral south Indians.
13 There were 16 such kingdoms, mostly in northern India. Among the more prominent ones were the Kosala and Magadha in the far north, the Pañcāla further east, and Avanti to the west.

control over the vast Indian expense. Muslim rule was introduced into the Subcontinent with the advent of the Delhi Sultanate, around the turn of the 13th century. Yet while the Sultanate was able to successfully resist the Mongol expansion that was occurring across much of the Eurasian continent at the time, for much of its rule, it controlled only a limited sliver of Indian territory. It took another Central Asian power—the Mughals, founded in 1526 by the Timurid descendant, Babur—to recover the remainder of the Gupta dynasty's holdings, before subsequently extending its supremacy over most of South Asia.

As successful as the Mughal dynasty was, it failed to resist European colonial conquest. The British first exerted their influence indirectly—a period known as the Company Raj (*rāj* being the Hindi word for rule)—in the mid-18th century, before the British government took direct control thereafter. Great Britain regarded India as the "Jewel in the Crown" of the Empire, and it ruled (or misruled) from afar, until independence and partition in the aftermath of World War II.

Incremental Economic Innovations Made India One of the Richest Ancient Powers

The Mauryan unification resulted in significant material and (especially) sociocultural advances, and was the basis for much of the economic strength that was to follow. Political cohesion brought military security, which in turn enabled trade and commerce to flourish. The Great Trunk Road—a major trade and communications route that linked Central Asia to the Subcontinent, and what would become part of the Silk Routes—traces back to this dynasty. Financial developments accompanied centralization, too. A single currency, in the form of punchmarked silver and copper coins, was used to facilitate exchange.

Following the mixed-economy principles of the *Arthashastra*—an ancient treatise on statecraft, analogous to Machiavelli's *The Prince*—public works abounded, funded by a strict-but-fair tax regime. Freed from arbitrary taxation by regional kings, agricultural productivity rose. Prosperity then enabled the development of arts and culture. The *Upanishads*—a late Vedic text that became the basis of not just Hindu religious tradition but also philosophy—dates to this time, and both Buddhism and Jainism emerged contemporaneously.

It was also during this period that the caste system (वर्ण, *varṇa*) became a mainstay of the Indian economy.[14] The four *varṇas*—*brahmins* (scholars or

---

14 The term "caste" does not originate in India, but is an English word deriving from the Spanish and Portuguese *casta* (which translates to "race" or "lineage"). Although the terms were historically distinct, the British classified all *jātis* into a *varṇa* supercategory in 1901. In modern usage, the term caste is sometimes used in India to refer to *jāti*, whereas English speakers tend to use the expressions *varṇa* and caste interchangeably.

priests), *kshatriya* (warriors or rulers), *vaishyas* (merchants and farmers), and *shudras* (artisans and servants)—prescribed the life purpose (or धर्म, *dharma*) of every Indian.[15] This subsequently shaped the sort of professions each individual could aspire to.

Beyond the *varnas*, the practical organization of Indian society revolved around various religiously-inflected informal institutions. The main economic grouping was the *jāti* (जटी, literally "birth"), which often prescribed one's hereditary occupation (but often also implied a geography and tribe) as well as constrained it. But other collectives existed; the *śreṇī* (श्रेणि) were associations of merchants or artisans, much like guilds,[16] while *pani* (पणि) were assemblies that regulated and managed trade.

The Gupta dynasty built on this foundation and became even larger and more sophisticated. Trade links became not just continental but intercontinental, and the economy during the time of the Guptas benefited immensely from Indo-Roman exchanges. India may even have sustained a trading surplus vis-à-vis the Romans, a possibility corroborated by hoards of Roman coins found in the Subcontinent.[17]

By the time the Muslim dynasties came around, the Indian economy was already well established, but growth had become stagnant over the medieval period. These dynasties heralded a period of even greater multiculturalism and cosmopolitanism than before. The Delhi Sultanate integrated the Subcontinent into the expanding global trading system, and encouraged technological transfer with the Islamic world. The spinning wheel, for instance, came to India via Iran.

The period was also one where government became more involved in the operation of the economy, at least compared to the Hindu administrations before it. The state would reserve certain sectors—such as horse trading and slave brokering—for itself, and instituted price and quantity controls on many goods. The willingness to impose controls on economic exchange would become a recurring theme in Indian political economy.

The Sultanate also opened migration to those from the Asian steppe; population doubled as a result. Non-Hindus were able to access positions in government and the military, on the basis of merit; this injection of diversity in human capital also helped reignite growth. But it was the Mughals that took India to the next level.

---

15 There is another unclassified *varna*, the *Dalits* (literally, "broken", although often translated as untouchable), who fall outside of the system (and are hence *avarna*). *Dalits* would perform "impure" work, such as working with leather (debased because of the sacred status of the cow in India), or sanitation work. Dalits are officially referred to as scheduled castes by the government of India, and today receive benefit from affirmative action policies.

16 *Śreṇī* could in turn organize jointly into *nigama* (निगम), similar to chambers of commerce.

17 Suresh, S., *Symbols of Trade: Roman and Pseudo-Roman Objects Found in India* (New Delhi: Manohar, 2004).

Protoindustrialization under the Mughal Empire

The Mughal Empire retained the cosmopolitan orientation of its predecessors. Administrators were recruited from across the Empire, including the fringes where Islam was more prominent. The non-Hindu ruling class stressed efficiency and standardization, and their evenhandedness in the handling of administrative affairs raised economic participation among the peasantry.

This not only boosted production in traditional agriculture, such as barley, rice, and wheat. New food crops—corn, potatoes, and tomatoes, which were brought in via the Columbian exchange—began to be planted (and integrated into daily life; it is hard to imagine Indian cuisine without potatoes or tomatoes today). Other nonfood cash crops—cotton, indigo, tobacco—were also introduced, which improved incomes in the agricultural sector.

The reform of property rights supported this transition. The Mughals adopted a three-tier, incremental framework for land rights: to cultivate, to levy taxes on cultivated land, and to grant the right to collect taxes, which accrued, respectively, to the farmer, the landlord (or *zamindar*), and the king or warlord.[18] Sharecropping arrangements—where landless peasants were promised a share of the crops, in exchange for their efforts at cultivating the land—helped align the incentives of tenants and landlords to maximize crop production.

As a result of these constructive efforts, India took her first, tentative steps toward protoindustrialization. Primary production started to climb up the value chain, from raw food into processed foodstuff, such as sugar, oils, and butter. But output went beyond agriculture, into manufacturing. A wide variety of textiles (cotton yarn, silk, and jute) and clothing were produced, as were forms of metalware and even shipbuilding. At its peak, India accounted for almost all of British—and a little less than half of Dutch—imports from Asia, and boasted a full quarter of global industrial output.[19]

Mughal military technology helped ensure a sort of *pax Mughalica* for over three centuries, at least within South Asia. Even though Europe had begun its global adventurism, which extended into the Indian Ocean, India was able to retain its sovereignty in part due to its control of heavy artillery, including some of the world's largest cannons.

As much as Mughal rule fostered economic advancement among the lower classes, the elite became increasingly disconnected from society, and were often engaged in conspicuous consumption. This is most evident, today, in the architectural achievements of the Mughals; the Taj Mahal, the Red Fort,

18 Roy, T., *Economic History of India, 1857–1947* (Delhi: Oxford University Press, 2011).
19 Clingingsmith, D. and J. Williamson, "Deindustrialization in 18th and 19th Century India: Mughal Decline, Climate Shocks and British Industrial Ascent," *Explorations in Economic History* 45(3) (2008): 209–234.

Figure 3.4 One of the most recognizable symbols of India today, the Taj Mahal, was built during the time of the Mughals, a mausoleum by Shah Jahan for his wife. While such forms of conspicuous consumption eventually doomed the Mughals to fiscal ruin, they remain some of the most enduring vestiges of their reign.
Source: © Yann Forget / Wikimedia Commons / CC-BY-SA 3.0.

and the Shalimar Gardens are just some of the testaments to the excesses of the time. The upshot of what are today considered heritage marvels was the enormous stresses placed on the Mughal treasury. The Taj Mahal was meant to be paired with a companion mausoleum—built in black marble—but this was never constructed, due to lack of financing (Figure 3.4). Such fiscal profligacy ultimately limited the outlook of the Mughal Empire, and an inexorable decline began not long thereafter.[20]

A Retreat from Industrialization under the British Raj

The British gained their foothold in India in 1757. The East India Company (EIC)—the main vehicle for the projection of British commercial and (para) military might around the world—had defeated the Nawab of Bengal (along with his French allies) at Palashi, in India's northeast. This allowed the Company to set up the first of its "Presidencies," private governing entities with the ability to levy taxes, formulate laws, and maintain armies. British rule would eventually expand into another two Presidencies and a Provincial

---

20 Some argue that this was due to the disastrous reign of Shah Jahan's son, Aurangzeb, who pursued greater Islamization of the Mughal state, and as a result undermined some of the stability that had resulted from a more tolerant approach to religion in society.

administration, exercising control over not just India but also British colonies in other parts of Asia.[21]

In line with the British Crown's proclivity for treating India as an extractive colony,[22] economic activity turned toward labor-intensive agriculture and handicrafts. To the extent that modern technology was deployed, it was to support natural resource extraction.

The EIC ruled with an iron hand, and the somewhat predictable result was routine famines (where it was not unusual for casualties to number in the millions) and frequent wars. Abuses by merchant-led town councils—responsible for the management of local affairs across the territories—were frequent, and unequal treatment, coupled with punitive taxation, was rife. Company corruption even found its way into British commercial and public life. These abuses came to a head with the Indian Rebellion of 1857, which almost toppled British control; thereafter, administrative control of the Subcontinent would come directly from the British government. The period of the British Raj would alter the trajectory of Indian economic development (many would argue negatively) in important ways.

After all, economic conditions in India—especially in the affluent financial capital of Bengal Subah—were ripe for takeoff. But the decision to realign production away from domestic textiles and flood the market with imported British cloth undermined any prospects for full-on industrialization. An economy that was exporting fine cotton and world-class silk in the 1750s was relegated to just opium, indigo, and raw cotton a century later.[23]

Despite this dismal record, not everything wrought by the British was negative. Extraction required infrastructure, and in this the colonial masters obliged. Over the course of almost 90 years of rule, the administration built and extended networks of mail, telegraphs, and trains; at the high-water mark of British India, there was more rail track there than anywhere else in Asia.[24]

---

21 The Calcutta (modern Kolkata) Presidency incorporated much of Eastern India—states such as Assam, Bengal, and Bihar—but also holdings further east, including Burma and the Straits Settlements. The Bombay (Mumbai) Presidency incorporated much of Western India—Gujarat, Maharashtra, and Sind (in modern Pakistan)—but also territories further west, such as Aden in Yemen, and some Omani islands. The Madras (Chennai) Presidency oversaw mostly southern states like Andhra Pradesh, Karnataka, Kerala, and Tamil Nadu, but also included states that were further north, such as Odisha. Finally, the Northwest Provinces covered central and northern states like Delhi, Punjab, Madhya Pradesh, and Uttar Pradesh.

22 Broadly speaking, colonial powers deployed two broad models: settlement colonies, such as Australia, South Africa, or the United States, saw the migration of settlers (and especially womenfolk), alongside the transfer of technology and institutions; while extractive colonies, which comprised the overwhelming majority, were designated more for resource extraction and transfer (some would say plunder) to the home country.

23 Tomlinson, B., *The Economy of Modern India: From 1860 to the Twenty-First Century* (Cambridge: Cambridge University Press, 2013).

24 An assessment of both sides of India's colonization experience may be found in Chaudhary, L., B. Gupta, T. Roy, and A. Swamy, *A New Economic History of Colonial India* (Abingdon: Routledge, 2016).

This connectivity of India to the industrialized and industrializing West was further enhanced by the opening of the Suez Canal, which reduced the distance to key European ports by at least thousands of miles. Connections such as these allowed India to participate in the global revolution in communications and transport that was unfolding at the time.

The British also consolidated the meritocratic system of administration that was already present under Islamic rule, and infused it with bureaucratic sophistication and centralized efficiency. As a testimony to its perceived importance, the Indian Civil Service was retained after independence, and is sometimes even credited with holding India together after partition.[25]

The Modern Indian Economy

Economic Independence, a License Raj, and the "Hindu" Rate of Growth

India—along with Pakistan—freed herself from the shackles of colonization in 1947. This occurred not only because of Indian agitation for independence. The political economy within India, as well as international conditions, had made the decline of the British Raj inevitable.[26]

But any hope that being freed from the fetters of colonization would translate into a sudden surge in Indian growth would be dashed over the course of the next three decades. In the post-independence period between 1951 and 1981, India grew at an average of between 3 and 4%. For those of us accustomed to advanced-economy growth rates, this may seem perfectly respectable; but recall, this was a population growing by 3% annually, which means that per capita incomes barely budged at all.

Moreover, India's anemic growth rate was disappointing when contrasted against the much-higher rates that newly-independent Asian nations, like South Korea and Taiwan, were posting (where growth ranged closer to 8% or 9% per annum). It was also disappointing for Indian liberals themselves, who came to call this a "Hindu" rate of growth.

To be fair, growth did not start off that poorly. Following independence, there was a nation-building phase, between 1951 and 1965, where annual growth rates fell on the higher end of that 3–4% range. The leadership at the time was led by Jawaharlal Nehru, an anti-colonial activist who became India's first

---

25 Some have strenuously objected to the notion that British rule ever brought anything positive to the country, and conclude that the effects of colonization had been unambiguously negative. See Tharoor, S., *Inglorious Empire: What the British Did to India* (London: Hurst Publishers, 2017).

26 Tomlinson, B., *The Political Economy of the Raj 1914–1947: The Economics of Decolonization in India* (London: Palgrave Macmillan, 1979).

post-independence prime minister. Scarred by the deindustrialization experience during the time of the British Raj, India's policymakers stressed economic independence. This desire to return to traditional economic strengths was so strong that the jenny (or *charkha*) was even encapsulated in the Indian flag, which features a spinning wheel (Figure 3.5).

The implication of this stress on self-sufficiency was a civil service that went into overdrive. The industrial regime became regimented: heavy industry (the so-called "commanding heights" of energy generation, heavy manufacturing, mining, and transportation) was the domain of the public sector, while regulation of the private sector investment was managed through an extensive system of licenses (which controlled the amounts that could be imported and distributed, or prices that could be charged). The inherent power of the bureaucracy became so great that they became known as the "License Raj." By the late 1960s, India's growth had slowed considerably, and would remain in the doldrums for another decade or so. Choosing the path of import-substituting industrialization, restrictions on production maximums applied to both domestic business houses as well as foreign investors were gradually

Figure 3.5 The spinning wheel (or *charkha*) became a symbol of economic independence for India after the nation was freed from British colonial rule. The country's founding father, Mahatma Gandhi, had used the *charkha* not just as a call for nonviolent struggle, but as a reminder of India's economic strengths in textile production, before the arrival of British imports.
Source: GandhiServe / Wikimedia Commons / Public Domain.

ratcheted up, and a ten-point socialist agenda was introduced by the then-prime minister, Indira Gandhi.[27]

Much like the case of China, while the initial stages of central planning did elevate investment, the complexity of resource allocation and coordination difficulties in a complex economy ultimately doomed such heavily interventionist economic policies. The License Raj was ineffectual when it came to adapting to external shocks that buffeted the Indian economy, which the period coughed up in abundance: drought in 1965–67, wars in 1965 and 1971, and oil price shocks, in 1973 and 1979.

It took an assassination—in this case, of Indira Gandhi by her Sikh bodyguards, in retaliation for a brutal suppression of an insurgency in Punjab state—before the nation reluctantly went on the road toward liberalization.

These nascent steps would commence under the oversight of Indira Gandhi's son. Rajiv Gandhi assumed the role of prime minister in 1984, after his mother's passing.[28] He immediately went about dismantling some of the controls that had been shackling the Indian economy. This "stealth" liberalization—which gradually unfolded over the subsequent half-decade—gradually returned economic decision-making power to the private sector.[29] But a full-blown economic crisis to sufficiently concentrate reformist mind it took, and reposition the country for an entirely new development strategy.

Accelerated Liberalization Revitalizes Indian Economic Potential

The economic crisis of 1991 was a watershed for the status quo model of the Indian economy. The crisis itself was a so-called twin crisis, involving both the public and private sectors. In the former, fiscal deficits had ballooned, owing to government borrowing for finance infrastructure and industrialization. In the latter, the Gulf War triggered an oil price spike and a resulting downturn in the West, which then led to a severe deterioration in the trade balance for an energy importer/goods exporter such as India. The hitherto overvalued currency began a precipitous drop, and at its nadir, the nation's foreign exchange reserves had whittled down so badly that it could barely muster 2–3 weeks of import cover. With precious few options available, the government made the momentous decision to formally embrace liberalization, deregulating markets, slashing import tariffs, and cutting taxes.

---

27 Arguably, this was the result of political insecurity. India was in the midst of several wars with Pakistan, and the latter had garnered U.S. support, which led India into the arms of the Soviet Union.

28 Rajiv Gandhi would himself later fall victim to an assassination as well, when he fell to a suicide bomber from the Tamil Tigers, a Sri Lankan militant group, in 1991.

29 This was by stealth not only because Gandhi's government faced stiff opposition to liberalization proposals, but also because such economic reforms were entirely absent from the party's election manifesto.

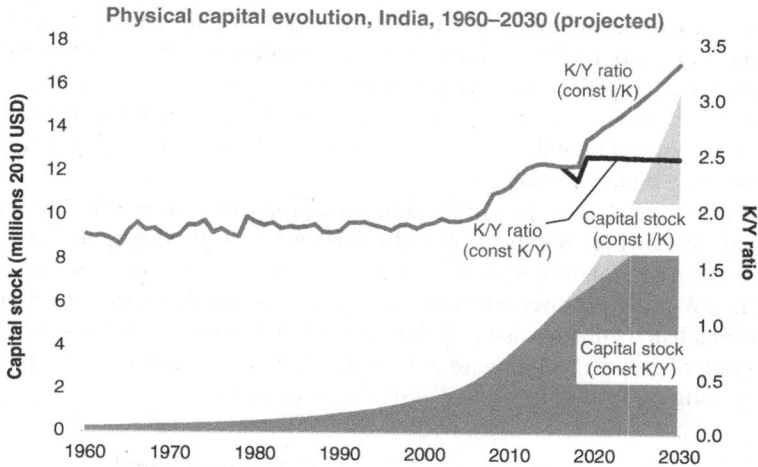

Figure 3.6 The steady accumulation of physical capital began relatively recently in India. After the economic crisis of 1991, India began opening its economy to financial globalization, but it was only in the 2000s—with the passage of various foreign investment laws—that the Subcontinent began its belated integration into world capital markets, and FDI policy only began to be liberalized, starting from 2005.

Once the storm was past, the Indian economy began to reap the benefits of this agenda. Investment (as a share of GDP) picked up steadily, from the low-to-mid 20s to 30% or more by the end of the decade. The process got another shot in the arm in the mid-2000s, with the passage of a number of laws and policies promoting foreign direct investment (Figure 3.6).[30] As a result, India enjoyed a spell of Chinese-level investment rates, peaking on the eve of the global crisis in 2007/08.

Investment rates have returned to earth, in no small part because Indian firms have lagged in terms of how much retained earnings are directed toward corporate investment. Well-known inefficiencies in the domestic financial sector have also exacerbated capital scarcity, as have occasional eruptions of hostility toward foreign investors via backpedaling in foreign investor protection laws. Still, investment rates are undoubtedly higher today than in the pre-liberalization years.

This heightened capital intensity has been complemented by an abundant, youthful population in their prime working years,[31] and one that is expected to

---

30 The first of these was the Foreign Exchange Management Act, which aimed to facilitate external trade and payments, in 1999. Additional legislation, including those related to anti-money laundering and majority (and eventually 100%) foreign ownership, were gradually rolled out, sector by sector, starting with the retail sector. See Lakatos, C. and T. Fukui, "The Liberalization of Retail Services in India," *World Development* 59 (2014): 327–340.

31 The age profile of India's population—which contributes to high household saving—has helped to partially offset the dismal saving rate of corporations, and dissaving by government.

continue expanding strongly, at least till the middle of the century. In addition to a still-rising labor force, the fact that its population exhibits a low rate of educational attainment—averaging around 8 years—means that there is still substantial room for building up human capital. Doing so will be critical, since the window of opportunity to harness the nation's workforce for productive purposes may be quite small.

Total factor productivity in India languished for a long time after independence, but—following liberalization and reform efforts—picked up in the 2000s, and has been on a gentle upward trend over the past two decades. As it was for China, reaping productivity gains after extreme misallocation of resources due to socialism is unsurprising. India's success in truly breaking free from the Hindu rate of growth will depend in no small part on its ability to fully harvest the low-hanging fruit of improved allocative efficiency.

Realizing the Demographic Dividend Through Human Capital Development

The key challenge facing India as it strives to exploit the dividend issuing from population growth is the fact that service delivery—including in the crucial areas of education and health—remains plagued with inefficiency, incompetence, and inequality. Until the quality of human development substantially improves across the country, the contribution from human capital to growth will always fall short of its true potential.

The efficiency of public education and healthcare in India is low, in turn, because of governance failures. These include additional side payments (both informal payments to facilitate access, as well as involuntary payments that result from poor service quality, such as the need for additional tutoring or out-of-pocket supplemental medical fees); human resource shortcomings (such as absenteeism—unauthorized absences during official schooling or facility operating hours—or time lost due to off-task activities, or inadequate degrees of effort); budgetary shenanigans (diversions of healthcare or educational funds due to upstream capture or downstream leakages, or the reporting ghost workers to seize larger-than-appropriate budgets); and perceptions of corruption that alter consumer behavior outright.

Absenteeism, in particular, is pervasive across Indian states, and especially in the northeast, where incomes are also lower and the incidence of poverty is greater.[32] And even when the absenteeism issue is addressed, other governance problems tend to bubble up. Effort is far from assured; teachers may

32 Chaudhury, N., J. Hammer, M. Kremer, K. Muralidharan, and F.H. Rogers, "Missing in Action: Teacher and Health Worker Absence in Developing Countries," *Journal of Economic Perspectives* 20(1) (2006): 91–116.

snooze on the job or be preoccupied with nonessential off-job functions. Well-meaning healthcare workers may be unable to provide the necessary care in overcrowded facilities that are not stocked with the necessary medications, or have medicines that have already expired.

Beyond inefficiency, service delivery is also compromised by incompetence. One should not paint this with too broad a brush, but many human development providers remain unqualified (or inadequately qualified) for their job. One in six elementary school teachers are not professionally trained,[33] and in rural areas, the quality gap may be even higher. More Indians die from poor quality healthcare—almost 122 per 100,000—than just about anywhere else in the world, including its South Asian neighbors such as Bangladesh (57), Nepal (93), Pakistan (119), and Sri Lanka (51).[34]

Finally, inequity of access is a perennial problem in any lower-income country with high levels of inequality. Schools and hospitals are often located far—more than 5 kilometers in distance—from residences and workplaces,[35] which is a major issue in a country where the rural population is quite large, and public transport connectivity remains limited. Privatization of basic services—which are meant to make up for service quality shortcomings—is in turn detrimental to equality.[36] This plethora of failures in human development has given rise to poor outcomes in education and health (Figure 3.7), even when headline quantitative metrics—such as school enrollment or public health facilities—may appear, on the surface, to be sound. For example, the level of reading and writing in English—admittedly a second language for many Indian students—remains woefully low, with students often performing several notches below their official grade levels. Similarly, since the presence of public health facilities per se does not guarantee that students and patients receive care (given how teachers and doctors are often absent), parallel private schools and clinics that actually *do* offer such services have been forced to emerge. More generally, the private sector in India appears to operate more as a *substitute for* the public sector, whereas in many countries, they tend to be a *complement*.

Governance failures of this sort can quickly become a self-fulfilling prophecy; when a teacher or doctor is absent or exerts insufficient effort on the job, students and patients do not receive the education or healthcare they require, which then puts them off from seeking schooling or treatment, and that in

---

33 Kundu, P., "To Improve Quality of School Education, India Must Spend More on Training Teachers," *IndiaSpend*, January 30, 2019.

34 Kruk, M., A. Gage, N. Joseph, G. Danaei, S. García-Saisó, and J. Salomon, "Mortality Due to Low-Quality Health Systems in the Universal Health Coverage Era: A Systematic Analysis of Amenable Deaths in 137 Countries," *Lancet* 392(10160) (2018): 2203–2212.

35 Kasthuri, A., "Challenges to Healthcare in India—The Five A's," *Indian Journal of Community Medicine* 43(3) (2018): 141–143.

36 Mahendru, A., A. Sekher, M. Dutta, P. Mishra, and V.S. Raman, *Inequality Kills: India Supplement 2022* (New Delhi: Oxfam India, 2022).

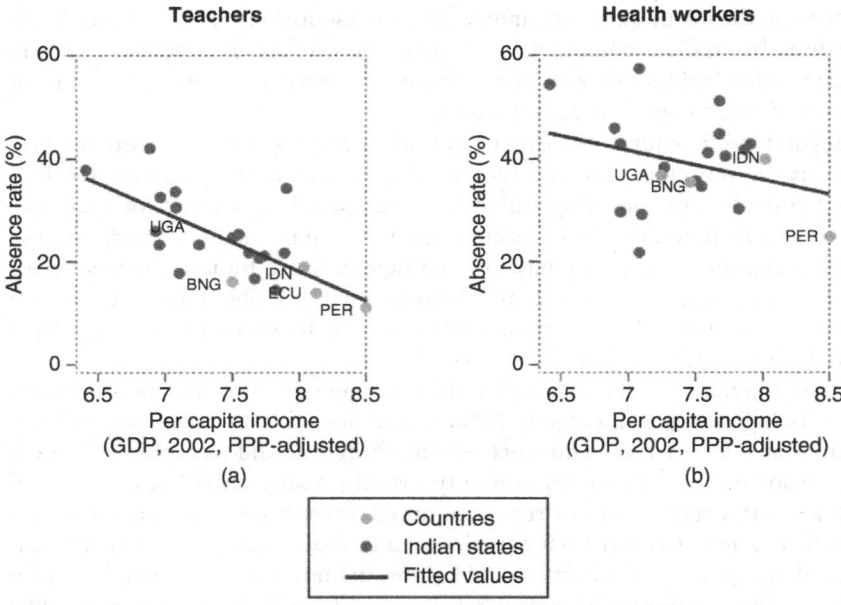

Figure 3.7 There is a strong and negative correlation between absenteeism in human development services, such as (a) education or (b) healthcare, and per capita incomes. While this relationship alone does not imply that governance failures cause underdevelopment, it is likely that a negative feedback loop exists.

turn leads to poor educational attainment or ill health that keeps them mired in poverty. The underdevelopment that results also works in the other direction: with low incomes, there is insufficient demand for quality education and health, which fosters continued underprovision.

To be clear, not all human capital development in India is shortchanged. The country has a network of institutes of national importance—of which possibly the most famous of these are the Indian Institutes of Technology—most of which provide high-quality education at the tertiary level. While most of these have yet to rise to the prominence commonly accorded to famous universities in the West, a number of these can justifiably be viewed as world-class. But, in general, higher education remains tightly regulated, which crimps the ability of these schools to charge sustainable fees, offer internationally competitive salaries, and operate autonomously.

Industrial Concentration in Large Business Houses

India's corporate landscape is dominated by large business houses. The three most enduring and successful ones are the Tata Group, the Birla Group, and

Reliance Industries (which is also frequently referred to as the Ambani Group). Unlike their counterparts in northeast Asia, however, such LBHs—while typically very diversified (in some cases, possibly over diversified, with holdings in largely unconnected sectors), as well as accounting for a sizable chunk of the economy—have mostly failed to distinguish themselves outside of India.

This could be the legacy of India's long flirtation with import substitution, as well as the presence of a very large (and still mostly captive) domestic market. Many LBHs were formed not long after independence, and have been able to consolidate their positions over time.

To be fair, the LBHs are relatively efficient. Returns on assets for such incumbents have consistently outstripped those of publicly-owned firms, often by a significant amount.[37] But therein lies the rub: while they are profitable *within* India, they may be less successful abroad. Foreign firms have generally turned in higher returns, an indication that these conglomerates may not be internationally competitive.[38]

What is possibly worse is how the profitability of new entrants may well have been weakened by the LBHs. With the presence of strong incumbents, these upstarts have generally been unable to garner decent profitability (Figure 3.8). This has potentially contributed to India's famous "missing middle" of a distinct lack of mid-sized firms in the manufacturing sector.[39]

The direct or indirect protection conferred by governments seldom helps. This is especially the case with state-owned enterprises. For example, Coal India—which has been profitable—may only be so because it had a monopoly on coal mining till 2021.[40] Jio Payments—a relatively new entrant established in 2015—was offered a strong foothold into the country's banking landscape, via a joint venture with the State Bank of India (the country's largest public-sector bank).[41] Others that have not been granted state-sanctioned monopolies nevertheless receive special preferences. As a result, many Indian businesses operate in a neutered competitive climate.

---

37 Alfaro, L. and A. Chari, "India Transformed? Insights from the Firm Level 1988–2005," *India Policy Forum* 6 (2009): 153–224.

38 Not all foreign competitors—even ones that are established elsewhere—have been able to successfully penetrate the Indian market, of course. American retailer Walmart famously failed in India, despite having a local LBH partner (Bharti Enterprises), and Coca-Cola and McDonald's have both struggled.

39 Krueger, A., "The Missing Middle," in Hope, N., A. Kochar, R. Noll, and T. Srinivasan (Eds.), *Economic Reform in India: Challenges, Prospects, and Lessons* (New York: Cambridge University Press, 2013), pp. 299–318.

40 Nayyar, D., "How India Can Sell Hundreds of Government-Owned Businesses," *Washington Post*, December 20, 2022.

41 Kant, R., "The Rise of the Monopolists in Modi's India," *Asia Times*, October 12, 2020.

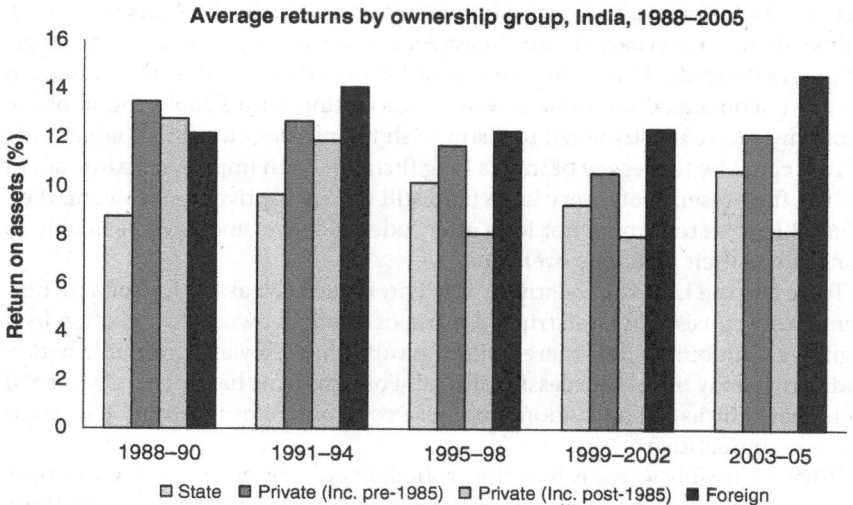

Figure 3.8 Although the return on assets for private sector incumbent firms (those incorporated prior to 1985) are clearly superior to that of the publicly-owned firms (and even new entrants in the private sector, those formed post-1985), they remain less competitive than foreign firms.

Policy Errors by the Modi Administration in Its Hunt for Growth

As India rapidly overtakes other advanced economies to ascend to the global perch of being the third-largest economy worldwide (and the second-largest emerging-economy giant), how smooth this journey will turn out to be will depend on keeping policy errors to a minimum. The recent record under the Modi administration, however, has not been encouraging.

The first major policy error was a demonetization effort in the winter of 2016. In an (ostensible) effort to curtail counterfeiting and tax evasion,[42] the government announced the overnight cessation of legal tender for ₹500 and ₹1,000 notes, which were to be replaced by new ₹500 and ₹2,000 bills. Existing holders of these denominations had 50 days to exchange their holdings, with a limit on the amounts that could be swapped daily.

The policy sparked long queues outside banks and ATMs, and led to a virtual standstill in many activities in the heavily cash-reliant economy. After all, the ₹500 note amounted to about $14—a fairly low value—at the time, and both denominations accounted for 86% of all cash in circulation. Yet by the time the exchange window closed, 99% of demonetized bills had been redeposited or

---

42 There was also speculation that the move was meant to cut off legitimate and illegitimate election-related spending for state-level polls in Punjab and Uttar Pradesh, with the latter being India's most populous.

converted, which raises questions about just how successful the entire exercise of stamping out so-called "black money" had been. Moreover, the policy appeared to accelerate the decline of an already slumping growth rate; estimates place the loss at around 2 percentage points of GDP.[43]

The episode did have a positive side. Usage of India's digital payments interface jumped upward immediately as the policy came into force, and steadily trended up thereafter. To the extent that the policy helped shift India toward the digital economy (even if inadvertently), that turned out to be an important benefit from an otherwise ill-informed policy.

The second policy mistake surrounded the federal-level goods and services tax (GST), which occurred in the summer of the following year. There had been much hope pinned on the unification and simplification of the tax regime, which had been widely viewed as an impediment to business and interstate commerce. But political horse-trading ended up yielding a fairly complicated variable-rate system, with states retaining taxation rights over certain goods,[44] as well as a smaller reduction in average rates than originally envisaged.

This botched effort to reform GST meant that the impediments to commerce resulting from the complex tax regime remained largely unresolved. Operational difficulties—such as substantial delays in refunds and an excessive documentation burden—compounded the problem.[45] Indian GDP took another dip.

The third error involved the initial handling of the COVID-19 response. The Modi government announced a nationwide lockdown in March 2020, with a curfew imposed on all except those providing essential services. Society ground to a halt, and—bereft of organized public transportation and without advanced warning—migrant workers began walking back to their home villages, in a scene some described as the greatest mass exodus since partition.

Indian growth—which had already been grinding lower since 2018—completely collapsed in the middle of the year, and GDP shed close to a third of its size, the worst drop ever in recorded history.[46] While economic performance did ultimately recover, the rebound was protracted, and output only returned to pre-pandemic levels two years after the shock.

---

43 Lahiri, A., "The Great Indian Demonetization," *Journal of Economic Perspectives* 34(1) (2020): 55–74.
44 There are five tiers—at 0%, 5%, 12%, 18%, and 28%—with key essential items, such as petroleum, electricity, and alcohol remaining under the tax jurisdiction of individual states.
45 To be fair, in spite of the underwhelming GST rollout, the regime has improved transparency and, perhaps more importantly, tax revenues have steadily risen since, to around 12% of GDP—the highest since 1974.
46 The disproportionate response to this first wave—which ultimately turned out to be much less detrimental to the country—is also worth contrasting to the more sanguine response of the government to the country's second wave, for which India was ground zero for the (much more transmissible) Delta variant.

Taken together, the administration's handling of these three major public policies dashed hopes that the government would be able to easily replicate the economic success of Gujarat state—which Modi oversaw as the chief minister for more than a dozen years prior to assuming the position of prime minister—for the rest of the country. At the very least, it dispelled any notions of Modi's invulnerability as an infallible architect of India's economic prosperity.

Indian Development in Comparative Perspective

India's Growth in the Rearview Mirror

By the time of the Gupta dynasty, India had already surpassed China to become the largest economy in the world, three times larger than the Roman Empire. Bhārat remained powerful and prosperous through much of the second millennium. Yet like China, the Industrial Revolution never visited its shores during the height of Indian economic prowess.

And like China, India had many of the preconditions necessary for industrialization, perhaps more. Protoindustrialization had begun, and wages in Bengal and South India were typically higher in the key textiles sector than they were in Britain.[47] Yet India failed to capitalize on this lead, perhaps due to an absence of any extrinsic pressure to compete in global markets.

Undeniably, once it relinquished this lead, there was little chance of quickly turning back the clock. Colonization had hollowed out Indian manufacturing, and made it impossible for growth to take off via the model adopted by other late industrializers like Australia, Canada, Germany, and the Netherlands.

But India was late to the party even by Asian standards. India and China did not begin their industrialization process in earnest until the 1980s, well after the NIEs were well into theirs. But even there, the two Asian giants eventually diverged (Table 3.1). This occurred despite liberalization policies being first proposed around the same time; China adopted "Socialism with Chinese Characteristics" in 1979, and India first documented its transition away from socialism in its Sixth Five-Year Plan of 1981. The acceleration of reforms likewise began concurrently: Deng's Southern Tour and the accession of Rajiv Gandhi to prime ministership both happened in 1992.

But it is clear, three decades hence, that while India has made solid progress in its development story, it has nevertheless underperformed expectations. On the upside, poverty reduction has been by impressive global standards, and India's—as well as China's—progress on this front is the overwhelming reason why *global* poverty rates have fallen as much as they have over the past four decades.

---

47 Parthasarathi, P., *Why Europe Grew Rich and Asia Did Not: Global Economic Divergence, 1600–1850* (New York: Cambridge University Press, 2011).

Table 3.1 Key development indicators for China and India after liberalization

	China	India
Saving/ Investment	High household/corporate saving with major FDI inflows	High household offset by corporate/government deficits
Poverty	Dramatic poverty reduction	Solid poverty reduction
Public goods	World-class infrastructure with good access to education/health	Backdated infrastructure with low-quality public services
Export model	Low value-added manufacturing	Skill/capital-intensive services
Policy approach	Top-down planning with bottom-up execution	Top-down policy poorly aligned with local incentives
Political economy	Autocratic (authoritarianism and corruption)	Democratic (populism and special interests)

Source: Author's compilation.

Indian households are also good savers. Indeed, household saving has often outstripped that of even their Chinese counterparts, and their thrift has kept national saving rates higher than the global average. If anything, it is the comparatively low rates of corporate saving—coupled with chronic deficits by the government—that has been a constraint on greater domestic funding of investment opportunities.

Another dimension where India has fallen far behind China is in infrastructure construction. This is most evident in railways, where India—due to its colonial legacy—once boasted a network that was three-and-a-half times more extensive. But by the turn of the century, China was spending three times as much as a share of its GDP on transportation priorities, and this has resulted in developments such as its high-speed *gaotie* (高铁) system, which stands in sharp contrast to the backward and decrepit Indian railway system. This is the case for other infrastructure projects, too. China's expenditure on power and telecommunications are both greater than that of India.[48] The one infrastructure element where India has made a concerted effort to improve—for good reason, if you have ever attempted to drive interstate in the country—has been in its highway network; the Subcontinent now has 150,000 kilometers of highway, compared to China's 130,000 km.

Where India differs most distinctly from China has been its choice to persist with a democratic regime—imperfect as it may be in practice—instead of eschewing it in favor of a more autocratic approach. This is anomalous not only compared to other developing countries; it is even different when contrasted against the development experience of the advanced economies of today,

---

48 Panagariya, A., *India: The Emerging Giant* (Oxford: Oxford University Press, 2008).

where the expansion of the franchise occurred alongside rising incomes.[49] While some would argue that there is still a fair amount of vote buying—as well as a tendency to "vote caste" rather than cast votes—democratic norms remain largely entrenched for a developing country.

Premature Deindustrialization

Most developing countries—in particular, those in East Asia—had relied on a tried-and-tested development strategy for accelerated growth: rapid factor accumulation, especially in physical and human capital, which enabled fast output expansion. Financing this effort was a combination of high domestic saving due to a youthful population, possibly supplemented by external saving from international financial inflows. These factors were directed toward complementing the large, comparatively low-wage labor force, which was channeled toward manufacturing goods that would be sold in global markets. In doing so, these nations were able to extricate themselves from their predominantly agricultural economies.

The approach had been repeated time and time again: first with Japan in its postwar growth miracle, followed by the Asian Dragons of Hong Kong, Singapore, South Korea, and Taiwan, before being emulated—to varying degrees of success—by the Southeast Asian Tiger Cubs, such as Indonesia, Malaysia, and Thailand, along with China. While the idiosyncrasies associated with each development story were slightly different, the lynchpin of gradually shifting a low-skilled, rural population into higher-skilled, urban manufacturing was always there.

This is where India bucks the trend. In 1985—at the dawn of its liberalization process—agriculture was about two-fifths of GDP (and close to two-thirds of employment), with industry accounting for about a quarter (and only a tenth of employment), and services the rest. But three decades later, while agriculture did shrink, the slack was taken up not by industry, but by services; the tertiary sector has grown to capture half of the economy (and a third of workers) (Figure 3.9). In contrast, the share of manufacturing has shrunk, and continues to fall: in 2011, it was 16%, dropping to 14% in 2021. India essentially skipped over the industrialization phase.

This is the case not just for the economy at large, but also for the largest non-financial firms.[50] While only accounting for a third of employment, services capture two-thirds of the wage share among formally-registered enterprises (by value-added, the imbalance is not as severe, albeit services still account for a larger share than industry) (Table 3.2). Information and communications

49 Lamba, R. and A. Subramanian, "Dynamism with Incommensurate Development: The Distinctive Indian Model," *Journal of Economic Perspectives* 34(1) (2020): 3–30.
50 Finance and banking are, of course, a service, and hence including data for such firms would further skew in wage and value-added balance in favor of the services sector.

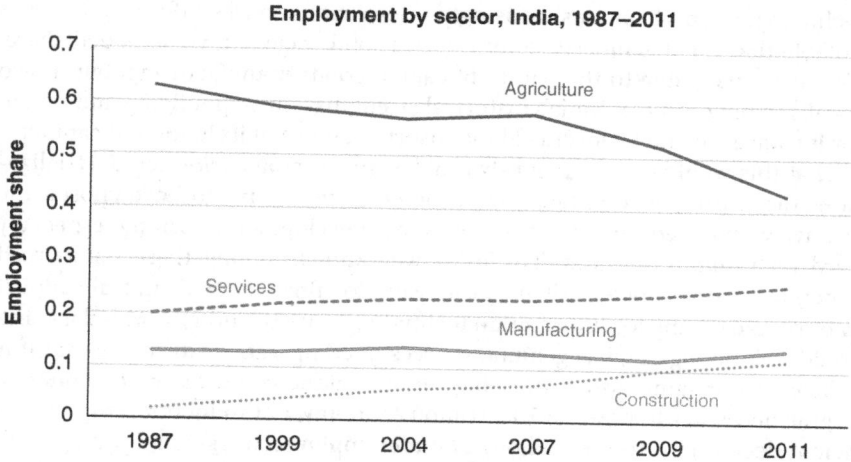

Figure 3.9 In the 1980s, agriculture dominated the economy, with two-fifths of output and two-thirds of employment. As the economy evolved over the subsequent three decades, agriculture shrank—to a fifth of output (and half of employment)—but the slack was taken up not by industry (which has remained mostly stagnant at a quarter of output and a tenth of employment), but by services, which has grown to half the economy and a third of workers.

Table 3.2 Wage and value-added shares among registered Indian corporations

Sector	Wage share (%)	Value-added share (%)
Industry	35	47
Construction	5	5
Consumer goods	8	9
Machinery	17	27
Raw materials	4	4
Other manufacturing	2	2
Services	65	53
Electricity	6	6
ICT	33	25
Real estate	1	1
Transportation	9	10
Other services	15	20

Source: Author's compilation, from Shah (2022) and CIME database.
Notes: Based on 26,040 nonfinancial firms for 2018–2019. Construction comprises construction materials and industrial/infrastructure construction; consumer goods comprise food, consumer goods, and textiles; electricity comprise electricity generation, transmission, and distribution; ICT comprises information technology and communications services; raw materials comprise chemicals, metals, and mining; real estate comprises hotels, tourism, and real estate; transportation comprises transport equipment and services.

technologies—perhaps unsurprisingly—dominate services offerings, but it is notable that the machinery sector seizes a solid wage and value-added share. This is partially due to the nature of capital goods manufacturing, but it also speaks to how some of India's historical strengths—in shipbuilding and repair, for instance—could be leveraged for absorbing more of its labor and capital.

That this would occur obviously rankles, since India's *prior* deindustrialization was entirely involuntary. Here, the economy seems to have chosen the relatively untested model of services-led development, leaning especially hard on *tradable* services. The most well-known among these outsourced functions—back-office auxiliary processing for finance, or technical support and routine coding for information technology—are (by now) world-class, and could well be regarded as genuine sources of comparative advantage. But it is difficult to imagine how exportable services alone could drive an economic engine necessary to power a $3.2 trillion economy, not to mention supply sufficient decent jobs to the millions of underemployed workers migrating from the Indian countryside. Regardless, the services trade is here to stay, not least because India now ranks seventh worldwide in exports of services (and only behind China among emerging economies).[51]

India therefore finds herself in the throes of premature deindustrialization: the secondary sector has retreated, well before the country has grown rich. This isn't to say that there is no hope for India to forge its own distinct growth model forward; after all, some research suggests that the development of services exports could stimulate other parts of the economy, including the export of goods.[52] Even so, it is valuable to recognize that the Subcontinent is wading into untested economic waters.

Relative Success with Poverty, But Less So with Inequality

When thinking about poverty, inequality, and growth, one is inevitably led to ask if this should (or shouldn't) be a preoccupation of economists and policymakers. One influential school of thought believes that India (like China) should simply focus on growth, and that this single-mindedness—if achieved—will do all the job of poverty reduction that is necessary.[53] But another school of thought challenges this notion, and argues instead that poverty reduction should be the *sine qua non* for evaluating India's development success.[54]

51 In 2022, services exports were valued at $323 billion (around 42% of total exports, and about 10% of GDP). This is slightly behind that of China ($338 billion), but far greater than the next emerging economy on the list, South Korea ($130 billion).

52 Loungani, P., S. Mishra, C. Papageorgiou, and K. Wang, "World Trade in Services: Evidence from a New Dataset," IMF Working Paper 2017/077 (Washington, DC: International Monetary Fund, 2017).

53 Dollar, D. and A. Kraay, "Growth is Good for the Poor," *Journal of Economic Growth* 7(3) (2002): 195–225.

54 Drèze, J. and A. Sen, *An Uncertain Glory: India and Its Contradictions* (Princeton, NJ: Princeton University Press, 2013).

After all, in spite of India's absolute success in raising incomes, progress in social metrics have diverged from that of other South Asian neighbors, and not in a good way. Although Bangladesh overtook India in per capita income terms only in 2019, key metrics of health—such as the under-5 mortality rate or stunting prevalence—and education—such as primary school enrollment or literacy rate—have been higher in the former for a prolonged period. Similarly, Nepal—a country with incomes around half that of India—has effectively caught up in terms of progress on a number of such social indicators.

Similarly, there is a well-established argument—known as the Kuznets hypothesis—that an inverted U-shaped relationship exists between inequality and development: inequality must first rise as a country gets richer, before eventually falling.[55] One should therefore simply accept rising inequality as collateral for what will eventually yield a payoff in terms of higher per capita incomes.

India's progress in poverty reduction—by almost any benchmark—has been remarkable. The share of India's population in extreme poverty—defined as those with incomes below the international poverty line of $2.15 per day—has fallen from close to 60% in 1981 to around 10% by 2019. Should it continue along this trend, India will be on track to eliminate poverty in another decade or two.[56] Just as important, India's (and China's) success are attributable more to domestic policy choices, rather than global factors.[57]

The Subcontinent's experience with income inequality has been far more circumspect. The Gini coefficient—a common measure of the distribution of income, where 0 represents maximum equality and 1 the opposite—has risen sharply since the 1990s.[58] Perhaps more worrisome is the enormous inequality of wealth in the country. The country's top 10% hold 77% of wealth, and the richest 1% own more than 40%. And this gap is growing wider, not narrower. In 2017, 73% of new wealth generated went to the top 1%, while the poorest half of the population received only a mere 1% increase. Just as damning, pandemic-related policy inaction resulted in inequality increasing as a result of the crisis—in stark contrast to many advanced economies, where government support provided a respite to rising inequality. Post-2020, incomes of households in the richest quintile increased by close to two-fifths, even as those in the lowest quintile halved (Figure 3.10).

---

55 Kuznets' explanation for rising inequality was not unlike that of Lewis' two-sector model; he believed that inequality would rise as rural labor migrated to urban areas, which would keep wages suppressed while capital benefited. But he added the twist that once a welfare state took hold in advanced industrialized economies, social mobility would increase again, and cause inequality to decline. See Kuznets, S., "Economic Growth and Income Inequality," *American Economic Review* 45(1) (1995): 1–28.

56 China did so in four decades, declaring victory in 2021. So while India is undoubtedly behind, its pace of poverty reduction remains astonishing.

57 Bardhan, P., *Awakening Giants, Feet of Clay: Assessing the Economic Rise of China and India* (Princeton, NJ: Princeton University Press, 2012).

58 In 1993, this was 0.32—having fallen from 0.33 in 1977—but it has since risen to 0.36 as of 2019.

Incomes have diverged sharply during the pandemic

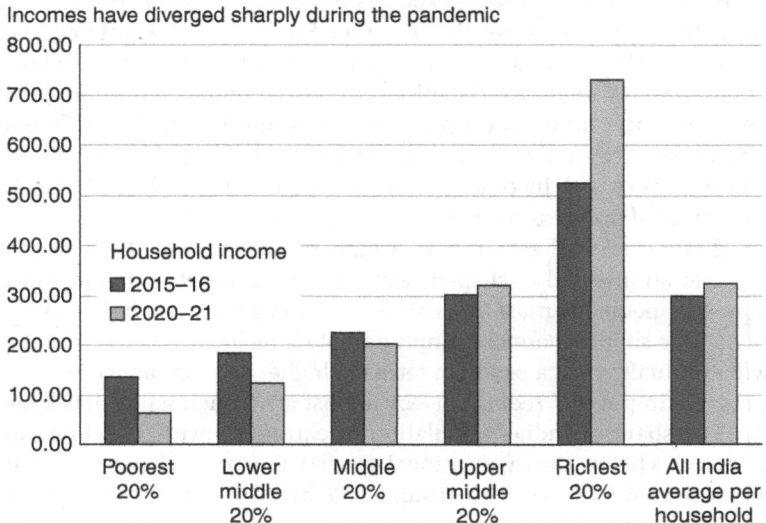

Figure 3.10 The incomes of the upper two quintiles rose during the COVID-19 pandemic, while that of the lower three fell, with that for the highest (lowest) quintiles rising (falling) by around two-fifths (half). This increase in inequality has otherwise been hidden by how average incomes rose slightly for all households.

India and the World Economy

Twin Deficits and Crises

The Indian government is frequently (one could go as far as to say virtually always) in deficit. To some degree, this is not necessarily detrimental; if government expenditures are directed toward growth-enhancing investment—especially in infrastructure—as well as human capital-improving services—such as education and health—then such spending can expand the economy and support development. The key question, of course, is whether the spending is productively deployed.

However, even a reliance on deficit financing has its limits—and the fact that India's expenditures have consistently exceeded revenue for the better part of a century and a half—raises the question of why government saving is so poor in the country. There are political economy reasons, such as the cost of subsidies for the rural and urban poor, along with the tendency to engage in patronage politics. But there are also more prosaic reasons, such as the inefficiency associated with a bloated bureaucracy.

Regardless of the reasons, the reality is that consistent fiscal deficits mean than public debt has built up over time, to a high (but still reasonable) 60% of

GDP. What is perhaps more disconcerting is that this public dissaving is also often accompanied by an excess of corporate investment over private saving.

Again, there is no issue, per se, with a country running a balance of payments deficit. Such imbalances are expected every now and then, and are the result of normal fluctuations in global demand conditions and investment opportunities, terms of trade, or exchange rates. There are even self-correcting mechanisms; a strong exchange rate will tend to reduce external demand for a country's exports, thereby helping restore equilibrium to the trade balance. And with generally higher returns available in emerging economies (such as India), a current account deficit is the natural consequence of accepting greater financial inflows.

Still, India's trade imbalances remain worrisome. This is especially the case vis-à-vis China, where total bilateral imports and exports is close to nine times in favor of China. Such chronic deficits in the balance of payments can eventually become problematic, giving rise to a loss of confidence in the ongoing viability of the economy, which could in turn trigger the sale of a nation's currency, which at worse would morph into a full-blown currency or financial crisis.

Fiscal and current account balances are tied together by the inexorable logic of the balance of payments identity, which requires that the current account always be equal to national saving—comprised of private saving and the fiscal balance—net of investment.[59] When both of these are in deficit—as India was in 1991—the onset of an economic crisis is almost inevitable (Figure 3.11).

India has come a long way since 1991, but given public dissaving, the economy has been reliant on foreign saving and household saving to finance its domestic investments. When either of these are challenged—perhaps due to a recession that prompts both foreign capital to withdraw, as well as households to draw down on saving to smooth consumption—investment would tend to be negatively impacted.

Indian Hesitancy in Further International Trade Integration

At the very tail end of the 15th century, the Portuguese explorer Vasco da Gama arrived at Kazhikode, a port on the Malabar coast in Kerala state. His entry opened the doors to trading links from India to Europe; the Dutch and English soon followed. By the 17th century, other nations had joined in the contest for the Indian Ocean trade, which subsequently extended to Southeast Asia.

Despite this long history of external relations with equal (or even more powerful) partners, India withdrew from this international trading order in the 20th century. It was only after the crisis of 1991—or the mid-1980s, if you count the stealth liberalization steps under Rajiv Gandhi—when the country began to reexamine its position, and even so, it has retained a certain hesitancy

---

59 More formally, the current account balance, CA, is equal to the sum of saving by the private (S) and public ($T - G$, which is the difference between tax revenue and government expenditure, or equivalently, the fiscal balance) sectors, net of investment (I). More formally, $CA = (T - G) + (S - I)$.

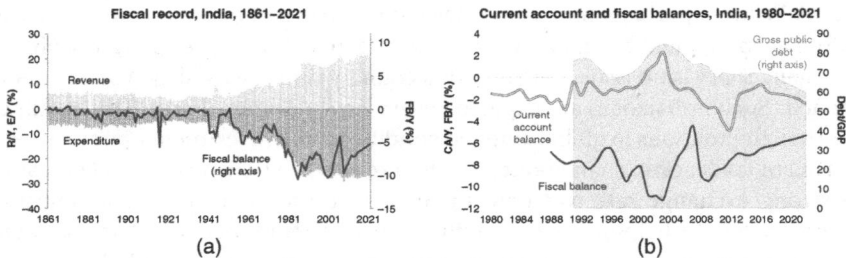

Figure 3.11 (a) India has run a chronic fiscal deficit for close to a century and a half, and this deficit has only become more marked after independence. (b) The country has also frequently run current account deficits in modern times. All this means that India's investment activity tends to be sharply curtailed whenever there are recessionary conditions, as both foreign capital and domestic households withdraw.

to international trade. This skepticism has remained, even as trade openness has increased dramatically over the past few decades, rising from a dismal 13% of GDP in 1985, to a peak of 56% in 2012 (before paring back to 45% as of 2021). One could go as far as to argue that expanded integration has occurred *in spite of*, rather than because of, the overall intransigence of the country, as it has demonstrated in World Trade Organization (WTO) negotiations, or, for that matter, other multilateral integration venues.

In July 2008, the Doha Round of the WTO was scuppered by a coalition of developing countries, led by China and India, over the types of measures these countries could adopt to support their poor farmers.[60] While it was true that offering such selective protection would have been a step backward—perhaps rolling back progress on liberalization by decades—it is simultaneously true that the sort of safeguards demanded by these countries against dumping of agricultural commodities would strike most as reasonable, given the large number of rural poor who may have been displaced from their already-near-subsistence living as a result of cheap produce imports. After all, countries like India could have reasonably expected that the round—which had been marketed as the Doha Development Agenda—should have been weighted more favorably toward their concerns.

---

60 To be clear, agricultural protectionism is rampant in both advanced and developing economies. The difference is that in the former, subsidies tend to go to large agricultural interests, which in turn encourages production of commodities that, sans subsidies, would not only be more expensive than that of their developing-country counterparts, but often even higher than global market-clearing prices. In the latter, subsidies tend to go to a large number of poor and otherwise not-formally-employed rural subsistence farmers. The desire of the former for market access to the latter's markets, and the fear held by the latter that this would lead to dumping of agricultural produce, are the crux of such disputes.

Efforts to revive the round in 2013 likewise ran into roadblocks due to Indian objections surrounding agricultural subsidies, and it led a number of other (mainly Latin American and African) developing countries[61] to push for additional concessions. Terms for the so-called trade facilitation agreement—which focused on the seemingly uncontentious program of streamlining global customs procedures—eventually acquiesced to public stockholding of commodities for food security purposes, but the mechanism was meant to be temporary in nature, and disputes remain about how to move forward.

The WTO has not been the only forum where India has demonstrated its discomfort with unfettered participation. In 2021, despite 8 years of negotiations, India chose to exit the Regional Comprehensive Economic Partnership (RCEP), a mega-regional trade agreement that would have brought together the 10 ASEAN nations with 6 of its major trading partners, all of which the group already had existing bilaterals.[62] Despite the hope that India would serve as a counterbalance to China, concerns that the Subcontinent was running trade deficits vis-à-vis as many as 11 of the RCEP members proved to be too much to overcome, along with the usual objection from agricultural interests.

Given the country's challenges with rural poverty, it is unsurprising that India has been less than enthusiastic in exposing its still-large primary sector to the vicissitudes of global factory farming. Still, one is left with a nagging suspicion that its reluctance has as much to do with historical vestiges of economic self-reliance, and the persistent effects of import substitution.

Yet this attitude of suspicion toward trade liberalization—as embodied in India's tendency to maintain higher average tariffs rates than its immediate neighbors (average tariff rates in 2020 were around 6.2%, and rates have hovered around 6% since 2008)—as well as its plodding pace in further entrenching Indian firms into global value chains, can be a hindrance to India's growth potential, as the economy gets excluded from lucrative regional value chains.

The Indian Outsourcing Juggernaut Gains a Second Wind

India is truly a trailblazer in the exportable services trade. As a service process outsourcer, the three giants—Infosys, Tata Consultancy Services, and Wipro—grew by 40% annually during the boom years in the second half of the 2000s.

---

61 The coalition of countries pressing for flexibility in developing countries to undertake limited market opening in agriculture is known as the G-33, which (despite the name) comprises 47 WTO member nations.
62 In addition to the 10 ASEAN nations, the six are China, Japan, and South Korea (sometimes known as ASEAN+3), along with Australia, New Zealand, and India.

Together with Cognizant and Tech Mahindra, two other major players, these firms drew revenues in excess of $60 billion in 2021, and—further bolstered by increased digitalization due to the COVID-19 pandemic—are expected to exceed $80 billion in revenues by 2023.[63]

The success of these firms—and, more generally, the grand experiment that is services-led industrialization—will hang on the country's ability to ensure that it excels in more and more of the sorts of services that are both marketable (that is, amenable to market pricing) as well as tradable (can be delivered across borders). After all, despite the overall tendency for services to lag manufacturing in terms of productivity growth, certain market services may exhibit comparable—or even greater—levels of productivity (Figure 3.12).

In doing so, it is necessary to shift the mindset beyond merely outsourcing—the notion of providing services, such as call centers or back-office processing, to another country by dint of lower costs—but to expand the offerings to include unique and in-demand market services. Tourism is the quintessential example, but certain functions within finance, logistics, design, and business operations also come to mind; building up a capability in these areas would offer India a comparative and competitive advantage in services that would otherwise be unobtainable elsewhere.

Such services-led growth is likely to result in a further exacerbation of India's already-adverse distributional outcomes.[64] Tradable services tend to require well-trained and highly-skilled workers, who in turn would already be earning higher incomes, not least by expanding the market available for their lucrative skills. Such expansion would exacerbate the overall trend—evident in emerging economies worldwide—of long-run technological change that favors skills and human capital.[65]

---

63 *The Economist*, "A Half-a-Trillion-Dollar Bet on Revolutionising White-Collar Work," April 2, 2022.

64 Fan, T., M. Peters, and F. Zilibotti, "Growing Like India: The Unequal Effects of Service-Led Growth," NBER Working Paper 28551 (Cambridge, MA: National Bureau of Economic Research, 2021).

65 The Stolper-Samuelson theorem—applied not to capital and labor as factors, but skilled and unskilled workers instead—predicts that trade liberalization will increase the relative price of goods that do not use skills intensively, which in turn will induce a more than proportional increase in wages for relatively abundant unskilled workers (and a decrease in skilled worker wages), at least in the developing country. The fact that this is not observed in India—or most developing countries—is an indictment of the simple Heckscher-Ohlin model, and one important reason why most economists favor skill-biased technological change as an explanation for rising wage inequality.

Sectoral Labor Productivity Growth, 2000–2010

(Difference with respect to economy-wide labor productivity growth, percentage points)

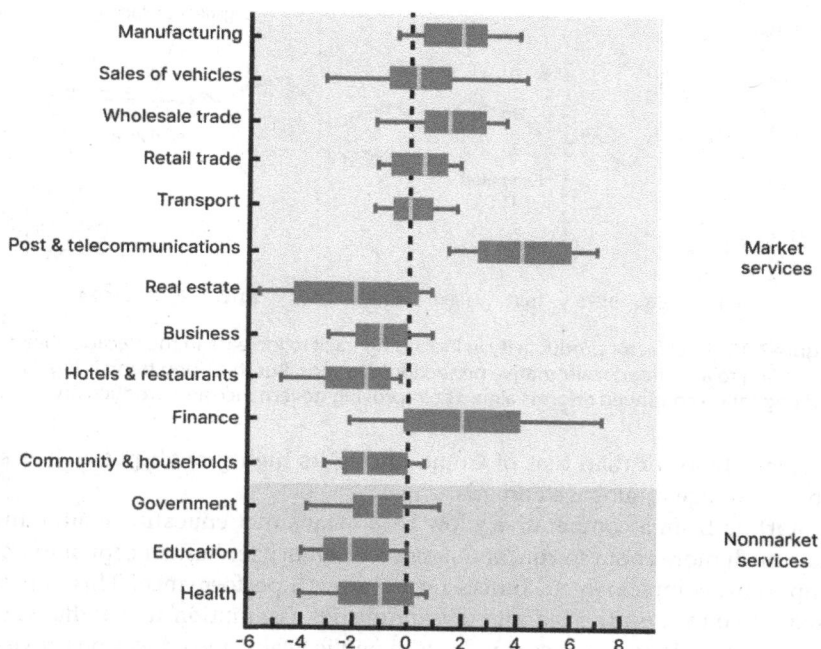

Figure 3.12 In contrast to the overall tendency of services to lag manufacturing in terms of growth in labor productivity, services that can be sold in markets may demonstrate comparable degrees of productivity.

Conclusion

The Future Success of Indian Growth Will Be Contingent on Continued Governance Reforms to Boost Productivity

On the basis of potential output alone, India looks likely to be among the fastest-growing major economies for many years ahead. This will likely come from a mixture of both physical and human capital expansion, but perhaps somewhat more from an increased contribution from TFP growth.

While investment rates are no longer as impressive as they were in the 2000s, the country's greater openness to international financial flows has allowed foreign saving to make up for a slowdown in domestic saving rates. This has enabled the economy to steadily increase the capital intensity of output, and while the overall rate of investment—standing at around 30% of GDP—remains

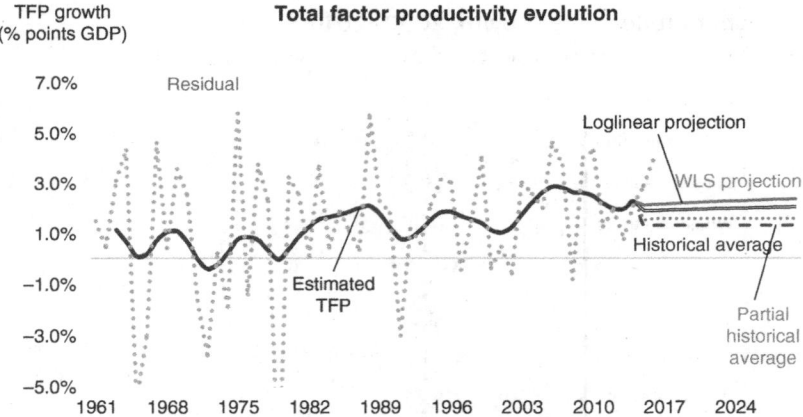

Figure 3.13 Total factor productivity in India is on track to increase in the decade ahead, according to a number of alternative projection methods. But this rising trend is highly contingent on continued reforms aimed at improving governance and productivity.

undeniably lower than that of China during its high-growth phase, it is still above-average by global standards.

Starting from a comparatively low base means that educational attainment has much more room to run, and hence we can expect human capital to be an important complement to India's future growth performance. This is premised, of course, on the (admittedly optimistic) assumption that India will be able to improve governance standards in public health and education provision (Figure 3.13). It will also require an improvement in female labor force participation in the workforce; currently, participation is a dismal 26%. This is unusually low not only compared to middle-income economies—where rates are around twice that—but also lower than China (at around 65%), and even India in its relatively recent past (it was as high as 38% at the turn of the millennium).

The major opportunity (as well as challenge) for the economy will, however, rest on not just sustaining but successfully raising productivity. Estimates have suggested that correcting existing resource misallocations could trigger TFP gains of as much as 40–60% in the manufacturing sector, an even larger gain than China, where estimates range from 30–50%.[66] Correcting such misallocations requires not only attention to removing restrictions on domestic economic relationships, but also liberalization of India's trade and financial links to the rest of the world.[67]

---

66 Hsieh, C.-T. and P. Klenow, "Misallocation and Manufacturing TFP in China and India," *Quarterly Journal of Economics* 124(4) (2009): 1403–1448.
67 Bau, N. and A. Matray, "Misallocation and Capital Market Integration: Evidence From India," *Econometrica* 91(1) (2023): 67–106.

There is also some belated recognition of the need to further leverage manufacturing. The Modi Administration launched a "Make in India" campaign in 2014, with a stated goal of boosting manufacturing's contribution to a quarter of GDP. But the decade hence has seen comparatively slow progress, with the share rising only by around 2 percentage points through till 2020. More support—in the form of production incentives and subsidies—was announced post-pandemic, as part of the government's *Aatmanirbhar Bhārat* (literally, "Self-Reliant India") package. But rather than economic isolation, successfully plugging into global value chains—especially in sectors like agriculture and food processing, chemicals, and electronics and semiconductors—appears to hold the most potential gain for increasing the nation's gross value-added from manufacturing.[68]

Recent policy has also pushed for the development of industrial corridors to support such efforts. These linkages will connect not just the principal cities, but also two lesser-known ones: Amritsar (in the northwestern state of Punjab, to Delhi and Kolkata), and Vizag (in Andhra Pradesh, to Chennai). Infrastructure projects to relieve transport costs along these corridors have also been planned, alongside a reduction of the corporate tax burden.[69]

Over the most recent decade, India has managed to partially fulfill some of this promise. Forecasts made in 2015, on the basis of India's economic complexity, predicted an annual growth rate averaging 7% through 2024.[70] While actual growth through 2022 has underperformed this somewhat—the average has been closer to 5%—this has still been very sound performance for a large economy, especially given the incidence of COVID-19. A future growth rate in the mid-5s to low-6s may thus be a more realistic projection. This would be premised on a TFP contribution of between 2% and 3%, which is attainable, albeit still higher than what has been consistently achieved in India since independence.

Still, having already overtaken the United Kingdom (the world's fifth-largest) in 2022, India will almost surely become the world's third-largest economy sometime in the 2030s (bypassing Germany and Japan). And population-wise, India already overtook China in 2023. But this combination of a still-expanding population alongside a growing economy means that per capita incomes will advance a great deal slower than if population growth were more contained. Hence, even after it takes on the mantle of the third-largest economy, it will likely do so as a developing nation.

---

68 Sankhe, S., A. Madgavkar, G. Kumra, J. Woetzel, S. Smit and K. Chockalingam, *India's Turning Point: An Economic Agenda to Spur Growth and Jobs* (Mumbai: McKinsey Global Institute, 2020).
69 EIU, *India's Manufacturing Moment* (London: Economist Intelligence Unit, 2023).
70 Center for International Development, "New Global Growth Projections Predict the Decade of India," Press release (Cambridge, MA: Harvard Kennedy School, 2015).

Policy Errors as a Symptom of Political Risk

India's recent policy stumbles—on demonetization, GST rollout, and the COVID-19 response—are a stark reminder of the risks inherent in strongman rule. As much as Modi has brought the Indian economy forward during his time at the helm, his bold strategic bets have also carried a greater possibility that mistakes become outsized, and thus not easily corrected.

It hardly helps that a number of recent policy moves—the revocation of special status for Jammu and Kashmir (which is territory under dispute with Pakistan), as well as requiring refugees to declare a religious affiliation in order to qualify for citizenship—have focused more on sociocultural control, which have stoked ethnic and sectarian tensions. More generally, the Hindu nationalist mindset of Modi's Bharatiya Janata Party[71] does not lend confidence to the administration's ability to manage an ethnically and religiously heterogeneous nation.

---

71 These date back at least to the time when, as Gujarat's chief minister, Modi appeared to approve of anti-Muslim riots—which led to thousands of deaths—on his watch.

4

Rest of South Asia: Finding Relevance in the Shadow of India

Extremism can flourish only in an environment where basic governmental social responsibility for the welfare of the people is neglected. Political dictatorship and social hopelessness create the desperation that fuels religious extremism.
>   —*Benazir Bhutto (1953–2007), Former Pakistan Prime Minister*

Gross National Happiness is more important than Gross Domestic Product.
>   —*Jigme Singye Wangchuck (1955–), former King of Bhutan*

The Sinhala state has, as never before, placed its trust on its military strength. It is living in a dreamland of military victory. It is a dream from which it will awake. That is certain.
>   —*Vellupillai Prabhakaran (1954–2009), founder and leader of Sri Lankan LTTE revolutionary party*

Introduction

Unlike India—their neighboring giant—the rest of the South Asian economies do not immediately conjure up images of economic prowess. If anything, they may be more typically associated with economic dysfunction and disruption due to civil conflict and terrorist activity (think Afghanistan, Pakistan, or Sri Lanka), or simply languishing as economic backwaters, reliant on the largesse of governments willing to extend foreign aid and tourists with a taste for the exotic (for Bhutan, the Maldives, or Nepal).

Such caricatures are exaggerations, no doubt, albeit clothed in some veneer of truth: the economies that comprise South Asia other than India are indeed relatively small when it comes to their global footprint. But by the same token,

Asian Economies: History, Institutions, and Structures, First Edition. Jamus Jerome Lim.
© 2024 John Wiley & Sons Ltd. Published 2024 by John Wiley & Sons Ltd.

they are often faced with developing-country challenges that, in turn, keep them small.

As former constituents of the regional giant India, Bangladesh and Pakistan entail sizable populations—of around 170 and 235 million, respectively—which have made their economies increasingly relevant. The former has grown rapidly over the past decade, making it a minor economic success story; it now boasts a higher per capita income than India. The latter has, likewise, embarked on the road toward (at least) semi-industrialization, although its progress has been somewhat less impressive. Both currently sit around the second quintile in the league table of global GDP—close to middle-income comparators like Egypt and the Philippines—but understandably have hopes of rising even further.

Such dreams of achieving economic prominence differ quite a bit for the other South Asian nations. They carry significantly smaller populations and exhibit less economic diversity; hence, the economic challenges they face are also different. Afghanistan and Sri Lanka fought long civil wars, which predictably frustrated their development efforts, and Bangladesh was born out of a war of independence with Pakistan. All are on tentative paths toward recovery, but social peace remains fragile, and there is a need to confront the difficult questions of reconciliation and reparations. The Nepalese have had to contend with extensive corruption among their ranks, while the Bhutanese have struggled with low levels of economic freedom, even as they transitioned away from the country's historical monarchy. Such political-economy challenges often inhibit sustained reform, keeping many of the region's citizens—already among the lowest-income earners in the world—mired in poverty.

In this chapter, we provide an overview of the economies of the region, but in a manner that (hopefully) divorces the discussion as much as possible away from the juggernaut that is India. While not always possible—shared history, culture, and even common economic shocks can make such differentiations artificial—we nevertheless wish to understand the rest of the region on its own terms.

Economic Geography of South Asia

The Rest of South Asia's Geography Is Extremely Diverse

The physical landscape of the rest of the other South Asian nations is as diverse as it is breathtaking. These span settlements at the "roof of the world"—the mist-shrouded buildings of Thimphu or the snow-capped mountains that frame Kathmandu—to low-lying areas by the sea, like the turquoise waters surrounding the picture-postcard beaches of the Maldives, the ancient windswept shores of Sri Lanka's southern coast, or the blighted floodplains of Bangladesh.

The nations which are crisscrossed by parts of the Himalayan mountain ranges—Afghanistan, Bhutan, Nepal (together with northeastern India)—may be regarded as "Highland" South Asia, while countries nestled closer to sea level—Bangladesh, the Maldives, Pakistan, and Sri Lanka—are more "Lowland."[1] This distinction oversimplifies, but is useful, because it allows us to recognize some of the key macroeconomic challenges each nation faces when it comes to sustaining long-run growth: Highland South Asia is constrained by being landlocked, and has to contend with limited arable space, whereas Lowland South Asia has to manage rural population explosions living at sea-level areas that will be severely impacted by climate change (and, as the increasingly frequent floods in Bangladesh remind us, this is already occurring).

The ranges have themselves shaped the surrounding landscape. The seasonal monsoon rains—which typically last from June through September—are the result of precipitation created when moist air from the Indian Ocean meets the Himalayas. This lowland plains of Bangladesh, Pakistan, and coastal Sri Lanka therefore experience some of the wettest conditions on Earth, of around 30 feet of rain annually, which is ideal for intensive wetland rice farming. In contrast, the highlands of the Himalayan and Karakoram belts, along with central Sri Lanka, are more conducive to the mixed cultivation of cereals, legumes, fruit, and vegetables, coupled with livestock.[2]

The Anomalous Distribution of Human Development

There is one important but underappreciated aspect of South Asian economic geography: the unusual distribution of human capital. For significant parts of the Himalayan Belt, the degree of human development is remarkably high—at levels comparable to the Southern Indian states—despite the fact that adjacent lowlands (whether in Bangladesh or India) regularly report among the lowest levels on the subcontinent (Figure 4.1). This is the case for Bhutan and Nepal, but also for certain Indian states (such as Arunachal Pradesh, Himachal Pradesh, and Mizoram), and disputed Indian-Pakistani territories (Gilgit-Baltistan, Ladakh,[3] and Jammu and Kashmir). Finally, although not part of the mountainous belt, Sri Lanka—which has highlands of its own—can also lay claim to comparatively higher levels of human development.

---

1 Pakistan sits at the intersection of three famous mountain ranges—the Himalayas, Hindu Kush, and Karakoram—but most of the population reside in the fertile plains of Punjab and Sindh provinces. Similarly, the northeastern part of Bangladesh (Sylhet and southeast Chittagong) has among the lowest population density in the country.
2 Dixon, J., A. Gulliver, and D. Gibbon, *Farming Systems and Poverty: Improving Farmers' Livelihoods in a Changing World* (Washington, DC: Food and Agriculture Organization and the World Bank, 2001).
3 Ladakh is also subject to competing territorial claims with China.

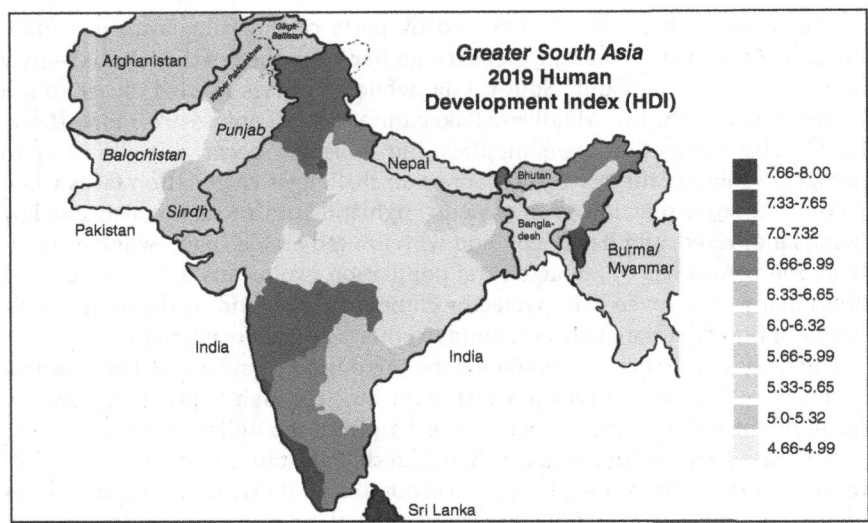

Figure 4.1 Unlike the surrounding regions of lowland South Asia, the regions in the highland Himalayan belt exhibit anomalously higher levels of human development, perhaps a testament to their missionary history and higher levels of infrastructure investment.

One possible explanation stems from the historical presence of Christian missionaries—who had stressed education in their outreach—as well as a greater attention to infrastructure development projects in these mountainous regions (by both India and Pakistan).

Economic History of South Asia

South Asian Nations Functioned in the Shadow of the Indian Economy

Much like how states in China's near abroad often saw their history overshadowed and influenced by developments in China, the other states in South Asia often saw their economic histories unfold in the shadow—or, at the least, the penumbra—of India.

For most of their past, Bangladesh and Pakistan—and significant parts of Afghanistan[4]—were directly woven into various Indian Empires (even if there

---

4 From the Middle Ages through the middle of the 18th century, the eastern regions— appropriately termed *Al-Hind*, were recognized as part of India. See Wink, A., *Al-Hind: The Making of the Indo-Islamic World*, Vol. 1 (Leiden: Brill Academic, 1996).

may have been some variations in their respective experiences).[5] As such, they do not offer much by way of distinct economic history.

But the others also saw their histories inextricably interwoven with the regional giant. Nepal was a tributary state of India for several periods, and Sri Lanka had to endure a number of invasions from southern Indian kingdoms. British India also waged wars against Afghanistan, Bhutan, and Nepal, which generally led to the cessation of some territory (usually with reparations)— although it should be noted that these nations were never fully conquered nor colonized.

Yet even for countries that remained steadfastly independent, many shared elements of culture, linguistics, and religion with India. In some cases—such as in Sri Lanka, where a significant minority of Tamils reside—they would have also lived alongside Indian ethnicities within their borders.

We therefore leave the discussion of the extensive economic history of South Asia, prior to the early 19th century, to Chapter 3 on India. Instead, we focus on the period thereafter, which is marked by the multifaceted influence that the British wrought after their arrival in the region, along with the implications of their rule and departure.

British Influence on the Rest of South Asia

The height of Great Britain's colonization of South Asia saw possessions that included not only the modern states that were part of the historical Indian Empire (India, along with Bangladesh and Pakistan), but also the Maldives and Sri Lanka. Afghanistan, Bhutan, and Nepal had also acquiesced to becoming protectorates, with foreign policy controlled by the Crown. This process began in the second half of the 18th century—with the expulsion of the Dutch from Ceylon and the Maldives by the British East India Company—and by 1880, essentially the entirety of South Asia had come under British influence, in whole or in part.[6]

The implications of this extended period of overlordship range from the more mundane (driving on the left side of the road, or an acquired taste for cricket) to the more economically consequential (deindustrialization, the

---

5 For example, during the reign of Darius I (522–486 BCE), the western Indus Basin (modern Afghanistan and Pakistan) fell under the Achaemenid Empire, while the Kushan Empire also extended into the middle Gangetic Plain (modern Pakistan and India) around 1 CE.

6 Afghanistan fell under British influence with the Treaty of Gandamak, signed in 1879. Similar treaties, often following wars, were signed by Bhutan (1865, Treaty of Sinchula), Sri Lanka (1815, Kandyan Convention), and territories that are today the nations of Bangladesh (1757, after the Battle of Plassy), India (1794, Battle of Buxar), and Pakistan (1839, with the capture of Karachi). Within British India, the so-called Princely States retained internal autonomy, but the British held suzerainty. Following the Indian Rebellion of 1857, most of these South Asian holdings formally came under the direct control of the British Crown and Parliament.

adoption of many aspects of the common law system,[7] and/or the formation of a professionalized civil service conferred with substantial power[8]). The effects of deindustrialization—discussed in Chapter 3 on India—were also present in the rest of South Asia; by the time of the British departure, the region mostly functioned as an agrarian economy (albeit one which included cash crops, ranging from cotton in northwest India and Pakistan, to opium poppies in eastern India and Bangladesh).

Colonial influence also affected the development of human capital, at both low and high ends of the distribution, and not always in a positive fashion. English-language public schools—many of them supported by Christian missionaries,[9] even as they ostensibly remained secular—steadily displaced the indigenous *gurukuls* or *madrasah*.[10] As a result, both traditional forms of schooling went into steep decline during the colonial era. Yet even as education became imbued with a "civilizing mission,"[11] primary education retreated in reality—falling to fewer than 3 schools for every 10 villages—accompanied by an increase in illiteracy.[12]

Science was deemphasized, in favor of arts and the humanities, depriving Indian graduates of the opportunity to channel their education toward professions that would contribute to productivity-enhancing innovation.[13] To the extent that science was taught, it was always done so with an eye toward the

---

7 In the region, only Afghanistan has not been influenced by English common law. Bangladesh, the Maldives, and Pakistan weave aspects of Islamic *Shariah* into the common law framework, Sri Lanka includes some Roman-Dutch civil laws in its common law backbone, while Bhutan and Nepal have Indian and religious influences in their common law systems. Certain states and territories in India (Goa, Daman, and Diu, and Dadra and Nagar Haveli) rely on a civil law system devised from Portuguese principles, but almost all of the country operates under English common law.

8 The East India Company first introduced the system of modern career public service to the subcontinent, but even after independence, many states in the region retained the essential characteristics of the civil service structure that had evolved from colonial times. See SAARC HRDC, *Comparative Study of Service Commissions in SAARC Nations: Bangladesh, Nepal, Sri Lanka, Afghanistan and Maldives* (South Asian Association for Regional Cooperation Human Resource Development Centre, 2014).

9 Bellenoit, H., *Missionary Education and Empire in Late Colonial India, 1860–1920* (Abingdon: Routledge, 2007).

10 *Gurukulam* (गुरुकुल) are publicly-supported (via donations) schools led by a teacher (*guru*), usually at his home (*kula*), delivering Hindu or Vedic education. *Madrasa* (مدرسة) are schools, often (but not always) focused on religious education in the Muslim tradition. Both these traditional forms were common in South Asia prior to the arrival of the British.

11 Watt, C. and M. Mann, *Civilizing Missions in Colonial and Postcolonial South Asia: From Improvement to Development* (London: Anthem Press, 2011).

12 Chaudhary, L., "Determinants of Primary Schooling in British India," *Journal of Economic History* 69(1) (2009): 269–302.

13 Kumar, D., "Science in Higher Education: A Study in Victorian India," *Indian Journal of History of Science* 19(3) (1984): 253–260.

commercial returns to colonial activities, in areas such as plantation agriculture or geology.[14] The pernicious effects of colonial rule likely even permeated the mindsets of indigenous elite leaders: of the four provincial governors first appointed after Pakistani independence, three were Britons.

Independence and Partition

The nations of South Asia freed themselves from the shackles of colonization after World War II. Indian independence occurred simultaneously with the separation of Pakistan. The latter initially comprised two exclaves—carved from the northwest and northeastern parts of British India—but eastern Pakistan subsequently declared its own independence, as Bangladesh. The remaining South Asian economies—most of which had hitherto been protectorates—also eventually regained their suzerainty, becoming independent states over the course of the subsequent two decades.[15]

For the new (one would hesitate to call them artificial) states—Bangladesh and Pakistan[16]—partition was a seismic event, and it ripped their economies asunder (Figure 4.2). Pakistan was bereft of industry, with more than half the economy (and two-thirds of its labor force) toiling in small-scale agriculture; Bangladesh, meanwhile, was entirely dependent on imports for raw materials. And with India preoccupied with its own internal economic challenges and turning inward due to socialism, even the former protectorates were not spared from the loss of trading relationships.

The breakup was further complicated by sociopolitical fractures. The provinces of Punjab and Bengal comprised nearly equal Hindu and Muslim populations, which resulted in the states being split, thereby compelling millions to relocate. The noncontiguous nature of eastern Pakistan also made nation-building difficult, and ultimately resulted in its declaration of independence. Still today, the region of Jammu and Kashmir (among others) remains a disputed territory between India and Pakistan.

Independence also brought difficult governance choices to the fore for the South Asian economies. The sort of strategic and developmental choices that Southeast Asian polities had to make in the aftermath of colonial

---

14 Kumaar, D., *Science and the Raj, 1857–1905* (Delhi: Oxford University Press, 1995).

15 This occurred between 1947 and 1971. Indian and Pakistan independence was gained in 1947. Sri Lanka gained independence in 1948, and the Maldives in 1965. East Pakistan declared its independence, as Bangladesh, in 1971. The other South Asian nations were not formally colonized, but Britain relinquished control of Afghanistan's foreign affairs in 1921, and Nepal in 1923. Bhutan's protectorate status was formally abandoned in 1949.

16 The name Pakistan, itself, is an acronym taken from the letters that comprised the letters from the provinces: *P*anjab, *A*fghania, *K*ashmir, *S*indh, and Baluchi*stan*, although notably (and perhaps foreshadowing the problems to come), this did not include the exclave of East Pakistan (composed of east Bengal).

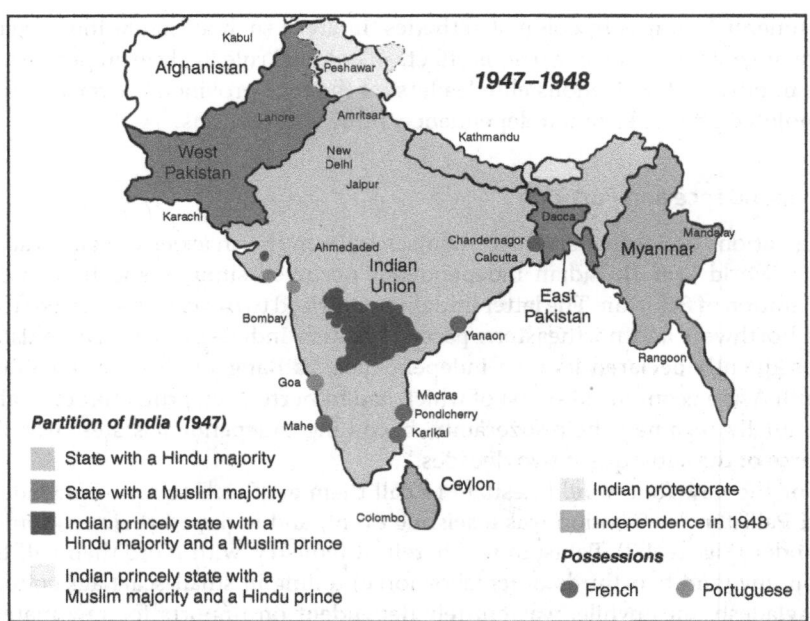

Figure 4.2 The partition of British India ripped an integrated economy asunder, with most of the newly-independent South Asian states left with a heavily agricultural economy. The breakup was further complicated by sociopolitical fractures; several states had comparable Hindu and Muslim populations, while the center of India contained a princely state ruled by a Muslim but comprising a Hindu majority.

departure—import substitution or export orientation, socialism or capitalism, authoritarianism or democracy—also confronted policymakers in the region.

South Asian Development in Comparative Perspective

The Burden of Civil Conflict for South Asian Development

Virtually the whole of South Asia has been wracked by civil conflict of some form or other. Afghanistan is the most prominent example, having been in a virtually incessant state of internal and external conflict since 1978.[17] Sri Lanka endured intermittent insurgencies—led by the so-called Tamil Tigers against the Sinhalese-dominated government—between 1983 and 2009, as did Nepal,

---

17 This started with the Soviet-Afghan War between 1979 and 1989, followed by the Afghan Civil War between 1989 and 2001, before the American-led War on Terror in 2001 through 2021.

which had to deal with a Maoist insurgency for a decade after 1996. Pakistan fought wars against India in 1947, 1965, 1971, and 1999, and ongoing border tensions between the two nations persist in the restive Kashmir region.[18]

Even the nations that have not had to manage repeated outbreaks of violence have had to contend with periodic civil unrest. After Bangladesh's War of Independence in 1971, the government faced coup attempts in 1975 and 1982. Pakistan has likewise confronted coups, but also political assassinations, such as the 2007 killing of twice-Prime Minister Benazir Bhutto. The Maldives experienced three attempted coups in the 1980s, along with protests and civil disobedience between 2011 and 2013.

Civil and interstate conflicts, as well as protests and unrest, are (for obvious reasons) immensely disruptive to economic growth,[19] leading to stagnant incomes and frustrating development efforts. But what is often forgotten is that fragile low-income economies and those suffering from slow growth are also more likely to descend into conflict.[20] The costs also show up in expended resources; in Pakistan, for instance, the economic toll of the War on Terror, between 2002 and 2018, is estimated at $127 billion (or two-fifths of GDP).[21]

Of course, not all such disruptions are uniformly detrimental to development. Pakistan's most impressive period of economic growth in the 1980s coincided with the military takeover by Zia ul-Haq. While rapid growth during that episode was sustained more by robust remittance inflows than enlightened policymaking, the administration at the time did shift away from socialism toward deregulation and privatization,[22] demonstrating that even for (some) coups, there could be a silver lining.

Still, the pervasiveness of such instability across South Asia has been one of the major factors that has held the region back from escaping the poverty trap. The proof is in the pudding: once freed from the ravages of civil conflict, many of these economies have subsequently taken off.

---

18 India, on its part, also faces periodic militancy in the Seven Sister States, and till today, even Indians require a permit to visit these states.

19 In addition to the outright destruction of capital and human capital, a more persistent and pernicious effect of fighting on development is that it interferes with *planning for the future*. This perception of instability can itself lead to chronic underinvestment, which undermines growth. See Thies, C. and C. Baum, "The Effect of War on Economic Growth," *Cato Journal* 40(1) (2020): 199–212 and Jha, S., "Civil and Ethnic Conflict in Historical Political Economy," in J. Jenkins and J. Rubin (Eds.), *The Oxford Handbook of Historical Political Economy* (Oxford: Oxford University Press, 2022), pp. C31P1–C31N21.

20 Blattman, C. and E. Miguel, "Civil War," *Journal of Economic Literature* 48(1) (2010): 3–57.

21 Finance Division, *Pakistan Economic Survey 2017–18* (Islamabad: Government of Pakistan, 2018).

22 Talbot, I., *Pakistan: A Modern History* (New York: St Martin's Press, 1998).

Governance Challenges Across South Asia

Beyond the legacy of civil conflict, South Asia faces myriad ongoing governance challenges (Table 4.1). On virtually every metric of overall institutional quality, countries in the region tend to score poorly, falling below zero on a scale of −2.5 to +2.5.[23] In most instances, the economies also fall short relative to India, albeit the regional giant's messy democracy remains among the most robust within the group.

Perhaps more worrisome is how, for some of these countries, the situation appears to have deteriorated. Corruption in Afghanistan and Sri Lanka is worse today than two decades ago, as is political stability in Bangladesh and Pakistan, and government effectiveness in the Maldives and Nepal. This has led some of these countries to slide further down global rankings of institutional quality, even while countries in other parts of the world have sought to bolster their own governance standards.

To the extent that these poor scores on governance detract from development and are a drag on longer-term economic prospects, it is difficult to imagine how these nations might eventually overcome the middle-income trap. It is certainly possible that these nations sustain reasonable—and, perhaps in certain years and decades, even pull off superlative—growth, just as the Tiger nations of Southeast Asia were able to. But fully transitioning into high-income status generally requires a sustained effort at maintaining high levels of governance, which appears to remain elusive for most economies in the region, for now.

Nor has higher income fully insulated countries from governance failures. In 2018, public officials in the Maldives—including then-President Abdulla Yameen—were implicated in a corruption scandal that saw no-bid leases offered on over 50 islands in the nation, ultimately resulting in losses estimated at tens of millions, and the eventual jailing of the tourism minister.[24]

The Modern South Asian Economies

Incomes in South Asia Mostly Remain Low, But This Has Not Inhibited Their Aspirations

Other than India, the two South Asian economies that dominate the regional economic landscape are Bangladesh and Pakistan, with GDPs that account for

---

23 As a percentile, the region does not do as poorly, since the global median for many governance metrics tends to be below zero. Still, it is typical for South Asian economies to likewise fall below the median on most indicators.

24 Belford, A., A. Down, and Z. Rasheed, "Paradise Leased: The Theft of the Maldives," *Organized Crime and Corruption Reporting Project Report* (Washington, DC: Journalism Development Network, 2018).

Table 4.1 Governance metrics from South Asian economies

	Control of corruption	Government effectiveness	Regulatory quality	Rule of law	Political stability	Voice and accountability
Afghanistan	1.3	2.2	−2.0	−1.8	−2.4	−2.0
	−1.1	−1.6	−1.3	−1.9	−2.5	1.6
Bangladesh	−1.2	−0.6	−0.9	−1.0	−0.7	−0.2
	−1.0	−0.6	−0.9	−0.6	−1.0	−0.8
Bhutan	0.6	0.6	−0.4	0.1	0.5	−1.1
	1.6	0.8	−0.4	0.6	1.0	0.2
India	−0.4	−0.2	−0.2	0.4	−1.0	0.4
	−0.3	0.3	−0.1	−0.1	−0.6	0.1
Maldives	−0.3	0.9	1.0	0.3	1.2	−0.8
	−0.4	0.4	−0.5	0.2	0.5	−0.2
Nepal	−0.6	−0.4	−0.7	−0.2	−1.2	−0.3
	−0.5	−0.9	−0.6	−0.5	−0.2	−0.1
Pakistan	−0.9	−0.5	−0.8	−1.0	−1.1	−1.2
	−0.8	−0.4	−0.7	−0.6	−1.7	−0.8
Sri Lanka	−0.2	−0.3	0.2	0.2	−1.9	−0.2
	−0.3	−0.1	−0.4	0.0	−0.3	−0.1

Source: Author's compilation, using World Bank (2022), *World Governance Indicators.*
Notes: The top row for each country are data for 2000, and bottom row for 2021. Scores range from −2.5 to +2.5, but percentile ranks vary. Estimates are accompanied by standard errors, which are not reported. India, discussed in Chapter 3, is provided for context.

around a tenth of regional output each. This is mostly a function of their population, but not solely so.[25] Bangladesh has distinguished itself as among the more dynamic economies in the region, boasting an annual growth rate of 6.5% since 2010 (and around 6 over the last two, proof positive that the past decade was no fluke). This accomplishment was achieved despite being branded as a "basket case" at the country's inception.[26]

Pakistan's track record is more mixed. Post-independence, openness to trade and cheap foreign lending coupled with military aid allowed the economy to

25 Bangladesh and Pakistan have the next largest populations after India, but the discrepancy between the two countries' GDP and that of the remaining economies is proportionately greater than their population differentials. Indeed, the nation with the fourth-largest population in South Asia is Afghanistan (around 42 million, or around 2% of regional population), but its GDP is lower than that of Nepal and Sri Lanka.
26 This characterization due to then-U.S. presidential advisor Henry Kissinger.

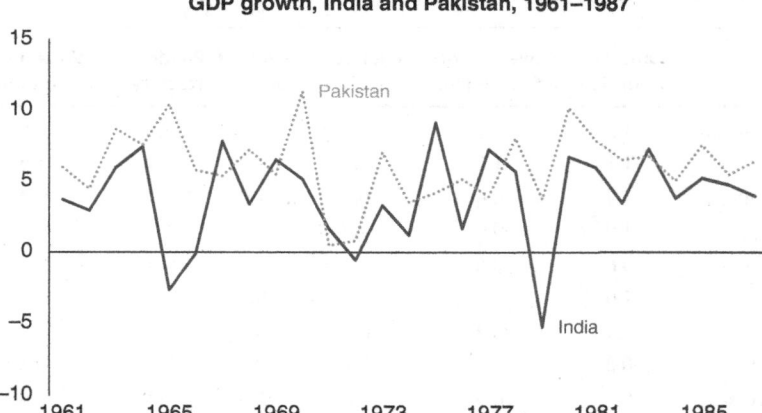

Figure 4.3 In the earlier decades, Pakistani growth handily outstripped that of India by around one-and-a-half times. However, there was a role reversal since the 1990s, with India's newly-liberalized economy outpacing that of Pakistan's, by around the same differential.

surge, in contrast to neighboring India (which had chosen to pursue a socialist, protectionist, import-substituting strategy). For two decades, GDP expanded by around 6% per annum, around one-and-a-half times that of India's "Hindu" rate of growth (Figure 4.3). But since the 1990s, the continued reliance on foreign aid flows—which enabled Pakistan to sidestep important but much-needed reforms, such as resolving infrastructural shortcomings and expanding the tax base—has resulted in a role reversal, with India's newly-liberalized economy able to outpace that of Pakistan's, by around the same differential.

The remaining South Asian economies have had more of a mixed run. The Maldives has recorded a solid average annual rate of 5.5% since the turn of the century, but its small, open—and heavily tourism-dependent—economy leaves the island especially vulnerable to external shocks (output plunged by a third in 2020 due to the pandemic, before rebounding by two-fifths the year after). Bhutan has likewise expanded at a fairly impressive 6.2% annual rate, but its economy is also exposed to tourism, and the other major contributing sectors—agriculture and wholesale-retail trade (the largest private sector employer)—are similarly volatile.

Of course, simple economic performance need not be the only metric for a nation's progress. Indeed, Bhutan has, since 2008, famously stressed the importance of looking beyond GDP. The country has even gone as far as to declare "Gross National Happiness" as the nation's guiding philosophy—it is explicitly written into its Constitution—while also shaping government policymaking. This makes for a different pace of life; Bhutan's capital, Thimphu, famously has no traffic lights. But this approach goes beyond such cutesy factoids; it encapsulates what academic research has increasingly emphasized as a credible national objective.[27] Hence, while the country remains among the poorer economies in the region, there is a certain logic to looking beyond GDP growth.[28]

Building an Industrial Base

The South Asian economies embarked on their independence journey with a footprint that was decidedly agrarian. Pakistan was hamstrung by a predominantly agricultural economy—it only received a tenth of manufacturing enterprises at the time of partition—while Bangladesh was likewise overwhelmingly rural—with the primary sector comprising around three-fifths of the economy—following its own independence from Pakistan.

Unlike India, however, most South Asian nations have steadily built up their industrial capacity. Over the half-century since 1960, primary production has been whittled down from more than two-fifths of the economy to around a fifth, with manufacturing generally taking its place (Figure 4.4). The notion that Bangladesh is an agricultural country has long ceased to be true, and by 2010, farm enterprises accounted for less than 15% of all household income.[29] In its stead, manufacturing enterprises—especially in textiles—have arisen, and the Bangladeshi apparel industry has also distinguished itself at the global level. Pakistan's economy also underwent its own structural transformation, which began in 1977, but accelerated in the 1980s and 1990s as the administration of Zia ul-Haq adopted a policy of deregulation and privatization.[30] As a consequence, Pakistan's industry now ranges from mining and fuel extraction,

---

27 See Oswald, A., "Happiness and Economic Performance," *Economic Journal* 107(445) (1997): 1815–1831 and Frey, B., *Happiness: A Revolution in Economics* (Cambridge, MA: MIT Press, 2008).

28 The counterargument to this line of thinking is that subjective wellbeing tends to be closely linked to its level of development, with some research going as far as to argue that there are no indications of a satiation point between per capita income and happiness. See, for the original argument of a diminishing return to income on happiness, Easterlin, R., "Will Raising the Incomes of All Increase the Happiness of All?," *Journal of Economic Behavior and Organization* 27(1) (1995): 35–47. For a rebuttal, see Stevenson, B. and J. Wolfers, "Economic Growth and Subjective Well-Being: Reassessing the Easterlin Paradox," *Brookings Papers on Economic Activity* 2008 (2008): 1–87. In reality, national happiness is likely to be determined by a wider range of factors than income alone; see Di Tella, R. and R. MacCulloch, "Gross National Happiness as an Answer to the Easterlin Paradox?," *Journal of Development Economics* 86(1) (2008): 22–42.

29 Khan, A., *The Economy of Bangladesh: A Quarter Century of Development* (Basingstoke: Palgrave Macmillan, 2015).

30 The episode is sometimes referred to as "corporatization." See Zaidi, S., *Issues in Pakistan's Economy: A Political Economy Perspective*, 3rd edn. (Karachi: Oxford University Press, 2015).

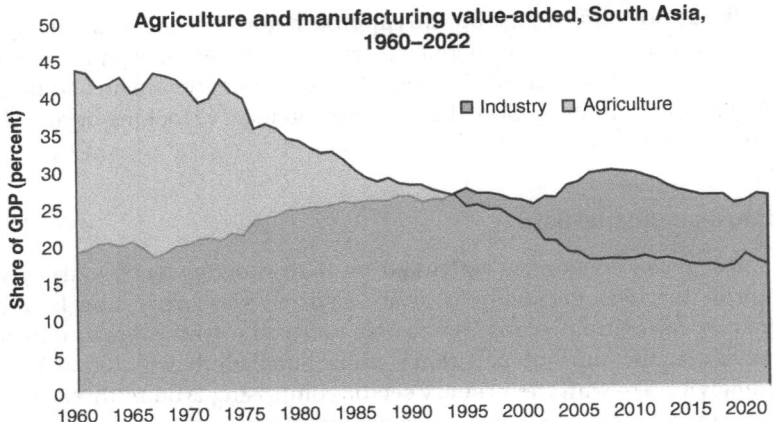

Figure 4.4 The South Asian agricultural sector has steadily crept down, and now comprises less than a fifth of the economy for the region at large. In its stead, industrial production has expanded, and is now a mainstay at around a quarter of output (and it would be greater if not for premature deindustrialization in India).

to textiles and garments, to automotives. Much of the advance in industrialization also occurred alongside a general shift toward export-oriented development, especially in Bangladesh, Pakistan, and Sri Lanka.

However, not all economies have made a decisive shift toward industrial activity, despite the overall regional trend. Nepal's economy—partly by dint of its natural endowments—still leans heavily on agriculture, which contributes a third to output (and two-thirds of employment); the same holds for Afghanistan and Bhutan.

The decline in the importance of the primary sector has been coupled with a demographic transition and urbanization. Fertility has fallen from 6 children per woman in 1960 to (the replacement rate of) 2.2 by 2021, while the urban population has concomitantly more than doubled, from 17% to 35% over the same period. These population movements formed the backbone to the region's manufacturing renaissance, echoing similar trends in East and Southeast Asia.

Overcoming Poverty and Fostering Human Development

Growth has enabled certain South Asian economies to make incredible progress in poverty reduction. For example, Bangladesh was able to pull more than 26 million poor out of impoverishment between 1991 and 2022, shaving the poverty rate down from 44% to 11%.[31] Along the way, it was able to overtake India not just in terms of per capita income, but also key metrics of human development, such as in educational attainment and health conditions.

---

31 World Bank, *Poverty and Shared Prosperity: Correcting Course* (Washington, DC: The World Bank, 2016).

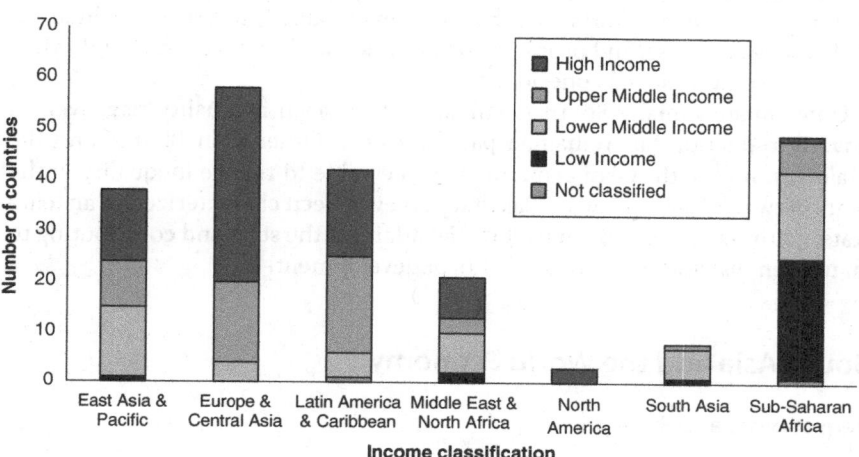

Figure 4.5 South Asia remains *sui generis* in that it is the only developing region with but one high-income economy, the Maldives, with the remainder still remaining either in low- or lower-middle income status. Given the gap in per capita income of the Maldives and the rest, it does not look like the discrepancy will disappear any time soon.

Even so, the South Asian economies almost all remain low or lower-middle income, except for the Maldives. There are proportionately fewer countries in the high- and upper-middle income categories in South Asia, than any other region in the world. Moreover, given the gap that still remains between the Maldives and the others, it is unlikely that the inequality in between-country incomes will close any time soon (Figure 4.5).[32]

This has meant that poverty rates in the region have remained significant. A third of the world's poor reside in South Asia. At the $3.65 a day (PPP) lower-middle income poverty line, the headcount for the South Asian economies—other than India and the Maldives—ranges from 40% (Pakistan) to 9% (Bhutan). Bhutan and Sri Lanka are ahead in their efforts to eradicate poverty, but the others have a way to go. However, when more holistic measures of multidimensional poverty[33] are considered, the region slips further behind, with countries

---

32 The GDP of the Maldives—the economy with the highest per capita income in the region—is around five times higher than that of Bhutan and Sri Lanka, the next two on the ladder. It is also an order of magnitude higher than that of the poorest economies, Afghanistan, Nepal, and Pakistan.

33 Multidimensional poverty captures the idea that deprivation for the poor tends to occur along multiple dimensions beyond income alone, to include education, health, and overall standard of living (e.g. lack of access to drinking water, electricity, housing, and sanitation). See Alkire, S. and J. Foster, "Counting and Multidimensional Poverty Measurement," *Journal of Public Economics* 95(7–8) (2011): 476–487.

like Bhutan and Pakistan also failing on this front.[34] Widespread poverty can complicate national efforts to enhance human capital, improve productivity and competitiveness, and promote consumption and aggregate demand, while also undermining social cohesion.[35]

Unfortunately, many South Asian states have seen inequality rise, even as poverty reduction has remained painfully slow. Other than Bhutan and the Maldives, no South Asian economy has been able to reduce inequality in the years between 1980 and 2015. Pakistan has even been characterized as an "elite state," with a small group controlling the affairs of the state and contributing to an uneven distribution of the benefits of development.[36]

South Asia and the World Economy

Remittances and Receipts

Anyone who has walked past a money transfer agent in the Middle East will be familiar with the long, snaking lines of South Asian laborers gathered on weekends to send money home. Such remittances are nontrivial. In Nepal, especially, as much as a quarter of GDP derives from inflows of current transfers from abroad. Even for the other South Asian nations, such receipts range from around 2% (Afghanistan) to close to 9% (Pakistan), which is significantly higher than either global (0.8%) or middle-income (1.5%) averages (Figure 4.6).

Remittances can play an important role in making up for the shortcomings of the state, as well as relieving poverty. Transfers fund the purchases of basic consumption goods, finance education and healthcare, provide capital for small businesses and down-payments on houses, and have become a key channel of development finance.[37]

Importantly, remittances are also usually countercyclical—they tend to increase when the destination country is undergoing a slowdown, to help cushion the effects of downturns experienced by recipient families—and are also less volatile than other forms of cross-border financial flows.[38] In that

---

34 For example, Bhutan and Pakistan's poverty gap (at $3.65 a day PPP) for the most recent available years (2017 and 2018) were only 2% and 9%, respectively, but their multidimensional poverty indexes were 37% and 38%.

35 The saving grace, if one may call it that, is that relative to India, these nations are all ahead in terms of human capital accumulation (despite India's higher per capita income than many of them), although this speaks more to India's failures in human development, than the successes of the rest of South Asia, *per se*.

36 Husain, I., *Pakistan: The Economy of an Elite State*, 2nd edn. (Karachi: Oxford University Press, 2020).

37 Maimbo, S. and D. Ratha (Eds.), *Remittances: Development Impact and Future Prospects* (Washington, DC: The World Bank, 2005).

38 In certain economies, they could also turn out to be acyclical or procyclical, which may exacerbate the effects of business cycles. See De, S., E. Islamaj, A. Kose, and R. Yousef, "Remittances Over the Business Cycle: Theory and Evidence," *Economic Notes* 48(3) (2019): e12143.

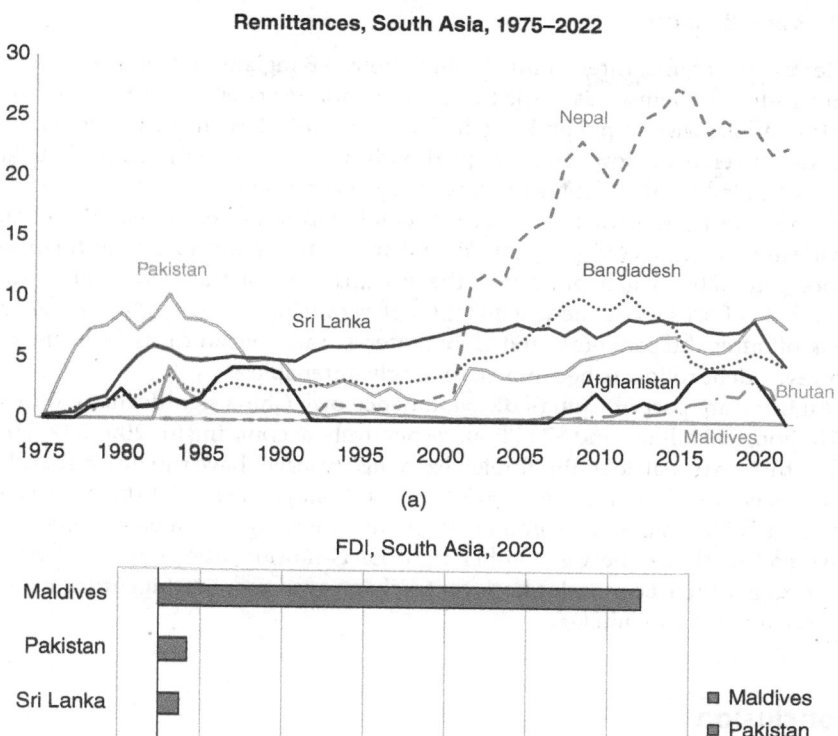

Figure 4.6 (a) South Asian economies are among the largest recipients of remittances globally—with Nepal in particular receiving as much as a quarter of its income from current transfers—while other South Asian countries also tend to receive inflows significantly above the global and middle-income average. (b) As a result, remittances may help offset the otherwise low levels of foreign direct investment in the region, which only the Maldives receives in significant volumes.

sense, they fulfill part of the role of FDI, which tends to be the standard reliable source of international capital for developing countries,[39] and for which only the Maldives receives any significant volume.

---

39 Data at the international level reveal that remittances overtook foreign aid and portfolio investment flows to developing countries, in absolute terms, in the late 1990s. Excluding China, remittance flows already significantly exceed FDI. See Yang, D., "Migrant Remittances," *Journal of Economic Perspectives* 25(3) (2011): 129–152.

Crises and Bailouts

After the pandemic, three South Asian nations—Bangladesh, Pakistan, and Sri Lanka—found themselves in the throes of economic crises. The context to this state of affairs was a rapid build-up in debt over the 2010s, fueled by easy credit offered at relatively low rates, coupled with willing external lenders. But the assets funded by this debt were not always economically viable. Sri Lanka's Hambantota Port, for instance, faced a combination of excessively optimistic projections of expected port traffic, and mismanagement of public finances more generally (which prompted the privatization of the port, and China Merchants Port's subsequent acquisition of a controlling stake). Once inflation took off after the pandemic and global interest rates began to rise inexorably, however, debt rollovers became increasingly untenable.

All three are part of China's BRI, and hence owe China significant amounts: $5 billion, $30 billion, and $7 billion, respectively, accounting for 20%, 30%, and 7% of their external debt. But foreign exchange reserves have run down sharply, which has forced them to seek IMF support. Policymakers find themselves in an intolerable situation—common to many emerging markets—where they have had to choose between either rigorous conditionalities imposed by the Fund to get their economies back on track, or even more stringent terms for loans extended by China.

Conclusion

With perhaps other than the conspicuous case of Afghanistan, South Asia appears to have left the legacy of internal conflicts mostly behind. This has allowed these nations to finally embrace the potential of their sizable populations—the so-called demographic dividend. Bangladesh, in particular, has experienced a prolonged spell of social peace, which has in turn allowed the economy to steadily grow, and even portend the possibility of breaking into upper-middle status sometime over the next decade.

Investment bank Goldman Sachs has argued that Bangladesh and Pakistan (along with Indonesia, Korea, the Philippines, and Vietnam) would be part of the "Next 11" wave of countries set to become among the largest emerging markets worldwide.[40] While such forecasts are almost always a fraught endeavor, it is notable that at least two of the South Asian economies are viewed by market watchers as holding the potential for global economic prominence.

Yet governance challenges abound, even among success stories. Under the current prime minister, Sheikh Hasina, Bangladesh's economy has become

---

40 Goldman Sachs Investment Research, *BRICS and Beyond* (New York: Goldman Sachs, 2007).

increasingly centralized, and institutional checks and balances have slowly been eroded. This could undermine the very basis for its accomplishments to date.[41] The constant threat of political instability can cast a pall over sentiment, which in turn will be a headwind for sustained domestic and international investment.

But South Asia seems to have found its own way, albeit in a somewhat unorthodox fashion. Unlike India, the region followed the more traditional path for the structural transformation of their economies, shifting labor and capital away from their large agricultural sectors and into industry, before services. But the source of financing has been less from foreign direct investment, and more from remittances. The challenge, then, is for such transfer flows to be directed into actual business and entrepreneurial endeavors, rather than simply funding consumption.

Alas, evidence from microfinance suggests that the latter is more likely. While institutions such as Bangladesh's famous Grameen Bank do provide much-needed microloans to (especially) rural communities and women—and the approach pioneered credible no-collateral lending—some of the promise of unlocking entrepreneurial spirit and investment has given way to more realistic expectations of supporting consumption smoothing.[42]

---

41 Quibria, M., *Bangladesh's Road to Long-term Economic Prosperity: Risks and Challenges* (Cham: Palgrave Macmillan, 2019).

42 The basic model of microfinancing relies on small loans to groups of tightly-knit borrowers, who apply social pressure to ensure repayment, thereby keeping loans performing even in the absence of collateral. See Morduch, J., "The Microfinance Promise," *Journal of Economic Literature* 37(4) (1999): 1569–1614.

5

NIEs: From Zero to Hero, but in Need of a New Economic Model

Most of East Asia's extraordinary growth is due to superior accumulation of physical and human capital. But these economies were also better able to allocate . . . resources to highly productive investments and to acquire and master technology. In this sense there is nothing 'miraculous' about the East Asian economies' success.
—*Lewis Preston (1926–95), Former president, World Bank Group*[1]

The newly industrializing countries of Asia . . . have achieved rapid growth in large part through an astonishing mobilization of resources. Once one accounts for the role of rapidly growing inputs in these countries' growth, one finds little left to explain . . . growth has been based largely on one-time changes in behavior that cannot be repeated.
—*Paul Krugman (1953–), Processor of Economics, City University of New York and Economics Nobelist*[2]

Introduction

Standing amidst the smoldering ruins of economies in the aftermath of World War II, one could scarcely have imagined that the two tiny city-states of Hong Kong and Singapore, along with the rump states of South Korea and Taiwan, would emerge as the winners in the competition for regional economic significance.

And yet they did. Starting in the 1960s, these Newly-Industrialized Economies (NIEs) of East Asia roared on to the global economic stage, sustaining extremely

---

1 Preston, L., "Foreword," in N. Birdsall, J. Campos, W.M. Corden, C-S. Kim, L. MacDonald, H. Pack, R. Sabor, J. Stiglitz, and M. Uy, *The East Asian Miracle: Economic Growth and Public Policy* (Oxford: Oxford University Press, 1993).
2 Krugman, P., "The Myth of Asia's Miracle," *Foreign Affairs* 73(6) (1995): 62–78.

Asian Economies: History, Institutions, and Structures, First Edition. Jamus Jerome Lim.
© 2024 John Wiley & Sons Ltd. Published 2024 by John Wiley & Sons Ltd.

rapid rates of growth—of between 7 and 9%—over more than three decades. These growth rates meant that their economies were doubling every decade.[3] Their impressive rise led them to be dubbed the "Four Asian Dragons."[4]

The Dragons were able to do so with a combination of an internationally-oriented trade strategy, an ability to harness both domestic and foreign savings for investment into equipment, machinery, and structures, and a disciplined effort to elevate the educational attainment of a young (but poorly-trained) workforce. It was a triumph of blood, sweat, and tears that enabled these hitherto "emerging" nations to actually emerge.

Looking at the various capitals today, one is tempted to forget how far they have come. Seoul is a vibrant, thriving megalopolis, host to world-famous multinationals such as Hyundai, LG, and Samsung, in stark contrast to its humble origins as a poor, war-torn town, battling urban congestion, rampant pollution, and housing shortages. Taipei was transformed from a small, forgotten provincial city into a wealthy, technologically-infused, globally-integrated metropolis, boasting more billionaires per capita than London, Los Angeles, and Sydney.

The Singapore of the 1950s was a malaria-infested, second-tier port, compared to the hypermodern, globalized trade and financial center it is today. And while Hong Kong was already renowned worldwide as a key gateway to the East—the very name, which translates to "Fragrant Harbor," clearly evoked that allure of the Orient—its people were still impoverished and uneducated, the economy was struggling to absorb the influx of refugees from China that numbered as many as 100,000 a month, and the city was grappling with organized crime triads. Visitors to today's Hong Kong are more likely to be awe-struck by the city's skyscrapers (the most in the world) and sophisticated public transportation network, its world-class services-led economy, and it's people's entrepreneurial dynamism.

Yet these nations—despite being commonly (and perhaps crudely) lumped together—are more heterogeneous in many dimensions than commonly believed. Both Hong Kong and Singapore were not only small island nations, but explicitly favored by their colonial masters as shining outposts of the British Crown. While national myths may paint a different picture, they did not start from the basement, but rather from a relatively solid base. Per capita incomes for the two, in contemporary dollars, stood at around $420 in 1960, almost

---

3 The rule-of-thumb often applied by economists is the so-called "rule of 70," which takes its name from the fact that, at a rate of g%, the economy would double every $70/g$ years. The rule itself derives from solving the formula $Y = Y_0\,e^{gt}$, where (Y_0) Y is (initial) GDP, and t is time.

4 They are also often referred to as the Four Asian Tigers, although the subsequent solid growth performance of the next wave of Asian industrializers—such as Indonesia, Malaysia, and Thailand—resulted in *these* economies being referred to as Tigers (in this text, we will retain the term "Dragon economies" for the original four NIEs, to avoid confusion). The term NIE itself has also been extended to nations beyond East Asia, including (but not limited to) countries such as Israel, Mexico, South Africa, and Turkey.

twice the upper-middle income average of $218 (in contrast, Korean and Taiwanese incomes were $160 and $150, respectively).

Similarly, while all the NIEs boast a number of home-grown multinational champions, the overall industrial landscape in Hong Kong and Taiwan—98% of which is comprised of small and medium enterprises (SMEs)—could not be more different from that of Korea and Singapore, which yields to the dominance of privately-held and government-linked industrial conglomerates, respectively.

A deep dive into the fast-tracked development experience of the NIEs requires not only an appreciation of the geographic and historical context from whence they emerged, but also a recognition of the key ingredients that were necessary for their meteoric rise, because it will reveal the sorts of challenges these nations will have to confront in the decades to come.

Economic Geography of the NIEs

Villages by the Sea

The NIEs are all relatively small, as far as global comparisons go. Of the four, South Korea is the largest: encompassing about 219,000 square kilometers, much of it mountainous, which constrains both population settlement as well as the amount of arable land available. Taiwan's 35,000 square kilometers make it one of the world's larger islands, although it still only ranks 39th worldwide, and the country has a smaller footprint than three of Japan's five main islands (save for Shikoku and Okinawa), as well as other Asian island nations, such as Sri Lanka.

Hong Kong and Singapore are city-states, so there is no genuine comparison. The former has, however, a hinterland—the New Territories—that make up the vast majority of what would otherwise be a tiny island and peninsula. As a result, the 1,100 or so square kilometers make it 1.5 times larger than Singapore (at 720 km^2).

Even a casual observer will discern how the four NIEs are surrounded by water (Figure 5.1). Hong Kong and Singapore are port cities, Taiwan is an island, and South Korea sits on the tail end of a peninsula. Access to the sea has been an integral part of each of these nations' cultures and lifestyles, and trade linkages have featured in their history, well before the modern era.[5] In addition to maritime access, Hong Kong and Singapore have also benefited from their

---

5 The exception, to the extent that it should be drawn, would be with Korea, which tended to limit its trading relationships mainly to China and Japan. Still, the peninsula had often been an economic intermediary between mainland Asia (principally China) and Japan, dating back to ancient times.

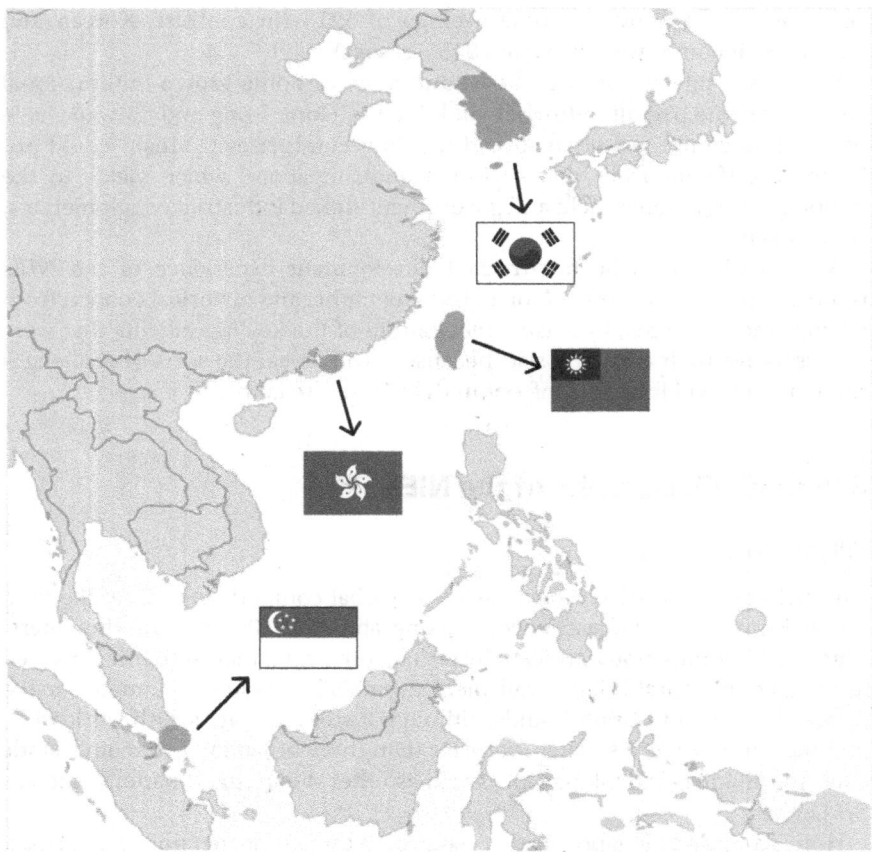

Figure 5.1 The most striking observation about the NIEs is how they are surrounded by water, which, in turn, has been an important conditioning factor behind their adoption of an export-oriented development model.

strategic locations—at the intersection of important shipping routes, allowing them to play the role of entrepôt—and their natural, deep-water harbors.

Accessibility to the sea has also helped these nations in their modern, export-oriented development strategies. It is useful to recall, after all, that despite massive advances in transportation technologies in the 19th and 20th centuries, the mass shipping of goods remains the cheapest, by ton, for ocean freight. The availability of low-cost shipping goes beyond the delivery of final goods; intermediate inputs can also be affordably shipped from other locales, allowing the disintegration of the supply chain that has been so much a feature of the East Asian production network.[6]

---

6 Feenstra, R., "Integration of Trade and Disintegration of Production in the Global Economy," *Journal of Economic Perspectives* 12(4) (1998): 31–50.

Most observers will also be aware that—with the exception of Korea—the NIEs fall within the tropics,[7] and hence do not exhibit the standard seasonal patterns. Hong Kong and Taiwan, being subtropical, do enjoy cooler winter weather, but none have to deal with the sort of harsher winter conditions that affect the Korean peninsula.

This is a blessing and a curse. While non-temperate climates relieve the need to deal with the effects of extreme cold and snow on buildings and other infrastructure, warm temperatures—even when they are not life-threatening—apply a steady, draining effect on productivity and political stability.[8] Singapore's founding father, Lee Kwan Yew, went as far as to muse that air conditioning was one of the "signal inventions of history."

Highly Urbanized Economies

The NIEs host relatively large populations, given their size. Korea—at about 77 million—is the largest, followed by Taiwan (24 million), Hong Kong (7 million), and Singapore (6 million). The combination of large populations within tight land masses means that the NIEs are among the most densely populated nations in the world.

They are also the most urbanized. As city-states, Hong Kong and Singapore are, of course, 100% urban, and certain parts—the Mong Kok or Kwun Tung districts in downtown Hong Kong, or residential neighborhoods like Sengkang or Yew Tee in the northeast and northwest of Singapore—have residential densities greater than Manhattan or central Paris.

But even the NIEs with comparatively greater land endowments tend to be extremely urbanized. About 80% of the population of Korea and Taiwan live in cities, and cities in these larger NIEs are also densely populated.

High urban density has resulted in the need to manage close living conditions. An example of this is the microapartments and nanoapartments (sometimes more disparagingly known as "coffin cubicles") of Hong Kong—claustrophobic flats that can be as small as 100 square feet. Entire families often squeeze into this tiny living space, and in spite of its size, many remain priced beyond affordability for the average Hongkonger (Figure 5.2).[9]

---

7 Strictly speaking, the island of Taiwan is bisected by the Tropic of Cancer, and the north of the island has a milder, subtropical climate, albeit still relatively humid. The mountainous east, however, is more temperate.

8 Dell, M., B. Jones, and B. Olken, "Temperature Shocks and Economic Growth: Evidence from the Last Half Century," *American Economic Journal: Macroeconomics* 4(3) (2012): 66–95.

9 Hong Kong has a perennial housing crisis, and is routinely ranked as the least affordable city in the world. Average house prices transact at more than 20 times median incomes, a ratio generally regarded as "severely unaffordable." See Cox, W., *Demographia International Housing Affordability* (Houston, TX: Urban Reform Institute and the Frontier Center for Public Policy, 2022).

Figure 5.2 Apartments in certain districts of Hong Kong can be exceedingly cramped, with the most extreme examples—sometimes referred to disparagingly as "coffin cubicles" where flats are illegally subdivided into 12–120 square foot units—housing entire families in a very small living space.
Source: stevecadman / Flickr / CC BY-SA 2.0.

While the Hong Kong example is admittedly extreme, the other major cities in the NIEs must likewise address the usual challenges associated with dense urbanization. Some of these challenges are prosaic and are of the kind associated with dense urban life anywhere: safeguarding the reliability of large-scale trash disposal and recycling programs, addressing noise complaints and other neighbor disputes, controlling and containing the spread of pests and diseases, and regulating traffic and safety. But it also means that the NIEs have become adept at dealing with the logistics of large crowds and persistent people flows. This can translate more broadly into expertise in urban management and development.

Mostly Lacking Natural Resources, But Also Free from Its Curse

All the NIEs have been endowed with very limited amounts of natural resources, but they are not entirely bereft. Of the group, Singapore has the least; virtually nothing beyond forestry land and marine fisheries, both of which are insufficient to support a modern economy (and, as the country has developed, these resources have also been whittled away). In contrast, Hong Kong—despite its small size—has had the fortune of nontrivial amounts of mineral deposits, some of which (such as granite and graphite) have been commercially exploited on a small scale. But the hills within which these resources are buried pose a separate problem: their positive *fengshui*[10] aside, they constrain the expansion of the city, since they abut downtown.

As larger land areas, Korea and Taiwan have been blessed with endowments of relatively common industrial metals (such as copper and iron), as well as small deposits of coal and petroleum. But while locally-sourced iron did feature in the early development of Korea's steel industry, most native sources of industrial metals and energy have since been depleted.

Perhaps more pertinent is that the *absence* of natural resources has freed the NIEs from the resource curse, or the tendency for countries with abundant natural resources to end up with poorer economic performance.[11] For the NIEs, this absence of competition over the very finite amounts of natural resources—coupled with a greater willingness to channel development efforts toward the accumulation of physical and human capital rather than resource extraction—has likely been a big part of why the NIEs have been able to circumvent the worst excesses of the resource curse.

---

10 *Fengshui* (風水, lit. "wind-water") is the Chinese practice of geomancy that seeks to improve one's fortunes via the configuration of the natural and built environment. In the context of Hong Kong, the harbor was traditionally regarded as bringing in wealth, while the hills would inhibit its leakage. *Fengshui* masters are also regularly sought by residents, and the city's modern skyline is heavily influenced by their recommendations.

11 There are many potential explanations for why this is so, ranging from how competition over said resources leads to political instability, a weakening of democratic accountability, an artificially-strengthened exchange rate (the so-called "Dutch Disease"), excessive income volatility, and a crowding out of human capital development. For an overview, see Torvik, R., "Why Do Some Resource-Abundant Countries Succeed But Others Do Not?," *Oxford Review of Economic Policy* 25(2) (2009): 241–256.

Economic History of the NIEs

From Dynasties to Division: A (Very) Brief Economic History of Korea

Korea's pre-Malthusian history was rich in culture and political intrigue, but less distinguished insofar as economic progress was concerned. The peninsula had undergone its own Three Kingdoms period—a mirror of what had happened in neighboring China[12]—but unification eventually brought the Baekje, Goguryeo, and Silla into one single power.[13] This unified Korea eventually transitioned to the Chosŏn dynasty, which then remained in power for another half-century.

What the Chosŏn oversaw was a largely agrarian peasant economy, hampered by poor control over water resources. Challenging climactic conditions on the peninsula placed a premium on public initiatives that would ensure that irrigation channels remained clear, and any damage from erosion was repaired, so as to avoid flooding. But the administration was chronically incapable of managing the nation's waterways, which resulted in low levels of agricultural productivity.

By the late 19th century, Japan's designs on Korea became increasingly evident, and this culminated in 1905, when the country eventually bowed to protectorate status. The official end of the dynasty occurred five years later, when Japan annexed the territory. Between 1910 and 1945, Korea functioned as a colony of Japan.

While devastating for Korea's independence and nationalistic self-esteem, the replacement of the crumbling bureaucracy of the Chosŏn dynasty with a developmental state—and one that had already experienced the fruits of industrialization—turned out to be just the sort of shot in the arm that the economy needed to transition into modern economic growth. Japan perceived Korea as part of its "core" holdings,[14] which implied a steady transfer of

---

12 In addition to two separate Three Kingdoms periods (the first from 57 BCE to 668 CE, and the second—sometimes termed the "Later"—Three Kingdoms period between 889–935 CE, both involving the same players), Korea also went through a Northern and Southern period. This actually overlapped with the two Three Kingdoms periods, after the South came under a unified Silla, and the North would fall to Balhae rule (itself having being formed out of the defunct Goguryeo state).

13 Despite the fact that the modern name of Korea derives from Goguryeo, it was actually Silla that first unified the disparate kingdoms in the 7th century. Rule was eventually handed over to the Goryeo—the successor to the Goguryeo—in the early 10th century, in what is sometimes referred to by historians of Korea as "true" national unification.

14 At the peak of Japan's territorial expansion during World War II, the empire occupied virtually all of Southeast Asia (stopping short at the southern end of Papua New Guinea), much of northeast Asia (including Korea, Manchuria, and a good swathe of northern and eastern China), along with many islands in the Pacific, ranging from half of Sakhalin (a Russian oblast), Guam (a U.S. territory), and the Solomon Islands (then a British protectorate). However, it really only viewed Korea, Manchuria, and Taiwan as part of "core" Japan.

manufacturing technology to the economy. Within three decades, GDP went from about a third in agriculture to two-fifths, with manufacturing growing to more than a quarter of the economy.

After the defeat of Japan in WWII, the victorious Allied powers divided the peninsula, along the 38th parallel, into Soviet and American-occupied zones, in the North and South respectively. While division was originally meant to be a temporary arrangement—at least until self-rule could be assured—the competing ideologies of the two superpowers led to two different governments set up in their respective zones, led by the anti-communist Syngman Rhee in the South, and the militarist dictator Kim Il-Sung in the North.

Unable to reconcile their differences, war erupted. The Korean War lasted for three years, and in the process, 1.5 million people perished, and a quarter of the capital stock was gone. At the time of division, Korea's industries were located in the prosperous North, hence many expected the rural South to struggle for economic relevance. And even though the North was entrapped by the limitations of a communist system, the South was hardly better; a military coup in 1961 installed Park Chung-Hee as authoritarian leader, where he remained in power till his assassination in 1979.

But South Korea baffled its detractors. Park presided over the "Miracle on the Han River"—a homage to the central role the river has played in Korean history, and a reference to the Miracle on the Rhine (where Germany and Austria rapidly rebuilt after World War II)—where real per capita incomes grew from around $1,000 in 1960 to more than $31,000, just 60 years later. During that period, the economy was able to sustain a growth rate that averaged a little shy of 9% for close to four decades.

Overrun Again and Yet Again, or an Economic History of Taiwan

As an island, Formosa has been occupied for an exceedingly long time. All but one branch of the Austronesian language family—a group that includes modern *Bahasa Indonesia* and *Melayu* (spoken in Indonesia and Malaysia), *Malagasy* (Madagascar), *Māori* (New Zealand), and *Tagalog* (the Philippines)—originated from the island, a testimony to the depth of human inhabitation there.[15]

Even in its more modern history, Taiwan has seen multiple transitions in overlordship. These include a foray by the Dutch in the early-to-mid 17th century, before they were forced out by a Chinese-Japanese warlord, Koxinga, in 1662. The Qing empire (1683–1894) and the Japanese (from 1895 till the end of World War II) also had a presence. The arrival of the Nationalists (國民黨, or

---

15 Trejaut, A., T. Kivisild, J.H. Loo, C.L. Lee, C.L. He, C.J. Hsu, Z.Y. Li, and M. Lin, "Traces of Archaic Mitochondrial Lineages Persist in Austronesian-Speaking Formosan Populations," *PLoS Biology* 3(10) (2005): e376.

Kuomintang) from the mainland in 1945 was therefore just the latest of a series of political regimes to govern the island.

Yet through this period of repeated conquest, Taiwan did not develop beyond a small number of settlements, and remained essentially an outpost for greater powers. Some of these were undeniably lucrative; at its peak, the Dutch East India Company derived a quarter of its profits from its Formosan operations. But the island remained largely entrenched in agricultural production—primarily sugarcane and rice[16]—and precious little energy was expended by these occupiers in developing the island.[17] Even so, the Japanese did plant a small number of factories, sowing the seeds of a subsequent industrial economy.[18]

The flight of the Nationalists to the island became permanent when their remaining territorial holdings on the mainland fell to the Communists in 1949. Taiwan, accordingly, retained the mantle of the Republic of China (ROC), whereas the mainland took on the more socialist-sounding *People's* Republic of China (PRC).

Through much of the 1950s, the economy was heavily reliant on aid from the United States, and this provided the foundations for a very rapid ramp-up in industrialization. By the end of the decade, under the oversight of revolutionary leader Chiang Kai-Shek, Taiwan was producing cheap light manufactured goods, such as textiles and electronics.

The main constraint preventing an even more decisive takeoff of the economy was a scarcity of foreign exchange. By the late 1950s, it was evident that this was due to an overvaluation of the currency. While Chile had its so-called "Chicago Boys"—economists, trained at the University of Chicago, who pushed for the adoption of pro-free market policies across Latin America—Taiwan had its own "Cornell Boys," a pair of economists,[19] educated at Cornell University, who urged a shift away from import substitution toward competing directly via exports to global markets. The signature move was the embrace of a more competitive exchange rate, which entailed a series of devaluations. This policy allowed the economy to reorient itself toward export promotion.[20]

The United States withdrew its support from Taiwan in 1965, and to add insult to injury, the country was unceremoniously booted out of the United Nations in 1971, when it became increasingly untenable to regard the government of

---

16 Ho, Y.-M., *Agricultural Development of Taiwan, 1903–1960* (Nashville, TN: Vanderbilt University Press, 1966).

17 Ho, S., *Development of Taiwan: 1860–1970* (New Haven, CT: Yale University Press, 1978).

18 Myers, R., "Taiwan as an Imperial Colony of Japan, 1895–1945," *Journal of Chinese Studies* 11 (1973): 425–454.

19 The two were Ta-Chung Liu and Sho-Chieh Tsiang, who persuaded key officials involved in economic affairs, Li Kwoh-Ting and K.Y. Yin, of the wisdom of an export-oriented development strategy.

20 Irwin, D., "How Economic Ideas Led to Taiwan's Shift to Export Promotion in the 1950s," NBER Working Paper 29298 (Cambridge, MA: National Bureau of Economic Research, 2021).

the small island as the official representative of the hundreds of millions living across the strait on the mainland. The world also fell into a recession, due to the 1973 oil price shock.

With the economy teetering on the edge, the administration turned to Keynesian-style pump-priming of the economy, with the launch of the so-called Ten Major Construction Projects (十大建設, *shídàjiànshè*). The building drive—which included the North-South Highway, Chiang Kai-shek International Airport, Kaohsiung Shipyard, China Steel integrated steel mill, and the Jinshan nuclear power plant—provided important infrastructure that was lacking at the time, while shoring up domestic demand.

Manufacturing quickly grew to become a mainstay of the economy, jumping from a fifth to more than a third of output by 1980.[21] Taiwanese electronics and electrical products—led by global leaders such as the semiconductor foundry Taiwan Semiconductor Manufacturing Company (TSMC) and electrical components supplier Foxconn—propelled the economy through the middle-income trap, and into the ranks of high-income countries.

Throughout this rapid-growth period, the ROC and PRC remained in a state of war, with a number of crises in the 1950s.[22] Cross-Strait relations began to thaw in the 1980s and 1990s, helped by stronger economic ties. While China has always retained its position that the island remains a part of China, the specific stance held by the island has vacillated between pro-independence and pro-reunification, depending on the electoral fortunes of the two main competing parties (with the Democratic People's Party supporting the former, and the *Kuomintang* the latter).

Hong Kong's Evolution from Low-Cost Factory to Services Hub

Hong Kong has, since ancient times, played the role of a gateway for the rest of the world—especially for European traders—into China. This is not to say that it was always as prominent as it is today; it languished as mostly a secondary pearl trading center after being incorporated into China by the Qin dynasty in 221 BCE. The region did enjoy a brief spell of prominence during China's Golden Age under the Tang (618–907), as the port—that is today part of the New Territories—also served as a naval base and salt production center for Guangdong province. But overall, the territory was lightly populated, and its role as an entrepôt meant little room for industrial development.

The island of Hong Kong (香港) was formally ceded to the British as a result of the First Opium War, while the Second Opium War—which followed 14 years later—handed over the area north of the island, Kowloon (九龍). The New Territories

---

21 Davis, I., "Taiwan: The Economic Significance of the Industrialisation Programme," *Australian Journal of Chinese Affairs* 6 (1981): 1–20.
22 The First and Second Taiwan Strait Crises occurred in 1954 and 1958, respectively, and involved air and sea engagements. Hostilities ceased thereafter, but no official treaty to end the war was ever signed.

(新界, or *sangai*) were then leased, on a 99-year basis, in 1898. This phase of direct colonial control would last for more than a century, during which the city rapidly developed as a globally-oriented center for financial and commercial services.

Under colonial administration, manufacturing activity also began to take root. Factories were initially entirely owned by the British, and focused on labor-intensive activities, such as shipbuilding and furniture. The Taiping Rebellion led to an influx of Chinese wealth and capital, expanding the scope (and ownership) of manufacturing into light consumer goods and electronics.

The British explicitly chose a *laissez-faire* development strategy, adopting policies that were among the most free-market in the world. This included low taxes, lax employment laws, free trade, and little government debt. The approach unleased the inherent entrepreneurial spirit of the population, and by the mid-20th century, Hong Kong had firmly established itself as an industrial hub.

Over the second half of the 20th century, however, the economic model of the city-state evolved. Rapid economic growth—from a comparatively higher base than Taiwan or South Korea—meant that the low-wage, export-intensive model was becoming more and more untenable. Throughout the 1970s, Hong Kong managed this pressure by diversifying its export basket, improving the quality of products, and expanding the number of target markets served.

By the 1980s, however, wages in nearby Shenzhen were starting to look irresistibly attractive, and Hong Kong's capitalists began financing the relocation of factories there. Hong Kong's economy quickly moved up the value-added ladder, toward a wide range of services, and deindustrializing at a rapid clip (Figure 5.3).

In 1997, the lease on the New Territories expired. Unsurprisingly, China declined to renew the terms. Concomitantly, the United Kingdom had become

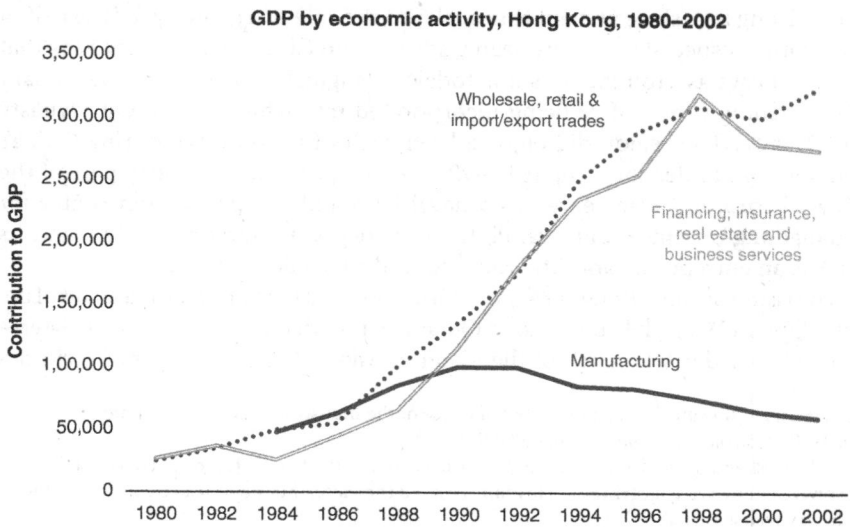

Figure 5.3 Even for a small, open economy, Hong Kong's deindustrialized process occurred extremely quickly. Until the late 1980s, manufacturing was growing at a comparable pace to services; but by 2000, Hong Kong had become a post-industrial economy.

a shadow of its imperial self, and the formal handover of all of Hong Kong's territories occurred over the summer that year. The city became a Special Administrative Zone (SAR) of China, with the (com)promise—enshrined in its so-called Basic Law[23]—that the existing legislative system and individual rights would be preserved for the following 50 years.

This was, in part, a push to ensure that the city-state's unique intangible advantages—in rule of law, investor protection, and system of government—would not be squandered, given their importance to the economy. After all, services had already grown to more than four-fifths of the economy by then.

Perspiration Over Inspiration: The History of Economic Transformation in Singapore

The island at the tip of the Malayan peninsula that is now Singapore was, for much of its early history, undistinguished, and heavily clouded by myth and legend (some manufactured, some not). The settlement—then known as Temasek[24] or Singapura[25]—fell under the control of various sultanates and empires between the 7th and the 16th centuries.[26] While its geographical position and natural deepwater port allowed it to rise to some prominence as a trading port, the settlement remained encumbered by piracy and a struggle with malaria. In 1613, however, the settlement became collateral damage in Portugal's colonial expansion in the region, and subsequently fell into obscurity, until its modern (re)founding.

This founding was attributed to Stamford Raffles. The British colonial officer negotiated into existence a small trading post in 1819, numbering around a hundred or so Malay and Chinese settlers. This was the genesis of the eventual colony that was formally established, half a decade later,[27] with Singapore

---

23 The Basic Law is itself a compromise, which (ostensibly) allows maximum flexibility of operations, within the rigid (but ultimate) control by the PRC. In some ways, it replicates Hong Kong's original colonial status, but under a different master. See Tsang, S., *A Modern History of Hong Kong: 1841–1997* (London: Bloomsbury Academic, 2004).
24 The etymology is likely from *tumasik*, which translates to "Sea Town" or "Sea Port," a moniker that has well summarized the *raison d'être* of the island since.
25 This is a portmanteau of the Sanskrit words *siṃha* ("lion") and *pūra* ("city"). Notwithstanding that there are no lions in Southeast Asia—the namesake animal was likely one of the island's native tigers—the name has stuck, as reflected in the modern name, Singapore.
26 Prior to the arrival of European colonial powers, Temasek was variously a vassal state of the Majapahit Empire (based in Java, modern-day Indonesia) and the Siamese Kingdom (modern-day Thailand) in the 14th century. In the 15th through the 16th centuries, it fell first to the Malacca Sultanate, followed by the Johor Sultanates (both in modern Malaysia).
27 The original agreement struck between the British and local leadership (the Sultan and Temenggong of Johor, in their capacities as head of state and head of public security, respectively) to establish the settlement was ratified via the Treaty of Singapore in 1819, but a second treaty—which fully ceded Singapore and its nearby islands—replacing the original was signed in 1824 (it was also in this year that the Anglo-Dutch Treaty demarcating the spheres of British and Dutch influence was signed). Hence, while 1819 remains recognized as the official founding of Singapore, 1824 is more properly regarded as when full colonial control was established.

forming a part of the so-called Straits Settlements (which included the Malayan ports of Malacca, Penang, and Dindings).[28]

Operating as a free port—exempt from port duties or heavy tariffs—Singapore welcomed not only goods, but also traders and migrants. Immigrants flooded in from around the world, including Westerners, Arabs, Chinese (including the Straits-born diaspora, known as Peranakans), and Indians. While it lent a certain vibrancy to commerce in the Crown colony,[29] the influx also meant the need to manage problems of tropical urban living: housing shortages, poor sanitary conditions, and general lawlessness. Still, driven by trade, the city thrived,[30] and by the eve of World War II, the port had become one of the most important in the world.

This was interrupted by the Japanese invasion. While Japanese occupation eventually proved to be fleeting, the conquest—which took all of eight days—provoked some serious introspection by the local population, as to whether the implicit protection supposedly guaranteed by British overlordship was as credible as previously believed.

After the war, this reexamination resulted in agitation for greater autonomy. Varying degrees of self-government followed,[31] including a flirtation with Federated Malaysia (1963–65). In August 1965, however, Singapore struck out on its own. The absence of a hinterland on which to draw resources or be a destination market—as well as continued challenges from overcrowding, unemployment, and civil unrest—led many contemporary commentators to consign the new nation-state to irrelevance.

This was not to be. Singapore confronted its shortcomings, head-on. The leadership cultivated a mindset of taking nothing as given, and urged the population to pull themselves up by their bootstraps. Workers plowed hours into labor, the young expended significant effort into education, and the youthful population channeled their savings into built-up capital. Complementing this

---

28 The Straits Settlements covered British possessions in Southeast Asia north of the Straits of Malacca—including Malacca, Penang, and Singapore—whereas the Dutch controlled territories to the south of the Malay archipelago (mainly Indonesia).

29 Crown colonies were directly administered by the British state from London. Singapore gained the status in 1857, following disappointment with Indian administration under the Calcutta Presidency.

30 In nominal terms, trade grew by two orders of magnitude, from $12 million in 1924 to $942 million in 1937, with the peak at $1.9 billion in 1926. Wong, L.K., "Singapore: Its Growth as an Entrepôt Port, 1819–1941," *Journal of Southeast Asian Studies* 9(1) (1978): 50–84.

31 This included local government under colonial administration between 1951 and 1955, partial internal self-government from 1955–1959 (where weak political stability prompted repeated racial riots), full internal self-government in the 1959–1963 period (that was threatened by communist elements), and as a state in the federation of Malaya during 1963–1965 (which was always going to be problematic, given how pro-Malay affirmative action policies would frequently run up against the city's pursuit of meritocracy).

massive resource mobilization crusade was a targeted plan to court foreign sources of capital and technology (especially by attracting FDI from multinational corporations (MNCs)),[32] including economic expertise.[33] It did so with massive investment into supportive infrastructure: industrial estates, and free economic zones, coupled with extremely favorable tax treatment.

This mix combined to produce one of the modern world's fastest economic transformations. From per capita incomes of the same level as Mexico or South Africa in 1965, it rose to a level past that of second-tier high-income countries like Portugal and Israel by 1990, before catching up to German and U.S. levels by 2015.[34]

From Forgotten Backwaters to First-World Nations

Despite their idiosyncrasies, there are common threads that tie together the historical experiences of the NIEs.

All four had a colonial history—Korea and Taiwan by Japan, Hong Kong and Singapore by Great Britain—but they were settlement colonies, rather than extractive ones. Consequently, there was substantial educational, technological, and institutional transfer,[35] which provided important initial conditions for these economies' subsequent takeoff. Although these differed qualitatively—Japanese institutions had a greater emphasis on technological capacity-building and bureaucratic efficiency, while British ones favored legal-political design and financial development—the impact of the transfers was nontrivial.

Perhaps in appreciation of this reality, anticolonial sentiment in these settlements also diminished relatively quickly,[36] and the resulting political stability allowed these economies to channel their energy and resources toward

---

32 Peebles, G. and P. Wilson, *Economic Growth and Development in Singapore: Past and Future* (Cheltenham: Edward Elgar, 2002).

33 The chief economic advisor was a Dutch economist, Albert Winsemius, who was not only instrumental in drafting the blueprint for Singapore's early industrialization push in the 1960s, but also continued to contribute to its development plans until the early 1980s. See Quah, E., *Albert Winsemius and Singapore: Here It Is Going to Happen* (Singapore: World Scientific, 2022).

34 Menon, R., "An Economic History of Singapore: 1965–2065," *BIS Central Banker Speeches*, August 5, 2015.

35 Kimura, M., "Standards of Living in Colonial Korea: Did the Masses Become Worse Off or Better Off Under Japanese Rule?," *Journal of Economic History* 53(3) (1993): 629–652; Chang, H.Y. and R. Myers, "Japanese Colonial Development Policy in Taiwan, 1895–1906: A Case of Bureaucratic Entrepreneurship," *Journal of Asian Studies* 22(4) (1963): 433–449; Onimaru, T., "Financing Colonial State Building: A Comparative Study of the 19th Century Singapore and Hong Kong," in T. Shiraishi and T. Sonobe (Eds.), *Emerging States and Economies: Emerging-Economy State and International Policy Studies* (Singapore: Springer, 2019), pp. 101–118.

36 Abramson, G., "Comparative Colonialisms: Variations in Japanese Colonial Policy in Taiwan and Korea, 1895–1945," *PSU McNair Scholars Online Journal* 1(1) (2004): Art. 5.

development. The general environment of low corruption also helped, even though the NIEs managed their underground economies in their own unique ways.[37]

Following independence, the NIEs pursued a clear development strategy: top-down directed development (often under fairly authoritarian regimes), where factor inputs were (sometimes coercively) summoned to serve the needs of export-orientated industries, and supported by state-funded infrastructure, financed with a combination of high domestic savings (some of which was forced) and undervalued exchange rates. Put this way, the model is straightforward. Yet it has been incredibly difficult to emulate, even by those neighboring countries faced with similar settings.[38]

NIE Development in Comparative Perspective

Growth Miracles or Brute Force Success?

Until the 1990s, most who had studied the track records of Hong Kong, South Korea, Singapore, and Taiwan perceived their growth model as a wild success. The World Bank even issued a triumphant report in the early 1990s, proclaiming (on behalf of the NIEs) that the East Asian experience was nothing short of a "miracle."[39]

Looking at how far and fast the NIEs have come, it is difficult to argue with this sentiment. However, the untrammeled accolades subsequently came into question. Economists who went through the painstaking exercise of decomposing the various contributors to growth (via growth accounting) discovered that close to four-fifths of the NIEs' output gains were due to resource mobilization.[40] Hence, only a small fraction of GDP expansion during their miracle years was attributable to total factor productivity (TFP) (Table 5.1). Put another way, the East Asian growth story was less a miracle than the result of sheer brute force.

Since that time, many more studies have been completed, updating, reanalyzing, and refining the original argument. The bottom line for these later works is

---

37 South Korea has had to deal with their iteration of the Japanese *yakuza* crime syndicates—the *geondal* (건달)—although their presence in the economy is nowhere as extensive as the *yakuza*. Hong Kong, Singapore, and Taiwan have had to manage criminal triad activity.

38 Quah, D., "Empirics for Growth and Distribution: Stratification, Polarization, and Convergence Clubs," *Journal of Economic Growth* 2 (1997): 27–59.

39 Birdsall, et al. (Eds.), *The East Asian Miracle*.

40 Young, A., "The Tyranny of Numbers: Confronting the Statistical Realities of the East Asian Growth Experience," *Quarterly Journal of Economics* 110(3) (1995): 641–680.

Table 5.1 Total factor productivity for the NIEs, 1991–2015 (%)

	Hong Kong	South Korea	Singapore	Taiwan
Economywide (1966–1991)	2.0	1.7	1.4	2.1
Manufacturing		3.0	−1.0	1.7
Services		1.7		2.6
Economywide (1991–2015)	0.2	0.6	−0.1	
Economywide (1966–2015)	1.0	1.2	0.6	

Source: Author's calculations, supplemented by Young (1995).
Notes: Sectoral and Taiwanese TFPs are drawn directly from Young (1995), which uses a slightly different specification to the calculation of economywide TFP applied here. Most estimates are comparable, except for Singapore, where Young's calculations for economywide TFP for the 1966–1991 period is only 0.2%, albeit dual estimates from Hsieh (2002) are as high as 2.1%.

that the essential message remains largely intact;[41] while TFP growth may have picked up for certain NIEs in certain brief spells, the overall contribution to output growth remains smaller than that of other advanced economies, where TFP expansion amounts for something closer to half of progress in GDP.

What's more, the global decline in productivity—especially in advanced economies since the 1990s[42]—has not spared the NIEs. To the extent that TFP in these economies remains suppressed, the global trend is likely to exacerbate the structural difficulties they will face in the future.

All that being said, it is important—even in light of the caveat advanced by the meticulous work of growth accountants—to recognize that input-dependent development does not completely overshadow the accomplishments of the NIEs. After all, rich is rich; even if their high per-capita incomes were arrived at via factor accumulation rather than TFP expansion, the constructed capital and educated

41 This view is not universally shared. Critics argue that the entire growth accounting exercise is inherently fraught, owing to difficulties in the measurement of the capital stock or TFP, or the sensitivity of estimates to assumptions about the form of the production function or the existence of (perfect) competition. Using the so-called "dual" approach to estimate TFP—relying on factor returns instead of input quantities—also yields higher TFP growth for Singapore and Taiwan, and explicitly accounting for land rental likewise raises the TFP contribution. Still, given the very high total growth rates, the TFP contribution remains a relatively small fraction, of typically less than a quarter. See Felipe, J., "Total Factor Productivity Growth in East Asia: A Critical Survey," *Journal of Development Studies* 35(4) (1999): 1–41; Hsieh, C-T., "What Explains the Industrial Revolution in East Asia? Evidence from the Factor Markets," *American Economic Review* 92(3) (2002): 502–526; and Bakker, B., "Unveiling the Hidden Impact of Urban Land Rents on Total Factor Productivity," IMF Working Paper 2023/170 (Washington, DC: International Monetary Fund, 2023).
42 Antolin-Diaz, J., T. Drechsel, and I. Petrella, "Tracking the Slowdown in Long-Run GDP Growth," *Review of Economics and Statistics* 99(2) (2017): 343–356.

workforce remain in place, and will continue to contribute to economic activity (albeit, like all capital, with the need for renewal due to normal depreciation). What is true is that the NIEs will now need to shift their tried-and-tested growth models toward one that is more sustainable in the longer term.

Another useful caveat to note is that—inasmuch as the sort of sustained growth over decades displayed by them remains exceedingly rare—many of these economies did not begin from absolute zero. Indeed, even though per capita incomes were only a fraction that of the developed world in the 1960s, they were still in the upper percentiles of the global GDP pecking order (Figure 5.4). This is most evident for Singapore, which moved from somewhere in the high 70th percentile to the 99th; still a remarkable jump, but not quite the miracle that it would be if it had started lower. If anything, the climb by economies that started substantially lower in the global distribution—such as that of China or Indonesia—while (still) admittedly incomplete, has been far more striking.

An admission of the advantageous initial conditions in Singapore and Hong Kong also goes a long way toward explaining why these two city-states now boast significantly higher per capita incomes vis-à-vis South Korea and Taiwan (the ratio between the former and the latter, in nominal terms, is around 1.5 times when measured relative to Hong Kong, and more than twice using Singapore as the benchmark).

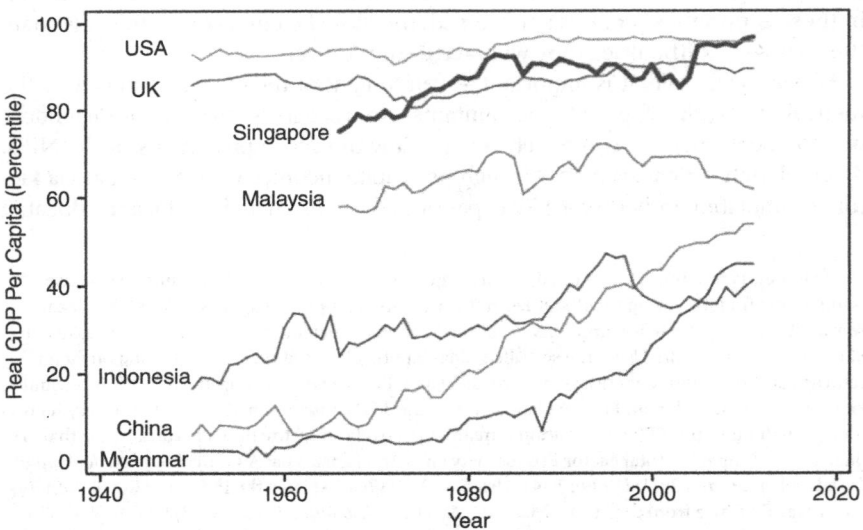

Figure 5.4 Although the growth of the NIEs was undeniably impressive, they started from a comparatively advantaged position, at least relative to other developing economies at the time. In 1960, per capita incomes in Hong Kong and Singapore were already in the top quartile worldwide, while that of South Korea and Taiwan were around the global median.

Export Orientation Versus Import Substitution

In the 1950s and 1960s, an intellectual contest raged between proponents of import-substituting industrialization (ISI)—the idea that trade protection should be offered to domestic firms so that they might have a ready market that would absorb their manufactured goods (rather than being flooded by potentially cheaper imports), thereby enabling industrialization—and those who supported export-oriented industrialization (EOI), where local firms were encouraged to compete at the global level by selling their manufactured products in a global market, possibly with government subsidies to support that endeavor.[43]

The champions of ISI—such as Argentine economist Raúl Prebisch and German economist Hans Singer—swayed policymakers around the world, but especially in Latin America, where many economies adopted the approach in earnest. However, most mainstream economists—along with international financial institutions, such as the IMF and the World Bank—tended to favor trade liberalization as a driver for growth, along the lines of EOI. While the contemporaneous choice between the two was far from clear, the NIEs mostly led the way in pursuit of export-led development (even if some, like South Korea, had brief flirtations with import substitution early on).

The EOI strategy did not occur in a policy vacuum. In addition to trade-oriented policy—and notwithstanding the competitive advantage already conferred by low-wage labor—the NIEs also marshaled exchange rate policy—such as capital controls and targeted undervaluation—to further bolster the appeal of their exports to the wider market. While controversial, such exchange rate manipulation was arguably as important for growth as the exporting machine alone, not least because a weak real exchange rate also confers benefits in terms of raising the returns to capital in the tradable sector, which is notorious for institutional complications that could undermine development there.[44]

Some observers have even gone so far as to argue that undervalued rates in the Asian periphery merely replicate the system that helped post-World War II Europe recover from the devastation of war, even as financial flows from said periphery to the center helped finance consumption demand that, in turn, supported export-oriented growth. This so-called "Revised Bretton Woods" system[45] would be relevant, therefore, not just for the NIEs, but for other economies that sought (or seek) to replicate the same development strategy.

Although an exhaustive assessment of the comparative success of EOI versus ISI lies beyond the scope of our discussion here, it is sufficient to note that

---

43 Krueger, A., "Import Substitution versus Export Promotion," *Finance & Development* 22(2) (1985): 20–23.
44 Rodrik, D., "The Real Exchange Rate and Economic Growth," *Brookings Papers on Economic Activity* 39(2) (2008): 365–412.
45 Dooley, M., D. Folkerts-Landau, and P. Garber, "The Revived Bretton Woods System," *International Journal of Finance & Economics* 9 (2004): 307–313.

the divergent performances of East Asia (which mostly adopted EOI) vis-à-vis Latin America (which generally went with ISI) lends a fair bit of support to the former approach. Even within Latin America, members of the more export-forward *Alianza del Pacífico* (or Pacific Alliance)—Colombia, Chile, Mexico, and Peru—have done comparatively better than their Mercosur cousins since 2012 (when the trade bloc was formed).

Another compelling piece of evidence comes from the divergent paths taken by the two Koreas. Recall that, at the time of division, it was the northern half of the peninsula that was relatively more prosperous. Yet a half-decade of pursuing socialist, inward-looking industrialization has now left the Democratic People's Republic as an impoverished shell, with the fruits of prosperity accruing to the capitalist-leaning, export-oriented (and actually democratic) Republic of Korea. The difference is so stark it can even be seen from space; night lights—symptomatic of economic activity—are spread across the South, while the North is almost entirely shrouded in darkness (Figure 5.5).

This is not to say that the pursuit of an EOI strategy amounts simply to unvarnished trade liberalization. Among the NIEs, the entrepôt economies of Hong Kong and Singapore were probably more zealous in the pursuit of *laissez-faire* trade; the former famously applies no tariffs on imports whatsoever, while the latter only maintains it on three lines.[46] In contrast, the remaining two NIEs—especially South Korea—liberally employ commercial policies that deviate from the free-trade ideal, including a stronger dose of infant-industry protection, state support for sectors deemed strategic, and more deliberate export promotion via subsidies and discounted credit.[47]

The NIEs' experience also became the template for other economies as they moved away from import substituting practices, especially for later industrializers in East, Southeast and Western Asia. When it became amply clear that the choice of embarking on a controlled (but significant) opening of their economies to global trade and finance would not induce a spiral of their economies into unmitigated chaos or global irrelevance (to the contrary), many other nations willingly boarded the EOI train.

The Developmental State

The economic advancement strategies of the NIEs go beyond the distinction between EOI and ISI. State involvement in the development process was, on balance, fairly intrusive (albeit the degree differed by NIE), with the active deployment of industrial policy.[48] This exercise of top-down control has been

---

46 These are customs imposed on beer, stout, and *samsu* (a Chinese rice wine), although excise is also charged on "sin" goods such as alcohol, tobacco, and fuel.
47 Chang, H.-J., *The East Asian Development Experience: The Miracle, the Crisis and the Future* (London: Zed Books, 2007).
48 Haggard, S., *Developmental States* (Cambridge: Cambridge University Press, 2018).

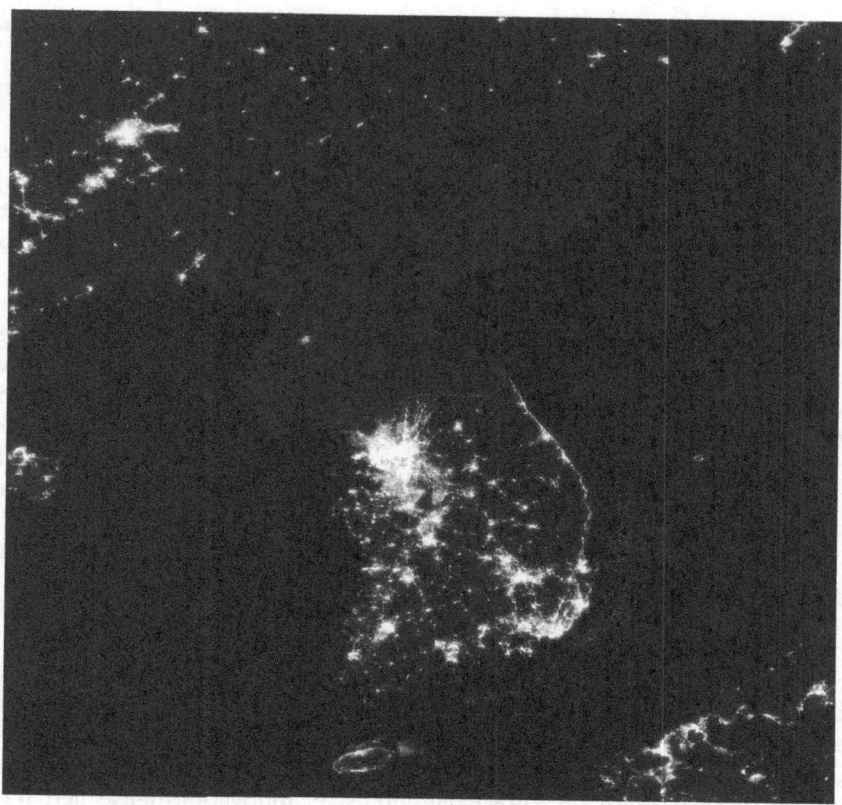

Figure 5.5 Despite starting off as the more advanced half of the Korean peninsula, North Korea is today an impoverished nation, compared to the economic powerhouse that is South Korea. This difference is evident even from the night lights of space, and is in no small part due to the divergent choices of ISI versus EOI adopted by the two Koreas.
Source: NASA / Wikimedia Commans / Public Domain.

most evident in the close control of the economy exercised by the first generation of its leaders: Park Chung-Hee (South Korea), Chiang Kai-Shek (Taiwan), and Lee Kwan Yew (Singapore) all maintained a certain authoritarian streak in their economic management (the first two were generals after all), albeit doing so while allowing market forces to mostly call the shots.

The hand of the state tended to be reflected in sectors where investment was directed. Separate from forced domestic saving or attracted foreign saving, the rapid capital accumulation was not always organic; state planners often influenced incentives with tax breaks for favored industries, as well as subsidized infrastructure (via industrial parks and export zones). By and large, these went to light manufacturing (especially of textiles or electronics) as well as information and communications technologies (especially computers and computer parts).

South Korea, for example, went through a "commanding heights" period in the 1970s, where steel and nonferrous metals production was paired with a push into the heavy chemical industry (HCI). While this could have been misguided at the time—there was hardly an automobile industry then to absorb domestic steel production, and the HCI drive was (at least in part) a vanity project of President Park—they have, with the benefit of time, turned out to be reasonable successes.

Today, South Korea's (constructed) comparative advantages in steel and heavy chemicals are legendary; the nation is the world's seventh largest exporter of steel, and its specialty chemicals rank fifth globally. Both have generated downstream spillover effects, into cars and semiconductors.[49] The approach speaks to the endogeneity of comparative advantage and a certain indeterminacy in the pattern of trade,[50] as well as the importance of how late industrialization often requires a difficult learning-by-doing phase, before becoming established.[51]

This is not to say that picking winners always pays off. Singapore has struggled with upgrading its biopharmaceutical sector—which it first targeted in the late 1990s—to the next level (while drug manufacture is a highlight, few blockbuster innovations can be traced back to the city-state), and the sector only contributes around 4% to national GDP, despite massive investment over two decades. Other late industrializers, like China, have also struggled.[52] More generally, the track record for targeted industrial policies has been fairly mixed.[53]

Although the developmental state applied a decidedly lighter touch in Taiwan, it was focused more on knowledge-intensive, innovation-dense activities. Indeed, science and technology policy was at the heart of industrial development, right from the country's post-separation days.[54] Technocratic direction

---

49 Amsden, A., *Asia's Next Giant: South Korea and Late Industrialization* (Oxford: Oxford University Press, 1992).

50 This was the observation of the so-called second-generation models of trade, where imperfect competition means that first-mover advantage—when coupled with increasing returns—can give rise to enduring export patterns, even in sectors where the country may not have an initial comparative advantage. See Helman, E. and P. Krugman, *Market Structure and International Trade* (Cambridge, MA: MIT Press, 1985).

51 Choi, J. and A. Levchenko, "The Long-Term Effects of Industrial Policy," NBER Working Paper 29263 (Cambridge, MA: National Bureau of Economic Research, 2021).

52 Branstetter, L., G. Li, and M. Ren, "Picking Winners? Government Subsidies and Firm Productivity in China," NBER Working Paper 30699 (Cambridge. MA: National Bureau of Economic Research, 2022).

53 Krugman, P., "Targeted Industrial Policies: Theory and Evidence," *Proceedings of the Economic Policy Symposium of the Federal Reserve Bank of Kansas* (1983): 123–155.

54 Greene, J.M., *The Origins of the Developmental State in Taiwan: Science Policy and the Quest for Modernization* (Cambridge, MA: Harvard University Press, 2008).

began in ICT—famously resulting in the emergence of the TSMC—but in more recent times has pivoted toward biotechnology.[55]

On its face, Singapore's economy does not immediately holler *dirigisme*. Economic freedom and ease of business indices routinely place the city-state in the top few worldwide,[56] and the government expenditure share—at around 15% of GDP—is on the low side for advanced economies.

All these leave the impression that the country operates largely on the basis of a light touch by the public sector. Yet. in reality, the long arm of the state is intertwined in almost all sectors of the economy. This was already the case during the nation's development phase—where the government had unabashedly declared its engagement[57]—as well as more recently, where nominally privatized entities[58] have controlling shares held by one of the state's sovereign wealth funds, Temasek. And while it is true that these bodies operate in competitive markets, the imprimatur of government ownership does lend these firms a certain credibility in their business dealings.

Even Hong Kong—the poster child of unfettered capitalism, at least until the past decade—was not exempt from active government policies in some areas. The public sector had always been heavily entwined in the real estate market—close to half of the population lives in rental or subsidized-sale public housing, after all—and land reclamation and infrastructure investment are comprised of significant government components.

The Modern Economies of the NIEs

Chaebol Rules in a Not-So-Small Open Economy

Today, South Korea is the thirteenth largest economy in the world (fourteenth in PPP terms). It is a diversified, industrialized economy, with two-fifths of output tied to manufacturing (the remainder is mostly services; agriculture accounts for a mere 2%). As the economy has developed, it has also transitioned away from a developmental state, toward greater market orientation. But this did not occur

---

55 Wong, J., "Re-Making the Developmental State in Taiwan: The Challenges of Biotechnology," *International Political Science Review* 26(2) (2005): 169–191.

56 The Heritage Foundation produces an index of economic freedom, which has placed Singapore among the freest economies since its inception in 1995 (with the nation taking pole position in recent years), as has the World Bank's *Doing Business* index (which was discontinued in 2020). See Kim, A., *Index of Economic Freedom* (Washington, DC: The Heritage Foundation, 2023) and World Bank, *Doing Business* (Washington, DC: The World Bank, 2020).

57 Huff, W., "The Developmental State, Government, and Singapore's Economic Development Since 1960," *World Development* 23(8) (1995): 1421–1438.

58 Like many countries around the world, the privatization drive occurred in the late 1980s and 1990s, when neoliberal ideology—championed by U.S. President Ronald Regan and UK Prime Minister Margaret Thatcher—spread around the globe.

instantaneously; Korean policymakers retained elements of protectionist trade and industrial policy at least until the late 1980s.[59]

The gap relinquished by state direction has been enthusiastically filled by the private sector, and in particular, the *chaebol* (재벌, or "wealthy clan"). These conglomerates are the country's equivalent of the *keiretsu*.[60] Despite their similarities—vertical and horizontal integration, with cross-shareholdings at the top—the *chaebol* are also distinct in some ways (Figure 5.6). They are often (still) run by founding families, rather than professional managers (which was the case even with the *zaibatsu*), and the structure does not require that a bank be involved (which is the case with *keiretsu*). In practice, the *chaebol* have also evolved less than the *keiretsu*, as the latter have become less exclusive in their business relationships in recent years, and have been more willing to both employ external contractors as well as service entities outside the group.

These *chaebol*—Samsung, Hyundai, LG, SK, and Lotte—are now household names globally, not least because they literally produce the refrigerators, televisions, washing machines, and other appliances that are common to many households, along with the snacks the children eat, and the cars the parents drive. This industrial dominance has paid off handsomely for the families that

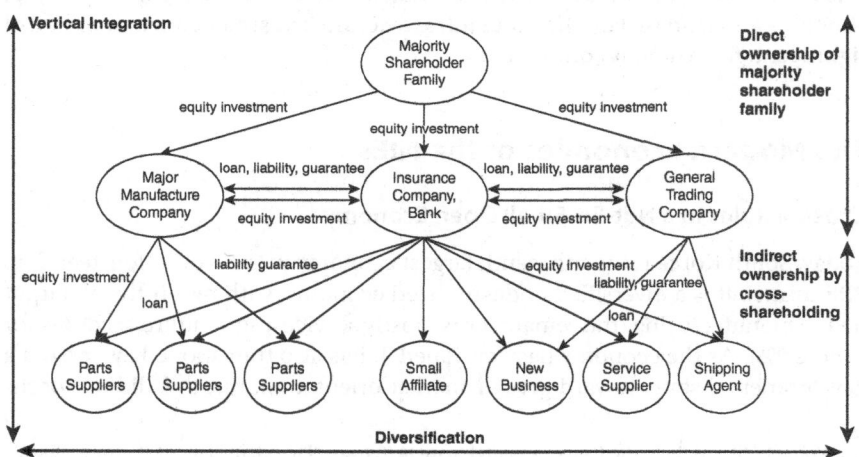

Figure 5.6 The *chaebol* conglomerate structure was modeled on the *zaibatsu*, and includes many similar characteristics, such as horizontal and vertical integration, along with cross-shareholding at the top level. However, ownership tends to be more centralized in a *chaebol*, and firms within the group rely as much on government loans and guarantees, as they do on the internal financial institution for credit.

59 Chang, H-J., "The Political Economy of Industrial Policy in Korea," *Cambridge Journal of Economics* 17(2) (1993): 131–157.
60 The parallels are not entirely coincidental; recall, during Japanese colonization, many institutional structures were copied, including the *zaibatsu*.

control the *chaebol*, as well as the economy at large: estimates suggest that the largest, Samsung, accounts for as much as a fifth of South Korea's economy.

The upshot of this dominance has been what some view as an excessive influence of the oligarchic class on the political scene. Chung Mong-Joon, the president of Hyundai Heavy Industries and member of a *chaebol* family, held a seat in the National Assembly for six years, and former president Park Geun-Hye was impeached and convicted of corruption charges related in part to *chaebols*. The country's recovery from the 1997/98 financial crisis was complicated by the need to execute large-scale bailouts for the *chaebols*—a third of the top 30 went bankrupt at the time—despite evidence of fraudulent accounting, and there was consternation over how much of the funds went toward controlling family shareholders, given low dividend payouts.

On the plus side, the horizontal integration of the nation's conglomerates has meant a very diversified export basket. South Korean exports span the industrial product space, and include electronics, machinery, transport (not just automobiles, but also shipbuilding), steel, and chemicals. And although the initial penetration of South Korean vehicles into global markets was characterized more by affordable (if somewhat inelegant) family saloons, quality has improved dramatically over the past few decades, and companies such as Hyundai and Kia (and, prior to its collapse, Daewoo) routinely won "Car of the Year" awards, with offerings ranging from ultracompacts to large-format sport utility vehicles, in formats that include internal combustion, electric, and hybrid engines. The family-led conglomerate structure has also enabled a certain tenacity in the pursuit of promising technologies that require a long gestation period; LG's position as a leading electric-battery producer owes its genesis to the stubborn vision of the *chaebol*'s founder's grandson, Koo Bon-moo. Taken together, *chaebols* have consolidated their position and improved the economy's resilience, especially after the Asian crisis.[61]

Despite its industrial dominance, modern South Korea is also slowly making a transition into a greater emphasis on services (which accounts for 70% of the labor force). Besides the usual suspects—such as finance and telecommunications—the country has had an extended push into tourism, and has sought to export its culture—an approach known as *Hallyu* (한류, a neologism that translates to "Korean Wave"). This has, perhaps surprisingly to some, gained traction well beyond Asian shores; Korean films are now viewed around the globe, K-pop bands like BTS and Blackpink have captured scores of fans worldwide, and Korean beauty and fashion brands have risen in prominence. The resulting boost to tourism receipts has been substantial, growing

---

61 Lee, K., J.Y. Kim, and O. Lee, "Long-Term Evolution of the Firm Value and Behavior of Business Groups: Korean *Chaebols* Between Weak Premium, Strong Discount, and Strong Premium," *Journal of the Japanese and International Economies* 24(3) (2010): 412–440.

to around 5% of GDP.[62] Altogether, the export of cultural content over the past decade has been massive, and its contribution may be as high as an estimated $6 billion a year.[63]

Industrial Linkages Have Allowed Taiwan to Become a Crucial Node in the Global Electronics Supply Chain

Modern Taiwan, despite its small geographical footprint, ranks 21st in economic size,[64] a little shy of Indonesia and Turkey, but well ahead of Argentina and Poland. Like the other NIEs, the economy put in an enviable growth record—between 1981 and 1996, it sustained GDP expansion at an average of 7.5% annually—but also in line with other NIEs, this rate has come down in the 2010s (to less than half that rate).

In comparison to South Korea's conglomerate-heavy economy, however, Taiwan's industrial structure is much less concentrated. Even though TSMC often grabs headlines—and its contribution of about 15% of the island's GDP is nontrivial—the overwhelming majority of other registered enterprises (1.25 of the total 1.28 million) are SMEs.[65]

This is not to say that Taiwanese SMEs maintain few links with each other. Science and industrial parks allow local firms to foster strong business ties with one another, while networks of regional industrial systems (RIS) also permit foreign firms—especially those located in Mainland China—to participate in such upstream and downstream links, in business clusters known as *chanye juluo*.[66] Despite their decentralized nature, it is clear that Taiwanese SMEs do not operate in isolation (Figure 5.7).

In part due to the strength of the different industrial networks, the country's export basket turns out to be fairly well diversified across different industrial categories, including electronics, ICT products, machinery, base metals, and plastics. Of course, semiconductors comprise the dominant share—and for this reason, Taiwan will always remain a crucial node in the global electronics supply chain—but it would be inaccurate to regard Taiwan's economy as a lopsided one.

---

62 This phenomenon also has a dark side; due to an emphasis on cosmetic surgery and idiosyncratic beauty standards, and an uncompromising cradle-to-grave process of training new stars, there has been pressure—especially within Korean society—to conform, leading to a score of high-profile suicides among Korean celebrities.

63 Park, J., "Measuring the Impact of *Hallyu* on Korea's Economy: Setting Off on the Wrong Foot." In: *Korea's Economy 2021* (Washington, DC: Korea Economic Institute of America, 2021).

64 This is in nominal terms; in PPP terms, it jumps to 19.

65 The more impressive statistic for TSMC is, perhaps, its global share of the semiconductor manufacturing market, where it routinely accounts for more than half (the next foundry, Samsung, accounts for a mere 15%).

66 This may also be translated as industrial cluster (産業聚落, *chǎnyè jùluò*). See Chen, L.C., "Building Extra-Regional Networks for Regional Innovation Systems: Taiwan's Machine Tool Industry in China," *Technological Forecasting and Social Change* 11 (2015): 107–117.

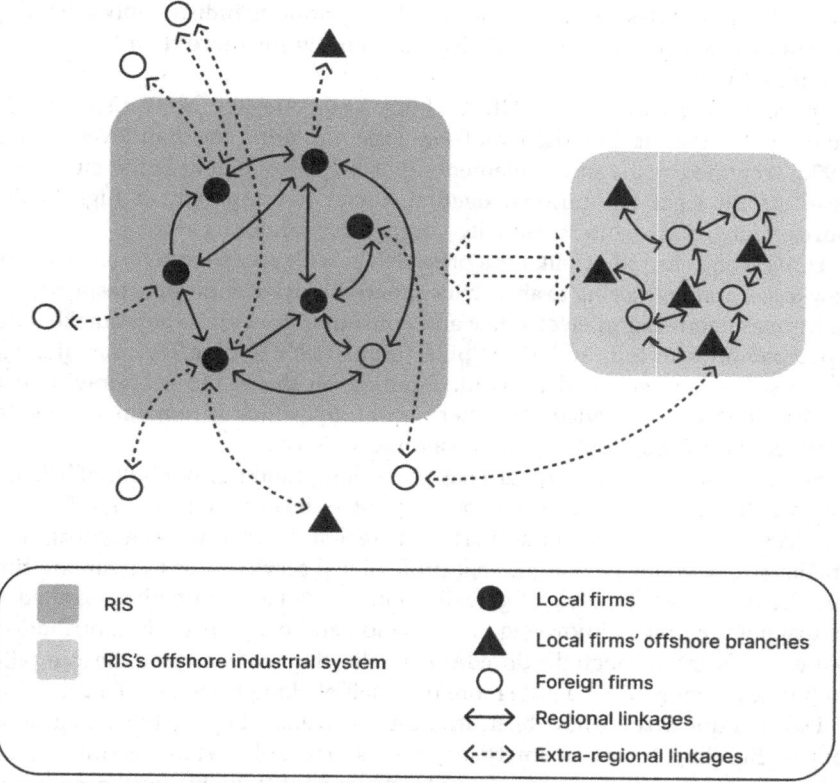

Figure 5.7 The Taiwanese industrial landscape may be comprised almost entirely of SMEs, but these firms do not operate in isolation, but are often part of networks—both within the country in science and industrial parks, as well as externally as part of regional industrial systems—which promote upstream and downstream linkages.

After all, the island's administration has displayed an adroit ability to handle economic policy challenges—most recently with its handling of the COVID-19 pandemic, where its strategies for managing the outbreak have been widely lauded as among the world's best—even while implementing active labor market policies—including strong union rights, high employment standards, and working hour provisions—that offer among the strongest degrees of worker protection among East Asian countries.

Hong Kong as a Postindustrial Economy

Steady economic growth of more than 7% per annum between 1962 and 1997 has allowed Hong Kong to ascend to becoming among the richest economies in the world (in PPP terms, per capita incomes are comparable to that of the United States). Even so, modern Hong Kong is indisputably a tertiary, postindustrial economy, with services accounting for more than 90% of economic activity.

In contrast to the larger NIEs, Hong Kong's legacy of British colonial rule meant that it inherited and—at least up until the handover in July 1997—retained many of the elements that helped distinguish the city-state's rise: strong legal institutions, deep financial development, a high-quality bureaucracy, and an internationally-competitive schooling system.

Hong Kong started off, like the other NIEs, with an economy that relied on low-wage manufacturing to absorb its underemployed labor force (especially in light manufacturing of electronics and consumer goods). It then quickly built up capabilities in four so-called "pillar industries": trading/logistics, finance, professional services, and tourism. Building on these, the economy quickly transitioned into a services-dominant economy, which it remains to this day (services now account for 90% of economic activity).

Some of these areas of strength have been longstanding, and built off the territory's natural advantages: trade logistics due to its entrepôt role, and financial services as the nominal counterpart to its real-side functions as a global intermediary (one could even argue that professional services and tourism are simply the two other channels of globalization where Hong Kong has excelled at, managing the flow of knowledge/information and people). Their contributions were significant; through the decade or so following the handover, the four pillar industries accounted for a little more than half of Hong Kong's GDP growth.[67]

Post-handover, there have been attempts to diversify beyond these traditional pillars. Building in part on emergent spheres that exploited the territory's free-wheeling spirit and encouragement of independent thought—well exemplified by the strides made by the film industry (which saw a flowering in the 1980s and 1990s), or the comparatively large number of tertiary institutions (22 with degree-conferring authority)—the Hong Kong administration now targets six new pillar industries, centered on tradable services: cultural/creative, education, medical, environmental, innovation/technology, and testing/certification. In doing so, it is hoping to rapidly climb the value-added ladder, offsetting the loss of comparative advantage that had previously accrued from low-cost, labor-intensive manufacturing.

This is not to say that old-school goods no longer feature in Hong Kong's trade. After all, Hong Kong's merchandise exports amounted to $126 billion in 2020 (including tradable services, this bumps up to $191 billion), with a strong global presence in electronic equipment as well as gold and other precious metals. But services are now the mainstay when it comes to Hong Kong's economy.

---

67 Research Office, "Four Pillars and Six Industries in Hong Kong: Review and Outlook," *Research Brief* 3 (Hong Kong: Legislative Council Secretariat, 2015).

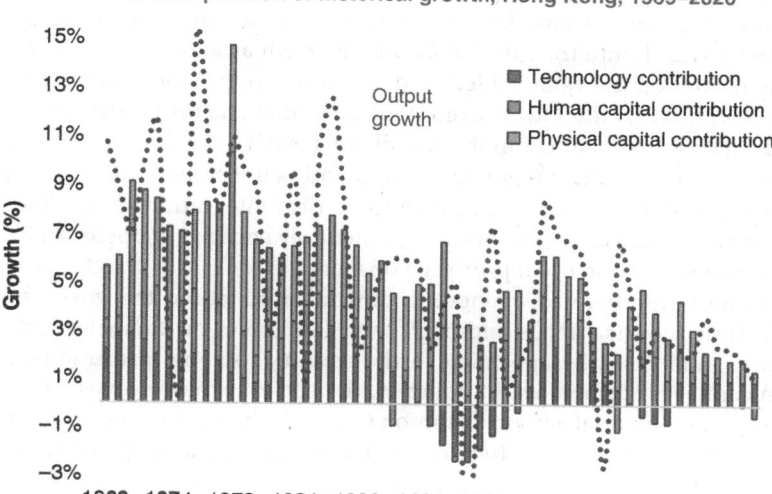

Decomposition of historical growth, Hong Kong, 1969–2020

Figure 5.8 Never large to begin with, TFP has been pummeled even further after handover in 1997, averaging rates of close to zero over the decade or so that followed. With the renewed focus of the economy on services—where productivity is notoriously low—prospects do not appear bright for a strong recovery in TFP any time soon.

The challenge, then, is how to sustain productivity growth in a sector that is notorious for being challenged on this front.[68] Indeed, post-handover Hong Kong has seen a clear diminution in its TFP; while its contribution to the territory's growth dynamics had always been relatively small, this dropped even more after 1997, averaging rates closer to zero (Figure 5.8). Till today, this has yet to recover.

Singapore: Small, Rich, But Unequal

Singapore's rapid growth years—in excess of 8% per annum until the 2010s—has slowed as it has become wealthier. Still, this is par for the course for a country that is today among the richest nations in the world: sixth for per capita income in nominal terms, and second when measured in PPP (behind Luxembourg).

---

68 Some recent research has begun to challenge this long-standing assumption that services are necessarily less productive than manufacturing; see Herrendorf, B., R. Rogerson, and Á. Valentinyi, "New Evidence on Sectoral Labor Productivity: Implications for Industrialization and Development," NBER Working Paper 29834 (Cambridge, MA: National Bureau of Economic Research, 2022) and Fan, T., M. Peters, and F. Zilibotti, "Growing like India: The Unequal Effects of Service-Led Growth," NBER Working Paper 28551 (Cambridge, MA: National Bureau of Economic Research, 2021).

For a high-income economy (and unlike Hong Kong), Singapore has retained substantial exposure to manufacturing activities—it accounts for about a quarter of output, and until the mid-1980s, was as much as a third—even as it has steadily moved up the value-added ladder in terms of products. For example, within ICT, it has shifted away from hard drive manufacturing (where it was once the global hub) and computer peripherals (such as keyboards, mice, and printers) to higher-end integrated circuits and semiconductors.[69] The city-state has also sought to retain as much as vertical integration as possible. Its biopharmaceuticals sector, for instance, is not only engaged in upstream R&D, but discoveries are also often produced onshore.

To support the drive to maintain industrial production, the government (still) actively courts MNCs, although with less stress on financial and tax incentives, and more by appealing to the country's strong institutional and human capital fundamentals. In doing so, the economy has reversed some of the decline in industrial activity common to many advanced economies, albeit its manufacturing activities exhibit more of a capital- and skills-intensive flavor (Figure 5.9).[70]

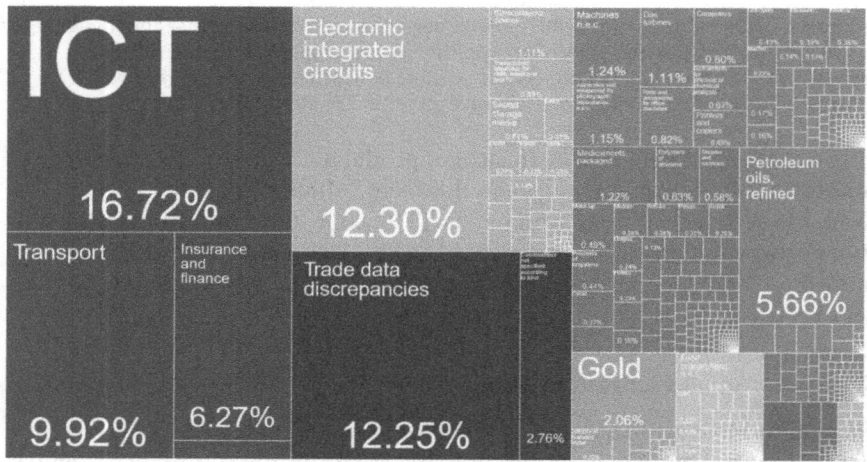

Figure 5.9 Singapore's export basket continues to reflect a large share of manufactured goods, especially in ICT and refined petrochemicals, although the nature of the goods has moved up the value-added chain as the economy has grown wealthier. Beyond merchandise, the island also exports a number of tradable services, in transport, tourism, finance, and ICT.

---

69 Wong, P.-K., "Leveraging the Global Information Revolution for Economic Development: Singapore's Evolving Information Industry Strategy," *Information Systems Research* 9(4) (1998): 323–341.

70 Emont, J., "How Singapore Got Its Manufacturing Mojo Back," *Wall Street Journal*, June 22, 2022.

Even beyond manufacturing, the city-state's industrial strategy has continuously realigned its direction. After a long period of targeting ICT in particular, the nation ventured more boldly into other areas, such as finance (as it liberalized the financial sector in the 1990s and 2000s, it also moved away from back-office functions into front-office roles, such as investment banking and, especially, wealth management), biotechnology (both pharmaceutical research and manufacturing, as well as medical services), and entertainment (high-end retail, concert, and convention facilities, headlined by the opening of casinos). In addition, tradable services now feature prominently in the country's export basket; some estimates place it at around a third. These include financial services but also ICT, transport, and tourism.

The reinvention goes beyond goods, but applies as well to the country's human capital. As the city climbed the global income ladder, the limitations of simply raising the educational attainment of its local population became ever-more evident; fertility rates were plunging, and no matter how high schooling quality would become, the proportion of the adult population able to acquire sufficiently high levels of human capital would be bound by normal distributions of talent. The erosion of the contribution from human capital was starting to show up in the data by the turn of the millennium.

The solution, then, was to import what the populace was unable to indigenously generate.[71] This has involved efforts at the low end—where low-wage migrant workers from other parts of Asia were granted work permits for fixed periods to perform menial tasks, such as cooking, cleaning, construction, and domestic care—as well as at the higher end, where foreign talent would be granted employment passes to embellish the white-collar work force. The resulting surge in effective labor—symbolic of the inroads made by the human capital importation policy—started to show up by the latter half of the 2000s, and would continue through the subsequent decade (Figure 5.10). Immigration restrictions imposed as a result of the COVID-19 pandemic—coupled with political backlash from the native-born population—revealed the shortcomings of this approach.

NIEs and the World Economy

NIEs Are Deeply Embedded in the Global Economy

As a direct consequence of the EOI strategy pursued a half-century ago, the NIEs are today fully integrated into the global economy. This is evident not

---

71 The policy was formalized in a government report, informally referred to as the Population White Paper, which projected an inflow of 100,000 migrants annually from 2013, to a population of as much as 6.9 million by 2030. The paper itself resulted in a political firestorm, as residents feared the consequences of urban overcrowding. As of 2020, Singapore's population stood at around 5.7 million, a little short of the projected 5.8–6 million outlined in the paper. See Strategy Group, *A Sustainable Population for a Dynamic Singapore* (Singapore: Prime Minister's Office, 2013).

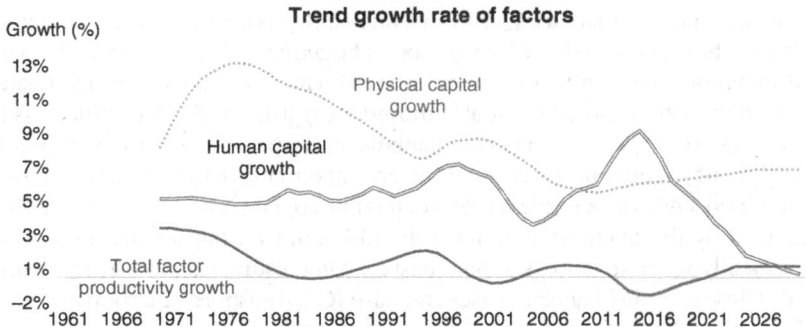

Figure 5.10 The importation of foreign talent led to a surge in the contribution of human capital to growth in the second half of the 2000s, after a marked decline in the earlier half of the decade. This persisted through till the middle of the 2010s, before declining precipitously thereafter.

only in terms of the usual metrics of trade openness—such as shares of imports and exports in GDP—but also in terms of the scope and importance of products made and exported by them.

Of course, it is wholly unsurprising that Hong Kong and Singapore—as global trade hubs *par excellence*—sustain massive trade flows, with their shares routinely coming up to several times GDP (peaking at close to four-and-a-half times previously). This is a function of their entrepôt models, where trade is not simply comprised of exports, but also *re*-exports (goods that are imported and subsequently exported without much processing or transformation)— which may exaggerate the true extent of trade. Nevertheless, trade has been, and remains, the lifeblood of the economic models of these two NIEs, and has been a major factor behind their prosperity to date.

But even the larger NIEs—which pursued more controlled trade exposure in their earlier development years—are now among the most open economies in the world, with trade shares of output at around 80% and 130% for South Korea and Taiwan, respectively. This reflects the nature of the East Asian production chain, of course, but is also in large part due to how parts and components produced by the NIEs are integral inputs in production processes elsewhere in the world, too. This should not detract, however, from the fact that import tariffs and production subsidies were key elements of their industrialization strategy, especially in the earlier stages of development.[72]

Furthermore, trade openness alone is insufficient to express just how embedded the NIEs truly are within the global system. To see this, one would have to examine the number of goods, range of product types, and comparative importance of these items in the global product map. When compared with its neighbors to

---

72 Chang, H-J., *The East Asian Development Experience: The Miracle, the Crisis and the Future* (London: Zed Books, 2006).

the North, for instance, South Korea clearly outperforms on all three dimensions (Figure 5.11). Analogous comparisons to other Asian economies—say, Central or West Asian nations that are resource-centric (think Uzbekistan or Saudi Arabia), or South Asian nations that have less diversified production capabilities (think Pakistan)—corroborate the same essential message.

Taiwan has an additional, complicating dimension in its international economic linkages: its relationship with mainland China. Yet while newspaper headlines often hyperventilate about vacillating cross-Strait relations—the health of which seems to depend on whether a pro-independence or pro-reunification party is in power in Taiwan[73]—*economic* ties have, till now, trended in essentially one direction: toward greater integration.

Until as recently as the mid-1990s, the share of total trade occurring between Taiwan and the mainland numbered only in the single digits. Much of this was routed through Hong Kong—which played its entrepôt role to a tee. Yet this intermediated trade peaked in 1994, and direct trade between China and Taiwan began to accelerate rapidly (this was undoubtedly further fueled by both the return of Hong Kong to China proper at the end of the decade, as well as China's entry into the WTO in the early part of the next). As of 2022, Mainland China and Hong Kong account for two-fifths of Taiwanese exports, while a fifth of its imports derive from China and Hong Kong.

A similar story may be told for financial flows. Close to three-fifths of the island's outbound foreign investment now heads to the mainland, even as it has

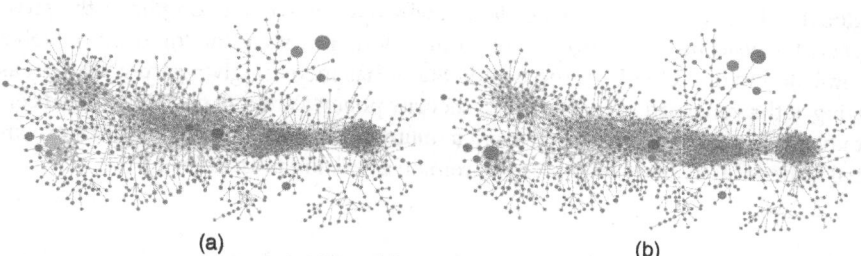

(a)   (b)

Figure 5.11 Comparing (a) South Korea to (b) North Korea, it is clear that the number of classes (counts of dots), range (dots of different colors), and importance (size of dots) of products exported by the South exceeds that of the North.

---

73 At risk of oversimplification, the so-called Pan-Green Coalition (泛綠聯盟, *fànlǜ liánméng*)—comprised of the center-left Democratic Progressive Party (the anchor), the Green Party Taiwan, the Social Democratic Party, the Taiwan Constitutional Association Taiwan Solidarity Union, and the Taiwan Statebuilding Party—tends to favor independence, while the Pan-Blue Coalition (泛藍聯盟, *fànlán liánméng*)—made up of the center-right *Kuomintang* (the anchor), the New Party, the Non-Partisan Solidarity Union, the People First Party, and the Young China Party—favors a Chinese-Taiwanese dual identity, with greater friendly exchange with the People's Republic with an eye toward gradual reunification.

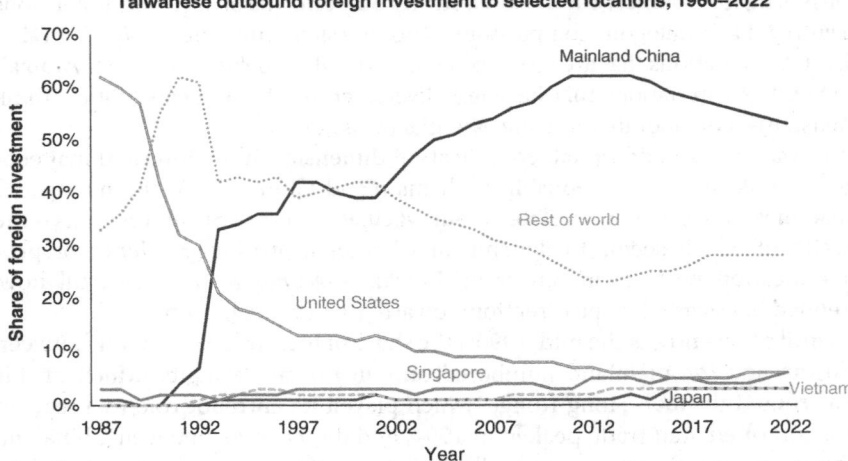

Figure 5.12 Taiwan's cross-Strait trade and investment have steadily grown since the 1990s, and economic ties with the mainland now account for about half of all bilateral trade from the island, even as its exposure to the rest of the world has scaled back.

scaled down its investment exposure to the rest of the world. Whatever views one may have about the geopolitical tensions between the two Chinas, their economic ties have seldom been stronger (Figure 5.12).

Yet recent saber-rattling prompted by the rapid rise of China has brought other global stakeholders back into the picture, which will inevitably complicate the prospects for peaceful integration in the future. With Taiwan at the forefront of global semiconductor technology, the United States has increasingly regarded Taiwan as lying at the vanguard of U.S. *national* security policy. While all parties involved certainly have a strong incentive to avoid a military outcome, the dark cloud of potential aggression in cross-Strait ties will remain a real and present fear.

NIE Challenges in Comparative Perspective

Inequality Has Risen Alongside Incomes

The spectacular rise of the NIEs has presented a dark underbelly: greater income and wealth inequality (Table 5.2).[74] If the Kuznets hypothesis of the inverted U-shaped relationship between inequality and growth were to be

---

74 Incomes are a flow, and measure an individual's or household's compensation received—whether actively in the form of wages from work, or passively via investment returns or property rental—whereas wealth is a stock, which is accumulated savings from unspent income plus dividend income, adjusted to allow for valuation changes.

refuted, it would surely struggle with explaining the changes experienced over time in (most of) the NIEs. Indeed, even while per capita incomes have gone from strength to strength in the Dragon economies—and nowhere near as breathtakingly as Hong Kong and Singapore—income and wealth distributions have remained askew (and especially so in Hong Kong and Singapore). This is well captured by the Gini coefficient, a gauge of the extent of disparity in income (where zero represents perfect equality, while one implies total inequality).

This is in part because the state has been far less redistributive in the NIEs; even after taking into account taxes and transfers, the decline in the Gini is only marginal, and in certain cases, fails to even match the Gini from earlier periods. In comparison, post-tax/transfer Ginis for other advanced economies are typically far lower than pre-tax ones; for example, Canada, France, Germany, and Japan have shaved their coefficients from 0.44, 0.52, 0.50, and 0.49 to 0.32, 0.27, 0.29, and 0.33, respectively.

Yet even statistics like the Gini—for all their merits[75]—may fail to capture the true extent to which income distributions have become more unequal in recent times. This has led to a focus on top incomes (and especially wealth); that is, the share of the national pie that goes to the top 1 or 0.1 or even 0.01% of the population.[76]

Distressingly, wealth inequality in the NIEs has largely remained unabated over the past few decades. Beyond the obvious political-economy tensions this introduces—losers from untrammeled globalization, rising inequality, and inadequate political representation have expressed their displeasure in street protests around the world, and Hong Kong's "Umbrella Movement" protests in 2014 may be seen as one in this vein—wealth inequality also manifests itself in less savory ways in daily life. This includes a glaring divide between cities competing for Michelin-star restaurant recognition, even as a meal for two at one of these distinguished establishments could easily amount to the monthly incomes of the lowest-income earners, or glitzy summer home and yacht shows serviced by locals who can only dream of retirement outside their home country due to exorbitant costs of living, or eye-popping transactions of property that easily amount to eight or nine figures (that, unfortunately, also have the unintended effect of escalating overall prices in domestic housing markets).

There has been increasing recognition among NIEs' governments that this state of affairs is untenable, but concerted action to address the widening

---

75 Gini-type indices, in addition to succinctly summarizing deviations of the distribution of income from perfect equality, also satisfy desirable technical axioms, such as anonymity (it does not matter who the high and low earners may be), scale (the size of the economy is irrelevant), and population (the size of the population is irrelevant) independence, and the transfer principle (transfers from a richer to poorer individuals lead to a more equal distribution of income).

76 For reviews, see Atkinson, A., T. Piketty, and E. Saez, "Top Incomes in the Long Run of History," *Journal of Economic Literature* 49(1) (2011): 3–71. An accessible (if lengthy) introduction is Piketty, T., *Capital for the 21st Century* (Cambridge, MA: Belknap Press, 2014).

Table 5.2 Income and wealth inequality in the NIEs

	Hong Kong	South Korea	Singapore	Taiwan
Income inequality				
Gini				
1980	0.43	0.31	0.44	0.28
Current	0.56	0.34	0.44	0.34
Post-tax/transfer	0.48	0.31	0.38	
Wealth inequality				
Top 1%				
1995	0.29	0.24	0.25	0.23
Current	0.55	0.26	0.32	0.31

Source: Author's compilation, supplemented by the World Bank Poverty and Inequality Platform, World Inequality Database, Kang (2001), Piketty and Li (2021), Schultz (1997), Singstat (2022), and Textor (2022).

Notes: Income inequality captured by the Gini index pre-taxes and transfers, while wealth inequality is captured by net top 1% wealth shares (except for Hong Kong, which is the top 0.001%). Current year differs due to data availability; for income inequality, these correspond to 2016 (Hong Kong, South Korea), 2021 (Taiwan), and 2022 (Singapore), and for wealth inequality, these correspond to 2020 (Hong Kong), 2021 (Singapore, South Korea, Taiwan). Both Gini and top percentages scaled as shares, ranging from 0 to 1.

divide has been unconscionably slow. One can sympathize with the difficulties of doing so while sustaining competitiveness—after all, the low-tax, pro-business model had been such a key ingredient to the development story of the Dragons—but one is left to wonder if the mindsets of the political classes have lost their bearings due to the trappings of their own manufactured successes.

Differences Between the NIEs Point to Impending Challenges

While the development strategies of the NIEs overlap in many ways, there are nevertheless idiosyncratic development patterns, which point to different economic challenges these economies could face in the future.

Trade openness has always been far greater in the city-states of Hong Kong and Singapore, and hence with the slowing of globalization—most evident in global goods trade, which has stagnated in the aftermath of the 2007/08 financial crisis—these entrepôts will find it more difficult to harness gains from trade to drive economic activity. They will also face upstarts and entities that receive favored support from their respective governments. For instance, the Ports at Klang and Tanjung Pelepas in Malaysia are now in head-to-head competition for transshipment business in Southeast Asia, and Hong Kong's financial standing is being eroded not only by Shanghai (in mainstream finance) but also by Shenzhen (in venture capital).

One might infer that this calls for production (and, by extension, export) diversification, but if anything, Hong Kong has gone somewhat in a different direction, embracing a greater disposition toward a service-dominated economy (albeit many of which are tradable). This was always going to be easier for the larger NIEs, since South Korea and Taiwan have an industrial base that includes heavy manufacturing and some capacity for the indigenous production of intermediate inputs. Whether the economic model of the two smaller NIEs will prove vulnerable in a deglobalizing world remains an open question.

Interestingly, the industrial structures in the NIEs do not cohere with the large-small economy distinction. Larger firms are more entrenched not just in South Korea (with its *chaebols*) but also in Singapore (with government-linked firms). Accordingly, they are more likely to seek out "national champions"—not unlike Japan—whereas the preponderance of SMEs in Hong Kong and Taiwan means that network effects and interfirm connections—made without the benefit of vertical integration—play an outsized role in these latter economies.

Conclusion

Getting Schooled on a Superaged Future

The flipside of the NIEs' remarkable corralling of human capital in their high-growth phase is the almost inevitable blowback in the form of diminishing returns. Every single one of the NIEs faces a problem of population implosion; fertility rates range from 0.8 (South Korea, the lowest in the world) to 1.1 (Singapore). Needless to say, these fall far short of the replacement rate.

Projections also suggest that the NIEs are on track to host some of the oldest people in the world. The elderly share of the population is already close to (or exceeding) a fifth of the population within the NIEs, and by the middle of the century, this could breach two-fifths. The dependency ratio—the number of working-aged (15–64 years) relative to youth (those up to 14 years old) and elderly (those 65 and above)—has already bottomed, and it is climbing at an alarming pace. Indeed, if the Japanese experience is any indication (Japan's dependency ratio bottomed in 1992, at around 43%), the ratio could easily double in a little more than three decades (it currently stands at 72%). The NIEs will not just be aged societies, but superaged ones.

The so-called sandwich generation—couples facing the need to support up to four elderly parents, while also trying to raise children of their own—have evidently already made the decision to reduce their burden by having fewer offspring. Pro-fertility policies have barely made a dent, and unlike Japan—where female participation rates were substantially lower at the trough of its dependency statistic—women are already more active in the NIEs, which in turn will inhibit how much policies that seek to elevate their involvement in the workforce can accomplish.

The challenges are amply evident when looking at the likely evolution of human capital into the future. For the NIEs, the boost to growth from the effective labor force will not only be negligible, given how much educational attainment had already been a contributor in the past; it will even turn negative (Figure 5.13). Short of an enormous immigration drive—akin to the sort that Germany absorbed in the form of Turkish migrants in the 1970s and early 1980s—the NIEs will need to rely on other factor contributions to offset this drag from a previously-positive drives.

The imperative to promote TFP gains as the solution to human capital woes will only become more pressing in the future, since wages—which are already noncompetitive when compared to even other upper-middle income economies, not to mention the usual lower-middle income suspects like India or Vietnam—can only rise sustainably with productivity improvements.

Nor can the NIEs hope to continue importing foreign technology as a means of harnessing low-hanging productivity gains, since their economies are already at the global production frontier. If the NIEs hope to continue improving the standard of living among their citizens, their policymakers will need to take on the belated task of making indigenous, innovation-led TFP matter.

The Perils and Promise of a Silver Economy

The silver economy will undoubtedly carry perils for the NIEs. A greater share of the elderly in the population—who will simultaneously live longer—is wonderful from a family perspective (who doesn't want their parents to live

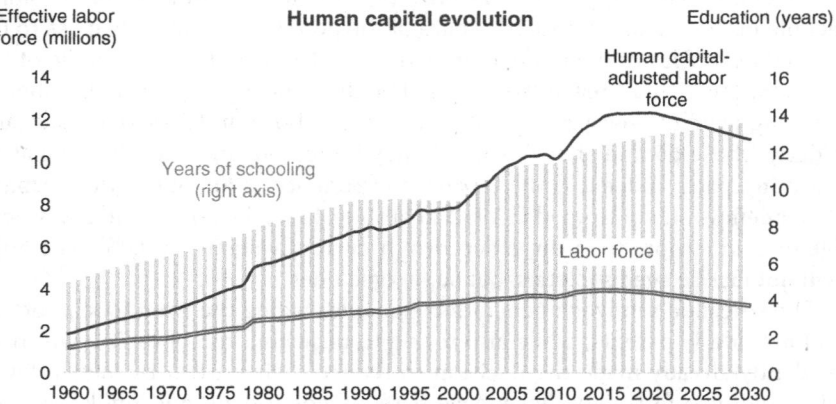

Figure 5.13 As a result of peaking in the size of the labor force around the 2020s, the contribution of Hong Kong's (as well as the other NIEs') effective labor force to economic growth in the decades ahead will not only be negligible, but could even be negative.

longer?), but could spell disaster for fiscal sustainability. Aged populations not only require greater medical attention and intervention—thereby drawing more on the national healthcare budget—but also dissave, which means drawing down on public pensions. There will be some offsetting effect from how low fertility allows reduced educational spending, but the effects would be modest in comparison. Altogether, fiscal sustainability will become a greater problem for the NIEs as they head into the future (Figure 5.14).

Yet NIEs can harness their greater exposure to an aging world by seizing opportunities in the silver economy, which will be present not just in Asia, but in the Western world as well. New enabling technologies as well as services tailored to the elderly will need to be provided, and there is little reason why these cannot emerge from the NIEs.

The fear that deglobalization will doom open economies such as Hong Kong and Singapore can likewise be channeled toward reinvention and a search for continued relevance. The networks of business, trade, and capital,[77] developed over centuries, remain present. There may be a need to shift toward a regional (rather than explicitly global) orientation, and a redoubling of efforts to boost productivity, but little about future economic prospects are set in stone. The Dragons have, after all, defied expectations more than once in their past.

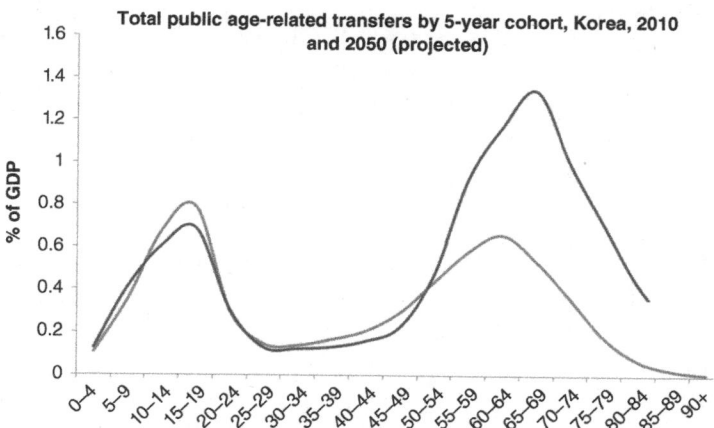

Figure 5.14 Like the rest of the NIEs, low fertility rates will relieve some of the fiscal pressure for public educational expenditures among the lower-age cohorts, but this will be more than offset by the need to substantially increase spending at the higher-age cohorts for public pensions as well as healthcare, especially as longevity increases alongside a rising share of the elderly in the population.

---

77 Meyer, D., *Hong Kong as a Global Metropolis* (Cambridge: Cambridge University Press 2000).

6

Southeast Asia: Can Underachieving Cubs Escape the Middle-Income Trap?

> *Southeast Asia has a real grip on me. From the very first time I went there, it was a fulfillment of my childhood fantasies of the way travel should be.*
> —*Anthony Bourdain (1956–2018), American celebrity chef and travel author*

> *You're talking about Rwanda or Bangladesh, or Cambodia, or the Philippines. They've got democracy . . . but have you got a civilized life to lead? People want economic development first and foremost. The leaders may talk something else. You take a poll of any people. What is it they want? . . . They want homes, medicine, jobs, schools.*
> —*Lee Kuan Yew (1923–2015), Former Prime Minister of Singapore*

Introduction

Close your eyes in the heart of any of the myriad capitals of developing Southeast Asia, and it's likely that you'll still be keenly aware of your surroundings, owing to the cacophony of vehicles honking, aromas by street-food vendors, and jostling by boisterous crowds. Whether it be Bangkok, Hanoi, Jakarta, or Manila, the ubiquity of dynamic (if occasionally chaotic) socioeconomic life is typical of populous middle-income nations, which encapsulate most of the region.

There is no singular way to describe the heterogenous economies of Southeast Asia, which have been at the crossroads of major Chinese, Indian, Muslim, and Western colonial powers throughout much of their history. These influences have indelibly rubbed off on the economic, political, and social fabric of each of the region's constituent nations, in varying ways.

Asian Economies: History, Institutions, and Structures, First Edition. Jamus Jerome Lim.
© 2024 John Wiley & Sons Ltd. Published 2024 by John Wiley & Sons Ltd.

We see it in the food, where Nusantara cuisine has long incorporated elements of Arab and Indian influence,[1] and French styles now mix happily with the earlier Chinese influence on Vietnamese food. We see it in the languages spoken, where Spanish loan-words pepper *Tagalog*, and English remains the language of law in Malaysia. We see it in the people, where—depending on the country—there are significant minority populations of Chinese and Indians among indigenous ethnic groups, along with admixtures that have evolved into subcultures, such as the Sino-Malay Peranakans or the Euro-Asian lineage of the Eurasians.

And, of course, we see it in the institutional structures that govern the economies of the region. The legacy of colonization—which was felt by all Southeast Asian countries, save Thailand—can be seen in the Christian schools that dot the educational landscape across the region, the European tradition in the design of political bodies such as parliament, and the formalism of bureaucratic strictures and legal frameworks.

Yet today, Southeast Asia—which had been consigned to play second fiddle, economically speaking, to the other nations that surround it—also stands on the precipice of a more promising (and prominent) future. This future matters enormously for the 680 million souls—comparable to the number of people in the European Union or Latin America—that inhabit the region, especially those residing on the islands of Indonesia, the most populous Muslim nation in the world.

Economic output for the Association of Southeast Asian Nations (ASEAN)—the political-economic grouping that includes virtually all countries in the region[2]—amounts to around $3.4 trillion, around that of India and the United Kingdom, but only a fraction of the European Union's $16.6 trillion. To date, the body remains more a convenient collective of economies rather than a cohesive economic unit, albeit one that has consistently pursued mutually beneficial trade and financial integration.

Moreover, there remains a wide disparity in incomes within ASEAN. Its poorest members—Myanmar and Cambodia—lay claim to production of not much more than $1,000 per head, while the upper-middle-income countries like Malaysia can boast incomes of an order of magnitude more. And, of course, Brunei and Singapore—the high-income economies in the list—are several times richer than even that.

---

1 The Indianization of the region occurred over a millennia, owing to Maritime Silk Road. The process began from around the 1st century CE, when Southeast Asia adopted Indian languages (Sanskrit), religions (Buddhism and Hinduism), governance and political-economic institutions and systems, and cultural elements such as arts and food.
2 Timor Leste was granted in-principle admission in 2022 (while remaining an observer), which only leaves Papua New Guinea—which has held observer status since 1976—as the only country in the geographic region that is not a member of the grouping. Sri Lanka—which may more appropriately be regarded as located in South, rather than Southeast, Asia—was initially invited to join ASEAN as a founding member in 1967, but it declined to do so (as it was pursuing a policy of nonalignment at the time).

Hence, while for many, Southeast Asia may still conjure up romantic images of a forgotten world—one portrayed in the very first travel guide published by the Lonely Planet franchise, *Southeast Asia on a Shoestring*[3]—the region has ineluctably moved on, and whether in economics, politics, or social affairs, is hardly satisfied with languishing in its past. So while we provide this all-important historical and institutional context to the region, we also stress the heterogeneity inherent in the modern economic structures, international economic relations, and future prospects of this incredibly diverse part of the world.

Economic Geography of Southeast Asia

Maritime Versus Mainland Southeast Asia

Most long-time observers of the region distinguish between "mainland" Southeast Asia—essentially, the south-eastern end of the Asian continent, ranging from the Mekong basin to the tip of the Malayan peninsula (and historically referred to as Indochina)—and "maritime" Southeast Asia, which encompasses the island nations (and traditionally called the Malay Archipelago).

But this taxonomic demarcation may oversimplify the harsh geographic realities of the region. Within the island complex of the maritime nations are further smaller archipelagos; Indonesia and the Philippines, in particular, are essentially seabound nations, comprised of island networks of their own. Indonesia, for example, has five main islands,[4] but there are some 18,000 smaller islands and islets (of which only around a third are inhabited). The Philippines has around 7,600 islands,[5] and even tiny Singapore's territory includes 64 offshore islands.

Moreover, even mainland Southeast Asian countries host strings of islands. Beyond the two states of Sabah and Sarawak—which comprise East Malaysia, and are located on a large island itself (Borneo)—Malaysia can count close to another 900 islands to its name, and Thailand has a little more than 1,400 off its two coasts.

The distributed nature of Southeast Asia means that the region's natives have always been seafaring folk, and heavily exposed to the (literal) winds of change. Every year, cold, high-pressure air originating from the Tibetan plateau enters from

---

3 Wheeler, T., *Southeast Asia on a Shoestring* (London: Lonely Planet, 1975). The book has remained in publication, and is now in its twentieth edition, with close to a thousand pages. The original was nicknamed the "Yellow Bible" by backpackers, for its iconic yellow cover and unparalleled travel advice.

4 These are, in order of geographic size, Sumatra, Java (the most densely populated), Kalimantan (which comprises around two-thirds of the island of Borneo), Sulawesi, and Papua (the western half of the island of New Guinea).

5 The three main island groups, from north to south, are Luzon, Visayas, and Mindanao.

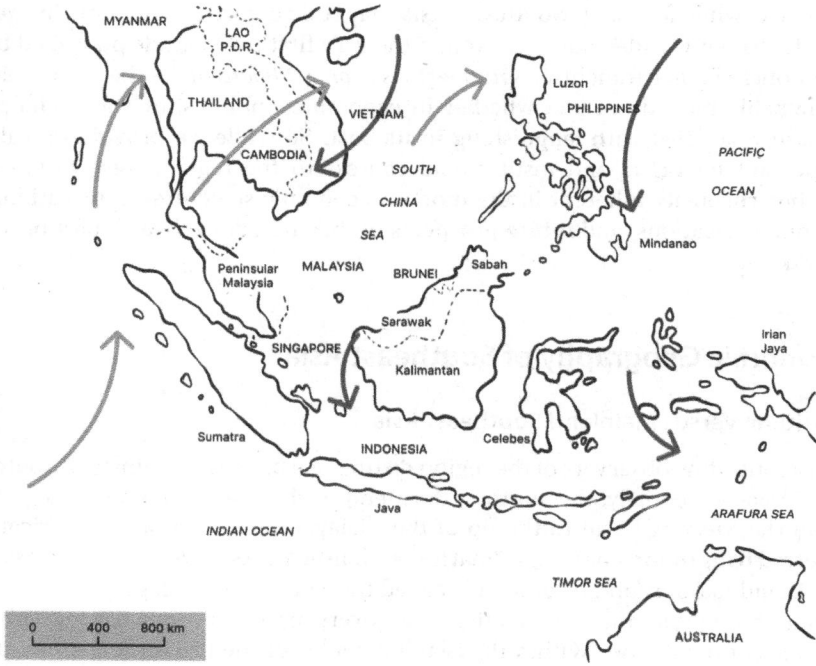

Figure 6.1 The annual monsoon cycle that envelopes Southeast Asia includes the northeast (or "winter") monsoon (downward arrows)—usually experienced between December and February—and southwest (or "summer") monsoon (upward arrows), which arrives between June and September. The monsoons not only bring natural irrigation, but have also influenced trade.

the northeast—in what is sometimes referred to as the "winter" monsoon, since it usually visits between December and February—as well as warm, moist air from the southwest—the "summer" monsoon, which arrives between June and September— both of which usher in a season of tropical storms and wet weather (Figure 6.1).[6]

These storms provide natural irrigation for primary production in the region, but their provenance goes beyond agriculture. Tradewinds have also historically brought trade and commerce from China and India, along with migrants, to both maritime and mainland Southeast Asia.

European Colonization Transferred Institutions, But to Different Degrees

Overlaid on the physical geography of Southeast Asia is a geopolitical one, reflecting the region's history of colonization. This is a heavily-colored map,

---

6 The Northeast monsoon manifests itself differently in northwest China (where it originates), being cold but dry there.

reflecting the fact that all but one country—Thailand[7]—was able to resist foreign domination.

The French controlled Cambodia, Laos, and Vietnam, the British held what is the modern countries of Myanmar, Brunei, Malaysia,[8] and Singapore, the Netherlands exercised nominal control over Indonesia, and even tiny Portugal held East Timor (Figure 6.2). The Philippines was colonized not once, but twice; first by the Spanish in the 16th century, then by the United States at the tail end of the 19th.

Most Southeast Asian nations were deemed extractive, rather than settlement, colonies. Hence, the colonial footprint was often comparatively

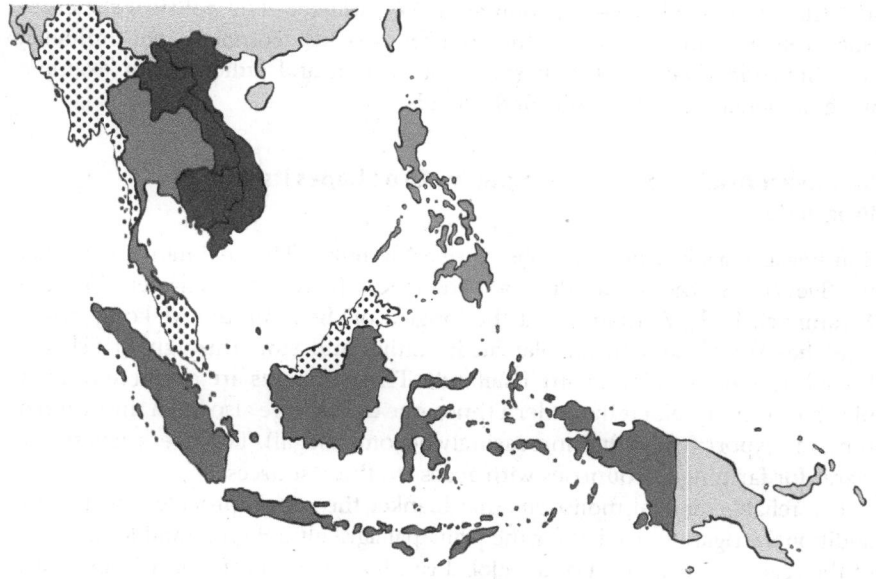

Figure 6.2 With the exception of Thailand, all of Southeast Asia has once been colonized. Mainland Indochina was split into British (dotted) and French (dark shaded) areas of control; the British also held what would become West and East Malaysia and Brunei. Maritime Southeast Asia fell under American, Spanish, Portuguese, and Dutch influence.

---

7 Siam was never brought under official European colonial domination, in part because of a compromise between the British and French to retain the area as a neutral buffer zone, and strategic diplomacy on the part of the contemporary Thai monarchs, Mongkut and his successor, Chulalongkorn. This did not mean that colonial powers exercised no influence on the kingdom. The Bowring Treaty, signed by Mongkut in 1855, granted extraterritorial rights to British subjects as well as the right to landownership in Siam, while the Franco-Siamese Treaty, signed by Chulalongkorn in 1893, ceded territory to the French (essentially the vassal state of Laos), in exchange for recognition of Siam's territorial integrity.

8 Parts of Malaysia were colonized earlier by other powers. Malacca first fell to Portuguese rule in 1511, before coming under the Dutch in 1641. In 1825, it was ceded to the British, and enfolded into British Malaya as part of the Straits Settlements.

light—even if it might have been far from gentle—insofar as the transfer of technology and institutions were concerned.

Still, the extent to which the colonial powers left a legacy would depend on the country and institution in question. Certain cities saw a greater establishment of missionary schools, some of which (perhaps by dint of their vintage) have grown to become among the better educational institutions. This was certainly the case for the University of Indonesia—originally founded to train doctors and public administrators in the Dutch East Indies—as well as the University of Santo Tomas, the oldest tertiary institution in Southeast Asia.

British legal and political traditions were often more wholly transferred, which is why Brunei, Malaysia, and Singapore follow a common law system, and the latter two have even adopted a Westminster-style political structure. But even in countries where the transfer was less complete, the influence remained indelible; the Indonesian legal system and judiciary, for example, were modeled on those of the Netherlands.

Southeast Asia's Economic Geography Also Shapes Its Primary Production

Southeast Asia has no shortage of river systems. The mainland is drained by five rivers: the Chao Phraya (Thailand), Irrawaddy, Salween (both in Myanmar), Red (Vietnam), and the longest of them all, the Mekong (which stretches from the Tibetan plateau in China and runs through British and French Indochina, along with Thailand). These systems are a source of complex biodiversity, albeit in modern times, the deltas have also been the origin of sand for export (which has increasingly become illegal). The rivers also supply water for farming in countries with access to these sources.

The reliable, annual monsoons that blanket the region provide much of the additional irrigation needed for the principal agricultural crop (and food staple) of the region: rice. A third of the global rice harvest is consumed within Southeast Asia, and Southeast Asian countries comprise half of the world's top 10 rice producers (after China and India, Indonesia is third, while Vietnam, Thailand, Myanmar, and the Philippines occupy the fifth through eighth spots, respectively).

Rice plants are cultivated in principally two ways: upland rice—grown in higher elevations and typically on the mainland—or wet rice (often referred to a *sawah* irrigation), which is grown in flooded, bunded fields, frequently on hillside terraces (Figure 6.3). Beyond rice and vegetables, the region's agriculture includes notable cash crops, such as cocoa, coffee,[9] palm oil, and rubber. For many of these crops, the region dominates global production. For example,

---

9 Most coffee grown in the region had historically been of the *robusta* varietal, and that is the type traditionally consumed by locals. Recent efforts to move up the value chain have also resulted in the growing of *arabica* beans, principally in Indonesia and Vietnam. The region also produces small amounts of *excelsa* and *liberica*.

Figure 6.3 Rice cultivation in Southeast Asia has frequently employed wet, or *sawah*, irrigation techniques, such as this terraced hillside in Bali, Indonesia. On the mainland, upland rice cultivation is also possible.
Source: Glen Scarborough / Flickr / CC BY SA 2.0.

Indonesia and Vietnam are among the world's top five coffee-growing nations, and—together with Thailand—are also the largest rubber producers. Nearly 85% of all palm oil originates from Indonesia and Malaysia, and virtually all Southeast Asian nations also export forestry products (although none more so than Indonesia and Myanmar).

The bounty is, unsurprisingly, not limited to what is grown on land. The region has long had a relationship with the sea—fishing and shrimping have historically been an integral part of the local diet, livelihood, and trade—although there are increasing risks of overexploitation, with no commercially viable marine organism left untouched, and no new fisheries left to be discovered.[10] Today, while fishing and fisheries comprise only a token amount of the economic output of most Southeast Asian nations, they remain important for many of them. Vietnam is the third-largest exporter of seafood (much of it via aquaculture), and Indonesia, Malaysia, the Philippines, and Thailand all sustain globally relevant fishing industries.

The region's natural wealth also extends into the ground. Indonesia is a major exporter of copper, cobalt, and nickel—key components of modern clean

---

10 Butcher, J., *The Closing of the Frontier: A History of the Marine Fisheries of Southeast Asia, c.1850–2000* (Singapore: Institute of Southeast Asian Studies, 2004).

energy technology—while Malaysian tin mining has a long and storied history, with the country being the world's largest producer in the late 19th century. Brunei's economy (and wealth) are almost entirely due to the exploitation of its vast reserves of oil and gas.

Economic History of Southeast Asia

Despite Broad Economic Independence, Southeast Asia Has Historically Remained Open

Due to its geography, Southeast Asia was, until the 1500s, largely a collection of individual settlements or city-states, operating mostly in economic isolation from each other. Societies were agrarian—centered on the cultivation of millet and rice—and supplemented farming with fishing. The focus was mainly on sustenance, with some excess being subject to trade.

The non-emergence of a large, unified state did not mean the absence of smaller kingdoms and principalities. Some of these came to exercise an expanded sphere of influence. On the mainland, Indochinese polities—the Pyu in Burma, Khmer in Cambodia, Ayutthaya in Thailand, and Văn Lang in Vietnam, for example—established themselves around various river valleys, and some remained in power for centuries (albeit not always contemporaneously). The archipelagos instead saw various Austronesian[11] thalassocracies—including larger empires such as the Srivijaya and Majapahit, smaller kingdoms like the Sunda and Mataram, and merchant sultanates of Aceh and Malacca, among others[12]—become influential.

The overall economic independence during this earlier period of Southeast Asian history did not mean that the region was closed. Since globalization at the time was more polycentric in nature—with distinct but overlapping economic spheres, connected through the movement of goods and people—relationships born of this exposure were rife. Even prior to "discovery" by European explorers, Southeast Asia was, as early as the 4th century BCE, part of the so-called Maritime Silk Road, which spanned not just China, Southeast Asia, and India, but went as far as the Arabian peninsula, Africa, and Europe.[13] Archeological

---

11 The Austronesians are a large group of people that may be regarded as the indigenous populations of Southeast Asia, together with Taiwan and the Pacific Islands (Melanesia, Micronesia, and Polynesia). The Austronesian language family also includes the languages spoken by coastal New Guinea and Madagascar, along with ethnic minorities in Indochina.
12 These were often heavily influenced by Arab and Indian culture—especially Buddhism, Hinduism, and Islam—and in a number of cases (such as, which were Hindu-Buddhic) resulted in syncretistic traditions.
13 Kwa, C.G., "The Idea of a Maritime Silk Road: History of an Idea," in V. Sakhuka and J. Chan (Eds.), *China's Maritime Silk Road and Asia* (New Delhi: Vij Books, 2016), pp. 99–110.

evidence strongly points to how Southeast Asia's oldest civilization—located at the Bujang Valley (in Kedah state in today's Malaysia)—had been engaged extensively in entrepôt trade since the 1st century BCE, which brought great prosperity to that kingdom.[14] By the early modern period—between 1500 and 1830—trade had become commonplace, facilitated by how the region lay naturally at the meeting point of the monsoon winds that blew between the Indian Ocean and the South China Sea.

Unsurprisingly, this meant that Southeast Asia came to be defined relative to others: as the East Indies (by the Occident), or *Nanyang* (南洋, literally "Southern Ocean", by China), or *Suvarnabhumi* (literally, "Golden Lands" by India[15]). But this has not been unidirectional; the people of Nusantara had frequently looked abroad, both for their sense of place in the world, as well as to imbibe new ideas and technologies, especially from the two dominant powers in their near abroad, China and India.

This is evidenced by how many Nusantara legends, myths, and stories prominently featured elements that reflected a deep desire to strengthen transcultural linkages.[16] Some tell of how the native princess would take a visiting prince from abroad as her partner, or how a local hero would travel in search of knowledge and wealth, returning with honor to wed the community's most beautiful woman, who cherishes such worldly experiences.

Such international exchanges generally reflected the comparative advantages at the time. Southeast Asia would export forestry products (wood, resins, rattans), along with seafood (especially valued by China), and herbs and spices (especially valued by India, and later by the West). In exchange, they would receive ceramics and textiles.

Hence, well before the arrival of European powers on the scene, the economies of Southeast Asia were already functionally open economies (even if said openness was not intensive), and thus well-positioned for what would become the dominant export-oriented development strategy of the region. Moreover, the close commercial ties would be the precursor of the vertically-integrated production systems that would characterize the East Asian production network.

Colonization Altered the Development Trajectories of Southeast Asian Countries

Before European intervention, the major Asian powers exercised some degree of influence over the Southeast Asian states. Between 111 BCE and 938 CE,

---

14 Murphy, S., "Revisiting the Bujang Valley: A Southeast Asian Entrepôt Complex on the Maritime Trade Route," *Journal of the Royal Asiatic Society* 28(2) (2018): 355–389.
15 Some have also referred to maritime Southeast Asia—or the islands within the Malay archipelago—as Insulindia, although this terminology is somewhat archaic.
16 Andaya, B. and L. Andaya, *A History of Early Modern Southeast Asia, 1400–1830* (Cambridge: Cambridge University Press, 2015).

northern Vietnam was effectively a vassal state of various Chinese dynasties, and many other polities in the region were at least tributary states to China[17] (indeed, part of the motivation for Admiral Zheng He's voyages in the 15th century was to collect tribute). The Indian Chola dynasty (200–1279 CE) also invaded and conquered the Srivijaya early in the 11th century. But these over-lordships either afforded substantial autonomy or were fleeting, and did not drastically alter the institutions or structures of the settlements in question.

Western colonizers first showed up in the East Indies in the 16th century, in search of the proverbial "God, Gold, and Glory" (although not necessarily and not in fact usually—in that order). This disrupted the region's relative economic homogeneity, and led each country on their own distinct development path, for the better part of two centuries.

The initial incursions by Europeans were confined to small territories. The Portuguese conquered Malacca (in modern Malaysia) and the spice islands of the Moluccas (modern Indonesia), but mainly operated out of the port cities, as their goal was to control the sea lanes plied by the spice trade. By the time the Dutch and the Spaniards arrived—around a century later—the colonizers began to impose an ever-larger footprint, gradually evolving from various chartered exploration and trading companies[18] toward centralized crown control via colonial offices. Thus began the divergence in economic fortunes of countries within the region, as different approaches and priorities came to the fore.

The colonial period commenced around the mid-1800s, and persisted through till the middle of the 20th century. This phase also saw a greater institutionalization of various economic functions: an organized bureaucracy, large-scale plantation agriculture, a more monetized trading economy (commerce had, hitherto, relied far more on barter; monetary systems improved the efficiency of exchange and enabled the rise of cash crops), and mission-based schools.

Post-Independence Economic Policy Choices

In the aftermath of World War II, nationalist movements sprang up across Southeast Asia. Some of this was inevitable; the war had revealed that one of the key implicit bargains between colonizers and their subjects—control in exchange for development and protection—did not hold water (it was difficult to believe, for instance, that Singapore truly represented the "Gibraltar of the

---

17 These included entities located in modern-day Brunei, Cambodia, Malaysia, the Philippines, and Thailand.
18 These were usually named various flavors of "East Indian Company," such as the British East Indian Company, the *Verenigde Oostindische Compagnie*, the *Compagnie Française pour le Commerce des Indes Orientales*, and the *Companhia da Índia Oriental* (the Dutch, French, and Portuguese equivalents, respectively).

East"—as touted by British Prime Minister Winston Churchill—when the battle for Singapore lasted all of a week).

The Dutch were the first to exit the region, in the late 1940s, and this was followed by the French in the 1950s, British in the 1960s, and Portugal—the final holdout—eventually relinquished Timor Leste in 1975. Nationalistic sentiments among Southeast Asian states varied, and their intensity depended, in part, on the idiosyncratic experiences each country had faced with colonization, as well as the degree to which Western institutional transfer had taken root among the population and elites.

Post-colonization occurred in tandem with a different, powerful force sweeping the globe. Marxist ideology readily filled the vacuum left behind by the departing Western powers. The defeat of the Americans in Vietnam seemed to reinforce the fears of the domino theory—the Cold War notion that democratic collapse in one country would shortly lead to communist takeovers in neighboring states, each falling like a series of dominos—but while French Indochina (Cambodia, Laos, and Vietnam) did ultimately succumb to communism, post-independence Burma went the (slightly more moderate) socialist route, and the tide was also stemmed elsewhere in the region (Figure 6.4).

Instead, the communist insurgency bolstered the dominant states in the rest of Southeast Asia, as they pursued state-led capitalism. Some economies—such as Malaysia and Thailand—briefly flirted with import-substituting industrialization, but virtually all economies in the region quickly moved to export orientation by the 1970s.

It is important to recognize that most Southeast Asian leaders were far more pragmatic than ideological when it came to development. Even in Vietnam, the so-called Vietcong (a portmanteau and abbreviation of *Viet Nam Cong San*, or Vietnamese Communists) were fighting not so much for communist principles, but for independence (first from the French, then the Americans). Far from ideology, it was more the practical policy choices of post-independence governments that would come to shape the contours of their development trajectories over the next half-century.

Figure 6.4 Domino theory held that the fall of Vietnam would eventually spread to the rest of Indochina, and eventually the rest of Asia. While it was true that the end of the Vietnam War was followed in quick succession by the rise of communist governments in Cambodia and Laos, Burma went the slightly more moderate route of socialism, and the insurgency failed to make headway in the rest of Southeast Asia.

Southeast Asian Development in Comparative Perspective

Elephants, Horses, and Tortoises in Economic Performance

When looking at the economic outcomes of Southeast Asian economies today, it is tempting to focus only on their average growth rate since independence, and infer that superlative economic growth is the major reason why economies like Singapore are prosperous today.

This is misleading, for several reasons. First, as mentioned in the Chapter 5 on the NIEs, Singapore started off from a superior initial position, being already among the upper end of the distribution of developing countries in the 1960s. Second, there are economies with a disastrous growth record—such as Brunei—which are still comparatively rich (at around $31,500, it boasts the second-highest per capita income in Southeast Asia, just shy of Japan and ahead of Hong Kong and Taiwan), by dint of the country's access to petroleum. And perhaps most importantly, other economies have been able to claim impressive growth outcomes over even a full decade. The average growth rates of the Philippines and transition economies in the 2010s were higher than that of the Lion City, and Malaysia in the 1970s and Thailand in the 1960s fared better than certain other decades in Singapore. And the award for the highest decadal growth belongs to Myanmar, at a blazingly fast average annual rate of more than 12% (Table 6.1).

Still, it has been the *consistent* growth of Singapore's economy, decade after decade, that has brought the economy to the heights that it stands at today. Indeed, such start-stop growth—which one may call growth spurts—is actually quite common, with all but the most advanced economies having undergone extremes in growth miracles and failures over substantial periods.[19]

It is also evident that the second wave of industrializers in Southeast Asia—the so-called "Asian Tigers"[20] of Indonesia, Malaysia, and Thailand—have earned that moniker through solid growth over the second half of the 20th century; certainly at least until the Asian financial crisis of 1997, and, for the Philippines, a belated catch-up in the new millennium.

As a result of these differing developmental journeys, observers of Southeast Asian economies broadly situate countries in one of three buckets:[21] a small group of (rich but slower-moving) "elephant" economies, comprising Brunei

---

19 Jones, B. and B. Olkem, "The Anatomy of Start-Stop Growth," *Review of Economics and Statistics* 90(3) (2008): 582–587.

20 To the extent that the original four NIEs are called "Tiger" economies, this next wave is then referred to as the "Tiger Cubs."

21 Lim, C.Y., *Southeast Asia: The Long Road Ahead*, 3rd ed. (Singapore: World Scientific, 2009).

Table 6.1 Decadal GDP growth for Southeast Asian economies, 1970–2020

	1961–1969	1970–1979	1980–1989	1990–1999	2000–2009	2010–2019	1961–2019
ASEAN-6							
Brunei		12.2	−2.4	2.1	1.4	0.5	**1.7**
Indonesia	3.5	7.2	5.8	4.3	5.1	5.4	**5.3**
Malaysia	6.5	8.2	5.9	7.2	4.8	5.4	**6.3**
The Philippines	5.1	5.7	2.1	2.8	4.5	6.4	**4.4**
Singapore	8.9	9.2	7.8	7.2	5.4	5.0	**7.2**
Thailand	7.8	7.5	7.3	5.2	4.3	3.6	**5.9**
Transition-4							
Cambodia				0.4	8.5	7.0	**6.0**
Laos			4.1	6.3	6.9	7.3	**6.4**
Myanmar	3.0	4.3	2.0	5.8	12.4	7.3	**5.9**
Vietnam			4.5	7.4	6.6	6.6	**6.5**
Observer							
Papua	6.4	3.9	1.4	4.3	2.8	5.3	**4.0**
Timor Leste					4.3	5.4	**4.9**

Source: Author's compilation, from World Bank (2023).
Notes: Values are simple averages of annual changes in real GDP, in %. For countries where data are only available from a given year onward, the mean was calculated based on available years. Brunei and Singapore are high-income economies, while the remainder emerging and developing.

and Singapore; a larger group of (dynamic and fast-growing) "horse" economies, which includes the next wave of industrializers, i.e. Indonesia, Malaysia, and Thailand, as well as (more recently) Vietnam; and a lagging tail of (poorer and usually slower-growth) "tortoise" economies, such as Laos, Myanmar, and Timor Leste (Figure 6.5).

Yet even within each group, there are differences. Brunei has traditionally relied on oil wealth to drive development, and while the country did run neck-and-neck with Singapore through the 1980s and 1990s, decades of relatively slower growth has seen it fall behind. While the economy is still rich by any means—and affords its citizens many of the welfare privileges common to high-income states—the diversification of the economy has remained painfully slow.

Nor is an economy consigned forever to a bucket. Until the past two decades, Vietnam was a laggard, as was the Philippines until the 2010s. But improved

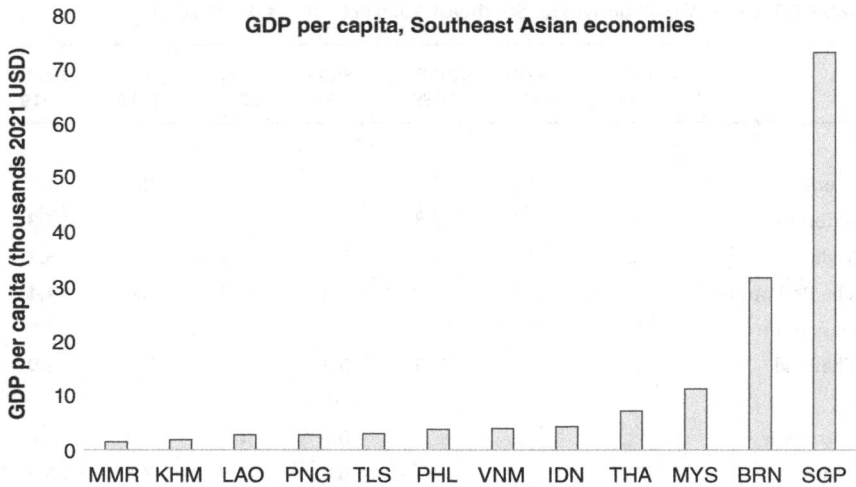

Figure 6.5 Based on their development journeys, Southeast Asian economies may be classified into groups on the basis of their current per capita income and growth rates; these include richer but decelerating "elephant" economies, more dynamic "horse" economies, and the poorer and slow-growth "tortoise" economies.

policy choices since then allowed growth to accelerate, which has in turn enabled them to join the ranks of the more dynamic economies of the region. And in the 2010s, it was the transition economies, such as Laos and Myanmar, that led the growth tables, albeit from a much lower base in terms of output.

Structural Transformation in the Southeast Asian Nations Follows the Standard Development Script

Over the course of the last half-century, the developing economies of Southeast Asia have closely followed the script for structural transformation common to developing nations around the world (Figure 6.6). To reiterate: the process kicks off by channeling saving (whether domestic or foreign) toward capital accumulation in the manufacturing sector, where higher wages then instigate a shift of the large (but underemployed) agricultural workforce toward the industrial production, which then expands to become an ever-larger share of the economy.[22] Wages remain low

---

22 To sustain agricultural production, there is also a sometimes a need for agricultural output to expand, to ensure food security. While smaller countries have been able to meet this with food imports, larger ones frequently need to simultaneously engage in land reform and support a green revolution, to improve agricultural yield. See Studwell, J., *How Asia Works: Success and Failure in the World's Most Dynamic Region* (London: Profile Books, 2013).

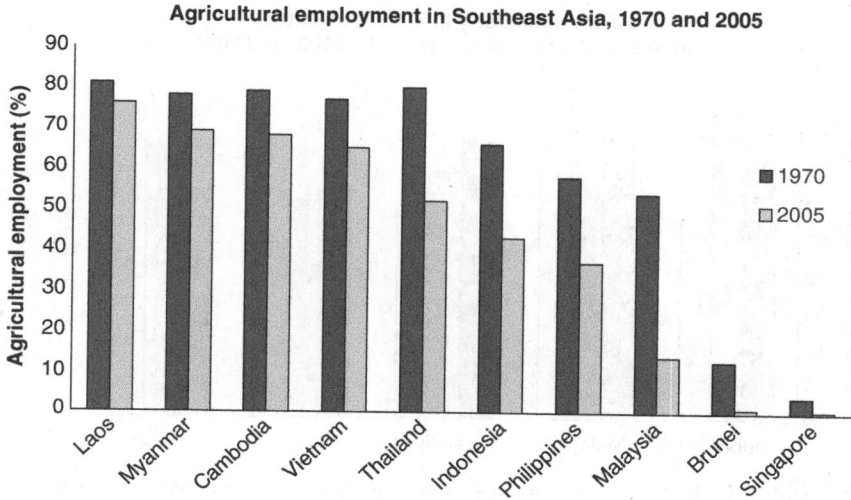

Figure 6.6 Employment in agriculture has fallen across Southeast Asian nations over time as they have developed, following the usual development pattern where excess labor in the primary sector is absorbed by manufacturing.

so long as there is still a steady inflow of labor from the countryside, before the exhaustion of this surplus manpower then prompts a steady rise in wages, which lowers the economy's international competitiveness, requiring a move up the value-added chain. In the meantime, rising incomes enable the expansion of the services sector, which grows to dominate the economy. Deindustrialization eventually stabilizes, and the country is now a post-industrial nation.

Since the 1970s, Southeast Asia has hewed to this model, albeit at a speed of transition that has varied across different economies. Primary-sector employment is currently virtually nonexistent in high-income Brunei and Singapore. Its share has also dropped sharply in the remaining ASEAN-6 economies—to below a third—from more than half around the time of independence. It is only in the Transition-4 economies—especially Laos, but also to some extent, Myanmar—where agriculture remains more of a mainstay, and still accounts for the majority (or close to the majority) of employed workers.

As agricultural labor has shifted toward manufacturing, the share of the economy devoted to industrial production has expanded in tandem. While the relationship is far from one-for-one, manufacturing output ramped up between the 1970s and 1990s, and only in the 2020s has this started to retreat within the ASEAN-6. Taking on the mantle has been the Transition-4 countries, where industrialization has become an ever-more significant part of production (Figure 6.7).

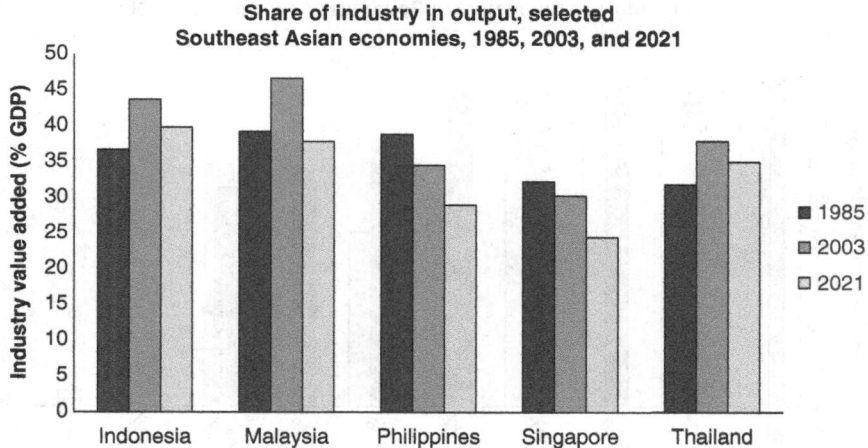

Figure 6.7 The middle-income economies have steadily increased the share of industry in GDP over time, while higher-income countries have slowly begun the process of deindustrialization.

The Potential of Physical and Human Capital Accumulation

In advanced economies, the distribution of talent at different levels of education tends to resemble a trapezoid: wide at the bottom due to universal or near-universal primary schooling, which tapers only slightly at the secondary level as most in the primary cohort go on to secondary education. It remains fairly broad at the top, as affordable (often public) tertiary education and quality high schools ensure that many youth take up tertiary studies.

In contrast, the talent structure of many developing countries is closer to that of a pyramid: wide at the bottom, but quickly narrowing near the top, such that those who go on to higher education remain a small fraction of each birth cohort. Even as public spending has been heavily devoted toward expanding primary schooling infrastructure and enrollment—for many such countries, education captures the largest component of government expenditure—the same does not hold at higher levels, due to a combination of resource constraints (on the supply side) and the high opportunity costs faced by poorer households in keeping their children in school (which diminishes demand).

As a result, human resource development is low, and high-skilled talent remains scarce. This is both a blessing and a curse. While one may fret about the enormity of the task in delivering education and training to large masses of the populace—along with the stresses of creating sufficient jobs to absorb new entrants to the workforce—it also means that these nations worry less about demographic decline due to a shrinking working-age population, and opportunities to channel workers toward economically-productive endeavors abound. Done well, rapid increases in schooling can yield the cherished "demographic dividend" of human capital contribution that the NIEs previously harvested (Figure 6.8).

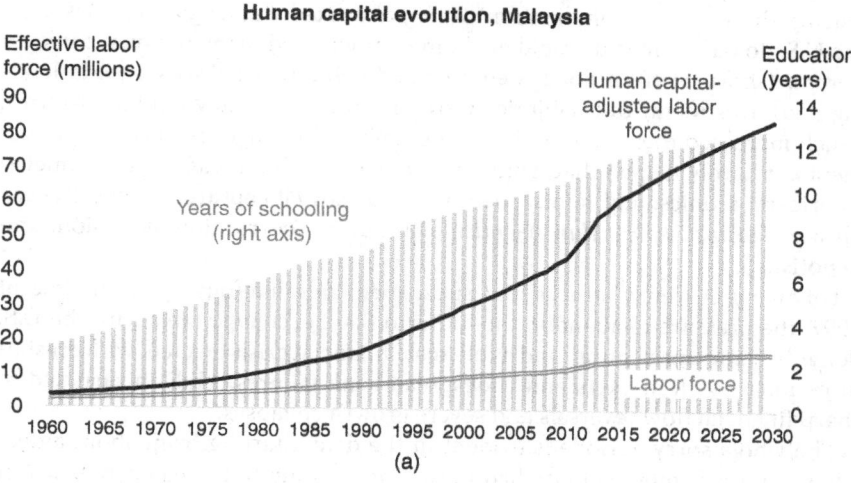

(a)

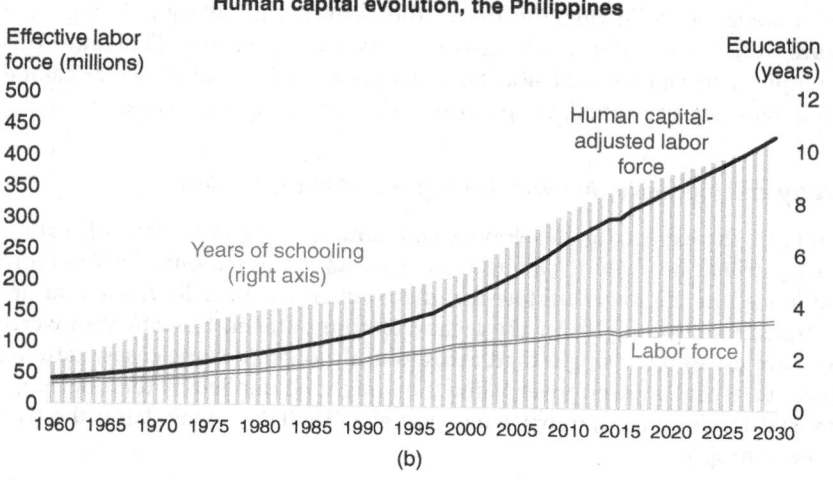

(b)

Figure 6.8 A major advantage possessed by the developing economies of Southeast Asia is that, should educational opportunities be seized, the increase in human capital accumulation will provide an important contributor to economic growth, unlike more advanced NIEs that will face a headwind from demographic decline. Both (a) Malaysia and (b) the Philippines illustrate this possibility.

The same can be said for physical capital expansion, but the road here has been far from smooth. While younger populations do indeed tend to save more—and regional financial institutions have, bolstered by financial repression, been able to channel this surplus saving into investment—the process has been more volatile (as investment is wont to be).

This is amply evident in the aftermath of the 1997/98 Asian financial crisis. During the runup, a combination of *de facto* fixed exchange rates (vis-à-vis the U.S. dollar), alongside rapid economic growth, led many regional banks to borrow (short-term) in dollar-denominated debt. This led to surges in lending and investment. But liabilities were in foreign currency (and long-term), which increased these economies' vulnerability to changes in currency movements. It hardly helped that, with liquidity awash, credit was often channeled to bribers, cronies, and family members; this is well captured by the *Bahasa* phrase "*korupsi, kolisi, dan nepotisme*" (literally, "corruption, collusion, and nepotism").

Following currency attacks and subsequent devaluations in the middle of 1997, the pressure to abandon the hitherto fixed exchange rates with the U.S. dollar became unrelenting, and a full-scale financial crisis ensued, with crashes in regional stock markets and widespread bank failures. This, in turn, led to sharp financial flow reversals and severe growth collapses.

The whole sorry episode is evident in the data. Starting from about a decade prior, investment activity had picked up, leading to a greater intensity of capital usage in the production process (as seen in rising capital-output ratios). But immediately following the crisis, the deployment of capital stagnated (Figure 6.9).[23] For some countries—such as Indonesia and Thailand—this interruption in capital intensification has yet to fully recover; while capital accumulation has resumed, the process of deepening appears to have stalled.

Poverty and Inequality Are Widely Distributed in the Region

As one might expect for developing economies, Southeast Asia still exhibits a nontrivial headcount of poverty across its many nations. This is more pronounced in the lower-middle-income countries, especially those that are still transitioning away from the legacy of communism. Elsewhere, poverty rates have crossed the single-digit threshold, although in some cases, national choices to accept a lower poverty line than might be implied by their development status—Indonesia, in particular, but also Thailand—may flatter the true degree of progress.

---

23 Capital intensity spiked in 1997/98, but this blip in the measure is a statistical artifact; the sharp decline in output (the denominator) is not accompanied by a concomitant drop in capital (since the numerator is a stock, and hence only erodes at the rate of depreciation).

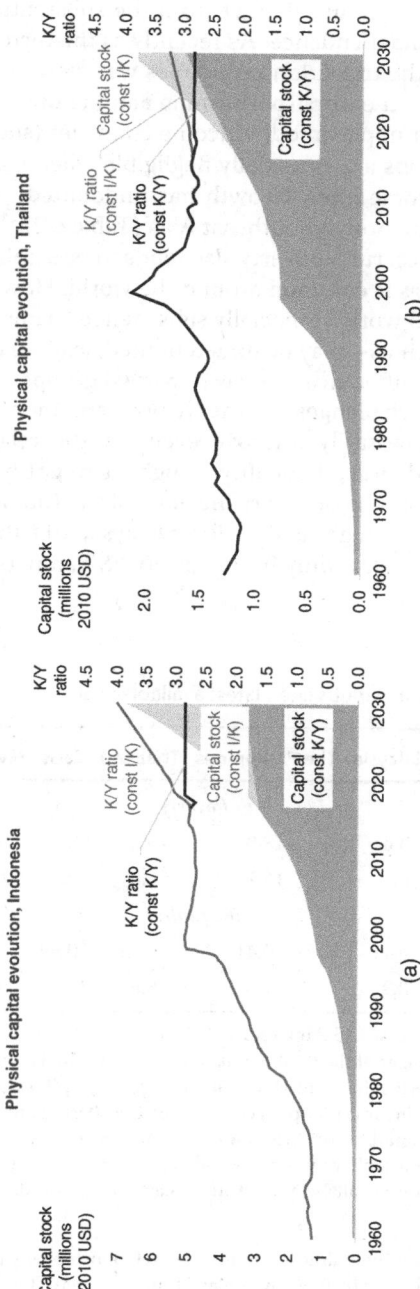

Figure 6.9 The Asian financial crisis led to an interruption in capital accumulation in many Southeast Asian economies, from which the region has yet to fully recover. In some instances, capital intensification—the ratio of capital to output in the economy—appears to have stalled in the two decades hence, as appears to be the case for (a) Indonesia and (b) Thailand.

Even so, these caveats should not detract from the substantial gains made by these economies since independence. As recently as the turn of the millennium, the poverty rate in the transition economies was close to a third of the population, whereas even in the worst-performing nation now (Myanmar), it is closer to a quarter. And for upper-middle-income countries (such as Malaysia and Thailand), poverty ratios are essentially negligible when computed using low and lower-middle-income lines. Growth has undoubtedly been a major contributor to poverty reduction in Southeast Asia (Table 6.2).[24]

In many of these countries, rural poverty also tends to be significantly higher than urban poverty rates, as is common around the world. However, it should also be noted that informal work—especially subsistence farming that is more pervasive in nonurban settings—may be undercounted, leading to a somewhat exaggerated picture of the differences between the two groups.

In contrast, inequality challenges in the region are more pronounced, and this issue doesn't necessarily improve even for the relatively higher-income economies. By and large, inequality is high, as might be expected for economies that appear to still be on the rising edge of the Kuznets curve. The Gini coefficient comes to as high as 0.41 for Malaysia and the Philippines, and even for the most equal economy in the group—Myanmar—the measure exceeds 0.3.

Table 6.2 Incidence of poverty at various lines, latest available year

	Indonesia	Malaysia	The Philippines	Thailand	Laos	Myanmar	Vietnam
			Poverty				
Income group	23.5	3.4	18.3	13.2	32.5	19.6	5.3
National	9.8	5.6	16.7	6.8	18.3	24.8	6.7
			Inequality				
Gini	0.38	0.41	0.41	0.35	0.39	0.31	0.37
S80/S20	6.5	8.3	7.9	5.6	6.6	4.5	6.7

Source: Author's compilation, from World Bank (2023).
Notes: Poverty ratios are percentages of the total population, while the Gini is an index ranging from 0 (perfect equality) to 1 (perfect inequality). Income-group poverty lines correspond to the lines for the respective country's income group, as classified by the World Bank, in 2021; these are measured in PPP terms, and amount to $2.15 (low-income), $3.65 (lower-middle), $6.85 (upper-middle) a day. National lines differ by country and depend on the specific threshold set by the country. Data are from the latest available year, from at least 2017 onward.

---

24 This argument—that there is a tight (almost one-for-one) relationship between growth and poverty reduction, was first made convincingly by Dollar, D. and A. Kraay, "Growth Is Good for the Poor," *Journal of Economic Growth* 7 (2002): 195–225.

Moreover, Gini indexes alone may mask more troublesome realities. Given Myanmar's extensive poverty, the comparatively lower Gini recorded there may simply be a function of households being equally poor, rather than shining examples of inclusive growth. For Malaysia, the share of income captured by the top quintile is far larger than that of the lowest, compared to other Southeast Asian countries with similar coefficients (such as Indonesia or Laos).

Crazy Rich Southeast Asians: Plutocrats and Family Business Empires

Many Southeast Asian conglomerates—both publicly-listed as well as privately-held—are controlled by a single family. While this structure harkens to the *chaebol* in South Korea or the *zaibatsu* in Japan, they differ in key aspects. Many emerged when enterprising immigrant founders—often originating from China or India—acculturated quickly, ingratiated themselves to local Malay elites and colonizers, and seized opportunities to build their domestic firms.[25] Many have now expanded abroad, creating family business empires.

While these founders were typically well-integrated into their home societies—in terms of language, culture, and society—like so many trading coalitions across history, they were able to exploit networks vis-à-vis their origin countries in the process of building up their business empires.[26] Indeed, the so-called "bamboo network" (竹网, *zhú wǎng*) of ethnic Chinese businessmen—and they are almost invariably men—exemplify how such social connections have been central to the rise and continued dominance business groups in Southeast Asia.

Today, such conglomerates are well established in their home economies. In Southeast Asia, they include household names such as Salim and Sinar Mas (Indonesia), Berjaya and Genting (Malaysia), KBZ and KT (Myanmar), Ayala, SM, and LT (the Philippines), Central and Charoen Pokphand (Thailand), along with Hoan Cau (Vietnam) (not to mention similar groups in Singapore, as well as Hong Kong, Macau, and Taiwan).

Notwithstanding their present success, the main challenge facing such groups has been managing succession. Many are already run by second-generation scions—who to their credit have often been capable stewards—but the entry of the third generation into the fold has not always been secured.

---

25 Studwell, J., *Asian Godfathers: Money and Power in Hong Kong and Southeast Asia* (London: Profile Books, 2010).

26 Such coalitions, by exploiting a multilateral punishment strategy, can enable trust in the absence of other formal contractual mechanisms to resolve commitment problems in trading relationships. For a detailed exposition, see Greif, A., "Contract Enforceability and Economic Institutions in Early Trade: The Maghribi Traders' Coalition," *American Economic Review* 83(3) (1993): 525–548. Social networks are reviewed more generally in Rauch, J., "Business and Social Networks in International Trade," *Journal of Economic Literature* 39(4) (2001): 1177–1203.

It is not unusual for these grandchildren of the original patriarch or matriarch to exhibit a distinct lack of enthusiasm for leading the business, even if they were able to resolve inter-family feuds over priority and rights. While the common aphorism of how wealth may not last beyond three generations may ring true to the casual observer,[27] it remains to be seen if this will doom the future vibrancy of economic enterprise in the region. At the very least, the entrenchment of such large business groups in their home economies means that weak corporate governance *within* the firm might eventually spill over into macroeconomic consequences, ranging from diminished innovation to poor economywide resource allocation, to dampened growth.[28]

Growth in Spite of Governance Challenges, But for How Much Longer?

Ensuring institutional quality is a perennial issue in emerging nations, and Southeast Asia is not much different in that respect. The region, understandably, lags behind high-income standards on a host of governance indicators, especially when it comes to democratic development. Yet its economies appear to have done well *despite* their challenges with governance.

This can be seen in a few ways. One is by examining the quality of institutions in the region vis-à-vis other parts of the developing world. For instance, while much of Southeast Asia ranks lower in the control of corruption as compared to Eastern Europe, it has chalked up much faster rates of economic growth over a comparable period.

Alternatively, notice how most of the larger Southeast Asian nations tend to exhibit lower levels of per capita income than the major emerging markets of Latin America, yet regulatory quality in the typical regional economy turns out to be at least as advanced.

These observations aside, it is probably worth recognizing that governance challenges are likely to be more and more pressing in the years ahead. There is a certain degree of endogeneity to this, of course—countries that attain higher levels of income tend to also raise their governance levels—but the sort of bottom-up, petty corruption that may have been a mild inconvenience to economic performance appears to be waning, and the region's economies

---

27 The notion that wealth will dissipate in three generations has been subject to academic scrutiny, and the conclusions are mixed. The belief, however, remains widely toted, especially as received wisdom (like the Chinese proverb, 富不过三代, literally, "wealth does not cross three generations"). The claim that wealth transitions face a 70% failure rate was made by R. Williams and V. Preisser, *Preparing Heirs: Five Steps to a Successful Transition of Family Wealth and Values* (Brandon, OR: Robert Reed, 2010). See Baron, J. and R. Lachenauer, "Do Most Family Businesses Really Fail by the Third Generation?" *Harvard Business Review*, July 19, 2021, for the contrary view.

28 Morck, R., D. Wolfenzon, and B. Yeung, "Corporate Governance, Economic Entrenchment, and Growth," *Journal of Economic Literature* 43(3) (2005): 655–720.

will need to face up to the more problematic issue of top-down weaknesses in governance—especially at the level of the bureaucratic and political elite—which could prove to be a greater impediment to future growth (Figure 6.10).

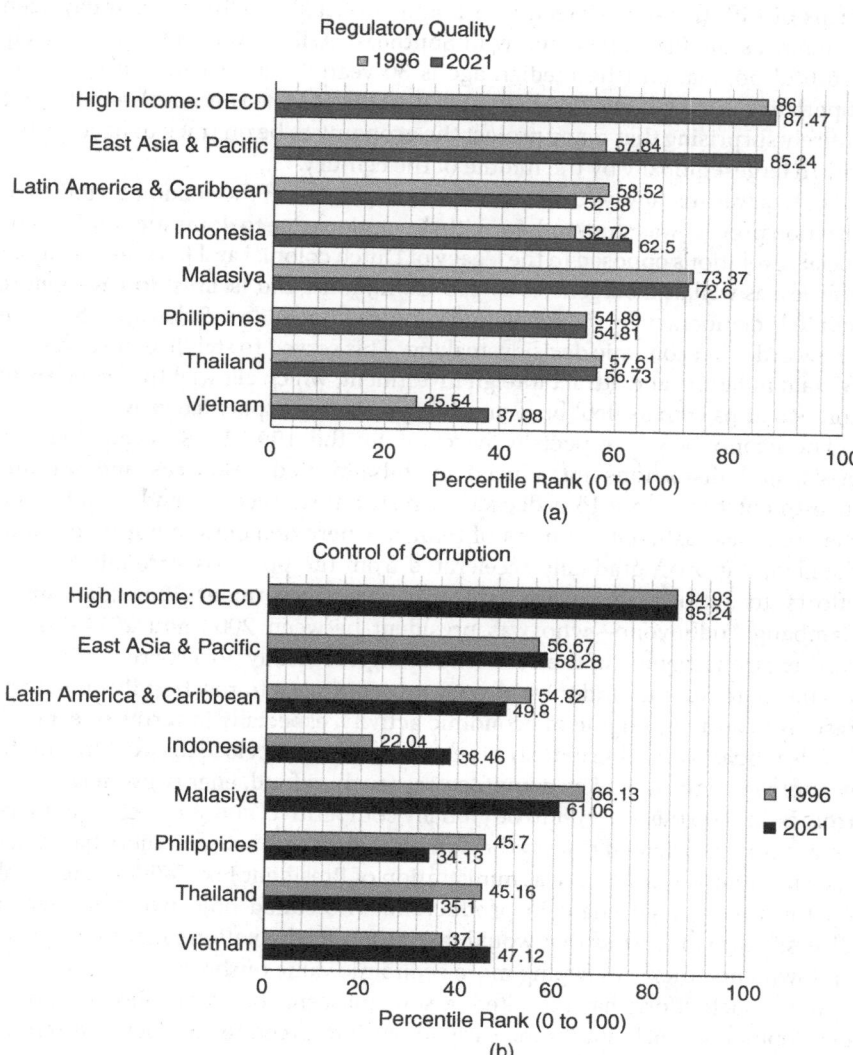

Figure 6.10 The strength of governance in developing Southeast Asia tends to lag that of advanced economies, but many countries do outperform their developing-country counterparts at a comparable income level, and economic growth does not appear to have been excessively hampered by shortfalls in institutional quality. This is exemplified by metrics such as (a) regulatory quality or (b) control of corruption.

The Modern Economies of Southeast Asia

Indonesia as the Next Regional Economic Powerhouse

As the largest economy in Southeast Asia—and seventh largest globally in terms of PPP (it ranks sixteenth in nominal terms)—Indonesia is today seen by many as the flagship economy in Southeast Asia. Layer on top a relatively youthful population (the median age is 30 years) and a steady—if not quite superlative—growth rate (averaging 5% over the past two decades), and it is not entirely surprising that many project the economy to be on track to become the fourth largest globally by the middle of the century.

Yet this was not always the case. After independence, the economy's industrialization process was stop-and-go, with disruptions due to domestic conflict—by social revolutions opposed to the legacy of Dutch colonial and Japanese occupier policies, as well as insurgencies by pro-Communist and Islamist forces—before "guided" democracy by the revolutionary-turned-president Sukarno ushered in a new order in economic decision-making. This served to stabilize the currency, contain inflation, and attract foreign investment, which allowed the economy to come to grips with its debt burden, while promoting export-led growth.

The economy was especially hard hit by the 1997/1998 Asian financial crisis, and distortions introduced by misallocated resources and forgone investment took close to a decade to restructure, recover, and rebuild. But the crisis also ushered in an era of reform, where democratic norms consolidated, and growth gradually accelerated from the post-crisis trough. Further efforts to rationalize government fiscal balances under President Susilo Bambang Yodhoyono—who was president between 2004 and 2014—saw a further strengthening of the economy, alongside steady poverty reduction.

The contemporary Indonesian economy continues to rely heavily on natural resources as a key engine of economic activity, especially in terms of exports. While it boasts a sizable industrial sector—amounting close to two-fifths of the economy—many of its key manufactures (such as food, energy products, electronics, and textiles) are yet to be globally competitive, and production in many areas remains oriented toward the domestic market. That said, there have been recent initiatives, led by the administration of President Joko Widodo, to climb up the value-added chain in production. The stated objective has been to diversify into industries that would take as inputs the nation's natural resource endowments, thereby keeping more economic value onshore.

While such efforts have resulted in some nascent (but promising) economic developments—including some early forays into green technology and renewable energy—traditional industry looks to retain its hold on economic activity over the medium term. With an estimated workforce of 120 million people—and one that is expanding at more than 2 million souls annually—such old-school manufacturing will likely remain an important absorber of the working-age population, and be an ongoing source of economic dynamism of the country.

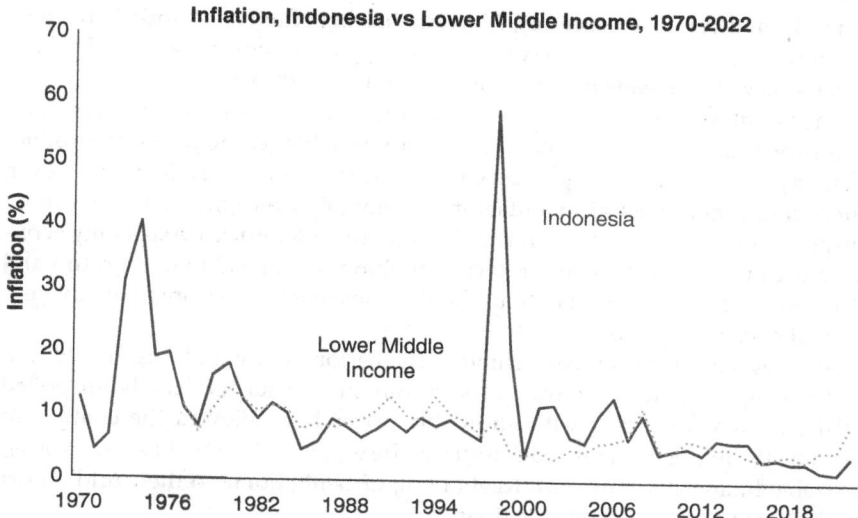

Figure 6.11 Inflation has been a recurrent bugbear for Indonesia. The economy went through a hyperinflationary episode between 1964 and 1967, and even in the years thereafter, there have been periods where inflation has clocked in as uncomfortably high.

The reservation is that modern Indonesia will simply be a repeat of its past, filled with disappointing performance and missed opportunities.[29]

A factor that has taken some of the wind out of the economy's sails has been inflation (Figure 6.11). The country has often struggled with the specter of rising prices. During the 1960s, there was a nasty hyperinflationary episode between 1964 and 1967, with prices jumping by as much as 1,136% at the peak (in 1966). Even after this settled in the decades hence, there have been periods where price increases went uncomfortably high, even by the standards of lower-middle-income economies. Thanks to its status as a commodity exporter, however, the period of global high inflation in the early 2020s did not manifest itself in Indonesia, affording it the wiggle room to stage a solid recovery from the pandemic.

Can Malaysia Avoid the Middle-Income Trap?

Modern Malaysia can rightly be proud of its position as the most economically advanced among the middle-income countries of the region, and with nominal per capita income a little more than $11,000, it finds itself on the cusp of high-income status (as of 2022, this threshold is around $13,000).

29 Booth, A., *The Indonesian Economy in the Nineteenth and Twentieth Centuries: A History of Missed Opportunities* (Basingstoke: Macmillan, 1998).

A modern, diversified economy, Malaysia has benefited substantially from its economic openness, which has fed both foreign investment—especially from Japan—as well as steady demand for its output.

The country is also an integral part of the East Asian production network, and over time, it has gradually moved into ever-higher value-added production, especially in electronics, electrical devices, and ICT products. However, success in other areas of manufacturing—notably transport—has been more suspect. While the country can rightly claim to be Southeast Asia's only economy with industrial capacity in terms of automobile production, Proton and Perodua are hardly the sort of household names that South Korean or Japanese carmakers have become.

Services have not been left behind in the nation's industrial rise. In addition to fostering its (natural) advantages in tourism—beautiful, largely unspoiled offshore islands coupled with affordable prices have allowed the country to become the tenth-most visited country in the world—Malaysia has also evolved a sizable financial sector, with Kuala Lumpur being home to the world's most sophisticated center for Islamic finance.[30]

Despite the maturity of the economy's industrial and services sectors, the Malaysian economy still receives a nontrivial contribution from primary production. Agricultural exports (such as palm oil and rubber), as well as the extraction of natural resources (especially tin and petroleum), are important exports.

Given the array of advantages that Malaysia enjoys, it may be surprising that it has not risen even further than it has. Some observers have attributed this to the significant governance challenges the country faces, especially in areas related to the economy.

Two, in particular, stand out. The first is the widely-derided New Economic Policy, an affirmative-action social policy, instituted in the 1970s, that conferred benefits to indigenous *Bumiputra* (literally, "son of the soil") Malays, in terms of economic ownership. This was not limited to property ownership or corporate equity, but also in education (with racial quotas in universities) and hiring (with minimum share targets for corporate hiring). Yet while the policy has likely contributed to a more equal distribution of income and wealth,[31] criticisms of its unmeritocratic premised and have been repeatedly leveled since its implementation.

The second has been in the management of national wealth. Until 2010, the government maintained an extensive range of subsidies and price controls over

---

30 Strictly speaking, the market share of Saudi Arabia—at around a third—is greater (in absolute terms) that that of Malaysia. However, the range of financial institutions and products are greatest in Malaysia (which holds around 15% of the global share), especially in the issuance of Islamic bonds, or *sukuk*.
31 Rasiah, R., *Malaysian Economy: Unfolding Growth and Social Change* (Shah Alam: Oxford University Press, 2012).

essential items, including grocery essentials and vehicle fuel. While ostensibly progressive,[32] these have led to strains on the public fisc, with balances firmly entrenched in deficit territory over the entire stretch of the 2000s. Consequently, public debt has steadily built up over that time, and is now hovering at about 70% of GDP, a level higher than many would regard as sustainable or desirable (Figure 6.12).

It hardly helps that the government continues to operate its public and sovereign wealth funds—Khazanah and Permodalan Nasional, 1Malaysia Development Berhad (1MDB), and the Employees Provident Fund (EPF)[33]—with an insufficient prudence and oversight, which has resulted in at least one major scandal at one of them. Misappropriation of funds at 1MDB eventually contributed, in part, to the downfall of then-Prime Minister Najib Razak's administration, along with his eventual conviction in 2022.

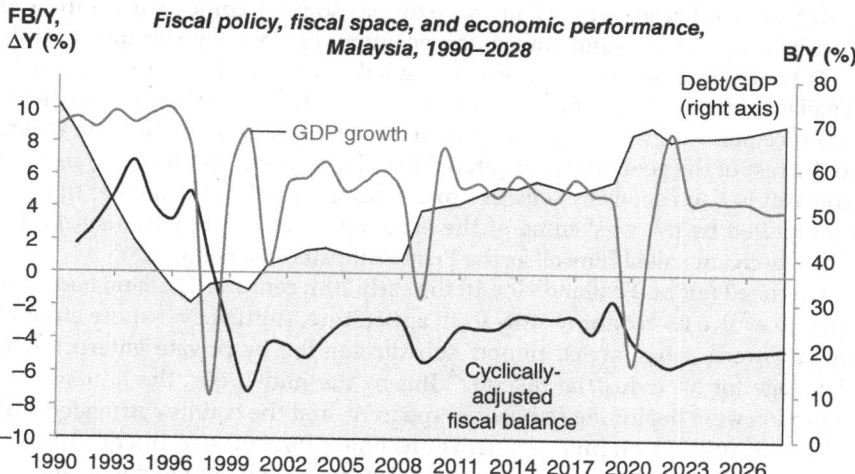

Figure 6.12 Fiscal space in Malaysia has been poor since the turn of the millennium, with chronic deficits resulting in a steady buildup of public debt—to around 70% of GDP—which is higher than typically viewed as sustainable.

---

32 The argument against blanket subsidies for essentials, however well intended, is that such policies may encourage excess consumption and often result in fiscal stresses. A more efficient redistributive effort would target the poor with direct transfers or tax relief (including negative taxes).

33 Permodalan, incorporated in 1978, manages $46 billion in assets, and is the oldest of the funds, but some of its subsidiary offerings are only accessible to *Bumiputra*. The EPF is a retirement fund, and with $143 billion under management, is the largest. Khazanah ($19 billion in assets) was incorporated in 1993, and was originally founded to take over the management of assets held by the Ministry of Finance. 1MDB started off as the strategic investment body of the state of Terengganu, before being taken over by the Ministry of Finance in 2009.

Such political economy failures have often been blamed for the economy languishing in the middle-income trap, despite a generous endowment in natural resources, and an abundance of unrealized economic potential.

Thailand: Excess Reliance on Tourism?

Thailand is Southeast Asia's second-largest economy (after Indonesia). As part of the next wave of Asian Tiger nations, it is a fast-growing, industrial economy, centered on the manufacture of electronics and electrical goods, as well as automotive parts and components. But while the secondary sector provides all-important ballast to Thailand's growth engine, the overwhelming driver of its present dynamism emanates from an $88 billion per annum (17% of GDP) tourism sector, which is projected to continue to grow to around a third of GDP by the 2030s.

But service-led growth reliant on external sources comes with a massive caveat: if foreign demand wanes, the economy can quickly run into trouble. COVID-19 became one such test. Extended border shutdowns—not just by Thailand, but also by China, a key source of tourists—meant a collapse in tourism receipts. And with a fifth of employment tied to tourism, flow-on effects to the rest of the economy precipitated in a sharp recession (of −6.2%) in 2020. Tourism is also especially sensitive to the need for political stability; this was exemplified by the weakening of the economy in 2014, after General Prayut Chan-o-cha installed himself as the Prime Minister in a coup.

This need not be Thailand's lot. In the early 20th century, Thailand had managed to evolve its economy away from agriculture, shifting ever-more employment toward urban areas. Import substitution led by private enterprise set the stage for an industrial takeoff.[34] But by the mid-1960s, the limits of the approach were beginning to become apparent, and the country struggled with a bevy of macroeconomic problems: declining foreign investment, frequent fiscal shortfalls, chronic current account deficits, high unemployment, and rising inflation.

This prompted the adoption of adjustment strategies, and a more decisive shift into export-oriented industrialization in the mid-1980s.[35] The Thai economy rapidly expanded its light and heavy manufacturing capabilities, supported

---

34 Anamwathana, P. and J. Vechbanyongratana, "The Economic History of Thailand: Old Debates, Recent Advances, and Future Prospects," *Asia-Pacific Economic History Review* 61(3) (2021): 342–358.

35 Thailand had a reasonably successful run with an import-substituting industrialization strategy in the 1960s, due to a continued emphasis on the market as a key guiding mechanism. But a strong exchange rate was becoming a constraint, and following several devaluations of the baht resulting from the Plaza Accord, policymakers embraced more firmly an export-oriented approach. See Unger, D., *Building Social Capital in Thailand: Fibers, Finance, and Infrastructure* (Cambridge: Cambridge University Press, 1998).

Figure 6.13 Labor markets in Thailand have traditionally relied on low wages as a key source of competitive advantage, but as the country has developed, its rate of increase has slowed (even as it has declined as a share of expenses), which has also prompted a creeping up of the unemployment rate.

by inflows of inward investment, especially from the NIEs. Foreign investors took advantage of low wages and a willing workforce, and Thai workers proved up to the task; unemployment stayed low throughout the 1990s and 2000s, without excessive upward wage pressure (Figure 6.13). Other sectors in the economy benefited from this manufacturing renaissance, especially finance and retail.

But it was tourism that ultimately established itself as the country's primary economic engine, and this remains so today. Despite sound fundamentals, the imbalance in its growth drivers, along with the continued threat of political instability, pose the key risks for future performance.

The Philippines: No Longer the Sick Man of Asia

For the longest time, the Philippines was often castigated as the "Sick Man" of Southeast Asia (an allusion to various western economies that have been deigned the "Sick Man of Europe"). To understand this characterization, it is necessary to hark back to the enormous economic potential of the island nation in the 1950s, during the period of mass independence across the region.

After all, at the turn of the 20th century, the Philippines was the second-richest economy in Asia (with a per capita income of around $1,033 in 1900, just behind Japan at $1,135). By the end of World War II, some of that earlier prosperity had dissipated. Still, the country boasted close economic ties to the richest nation in the world (due to American occupation), a population conversant in English, a relatively sophisticated educational system (made up of an extensive network of mission schools and tertiary institutions that dated back to the 17th century, owing to Spanish colonization), a large, young population, and a republican system of government.

But economic growth over the course of most of the 20th century turned out to be disappointing. Growth through the 1970s through 1990s would end up half that of its Southeast Asian counterparts. Much of this is attributable to economic mismanagement, first under the Marcos and then Aquino administrations. The excesses of the era were well illustrated by First Lady Imelda Marcos, who lived a lavish lifestyle at the expense of the national treasury; after being deposed in 1986, it was revealed that the couple had amassed a fortune estimated at $5–10 billion, which included art, jewelry, and (infamously) 3,000 pairs of shoes.

Any halting progress under the subsequent administrations would be derailed by the Asian crisis, where the Philippines was among the major casualties. Even following the crisis, recovery was anemic, at least until the presidency of Gloria Arroyo. An economist by training, her two terms helped the economy find a firm footing—evidenced by doubling of growth relative to prior decades—and ride through the global crisis of 2007/08. Over the most recent decade, the nation even outgrew the other ASEAN-6 nations, something that would have seemed inconceivable as recently as the 2000s.

Industrialization took hold in the 1960s and expanded its share of GDP until the 1980s. But while agribusiness and manufacturing remain mainstays in the economy, the nation's traditional strengths in electronics, pharmaceuticals, and shipbuilding have receded in importance. This has been displaced by services, especially tourism, but also business process outsourcing (think of the quintessential call centers providing customer support, especially to the United States) (Figure 6.14).

A less-appreciated aspect of tradable services has taken the form of permanent, temporary, and irregular migrants; these range from domestic helpers and nursing staff to seamen and construction crew. The upshot has been a remittance flow into the country of close to 10% of GDP, but this has also meant the inevitable brain drain of talented Filipinos to economies elsewhere in the world.

Vietnam and the Transition Economies: Plugging into Regional Value Chains

For much of their modern economic history, the Southeast Asian nations of the Mekong Basin—Cambodia, Myanmar, Laos, and Vietnam[36]—were heavily agrarian economies. Within the group, Vietnamese civilization did rise to become among the more important economic powers in the region, but a closed-door policy[37] at the turn of the 19th century led to stagnation, before its eventual colonization by the

---

36 The term Mekong Basin often refers not only to the four transition economies, but also to China and Thailand. Here, the expression will be used interchangeably with just the four.
37 In 1806, the Emperor Gia Long of the Nguyễn dynasty chose to impose a "sea ban," which prohibited Vietnamese merchants from pursuing overseas business, while Western merchants were also stopped from entering Vietnam.

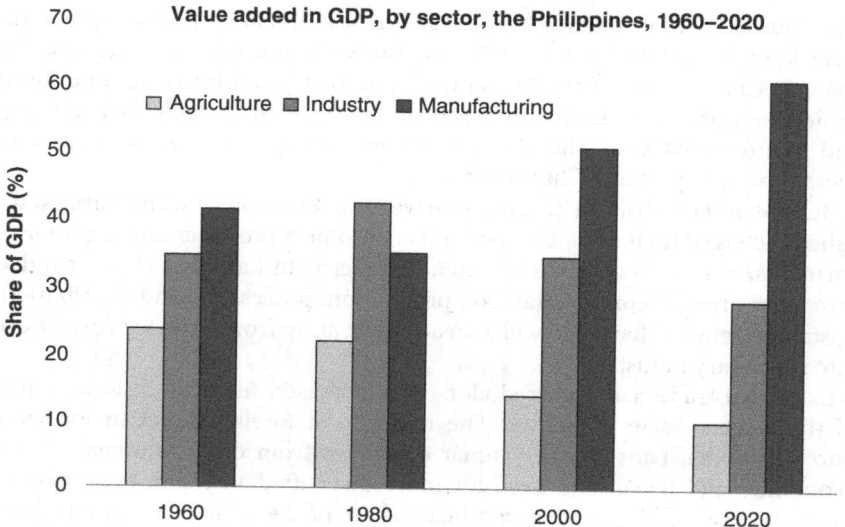

Figure 6.14 As the Philippines has developed, there has been a typical decline in the agricultural share of the economy. However, while the industrialization process did take hold in the 1960s and advanced through the 1980s, it began to retreat prematurely thereafter, replaced by a sharp expansion in services.

French. The French also seized neighboring Cambodia and Laos, while the British incorporated Myanmar (as Burma) into British India.

Following independence, these nations turned to communism—often after brutal civil wars—after which external economic relations were mainly with the Soviet Union and its allies (typically under the auspices of the Council for Mutual Economic Assistance, or COMECON). By the time the transition economies turned away from purely socialist economies toward market socialism, they had fallen substantially behind the rest of ASEAN. However, the absence of legacy restraints eventually allowed leapfrogging, which resulted in an acceleration of structural transformation, economic growth, modernization, and a shift toward middle-class status.

Within the group, Vietnam—by dint of its relatively more mature civilization, larger population, and cultural proximity to the growth powerhouse that is China—has always been the economic leader. Vietnam's workforce is frequently perceived as somewhat more industrious than those of its other immediate neighbors; an old (disparaging) French saying quips that "the Vietnamese plant the rice, the Cambodians watch it grow, while the Laotians listen as it does so."

It is therefore little surprise that Vietnam is also leading the group into a more ASEAN-oriented economic model. A key part of this strategy is integration with trade and financial networks of the region. On the trade side, they have sought to become part of the East Asian production network; here, Vietnam is the clear winner, having taken on much of the labor-intensive work that Southern China relinquished as wages rose there, in industrial agglomerations known as *khu công nghiệp*. It has also been an unwitting beneficiary of the U.S.-China trade war, since its exports to the United States have not been subject to tariff action; international corporations, such as Apple, Dell, Google, and Microsoft have all shifted parts of their supply chain to the country in recent years, as part of a China+1 strategy.

But the other transition economies have also not stood still, and have established niches of their own. Cambodia has become a producer and exporter of garments, as has Myanmar. The latter, together with Laos, has also expanded into more areas of commercial food production, processing, and distribution. Sustained reforms have allowed a steady shift away from primary agriculture into secondary industry.

Expanded trade has occurred alongside increased financial inflows, much of these intra-Asian in nature. The majority of foreign direct investments into Cambodia, Laos, and Myanmar originates from other Southeast Asian economies and Japan (and even for more-diversified Vietnam, they account for around two-fifths), with a significant share of the remainder coming from China and South Korea. Like the NIEs and China before them, foreign savings have provided an important source of financing for investment into factories, machinery, and vehicles, kickstarting these countries' industrialization processes. This has allowed the transition economies to increasingly ensconce themselves into the East Asian value chains, although remaining open to FDI, including in services, will be necessary to keep momentum going (Figure 6.15).

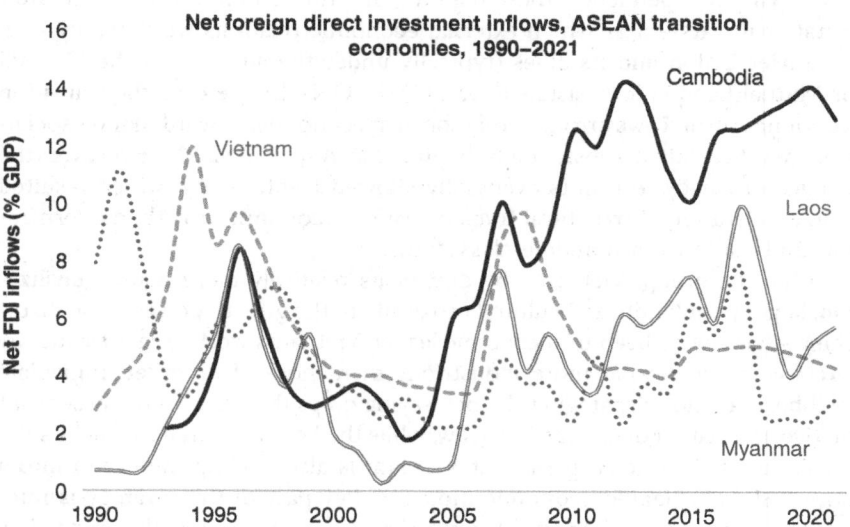

Figure 6.15 The transition economies of Southeast Asia have benefited from financial inflows from other Asian economies, and this has resulted in the ability to expand investment in industrial activity.

But in the longer run, the success of these economies will also require policymakers there to do their part. They will need to expand capacity—especially in critical infrastructure (nothing says not ready to do business as being unable to keep the lights on)—and gradually allow their workers to develop the sort of skills and human capital necessary to serve the needs of modern manufacturing processes, as well as climb the value-added chain, especially in services.[38]

Southeast Asia and the World Economy

Southeast Asian Exports Have Relied Heavily on Countries' Comparative Advantages, But This Is Changing

Historically, the economies of the region have often leaned hard on their traditional comparative advantages in their approach toward trade: exporting either raw materials for which they had been richly endowed, or by specializing in the manufacture of labor-intensive goods, taking advantage of their relative abundance of workers.

This pattern is evident in the evolution of the export baskets of the region. Even as these have increased substantially in value over time, they have remained consonant with their economies' underlying comparative advantage. Indonesia has exported ever-more agricultural products (including palm oil, natural rubber, and spices) over time, along with mineral commodities (especially iron, copper, and nickel; with global demand for the last especially robust, given how it has become a mainstay of modern green technologies). Nearby Thailand, blessed with less by way of natural resources, has nevertheless focused on plugging into the East Asian production network by offering low-wage, low-skilled workers engaged in labor-intensive production.

But this pattern is gradually changing, as countries wise up to the enormous untapped value in more downstream activities, many of which they now have the ability to move directly into, due to the international diffusion of technology, know-how, and financial capital. In 2022, Indonesia went as far as to ban certain mineral exports (starting with nickel, but this is expected to extend to others, such as bauxite, copper, and tin), in an effort to (re)capture the added value by keeping refinement and resource-intensive industrial activity onshore (Figure 6.16). This attempt to move into allied sectors in the global production space has some support from recent research in international trade.[39] Hence, it

---

38 World Bank, *Taking Stock: Harnessing the Potential of the Services Sector for Growth* (Washington, DC: The World Bank, 2023).

39 Hausmann, R. and D. Rodrik, "Economic Development as Self-Discovery," *Journal of Development Economics* 72(2) (2003): 603–633; Hausmann, R., J. Hwang, and D. Rodrik, "What You Export Matters," *Journal of Economic Growth* 12 (2007): 1–25.

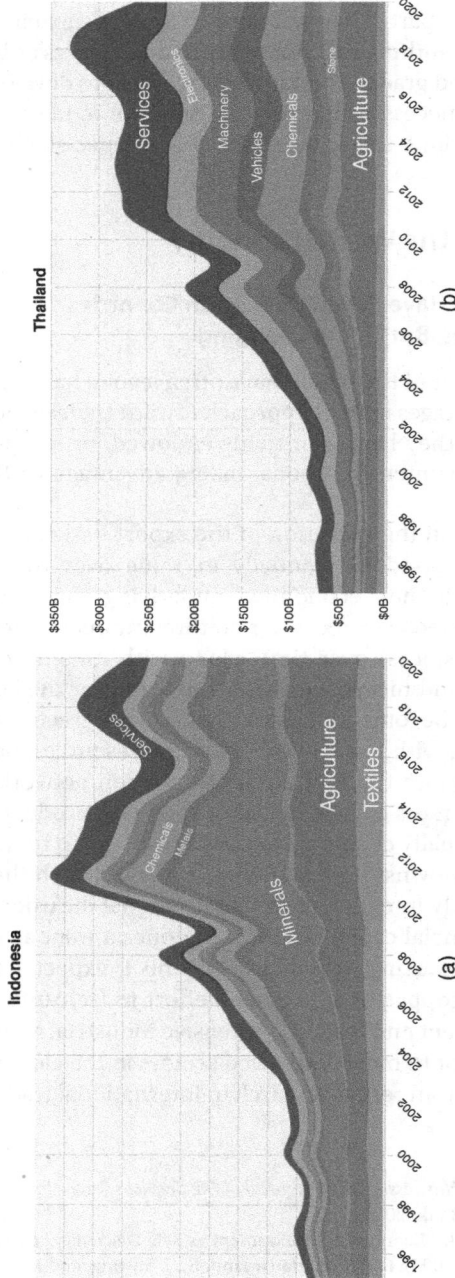

Figure 6.16 (a) While Indonesia's export basket has undeniably evolved over time, it is still heavily reliant on agricultural goods as well as mineral commodities. (b) Similarly, as Thailand has industrialized, it has produced mostly labor-intensive manufactured goods, consonant with its low-wage workforce. More recently, Southeast Asian economies have sought to capture more value-added activities within their borders, including onshoring more downstream processes.

is unsurprising that economies with the capacity and potential to do so would leverage such a development strategy, although the devil is in the details.

This move has, nevertheless, caused consternation among economies that have previously relied on Indonesian mineral exports as a means for their *own* production processes. Some have suggested that this could harm the nation's credibility as a trading partner,[40] and, unsurprisingly, this issue has been raised in the WTO.

Nor is the process of autarky-for-independence as straightforward as slapping on a unilateral export ban. To produce electric vehicle batteries, it is not just nickel that is required, but also lithium; but the latter is in short supply in Indonesia (it is, however, abundant in neighboring Australia, as well as in African nations such as Namibia), which means the need for their import. But competitors have not stood still, and China, in particular, has pulled ahead in securing African supply chains.[41] Furthermore, the technological knowhow for efficient battery production frequently resides in trading partners—Japan or South Korea, for example—who cannot be alienated. The bottom line is that the nation cannot simply dissociate itself from existing international trading norms and institutions, even as it seeks to onshore more lucrative economic activity.

Trade Policies and Integration in Southeast Asia

The lynchpin for international trade in Southeast Asia is ASEAN. Although the arrangement was initially conceived as a forum for navigating the potential recriminations that could arise due to the Cold War environment, it quickly evolved into a shop for discussions surrounding economic integration. Under the auspices of the common market,[42] ASEAN has gradually dismantled its tariffs among members, which in turn have resulted in some of the highest levels of intraregional flows of goods, services, and financing worldwide (exceeded only by the European Union) (Figure 6.17).

---

40 Hendrix, C., "Indonesia Wants to Sell Nickel to the US, But First It Should Scrap Its Export Bans," *Realtime Economics*, April 26 (Washington, DC: Peterson Institute for International Economics, 2023).
41 Dempsey, H. and J. Cotterill, "How China Is Winning the Race for Africa's Lithium," *Financial Times*, April 3, 2023.
42 Economic integration occurs in various stages. Preferential trading agreements (PTAs) are the least integrated, allowing partial goods, services, and financial movement, whereas free trade agreements (FTAs) allow substantial goods movements, while still retaining restrictions on services and capital flows. Economic partnerships (EPs) go further, and allow for substantial goods, services, and capital movements. When FTAs and EPs adopt a common external barrier (usually in the form of a unified border tariff regime), these become customs unions and common markets, respectively. ASEAN is today a common market, much like the European Coal and Steel Community (which was the integration arrangement that preceded the European Union). Deeper integration that permits significant flows of labor are economic unions, followed by monetary unions (a common currency and monetary policy, as the EMU is today), and, finally, full economic integration (the case of the United States).

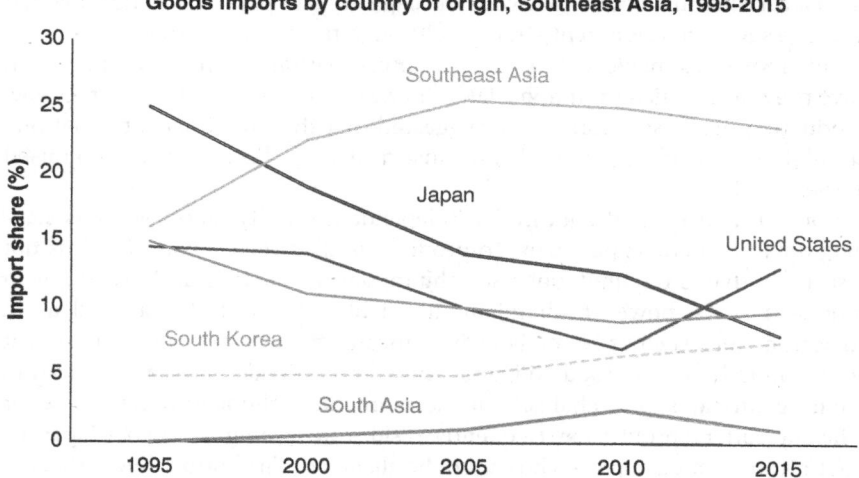

Figure 6.17 Although not as integrated as more comprehensive agreements such as the European Monetary Union, ASEAN has fostered deep economic relationships among its member nations, to the point where intra-regional trade dominates its exchange of goods (although China has become increasingly important).

The expansion of ASEAN-6 to the current membership (including the transition economies and, most recently, Timor Leste) has also spurred a greater relaxation of the tariff regime in those economies as well (Table 6.3). Indeed, with ASEAN as a cornerstone, trading agreements have been extended to additional partners. These include the so-called ASEAN+3 (ASEAN with China, Japan, and South Korea) and ASEAN+6 (the ASEAN+3 plus Australia, New Zealand, and India). The original conceptualization of the Regional Comprehensive Economic Partnership (RCEP) was to bring together the plus-6 nations into a mega-regional bloc. One would have thought that this would be a straightforward process—ASEAN already has bilateral free trade agreements with each of the six—this has been anything but.

RCEP negotiations quickly became embroiled in broader global geopolitics. The United States came down on the side of emphasizing open regionalism, centered on the Asia-Pacific Economic Cooperation forum, while also stressing the importance of higher-standard trade rules, as it did with the Trans-Pacific Partnership (before this was abandoned during the Trump administration).[43]

---

43 The Trans-Pacific Partnership (TPP) eventually went ahead without the participation of its largest (and most lucrative) market, the United States, after being renamed the "Comprehensive and Progressive Agreement for Trans-Pacific Partnership" (CPTPP), and relinquishing some of the provisions (mainly regarding intellectual property, but the CPTPP also suspended certain provisions on labor and the environment) that the U.S. had initially insisted on. The United Kingdom has since applied—and was approved for—accession to the CPTPP (in 2023), which would make it the second-largest member economy, after Japan (the UK qualified on the basis of its sovereignty over the Pitcairn Islands, located in the Southern Pacific).

Table 6.3 Effective tariff rates in the ASEAN-6, 1989, 2004, and 2019

	Effective tariff rates (%)			Change 1989–2019 (%)
	1989	2004	2019	
Brunei	4.4	6.1	0.0	−540
Indonesia	14.5	4.0	2.0	−198
Malaysia	14.4	5.4	3.6	−139
The Philippines	22.5	2.9	1.7	−260
Singapore	3.3	0.0	0.4	−212
Thailand	33.7	6.0	3.5	−226

Source: Author's compilation, from World Bank (2023).
Notes: Effective tariff rates are the weighted averages of applied rates, weighted by the product import shares corresponding to each partner country. Where data for the specific year were unavailable, the nearest year was chosen; these was the case for Brunei (1992 instead of 1989), Malaysia (1988 and 2020 instead of 1989 and 2019, respectively), and Thailand (2015 instead of 2019).

Membership in RCEP also excluded India—an original negotiation partner—after the nation opted out in the final stages, ostensibly due to its concerns over the lack of protections for its domestic agricultural and industrial sectors. This caused not a small amount of distress among the remaining economies, in part because they had hoped for India to be a natural counterweight to the immense economic might of China.

Hence, inasmuch as trade integration has been a central driver in the region's economic fortunes in the past, there is a risk now that this important engine will recede in the future. If so, Southeast Asia will simply be following the somewhat unsavory trend of deglobalization, and it will be the economies most in need of sustained trading relationships seeking to embed themselves into regional value chains—the transition economies and observer nations—that will be the worst off for it.

Southeast Asia and the Asian Financial Crisis

Regional financial flows have moved much in lockstep with expanded trade, in accordance with the evolution implied by the "flying geese" model. The earlier phase—mainly in the second half of the 20th century—saw foreign direct investment channeled to the NIE Dragons (Figure 6.18). By the 1990s and 2000s, those economies had assumed the baton and begun directing their own FDI toward the Tigers and, most recently, the transition economies.

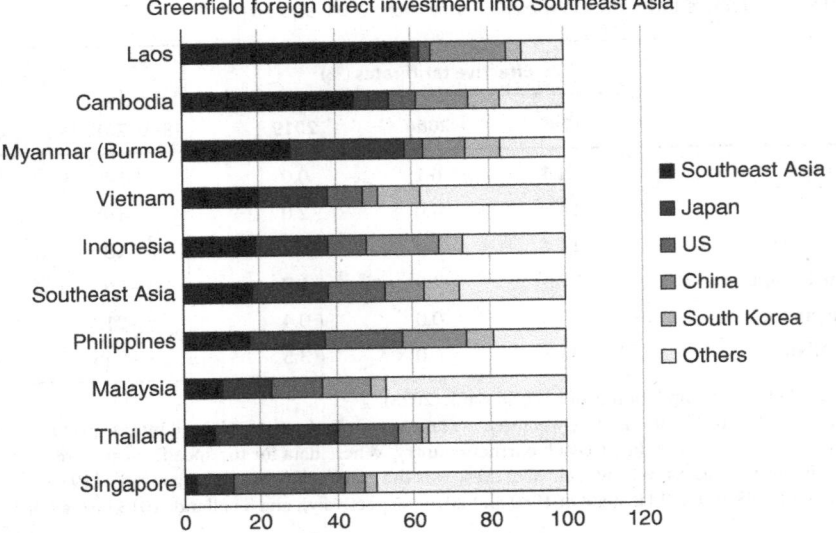

Figure 6.18 Financial flows in the region, inspired by the Japan-led "flying geese" model, have generally been an important channel for development. In more recent times, this has disproportionately benefitted the transition economies, which had previously been cut off from financing.

While the latest wave of FDI has also increasingly featured China, these flows tend to be qualitatively distinct; in contrast to investment into a diverse array of industrial activity—along with real estate—that is the thrust of ASEAN investors, China tends to focus on sectors like mining and energy.

More recently, ASEAN investment in services—especially in finance and ICT—have also picked up. But these tend to concentrate in the NIEs, and Singapore, especially, has become a major recipient of FDI in the IT services. Clearly, expanded intra-regional FDI is not limited to just the emerging economies, but also advanced ones. This is not a bad thing, given the track record of FDI as a contributor to long-run development.

The import of reliable financial inflows were brought to the fore during the Asian financial crisis of 1997/98. At the time, the region adhered to a Dollar Standard, where most ASEAN currencies were (implicitly if not explicitly) pegged to the U.S. dollar. But this also allowed double mismatches—where short-term liabilities took the form of dollar-denominated debt, even as lending to local firms was priced in local currency and had long maturities—to form. When the exchange rate pegs were ruptured in the summer of 1997, triggered by the collapse of the Thai baht, the dominoes quickly fell. By the beginning of 1998, the fire had even spread to other parts of East Asia, including Hong Kong and South Korea.

The Asian crisis followed a different script from crises past. The so-called "first-generation" crises—the ones observed in Latin America in the late 1970s and early 1980s—resulted from insufficient fiscal rectitude, where profligate spending by governments, coupled with central bank acquiescence, led to a speculative attack on the currency.[44] Yet on the eve of the crisis, many Asian governments were not running outrageous deficits on their balance sheets (which they subsequently had to due to crisis conditions).

Nor was the crisis one purely of the "second-generation" sort—which plagued the European Monetary System in the early 1990s—when central banks with conflicting objectives on inflation and growth ended up being "gamed" into relinquishing the fixed rate regime, because everyone expected this to occur, ultimately making the crisis self-fulfilling.[45] While expectations played an important role in the Asian crisis, fundamentals were weak, too.

The Asian crisis actually gave rise to a "third generation" of financial crisis, characterized by a double mismatch—of foreign currency-denominated, short-term liabilities coupled with long-term local currency assets—by private firms, which became intolerable once the implicit guarantee of a fixed exchange rate was no longer there. Banks would become illiquid, raising the specter of default. Governments would be dragged in, as they were forced to bail out their banking systems to prevent a complete implosion of the economy.[46]

Thankfully, most of the region experienced a V-shaped recovery, with a solid rebound in GDP after deep declines in 1997. Of the four hardest-hit economies (Indonesia, Malaysia, the Philippines, and Thailand), only Indonesia had to endure a protracted climb out of the troughs. Still, the lessons from the

---

44 First-generation models boil down to a few key elements: a fiscal authority that maintains fiscal deficits, which is fully monetized by the central bank; this sparks inflation, and given purchasing power parity, there is depreciation pressure on the (presently) fixed exchange rate. The fixed rate can only be sustained by the sale of reserves, but these steadily erode, until the exchange rate level that will otherwise prevail in a floating rate regime (the "shadow floating rate") surpasses the current rate; at this point, there is a sudden exhaustion of reserves, as speculators simultaneously sell the domestic currency. See Krugman, P., "A Model of Balance-of-Payments Crises," *Journal of Money, Credit, and Banking* 11(3) (1979): 311–325.

45 Second-generation models result from multiple equilibria: a monetary authority, facing a loss function that seeks to balance both inflation and tax collection objectives, may be "gamed" into pursuing a float, because if enough agents expect the central bank to pursue an inflation-tax tradeoff associated with a floating exchange rate equilibrium (over the prevailing one consistent with a fixed rate), then that shift in expectations itself becomes self-fulfilling. See Ostfeld, M., "The Logic of Currency Crises," *Cahiers Economiques et Monétaires* 43 (1994): 189–213.

46 See Caballero, R. and A. Krishnamurthy, "International and Domestic Collateral Constraints in a Model of Emerging Market Crises," *Journal of Monetary Economics* 48(3) (2001): 513–548; Chang, R. and A. Velasco, "A Model of Financial Crises in Emerging Markets," *Quarterly Journal of Economics* 116(2) (2001): 489–517.

crisis—on the importance of reserve backstops, limiting government guarantees, preferring a loose managed float instead of a tighter adjustable peg, and establishing a system of currency swap arrangements[47]—remain central to the evolving institutional framework of the region.

Conclusion

The Importance of Leadership and Development Strategy

Singapore's late founding father, Lee Kwan Yew, is said to have responded to a question by China's Premier about the island nation's success: "You have bigger land, more resources, and more people and talent than us, whatever Singapore has done or can do, you can do it bigger and better."

The same applies, one would argue, to all the other larger, more naturally endowed, and economically promising nations in the rest of Southeast Asia. What has been the incontrovertible challenge has been one of governance: both in terms of visionary, committed leadership at the very top,[48] together with ensuring that the quality of institutional governance—controlling corruption, maintaining an effective government, safeguarding political stability, respecting the rule of law, and the like—permeates at all levels.

Sound Fundamentals Favor Future Growth

Southeast Asian economies will still enjoy favorable demographic tailwinds in the years ahead. Many still have young populations, which are both able to contribute to an expansion of the labor force, as well as younger working-age propensities toward saving (which will provide critical financing for investment). These young workforces will also have a runway for building up human capital, since human resource development remains relatively unexploited.

The major challenge is to ensure that governance weaknesses do not become too much of a distraction. Historically, productivity has been poor not due to its complete absence, but rather because positive TFP shocks have frequently

---

47 This took the form of the Chiang Mai Initiative, which established a system of bilateral currency swaps among the ASEAN+3 economies, effectively pooling the reserve resources of regional economies to withstand liquidity shortages due to speculative attacks.
48 The importance of leadership for growth and development was made convincingly by Jones, B. and B. Olken, "Do Leaders Matter? National Leadership and Growth Since World War II," *Quarterly Journal of Economics* 120 (2005): 835–864.

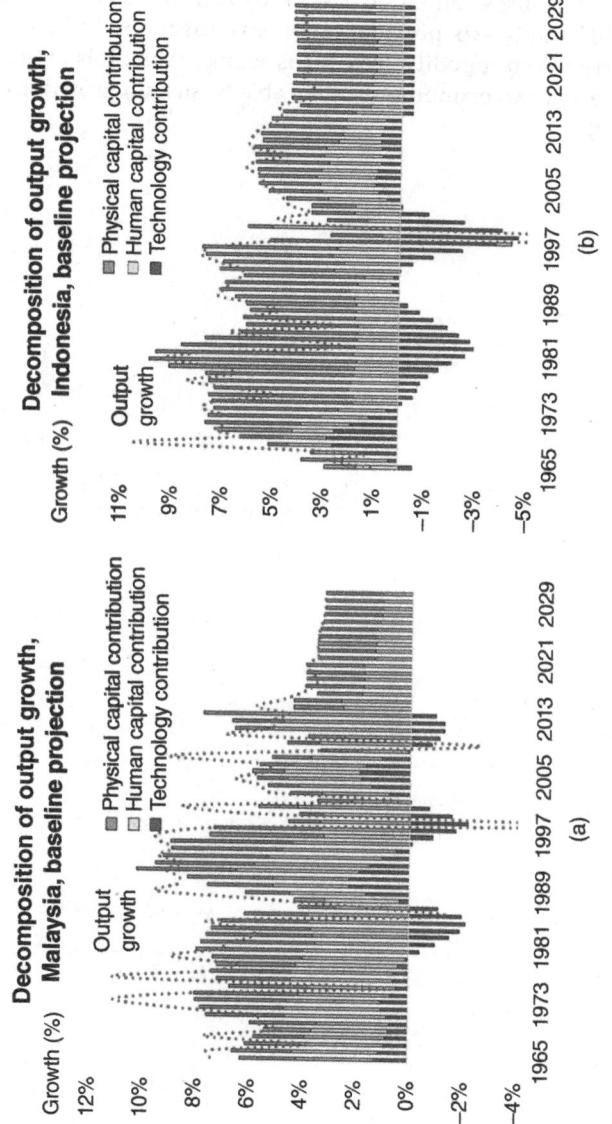

Figure 6.19 Favorable demographic profiles, still-underdeveloped human resource structures, and working-age populations in a position to save to finance domestic investment place Southeast Asian economies in good stead for sustained future growth, so long as governance challenges do not get in the way. The potential of nations like (a) Malaysia or (b) Indonesia is great.

been offset by negative ones. By a similar token, these natural resource-dependent economies should not allow occasional favorable terms of trade to induce excess consumption, perpetuating volatile cycles. Instead, fiscal and current account surpluses can be saved—perhaps in the form of accountable sovereign wealth funds—to provide useful macroeconomic ballast during downturns where the commodity cycle turns against them. It is in this manner that the Southeast Asian economies will be able to sustain growth in the long run (Figure 6.19).

7

Central Asia: Crossroads in a Globalized World

Trade occurs while you are stroking your beard.
—Kazakh proverb

Everything I have heard about the beauty of this city is indeed true, except that it is much more beautiful than I imagined.
—Attributed to Alexander the Great, Macedonian king and conqueror

I cannot forecast to you the action of Russia. It is a riddle, wrapped in a mystery, inside an enigma; but perhaps there is a key. That key is Russian national interest.
—Winston Churchill (1874–1965), British Prime Minister[1]

Introduction

Central Asia has, through much of human history, promoted civilizational exchange, with trade deeply infused into the identity of the region. These lands were also integral to *Pax Mongolica*, which opened trade between China and Europe for the first time in the 13th century, and formed the basis for the Italian merchant Marco Polo's famous travels. The Berber explorer, Ibn Battuta, likewise made his way across the Muslim world of the 14th century—passing through Central Asian territories that succeeded the Chagatai Khanate, the Golden Horde, and Ilkhanate[2]—sharing

---

1 Churchill, W. "The Russian Enigma," BBC Broadcast. London: British Broadcasting Corporation, 1939.
2 The Chagatai Khanate was ruled by Chagatai, the second son of Genghis Khan, and its territories covered what is today mostly Uzbekistan, together with parts of Kazakhstan and Tajikistan. The Golden Horde (also known as the Kipchak Khanate), founded by Batu Khan (a grandson of Genghis), included Asian holdings that are parts of modern Kazakhstan and Turkey. And within the Ilkhanate, founded by another Genghis grandson, Hülegü, was the core that is today Azerbaijan, Iran, and Turkey, but included Afghanistan, Pakistan, Tajikistan, and Turkmenistan at its greatest territorial extent.

Asian Economies: History, Institutions, and Structures, First Edition. Jamus Jerome Lim.
© 2024 John Wiley & Sons Ltd. Published 2024 by John Wiley & Sons Ltd.

knowledge of exotic food, wares, and practices with Islamic civilization. Cities like Almaty (in modern-day Kazakhstan), Merv (Turkmenistan), Osh (Kyrgyzstan), and Bukhara (Uzbekistan) were key stops along the various Silk Roads, and crown jewels like Samarkand have inspired figures across history as varied as the Macedonian conqueror Alexander the Great and the Chinese explorer Zhang Qian.

The economic potential of the region was also well recognized by Russia, which first arrived as colonizers, before enmeshing the region behind the Iron Curtain.[3] As Soviet Republics, these nations provided much of the raw materials and mineral resources that contributed to the might of the USSR, as well as agricultural commodities—especially cotton—that would be made available to Russian mills and markets. In return, the Soviet Union laid down much of the road and railway infrastructure across the region, as well as previously-unknown industrial capacity.

Yet thirty years after the break-up of the USSR, Central Asia is frequently overlooked by analysts of the global economy and travel guidebooks alike. The transition from central planning to market economies has been rocky, and the region's economies remain small relative to the rest of the world. Combined, aggregate GDP amounts to around $348 billion—similar to that of much smaller countries like Chile, Hong Kong, and the UAE, making the entire region seem like a footnote. And while certain countries in the region (Kazakhstan and Turkmenistan) boast per capita outputs that are starting to approach the threshold for high-income countries, income inequality is significant, and appears to be widening.

Could this situation change? There are solid reasons to believe that it will, and this chapter explains why. After all, the region holds the potential to become an ever-more important part of the world, not least because of its still-abundant natural resources, and continued openness to fostering trading relationships. While often subject to geopolitical pressure from Great Power rivalry—and still ruled by strong, authoritarian governments—Central Asian societies are gradually becoming more pluralistic. That said, Central Asians' visions of a democratic society are likely to differ from those of the West, and tend to be focused more on improvements in the quality of life, the proper provision of social services, and reducing the gap between the rich and poor.[4]

---

3 Most Central Asian states became official Soviet Republics in the late 1910s and early 1920s, and remained so till the dissolution of the USSR in the early 1990s.

4 Stronski, P. and R. Zanca, "Societal Change Afoot in Central Asia," Carnegie Research Article (Washington, DC: Carnegie Endowment for International Peace, 2019).

Economic Geography of Central Asia

A Land Well-Traveled

Central Asia is generally taken to comprise five countries: Kazakhstan, Uzbekistan, Kyrgyzstan, Turkmenistan, and Tajikistan.[5,6] All are landlocked.[7] However, two major rivers traverse the vast steppe landscape: the Syr Darya—which passes through Kyrgyzstan, Uzbekistan, and Kazakhstan—and the Amu Darya, which crosses Tajikistan, Uzbekistan, and Turkmenistan.[8] The rivers rise in the high mountains in the southeast, and drain into the Aral Sea (although excess usage now threatens the endorheic lake with risk of disappearing altogether within the next two decades). Kyrgyzstan and Tajikistan are generally regarded as "upstream" countries, while the remainder are "downstream."

Despite the geographic reach—the total landmass is about the same as that of the European Union, and about a quarter times larger than the Indian subcontinent—it is lightly populated, with the largest cities only about 2 million in size.[9] Kazakhstan is, by far, the largest country—it is more than twice the combined size of the other Central Asian states—but Uzbekistan accounts for around half the region's population of 78 million (which in turn is just 1% of the global total).

While not quite dead center of the Eurasian supercontinent, Central Asia has always been heavily traversed, since it has lain between the civilizations of the West and East. Trade has been and remains a mainstay of the region's economies. While it lags behind the level of integration achieved in East or Southeast Asia, Central Asia's trade beyond the region's boundaries is greater, in proportionate terms, than these two regions (where *intra*regional trade is more pervasive). With increasing recognition of the region's economic potential in terms of primary exports, this is set to increase in the years ahead.

Abundant Natural Resources in Lands That Abound

The names of Central Asian nations all prominently display the Persian-origin suffix "-stan" (ستان), which means "places abounding in." This is subtly

---

5 Prior to independence, the region was often referred to as Turkestan, although that would include an eastern part, Uyghuristan, which is today Xinjiang Province in China.
6 Afghanistan, while abutting three Central Asian economies (Tajikistan, Turkmenistan, and Uzbekistan), and sharing the same "-stan" suffix, is typically regarded as part of South Asia.
7 Although two, Kazakhstan and Turkmenistan, border the Caspian Sea, the world's largest inland body of water.
8 The rivers' traditional names were the Jaxartes and Oxus rivers, respectively.
9 These are Almaty and Tashkent, with both around 2 million. Consistent with Zipf's Law, city sizes quickly fall: the next three are Bishkek (900,000), Ashgabat (728,000), and Dushanbe (680,000).

appropriate, given the abundant natural resources that may be found in the region.

Kazakhstan is the sixth-largest oil producer among non-OPEC countries (and the twelfth-largest worldwide), cranking out more than 1.7 million barrels a day. Turkmenistan and Uzbekistan rank eleventh and sixteenth, respectively, in terms of global natural gas production, and all three have potentially underexplored coal deposits. As upstream countries, Kyrgyzstan and Tajikistan possess underdeveloped hydropower potential, which could be exploited at relatively low cost.[10] Reserves of uranium, at least in Kazakhstan and Uzbekistan, are also substantial, should the energy source regain favor as a transition fuel worldwide.

Central Asia is also rich in deposits of many industrial metals that will be crucial for the renewable energy transition; these include around a third of global manganese and chromium reserves, along with nontrivial shares of cobalt, copper, molybdenum, titanium, and zinc (Figure 7.1).[11]

Mineral Deposits of Central Asia

Figure 7.1 Central Asia is a geologist's paradise, with an A–Z of mineral deposits (including key green technology commodities), along with an array of nonrenewable and renewable energy resources, such as coal, natural gas, oil, uranium, and water.

---

10 While renewable, hydropower in the region tends to become unavailable, due to freezing. In lieu of this, the region has explored replacement power in the form of thermal, for winter energy and heating needs.

11 The shares are around 5% for copper, cobalt, and molybdenum, 9% for titanium, and 13% for zinc. See Asian Development Bank, *Central Asia Atlas of Natural Resources* (Manila: Asian Development Bank, 2010).

Unfortunately, the geology that has yielded what lies beneath the earth has largely precluded what lies above. The scattering of desert and grassy steppes—while hauntingly beautiful—often means little arable land, with only a fifth of land in the region suitable for agriculture overall (and for some countries, such as Kyrgyzstan and Turkmenistan, the total land dedicated to cultivation is in the mid-single digits).

Economic History of Central Asia

Ancient Economies with Global Connections

Central Asia's recorded linkages between East and West date back to the Classical epoch. In the 4th century BCE, Alexander the Great extended his conquests to the region, on his way to India. In his wake, Alexander's Seleucid successors established various Greek settlements in the Oxus valley, but these did not last.[12] By the 1st century BCE, the Kushans[13]—a nomadic people from western China—had begun to gradually displace the Hellenistic kingdoms. The dynasty they formed ruled the region for more than three centuries, and intermediated trade between the Romans and Chinese. This brought prosperity, evidenced by the gold coins minted by the Kushanese treasury (Figure 7.2).

Figure 7.2 Kushan gold coinage, which captured the images of their kings, were a testament to the Empire's prosperity and reliance on trade and exchange. They also inspired the use of coins in neighboring states, such as the Gupta Empire in India, and the Sasanian Empire in Persia.
Source: Classical Numismatic Group / Wikimedia Commans / CC-BY-SA 3.0

---

12 Bernard, P., "An Ancient Greek City in Central Asia," *Scientific American* 246(1) (1982): 148–159.
13 These were known to the Chinese as the *yuezhi* (月氏).

After their decline, the remnants of the empire would sink back into the periphery of history. External powers—such as the Sasanian and Parthian Empires, came to dominate trade, until the subsequent arrival of the Arabs, followed by the Mongols, then the Timurids.[14] Fragmentation would follow, and the region would slide into being ruled by various emirates and khanates.

The tight connectivity of Central Asia with the wider world would begin to erode in the 15th century. Long-distance trade increasingly took to the seas, birthing maritime powers like the British and the Dutch. This bypassing upended the traditional *raison d'être* of the region as the crossroads of civilizations and graveyard of empires.

As Part of Imperial Russia and a Cog in the Soviet Economic Machine

In the mid-19th century, Imperial Russia began to exert greater control over Central Asia. This culminated in conquest, and the region became Russian Turkestan (Русский Туркестан, *Russkiy Turkestan*). Modernization would not accompany colonization, however, as the Tsarist powers favored keeping the region backward to reduce opposition to their rule.

After the Russian Revolution in 1917, these economies of Central Asia were officially absorbed into Soviet Central Asia (Советская Средняя Азия, *Sovetskaya Srednyaya Aziya*). By and large, the region remained largely autonomous, but as distinct republics, borders—which had only been loosely-defined until then—were drawn, and an internal passport system was instituted.

Although politically contentious, this was a period of solid economic development, as the region became a part of the Soviet system. Agricultural cultivation moved toward cash crops—in particular, cotton—which became the dominant export for several states (it constituted 85% of all cotton produced in the Soviet Union). The Soviets also brought the necessary investment and technology that allowed manufacturing and industry to take root. Kazakhstan was rapidly industrialized after World War II, and oil prospecting was launched across the territory. Hydroelectric power stations sprang up in the upstream republics, as well as eastern Kazakhstan. The region even hosted a spaceport—the Baikonur Cosmodrome—which continues to operate under rental to Russia.

The Soviet developmental state also ushered in educational advances.[15] Basic education was expanded, with literacy—albeit in Russian—ramped up to close to 100%. Meanwhile, the migration of technical personnel from European parts of the USSR helped bolster the human capital formation at the higher

---

14 The Timurids were founded by the Mongol-Turkic conqueror Timur-e-Lang (or Tamerlane), and perceived their dynasty as the successor to the Chagatai Khanate. At the height of the Empire, Timur was the most powerful ruler in the Muslim world, having defeated not just the khans of the Chagatai (Central Asia), but also the Golden Horde (Caucasus and Southern Russia), the Mamluks and the Ottomans (Western Asia), and the Delhi Sultanate (India).

15 Shorish, M., "Soviet Development Strategies in Central Asia," *Canadian Slavonic Papers* 17(2/3) (1975): 404–416.

end. In just a half a century, these strategies transformed the region into a far more economically viable one.

Exit, Stage Right

On Christmas Day in 1991, the flag of the Soviet Union was lowered for the final time, and the former republics in Central Asia were officially recognized as independent nations (many had declared sovereignty in the months prior). From an economic perspective, it was an exceedingly acrimonious break-up.

Central Asian economies promptly fell into a recession. Trade unwound quickly; flows to the former Soviet Union shrank from $69 billion, pre-break-up, to a trough of $11 billion by the middle of the decade.[16] Prices rose, and quickly accelerated into hyperinflation. In Turkmenistan, monthly inflation between the start of 1992 through the end of 1993 peaked at 429% *per month*; this was equivalent to prices doubling every two weeks. Episodes in the other republics weren't much better; Tajikistan saw rates peaking at 200%, and the others all had peaks of more than 100%.[17] And inflation continued to ravage Central Asian economies over the subsequent years. Kazakhstan, for instance, clocked annual inflation of 1,878% in 1995.

The rocky exit from the Soviet Union had as much to do with policy missteps, as it did with the wrenching dislocations that resulted from a sudden, forced transition of the macroeconomy away from central planning toward a decentralized system. The initial decision by the former Soviet republics to retain the Russian ruble as their currency exacerbated the shock of exit by taking away the exchange rate as an insulating and stabilizing tool, while also contributing to inflation.[18] Over the course of 1993, progressively more economies left the ruble zone; this began with Kyrgyzstan in the middle of the year, but Kazakhstan, Turkmenistan, and Uzbekistan would follow by that year-end.[19]

Many difficulties currently faced by Central Asian economies may be traced back to this period. Soviet rule had led to a disproportionate expansion of cotton monoculture, which has led, among other things, to economic stagnation, labor exploitation, widespread poverty, political repression, and environmental degradation.[20] Today, Tajik, Turkmen, and Uzbek small-holding farmers are generally located at the beginning of the international production chain, which means that payments received amount to only a small fraction of international

---

16 These were not made up by flows to the rest of the world, which mostly remained between $6 billion and $9 billion over the same period. See Islamov, B., "Central Asian States: On the Way from Autarchic Dependence to Regional and Global Interdependence," *Hitotsubashi Journal of Economics* 40(2) (1999): 75–96.

17 Hanke, S. and N. Krus, "World Hyperinflations," in R. Whaples and R. Parker (Eds.), *Handbook of Major Events in Economic History* (New York: Routledge, 2013).

18 Pomfret, R., *The Economies of Central Asia* (Princeton, NJ: Princeton University Press, 1995).

19 Tajikistan eventually adopted the Tajik ruble as the sole legal tender in 1995.

20 ICG, "The Curse of Cotton: Central Asia's Destructive Monoculture," *Asia Report* 93 (Brussels: International Crisis Group, 2005).

prices; their meager incomes are therefore effectively inelastic vis-à-vis global cotton prices. Kazakh and Kyrgyz farmers—with larger, privately-held farming operations—tend to do better, but this is also because of their relatively lower dependence on the crop for export revenue.

The vestige of Soviet authoritarianism also reveals itself in the contemporary political economy. Except for Kyrgyzstan—where then-President Akayev embraced the advice of Western institutions and implemented the most liberal regime in the region—the other polities remain autocracies,[21] where they are headed by strongmen presidents. These myriad governance challenges were further exacerbated by elite competition over natural resource rents.

The Modern Central Asian Economies

The Collapse and Rebound of Central Asian Production

Today, the region's combined share of global GDP amounts to less than 1%. Kazakhstan dominates the group, gobbling up more than two-thirds of regional output. Turkmenistan and Uzbekistan each have economies about a third that of the regional giant, while output in Kyrgyzstan and Tajikistan is an order of magnitude lower.

While growth remains volatile—even for non-energy exporters[22]—economic activity has recovered neatly after plunging in the immediate aftermath of separation from the Soviet Union (as was the case for virtually all former countries of the USSR, including Russia) (Figure 7.3). In the first two decades of the new millennium, growth averaged more than 6% for the region. This allowed the two major energy exporters, Kazakhstan and Turkmenistan, to post per capita incomes that are now pushing close to high-income status.[23] Uzbekistan—the third energy exporter of the group—also cranks out substantial output (it is higher than Turkmenistan in absolute terms), but its massive population—accounting for a little less than half of the region—means that this production is spread over a larger base (in that sense, its disproportionate population share is analogous to the out-of-proportion GDP share of Kazakhstan).

But the steady progress of the Central Asian economies in economic performance has not been solely due to the fortune of improved terms of trade from elevated commodity prices (which in turn was because of the global

---

21 Indexes of democratic development place Tajikistan as a closed anocracy, but it leans more toward autocracy than democracy.

22 This is a similar situation with Western Asia, where even non-energy exporters are affected by commodity price volatility, due to spillovers via FDI and remittances. But in this case, fluctuations in the prices of raw materials affect the non-energy exporters directly as well, since they are also commodity exporters of some form.

23 The latest available GDP per capita figures for Kazakhstan and Turkmenistan are $12,306 and $13,065, for the year 2023 (according to IMF estimates). While the high-income threshold is adjusted yearly, the 2022 figure was $13,205 (based on the World Bank classification).

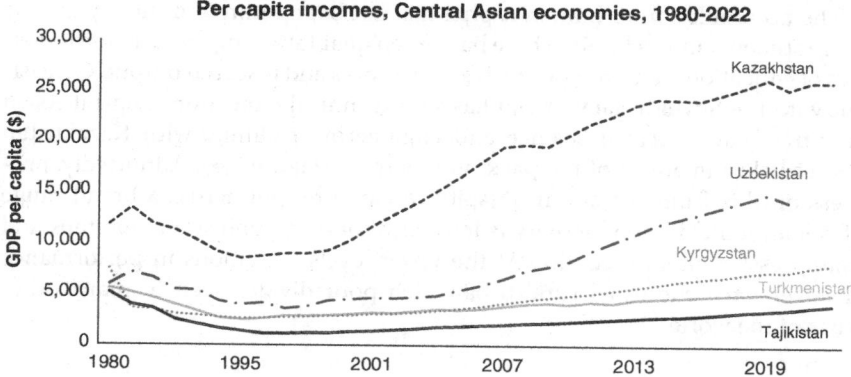

Figure 7.3 GDP growth plunged in the immediate aftermath of the breakup of the Soviet Union, and remained low for the half-decade thereafter. But the 2010s were a period of solid growth, boosted by elevated global commodity prices.

supercycle). Policymakers have worked hard to attract foreign direct investment, which multiplied by a factor of 17 between 2000 and 2021.[24] Education has also been expanded, especially at the secondary and tertiary level, with enrollment rates for the secondary level increasing by around 25 percentage points for most countries since the turn of the century (although still falling short of ratios reported during Soviet times) (Figure 7.4).[25]

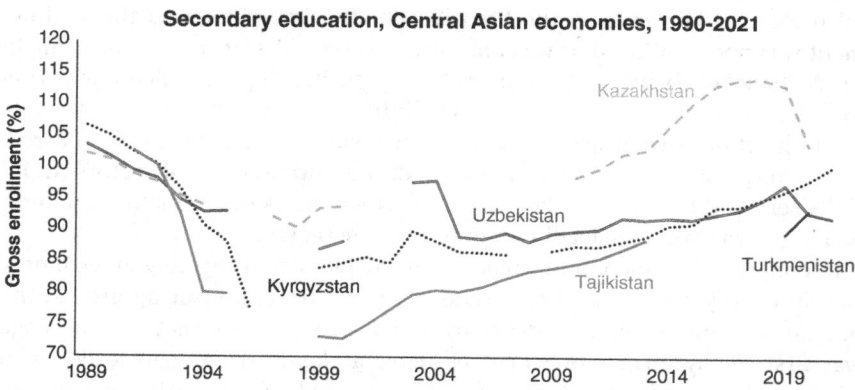

Figure 7.4 Enrollment rates in the Central Asian economies have steadily increased over the past two decades, although in most cases, these have yet to recover ground that was lost following their exit from the Soviet Union.

24 Vinokurov, E. (Ed.), "The Economy of Central Asia: A Fresh Perspective," *EABR Reports and Working Papers* 22/3 (Moscow: Eurasian Development Bank, 2022).
25 The failure to reach levels reported in the late 1980s may be due to a genuine lack of progress, outmigration (especially from more affluent and better-educated households), and/or improved recording and reporting (today compared to during the Soviet era), although the truth is probably some combination of all of these explanations.

The accumulation of human capital has not been limited to merely getting more students into schools. There have been qualitative improvements in metrics of educational attainment, such as test scores and research output. Consistent with the Soviet legacy of emphasis on technical education, Central Asian countries have stressed science and engineering training, with Kazakhstan and Uzbekistan ahead of the pack on this front (Figure 7.5). Admittedly, progress on this front is uneven. Despite research output across a broad range of scientific fields, productivity is low, with modest publication volumes and unimpressive citation counts. At the lower levels, variations in performance have reflected the usual rural-urban, rich-poor divides seen in many other parts of the world.[26]

Nation-Building in the Aftermath of Communist Centralization

While it is convenient to classify them all as economies in transition, the different paths to political-economic transformation pursued by each state since independence have meant differential progress. Kazakhstan and Kyrgyzstan are furthest along in terms of adopting market reforms, while Turkmenistan and Uzbekistan are relatively far from completing their transitions to market economies; Tajikistan is an intermediate case (Figure 7.6).[27] By the same token, these differences offer insight into how the economic strategies adopted by each country have contributed to nation-building and development.[28]

The Kazakh economy has benefited immensely from its abundance of natural resources. However, in the first decade after independence, this endowment was poorly utilized. It was only after a series of reforms—culminating in the *Nurly Zhol* (Нұрлы жол, literally, "Bright Path") plan, rolled out during the Nazarbayev administration, for infrastructure and social services modernization—when growth began to consolidate, and take-off occurred. The strong market orientation has also allowed nontraditional sectors (especially services) to become a key driver of growth in its modernizing economy, making Kazakhstan the leading economy of the region.

In contrast, Turkmen policymakers—while likewise navigating an economy rich in energy resources—have eschewed liberalization, favoring instead the pursuit of economic independence by way of strong state direction. The stage was first set by former president Niyazov, a classic strongman leader who adopted the grandiose title *Türkmenbaşy* ("Head of the Turkmen") during his administration. The post-independence economy came to be structured

---

26 Egéa, D. (Ed.), *Education in Central Asia: A Kaleidoscope of Challenges and Opportunities* (Cham: Springer, 2020).
27 Batsaikhan, U. and M. Dabrowski, "Central Asia—Twenty-Five Years After the Breakup of the USSR," *Russian Journal of Economics* 3(3) (2017): 296–320.
28 Pomfret, R., *The Central Asian Economies Since Independence* (Princeton, NJ: Princeton University Press, 2006).

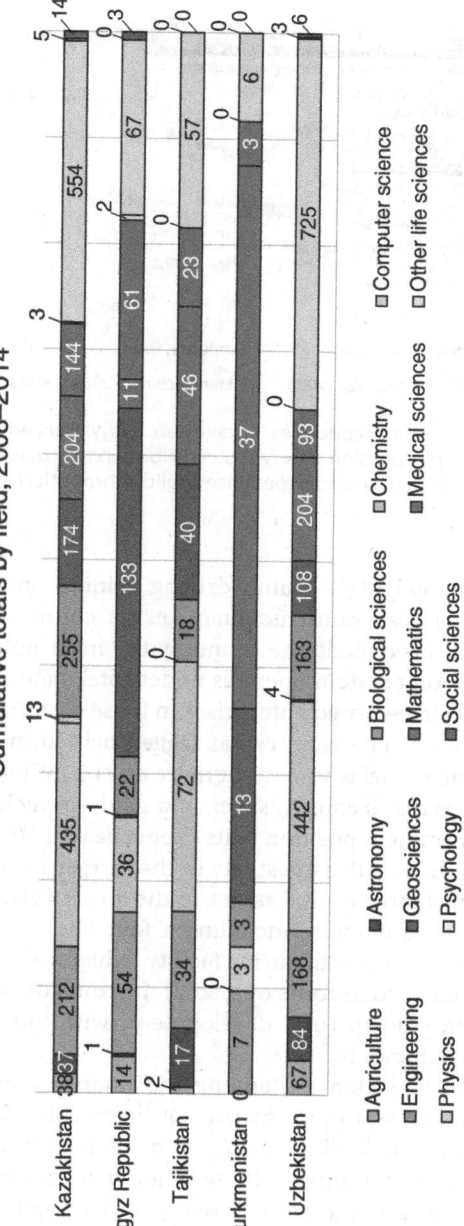

Cumulative totals by field, 2008–2014

Legend: Agriculture ■ Astronomy ■ Biological sciences ■ Chemistry ■ Computer science ■ Engineering ■ Geosciences ■ Mathematics ■ Medical sciences ■ Other life sciences □ Physics □ Psychology ■ Social sciences

Figure 7.5 The most prolific countries for scientific output—Kazakhstan and Uzbekistan—tend to specialize in physics and chemistry, while Kyrgyzstan and Turkmenistan exhibit pluralities in geosciences and mathematics, respectively.

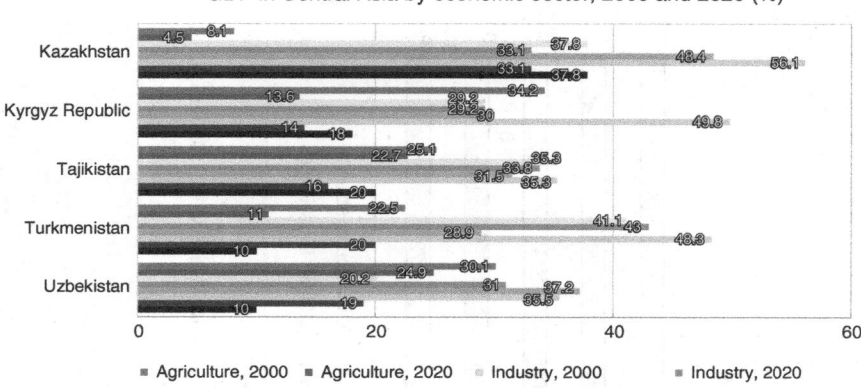

Figure 7.6 Among the Central Asian economies, Kazakhstan, Kyrgyzstan, and Uzbekistan have seen the most substantial expansion of services' contribution to growth. With the exception of Tajikistan, the others have also experienced solid contribution from industrial production, especially in Turkmenistan.

around the "commanding heights"—mainly drilling, mining, and refining, but also secondarily from chemicals, construction materials, cotton, and electricity generation—all of which have made the economy the most industrialized in the region. Even the banking system operates under total state control, channeling financing toward state-owned enterprises in these sectors.

Uzbekistan is in-between. The country has lagged behind in its transition process, but its economic model is somewhat more diverse. While the country has deposits of oil and gas, it is copper, silver, and gold—especially the last—that occupy the most prominent position in its export basket. With the capital, Tashkent, having being the fourth-largest city in the former Soviet Union, the nation also inherited substantial capital assets, in the form of civil and military transportation plant and equipment, including a four-line metro (built way back in 1977) and an aviation manufacturing facility (which has, unfortunately, been allowed to depreciate and become outdated). But outside of urban areas, little attention has been paid to rural development, with job opportunities especially scant in the countryside.

Both Kyrgyzstan and Tajikistan are among the poorest countries in the world, and it shows in terms of other metrics of human development, such as health and education. The Tajik economy remains heavily dependent on migrant remittances—by one estimate, these amount to close to a third of GDP—and exports of minerals and cotton are especially fragile, as well. Economic challenges have been compounded by repeated political unrest; right after independence, a five-year-long civil war wracked the country, and the rehabilitation of former combatants drained the fiscal coffers. Still, belated reforms undertaken since 2000 have placed the economy on more solid footing, allowing it to rapidly whittle down the poverty rate, from more than a third in 2003 to around a quarter in 2021.

As the poster child for rapid economic liberalization in the region, the Kyrgyz economy is a fascinating case study for the sort of challenges such a strategy may throw up. Starting from a very low base—Kyrgyzstan was among the poorest of the former Soviet Republics, and the most rural—the economy has nevertheless mustered an almost fivefold increase in per capita incomes since. Like Tajikistan, GDP is still excessively reliant on remittances (the contribution is around a quarter), but it has come a long way, steadily diversifying away from agriculture into both industry and services. Kyrgyzstan has also actively sought to embed itself in the global trading system—the nation was the first Central Asian economy to join the WTO—and it now boasts a wide array of international trading partners. This feat is all the more remarkable since, at the point of independence, some 98% of its exports were destined for other parts of the USSR. The jury is certainly still out as to whether the country's more liberal development strategy will pay off, but the emerging evidence has, thus far, been promising.

Central Asia and the World Economy

The Mixed Record of Regional Cooperation Initiatives

The region's propensity toward free trade and intermediation trace back to the ancient world. The Silk Roads, of course, had traversed Central Asia since the 2nd century BCE, linking the riches of China and India to Africa and the then-underdeveloped West.[29] Kushan middlemen—said to control important transregional and long-distance trade routes—are often credited with bringing power and prosperity to the Kushan Empire.[30]

But following the shift toward seaborne international trade after the 1500s—which was further accelerated with the container revolution in the 20th century[31]—the status of Central Asia as a landlocked region became a handicap, and a steady erosion of the region's traditional intermediary role followed. Trade costs in the region, which are today the highest in the world, have now became a real and major impediment to further trade expansion.

---

29 Frankopan, P., *The Silk Roads: A New History of the World* (London: Bloomsbury, 2015).

30 Morris, L., "Constructing Ancient Central Asia's Economic History," in S. von Reden (Ed.), *Handbook of Ancient Afro-Eurasian Economies*, vol. 1 (Berlin: De Gruyter, 2020), pp. 669–692.

31 Estimates suggest that the container was a key driver of 20th-century economic globalization. See Bernhofen, D., Z. El-Sahli, and R. Kneller, "Estimating the Effects of the Container Revolution on World Trade," *Journal of International Economics* 98 (2016): 36–50.

Moreover, despite the fairly broad distribution of natural resources across the territory, the effects of external orientation on the different economies have been far more varied. Oil has enabled the major exporters—Kazakhstan and Turkmenistan—to surge ahead in incomes, while trade exposure has availed development opportunities to populous Uzbekistan. Meanwhile, economies like Kyrgyzstan and Tajikistan have become heavily dependent on remittances and spillover investments from the oil-rich states.[32]

Given the residual frictions, the economies in the region have sought to promote trade through more institutionalized channels, although the track record for these efforts have been mixed (Table 7.1). Kazakhstan and Kyrgyzstan, for instance, are members of the Eurasian Economic Union,[33] which has run into problems following the Russian invasion of Ukraine in 2022. The Economic

Table 7.1 Economic integration agreements for the Central Asian economies

	Kazakhstan	Kyrgyzstan	Tajikistan	Turkmenistan	Uzbekistan
Central Asian Regional Economic Cooperation Program (CAREC)	✓	✓	✓	✓	✓
Commonwealth of Independent States (CIS)	✓	✓	✓		✓
Economic Cooperation Organization (ECO)	✓	✓	✓	✓	✓
Eurasian Economic Union (EAEU)	✓	✓			
Organization for Security and Cooperation in Europe (OSCE)	✓	✓	✓	✓	✓
Shanghai Cooperation Organization (SCO)	✓	✓	✓		✓
World Trade Organization (WTO)	✓	✓	✓		

Source: Author's compilation.
Notes: Uzbekistan holds observer status with the EAEU. The OSCE and SCO are primarily security cooperation organizations, but comprise notable economic components.

---

32 Pomfret, R., *The Central Asian Economies in the Twenty-First Century: Paving a New Silk Road* (Princeton, NJ: Princeton University Press, 2019).
33 The other members are Armenia, Belarus, and Russia. Uzbekistan holds observer status, as do Cuba and Moldova.

Cooperation Organization includes all five Central Asian states,[34] but the group has mainly spawned a patchwork of bilateral agreements. The most extensive initiative has been the Central Asia Regional Economic Cooperation Program (CAREC), but it functions less as a full-fledged regional trading agreement than a forum for cooperative dialog.

New Connections: the Eurasian Land Bridge and the Belt and Road Initiative

China's increasing presence in the region has revitalized Central Asian trade relations beyond Russia. Trade and financial flows between China and the region overtook that of Russia in the 2010s, and it does not look like this will reverse (Figure 7.7). Flows are dominated by the export of commodities from the region—consistent with China's trade patterns vis-à-vis other resource-intensive countries—although neither country is the major trading partner for Kazakhstan or Turkmenistan.[35]

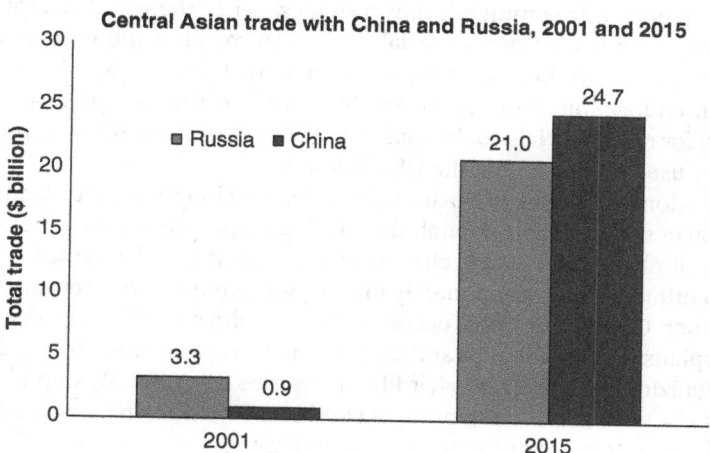

Figure 7.7 China overtook Russia as a trading partner for Central Asia in the 2010s, although most of this trade is dominated by commodities. A similar overtaking has occurred in terms of foreign direct investment.

---

34 The group began as an Iranian, Pakistani, and Turkish enterprise, and currently also includes Afghanistan and Azerbaijan.

35 These are the EU (Kazakhstan) and Turkey (Turkmenistan). China and Russia are the top two partners for Kyrgyzstan and Uzbekistan (in that order), while Russia is the top trading partner for Tajikistan.

Furthermore, the Belt and Road Initiative (BRI)—officially announced in 2013 in Kazakhstan, which itself stands as a testimony to the importance China places on the region—has led to a host of new infrastructure projects that will further consolidate Central Asian linkages with the Middle Kingdom. These include oil and gas pipelines, as well as rail connections. Connectivity was also boosted by the Eurasian Land Bridge, a transcontinental route for moving freight between China and Russia, which passes through Kazakhstan. These have been market-driven, with governments mainly playing a facilitator role.[36] The connections may eventually prove to be self-reinforcing; agglomeration economies playing out across Eurasia, coupled with associated labor migration toward hubs of economic opportunity, may be the very sort of stimulus that is needed carry the region to the next phase of development.

Conclusion

Despite being on the periphery of many contemporary observers, Central Asia has a long history of finding a niche in the global trading system. Although the region currently commands only a small sliver of the world economy, size need not imply irrelevance, especially when so much of the region's natural resources are set to become integral to modern technologies. After all size is, itself, endogenous; continued steady growth in the face of steady global demand for raw materials could easily return these economies to the important role they used to play within the USSR's ambit.

The region's exposure to Soviet-style industry, along with the steady accumulation of skilled human capital, also offers the opportunity for Central Asian firms to climb the value-added chain of mineral refining and processing, instead of contenting themselves on merely mining and exporting raw resources.

Whether these transitions occur quickly or slowly will likely depend on reform plans moving forward and taking root. Kyrgyzstan has already dangled the tantalizing possibility of what liberal reforms can offer. It is up to policy-makers elsewhere in the region to seize them, or risk being ensnared in the natural resource curse or the middle-income trap.

---

36 Pomfret, R., "The Eurasian Landbridge and China's Belt and Road Initiative: Demand, Supply of Services and Public Policy," *The World Economy* 42(6) (2019): 1642–1653.

8

Western Asia: An Economic Arab Spring?

> *Throughout history many nations have suffered physical defeat, but that has never marked the end of a nation. But when a nation has become victim of psychological defeat, then that marks the end of a nation.*
> —*Arab social scientist, Ibn Khaldun (1332–1406)*[1]

> *The Arab Spring, I think we will look back whether it's two years, five years, ten or fifteen . . . [a]nd say that it is a good thing.*
> —*Abdullah II bin Al-Hussein, current Hashemite King of Jordan*

> *This is the Middle East, where every week you have something new; so whatever you talk about this week will not be valuable next week.*
> —*Bashar al-Assad, current President of Syria*

Introduction

Mention the term "Middle East" and, for most, this would conjure up either images of the dry and dusty hillsides of Damascus or Jerusalem, or more recently, the glitz and glamor of towering skyscrapers in Doha or Dubai. But the Middle East is also the home to the rugged beauty of oases amid *wadis* in Oman, the modern buzz of trendsetters in Beirut or Tel Aviv, and the unmistakable grandeur of the Hagia Sophia in Istanbul or the pyramids at Giza. These are the sights and sounds of the Orient.

Yet, for much of its past, the part of the world we today call the Middle East (or Near East) was not even defined relative to the Western world, but as an intrinsic part of Asia. Sitting on its far western reaches, the region would extend its culture practices, and traditions toward the East, rather than the West.

---

1 Ibn Khaldun, *The Muqaddimah: An Introduction to History* (Princeton, NJ: Princeton University Press, [1377] 2015).

Asian Economies: History, Institutions, and Structures, First Edition. Jamus Jerome Lim.
© 2024 John Wiley & Sons Ltd. Published 2024 by John Wiley & Sons Ltd.

After all, Western Asia saw not only the birth of civilizations, but also the intersection of empires, and these empires, in turn, had frequently spread their influence toward the Subcontinent and Far East, via trade linkages that carried not only goods (coffee, dates, honey, and olive oil) but also ideas and knowledge (astronomy, algebra, and surgery), technological advances (such as prototypes of a flying machine, and the crank), and sociocultural and religious influences (from music to art to, of course, Islam) to distant lands.

Today, many think of the region principally from the perspective of either hydrocarbon exports—the Middle East has almost become synonymous with oil—or in terms of wars and religious extremists. Yet this is a jaundiced view of a part of the world steeped in a rich, deep, and storied history, and bearing marks of tremendous diversity in economic and sociopolitical organization.

After all, not one but two of the pristine civilizations emerged from the area we now call the "Fertile Crescent,"[2] a C-shaped fringe stretching from the edges of modern Iran in the east, through the Jordan valley, and on to the Mediterranean in the west. The Egyptian and Mesopotamian civilizations were established several thousand years before anywhere else in the world,[3] although each adopted distinct models for social organization: the former exhibited features of a structured, dynastic hierarchy, while the latter was characterized more by free-wheeling, independent city-states.

But the discovery of natural resource riches would change the region's political-economic calculus forever. Today, Western Asia includes some of the richest economies in the world—the tiny emirate of Qatar, by dint of its vast gas resources, boasts a GDP per capita a few thousand dollars higher than that of the United States—as well as some of the poorest (Yemen, at the southwestern edge of the Arabian peninsula, is among the world's poorest nations, with incomes comparable to that of Malawi, North Korea, and Somalia). And far from just a treasure trove of oil, major exports from Western Asia now include apparel as well as agricultural produce.

Also in stark contrast to the widely-held notion that overpopulated Western Asia is teeming with disaffected youth, eager to perpetuate extremist acts of violence, the working-age population for the region as a whole peaked around 2010. Elderly dependency ratios—the ratio of those aged above 65 to those between 15 and 64—are currently higher than they have been since the middle of the last century. Hence, while it is true that youth unemployment (and underemployment) remain a challenge for policymakers, the demographic

---

2 Breasted, J.H., *Ancient Times, a History of the Early World: An Introduction to the Study of Ancient History and the Career of Early Man* (Boston: The Atheneum Times, [1914] 2016).
3 The Indus Valley civilization was the third of the pristine civilizations that date significantly earlier than the other three—the Yellow River (modern-day China), Mesoamerican (Mexico and Central America), and Andean (Peru and parts of Argentina, Chile, and Colombia), although the earliest settlements in the Indo-Gangetic plain only date to around 7000 BCE, still around a half-millennium after Mesopotamia and the Nile Valley.

transition has already occurred across most of the region, resulting in more stable populations with an interest in high-quality growth.

Western Asia is therefore not only a part of the world that defies common misconceptions, but also one where any simple narrative of a monolithic region is not only inaccurate, but unjustifiable. This chapter paint a broad picture of key commonalities in the economic features of the region, but also emphasize the distinctive nuances of key countries, drawing on their history and geography to enlighten us on their present structures and future prospects.

Economic Geography of Western Asia

The Blessings of Resources Above and Below the Earth

Western Asia—or perhaps more accurately, Southwest Asia (although neither term remains in common use today)—is often defined as a region that spans the eastern edges bounded by the Caucasus mountains and the Hindu Kush, through to the western flanks that include the Sinai peninsula and Asia Minor (Anatolia).

The eastern parts—often referred to as the Mashriq (أَلْمَشْرِق, poetically "place where the sun rises")—reside in Asia, and comprise the Arabian peninsula (الخليج, *Al Khaleej*, or "the Gulf"),[4] along with the Levant (modern Israel, Jordan, Palestine,[5] Syria, and parts of Turkey) and Northeast Africa (Egypt and Sudan). The western segment—the Maghreb (الْمَغْرِب, "place where the sun sets")[6]—is often regarded as part of the broader Arab world, but falls beyond the scope of Asia (and hence this book).

Within this space is an often self-contained world, encompassing immense natural resources and human diversity. At risk of an excessively crude characterization of the diverse sociocultural geography of the region, there are two important dimensions along which one may think about the economies therein: based on their access to natural hydrocarbon resources (principally oil, but also natural gas), and their labor endowments[7] (Table 8.1).

Certain economies are both resource-rich, as well as labor-abundant; these are principally Iran and Iraq—known oil reserves in the two amount to around

---

4 The Gulf, itself, is a contested term, depending on whether one draws reference from Saudi Arabia (the "Arabian Gulf") or Iran (the "Persian Gulf").

5 We use the term Palestine not so much as a political term, but because of its common usage in the region. Modern Palestine is comprised of the West Bank and Gaza, although the displaced Palestinian population can also be found in significant numbers in Israel and Jordan.

6 Stretching west from Morocco through to Algeria, Tunisia, and Libya, but sometimes also taken to include Mauritania and the disputed region of Western Sahara.

7 Cammett, M., I. Diwan, A. Richards, and J. Waterbury, *A Political Economy of the Middle East*, 4th ed. (New York: Routledge, 2013).

Table 8.1 Classification of regional economies based on natural resource and labor abundance

Category	Countries
Resource-rich, labor-abundant (RRLA)	Iran, Iraq, Saudi Arabia, Sudan
Resource-rich, labor-scarce (RRLS)	Bahrain, Kuwait, Oman, Qatar, the UAE
Resource-poor, labor-abundant (RPLA)	Egypt, Israel, Jordan, Syria, Turkey, Yemen
Resource-poor, labor-scarce (RPLS)	Lebanon, Palestine

Notes: In most cases, labor abundance is defined as economies with workforces of 6 million or less, with the exception of the UAE, where the Emirati population is only an estimated 11% of the total population of 9.4 million, and hence has been classified as labor-scarce. Sudan is not a part of Asia but has been listed for comparative purposes, due to its usual inclusion as part of the Mashriq.

a tenth of the global share (third and fifth worldwide),[8] respectively—but by dint of their sizable populations, such wealth has to be shared among a far larger group of beneficiaries (while this would also apply to Saudi Arabia, its resource abundance, relative to population of around 22 million nationals, has enabled a more sustainable sharing of the Kingdom's resources).

Most of the nations on the Arabian peninsula are resource-rich yet labor-scarce; these include the remainder of the Gulf Cooperation Council (GCC) nations. Among these, Qatar is notable in that it is abundant not so much in petroleum but in natural gas (proven reserves are third globally, after Russia and Iran, albeit production stands at sixth).

Lebanon and Palestine are nations that are not only resource-poor, but are in possession of fairly small populations. This places them in a small group of countries in the region that have had to rely on developing human capital as the foundation of economic growth. Human capital is, however, mobile, and the tendency for outmigration points to the difficulties these countries face in talent retention amid domestic political instability, resulting in a greater scarcity of labor than might otherwise have been the case.

Finally, there is a large group of resource-poor but labor-abundant economies. This isn't to say that these nations have no natural resources whatsoever—Syria, for instance, was once a net oil exporter,[9] and Yemen has nontrivial deposits of copper, gold, and silver—but, by and large, the larger populations

---

8 Political-economy challenges in both have also meant that production has been significantly lower than potential; Iraq's production is fifth globally in terms of barrels per day, while Iran's falls to ninth.
9 A combination of reserve exhaustion, international sanctions, and government mismanagement led to the economy turning into a net oil importer around 2010.

in these countries have resulted in greater emphasis on their workforces. Many have chosen to leave their home countries in search of better opportunities; the Egyptian, Jordanian, and Turkish diasporas can be found across the region (as well as the rest of the world).

Within this group also lie the two industrialized economies of Western Asia: Israel and Turkey. The former's economic prowess lies in certain specialized industries (chemicals and pharmaceuticals, polished diamonds, and arms), as well as its internationally-distinguished high-technology sector; Israel's central technology hub—"Silicon Wadi"[10]—is a rich ecosystem of complementary innovation-oriented startups, venture capital, and educational and research institutions, much like its Californian counterpart. Turkey, in contrast, has a somewhat broader industrial base, which includes lower-end manufacturing (textiles and consumer electronics) as well as more sophisticated products (military technology, including aerospace).

Heavy and Sour, But Gold Nonetheless

Hydrocarbon deposits aren't the whole picture in terms of Western Asia's natural resource gifts, but they account for much of the story. Of the top 10 oil producers, half are in Western Asia; the region also accounts for three of the top 10 gas producers.[11]

Much of the oil extracted from the region is of the heavy (highly viscous) and sour (containing greater levels of sulfur) variety, which results in the need for greater processing. Consequently, the benchmark price for oil from the region—Dubai Crude—tends to trade at a discount relative to light, sweet benchmarks, such as Brent or West Texas Intermediate (WTI) (Figure 8.1).[12]

Western Asia commands around a third of global reserves of natural gas deposits, but only generates a tenth of its production. Since natural gas must be transported by pipelines or liquified for transport on purpose-built ships, the region's physical distance to the major markets of East Asia, Europe, and the United States has limited its export options to liquefaction, which has left the main gas fields of the Gulf less competitive than elsewhere.

Still, while the region does not clearly *dominate* global oil and gas production, it tends to be the *swing producer*—the one that matters at the margin—due to production than far exceeds domestic consumption, as well as an ability

---

10 The Hebrew term *wadi* (נחל), common as well to Arabic, translates to valley or stream.

11 These are, in order of production, Saudi Arabia, Iraq, the UAE, Iran, and Kuwait (for oil), and Iran, Qatar, and Saudi Arabia (for gas).

12 Brent is the standard global reference rate, for which around two-thirds of all global contracts are priced, and tends to be applied to light, sweet crude. WTI is the usual standard for U.S. oil (which is also light and sweet), but due to storage and shipping problems, the WTI may diverge from Brent pricing.

Density and Sulfur Content of Selected Crude Oils

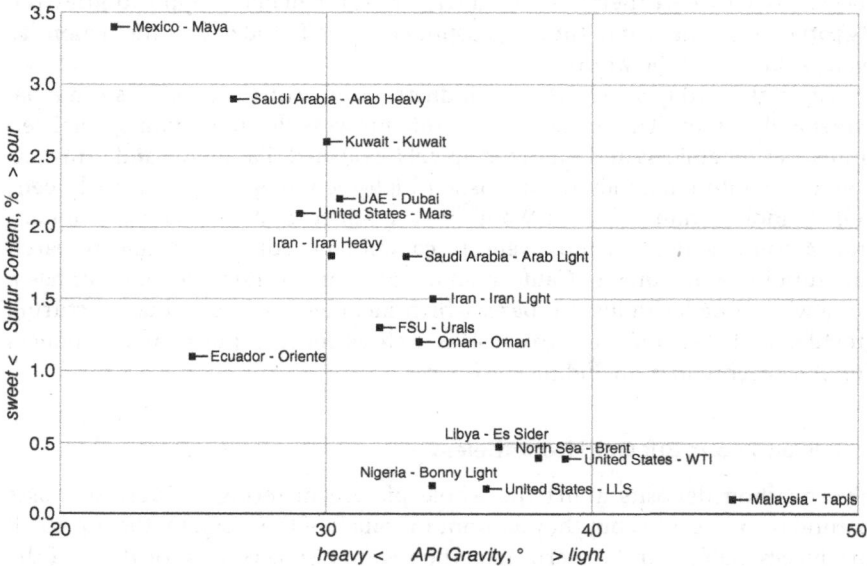

Figure 8.1 The oil produced in Western Asia tends toward the heavy, sour variety, which requires greater processing, and as a consequence tends to be sold at a discount relative to light, sweet crude.

to ramp up (or down) production more quickly. This makes Western Asian economies key global exporters.

Primary production in the region extends beyond just oil and gas. For example, Egypt is a niche cotton producer, and Iran a global fruit powerhouse. In terms of other mineral resources, Jordan and Saudi Arabia are internationally-recognized phosphate producers, while Turkey is a key zinc exporter. Still, it is undeniable that hydrocarbons—and related petrochemicals and byproducts—define Western Asia, and many economies, especially those in the GCC, have become enormously wealthy because of it.

There is one other natural resource that is of great importance to the region, defined more by its scarcity than abundance: water. The geography of the region has always been arid or semi-arid to begin with; after all, the Fertile Crescent is so named more for the rich river deposits accumulated over millions of years—which permitted agricultural cultivation and state-building when coupled with ingenuity—rather than a lush, verdant landscape, even in the past.

But the forbidding (and fragile) land across much of Western Asia presents new problems today. A still-rising population—amounting to around 290 million souls—has placed the region's aquifers under great duress. The Tigris and

Euphrates—both of which flow southeast across the region, and border most of the original settlements[13]—have both experienced decreases in water quantity and quality. Both are forecast to have reduced water flows (of 30% and 60%, respectively) by the end of the century. The north-flowing Nile—which crosses through Egypt before emptying into a large delta at the Mediterranean—is likewise drying, with dam projects and other upstream diversions contributing to a steady reduction in river flow.

Continuing changes in the climate—resulting in decade-long drought conditions in some countries, such as Egypt and Syria—and additional water demands associated with development have now applied further pressure, leaving the region on the verge of a water crisis.

Wealth Has Enabled Economic Diversification

While Western Asian economies are, today, more diversified than several decades ago, the region remains dependent on oil exports. Measures of economic diversification[14] indicate that, relative to the 1980s, many economies are only between 10% and 15% more diversified.[15] This has been disappointing, not least because the lack of production diversification has worsened business cycle-related output fluctuations, and all the more given the fickle nature of global energy prices.

This desire to hedge against output volatility has provided a strong impetus to pursue restructuring. Where diversification has been realized, it has been due to increased forward participation; that is, by building industrial capacity that would enable these economies to become intermediate goods suppliers for other countries (in contrast, the Southeast Asian economies have sought to increase backward integration of their products, by incorporating previously imported intermediate goods into their domestic production chains).

As it turns out, the sort of structural policies required for successful diversification tend to be more easily adopted in the higher-income economies (Figure 8.2). This is unsurprisingly the case for Israel and Turkey, which are already high-income and industrialized. But the GCC economies—especially

---

13 The term Mesopotamia literally means "land between two rivers," in references to the Tigris and Euphrates.

14 The most standard measure of economic diversification is the so-called Herfindahl-Hirschman Index (HHI), which takes the sum of squares of market shares of each sector in the economy (s_i), such that $HHI = \Sigma_i s_i$. Higher HHI measures indicate greater concentration (less diversification), with measures above 0.25 (below 0.01) typically regarded as excessively low (high) diversification.

15 Mazarei, A., "Efforts of Oil Exporters in the Middle East and North Africa to Diversify Away from Oil Have Fallen Short," *PIIE Policy Brief* 19-6 (Washington, DC: Peterson Institute for International Economics, 2019).

Level of diversification of goods exports (2010–2014)

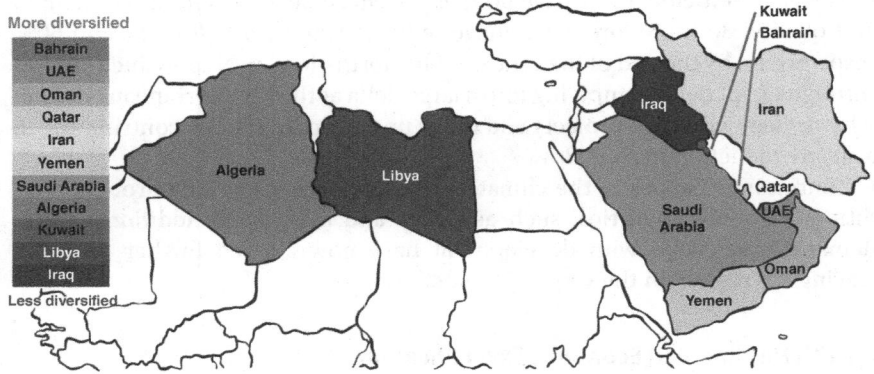

Figure 8.2 Economic diversification has been limited and erratic in the economies of Western Asia, and to the extent that this has occurred, it has been most successful in the higher-income countries.

Bahrain and the UAE (largely due to the emirate of Dubai)—have steadily deployed their natural resource rents toward expanding their production capabilities too, and are now much more diversified in their exports, especially compared to nations like Iraq or Yemen.

One major reason for this positive relationship between per capita GDP and diversification is that higher incomes tend to be accompanied by stronger economic incentive systems that enable firm growth, improved macroeconomic policymaking, and higher-quality governance. Yet it is, arguably, the least-developed countries that are in greatest need of more diversified economies.

Economic History of Western Asia

West Asia as the Cradle of Civilizations and the Clash of Empires

The first known civilization, Sumer, was located in southern Mesopotamia (modern Iraq). Sumer emerged around the 6th and 5th millennium BCE, and included multiple city-states. Sumerian civilization was eventually absorbed into the Akkadian Empire, the first ancient empire in the region, circa 2300 BCE.[16]

Similar developments were occurring along the banks of the Nile. A Neolithic culture took hold around the 6th millennium BCE, and gradually expanded, until about 3150 BCE, when the first unified kingdoms were founded. Ancient

---

16 The Sumerians and Akkadians, in turn, eventually evolved into the Babylonian and Assyrian civilizations.

Egypt then underwent a slew of dynastic periods,[17] before being intertwined with Western civilizations under the Ptolemies and Romans.[18]

The settled cultures were enabled by sedentary agriculture and animal domestication. Starting around 3500 BCE, humans began the transition away from hunting-gathering by devoting their energies to the farming of cereal; these were mainly emmer and einkorn wheat, along with barley, pulses like lentils and chickpeas, and flax. Husbandry of sheep and goats also turned out to be far more efficient as a source of meat, compared to hunting. The food surpluses that resulted enabled the emergence of specialized professions—such as scribes, soldiers, priests, tradesmen—which are the origins of non-agricultural labor in the economy.

Many elements of modern economic organization can be traced back to ancient Egypt and Mesopotamia. These include property rights—used to demarcate fields for agriculture, and temple land for worship—and the payment of wages (often in the form of, believe it or not, beer), for labor in the fields (Figure 8.3). Invariably, taxation followed; temples required payments, which were made possible given wages from work and surpluses from the

(a) (b)

Figure 8.3 (a) A clay tablet demarcating property ownership of fields, towns, and palaces around the ancient Sumerian city of Nippur in Mesopotamia, and (b) a tablet inscribed in cuneiform indicating wages to be paid in the form of beer.
Source: (a) Mary Harrsch / Wikimedia Commons / CC BY 2.0, (b) Osama Shukir Muhammed Amin / Wikimedia Commons / CC-BY-SA 3.0

---

17 Egyptologists number these at 31, although the chronology is usually defined as the Early Dynastic (1st and 2nd dynasties), Old (3rd–6th), Middle (12th and 13th), and New (18th–20th) Kingdoms, followed by the Late (26th–31st) Period, with three intermediate periods of greater dissension between kingdoms.
18 The Neo-Assyrian Empire came to an end with the fall of Nineveh in 612 BCE, while the Neo-Babylonian Empire ended after Babylon was conquered in 627 BCE.

fields. For those temporarily unable to pay (or in possession of excess), savings and credit were made available with a proto-banking system. Even the idea of government came about at this time, led by the priests who served as intercessors to the gods, seeking to guarantee a good harvest.

The stable but slow progress in economic growth eventually led to the dominance of the region by other civilizations. The Greeks, especially under Alexander the Great, extended Macedonian influence through Egypt, Asia Minor, the Levant, and eventually, ancient Persia.[19] The Sasanians—a Southern Iranian people—followed, with the (re)conquest of Persia, before expanding westward toward Egypt, the Levant, and Arabia.

But what brought Western Asia firmly back into the global conversation was the rise of Islam. During the Caliphate period[20]—which spanned the early 7th century until the mid-beginning of the 16th century—Muslim power stretched from Persia and central Asia to the east, across the countries of the Eastern Mediterranean, through to North Africa and Southern Spain in the west.

This was the Golden Age of Islam. Militaristic expansion had led to a rapid accumulation of wealth and power, and Baghdad—the capital during the time of the Abbasids—even attained the enviable status of being the richest city in the world. Wealth was accompanied by significant advances in knowledge and learning. Islamic scholars seized on texts from the Greeks and Romans, and cities across *Dar al-Islam* (دار الإسلام), the "House of Islam")—Baghdad, Córdoba, Seville, and Shiraz all had intellectual classes—expanded scientific inquiry in several different fields. The legacy of knowledge transfer cannot be understated. Indeed, much of the innovation and discovery that emerged during Europe's Renaissance and Age of Enlightenment was built on ideas that were translated (and in some cases, re-translated back) into European languages, having been preserved by Arabic scholars during this time.[21]

---

19 There was also a two-year campaign, waged between 327 and 325 BCE, which saw the expansion of the empire into the Indian subcontinent (into what is modern-day Pakistan). The Macedonians would hold onto the territory even after the death of Alexander, under satraps of the Seleucid Empire, until the reconquest during the Mauryan Empire.

20 The first three successive caliphates were the Rāshidun (661–632, الراشدة CE, led by the so-called "Four Righteous Caliphs" of Abu Bakr, Umar, Uthman, and Ali), the Ummayad (750–661, الأموية), and the Abbasid (1517–750, العبّاسيّة). These were based, respectively, in Medina (then Kufa), Damascus, and Baghdad. There is no real scholarly consensus on the end of the Abbasid, as there were a number of contending successor regimes: the Fatimid (909–1171), Córdoba (929–1031), Almohad (1147–1269), and Ayyubid (1171–1260) all present overlapping claims, although the Mamluk Sultanate (1261–1517) was the longest-lasting.

21 These were in domains ranging from astronomy, to biology and medicine, and to mathematics, among others. For example, refined planetary models with the sun at the center of the solar system were first made in 837 CE by Abū Ma'shar Ja'far ibn Muhammad ibn Umar al-Balkhi, 707 years prior to Nicolaus Copernicus's model of heliocentric model of the universe in 1543. The earliest-known example of a trial with a control group was by Abū Bakr Muhammad ibn Zakariyya al-Rāzi in 890 CE, 910 years before James Lind conducted his first clinical trials on scurvy in 1747. In 1011 CE, Abū Rayhân al-Bīrūni had developed mathematical techniques for solving cubic equations and extracting numerical roots; it took another 192 years before Fibonacci provided a positive solution to the cubic equation, in 1202.

The Magnificence of the Ottomans, and Its Less-Than-Glorious Decline

The next power to cast their shadow over the region were the Ottomans. Founded by the tribal leader Osman—from which the term Ottoman is derived—at the turn of the 13th century, the empire would come to extend its control over significant parts of Western Asia, North Africa, and Southeastern Europe. These included the conquest of Constantinople around the mid-15th century, and two (ultimately unsuccessful) sieges of the Habsburg city of Vienna. At the apex of the empire's economic, military, and political power (under Suleiman the Magnificent), Ottoman cities were global hubs for art, science, culture, and religion.

This military and economic prowess was supported by the remarkable ability of the Ottomans to absorb human capital from across the multiethnic and multicultural empire. For instance, the fearsome *janissary* (*yeniçeri*)—an elite infantry that was the first standing army in Europe—were often from the Balkans, and even the Grand Vizier—the effective head of government—was not always of Turkish ethnicity.[22]

Still, after several centuries, internal divisions translated into a drawn-out decline, which culminated in an ignominious partition at the hands of European powers at the start of the 20th century. The weakness of the late Ottoman Empire, therefore, set the stage for the political economy of Western Asia, as we know it today.

Negative European influence began as early as the 19th century. An insistence on unfettered trade access allowed the more productive Industrial Revolution factories to flood—and eventually crowd out—local industry, which had originally managed to embark on proto-industrialization, even attaining self-sufficiency in cotton and woolen textiles. Even before formal conquest and dissolution, the Ottomans had begun to develop an unhealthy financial dependency on various European powers. The double whammy of deindustrialization and dependence meant that, by the time of partition—in the form of the infamous Sykes-Picot Agreement that carved up the remnants of the empire into British and French (and to a lesser extent, Italian, and Russian) spheres of influence—the mighty Ottoman Empire had already been all but hollowed out (Figure 8.4).

Partition itself left an indelible legacy, having occurred with little attention to centuries-long ethnic or institutional fault lines. Such careless artificial boundaries would come back to haunt the region, in the form of civil wars and cross-border conflicts. It would also shift the modern economic leadership of Western Asia—which had historically resided in economies located either in the Eastern Mediterranean or Persia—elsewhere.

---

22 This was also somewhat necessary, given how the practice of fratricide—where a new Sultan would subsequently kill all his sons and nephews since they were potential contenders to the throne—often eliminated a valuable pool of elite human capital that could provide crucial support for governance.

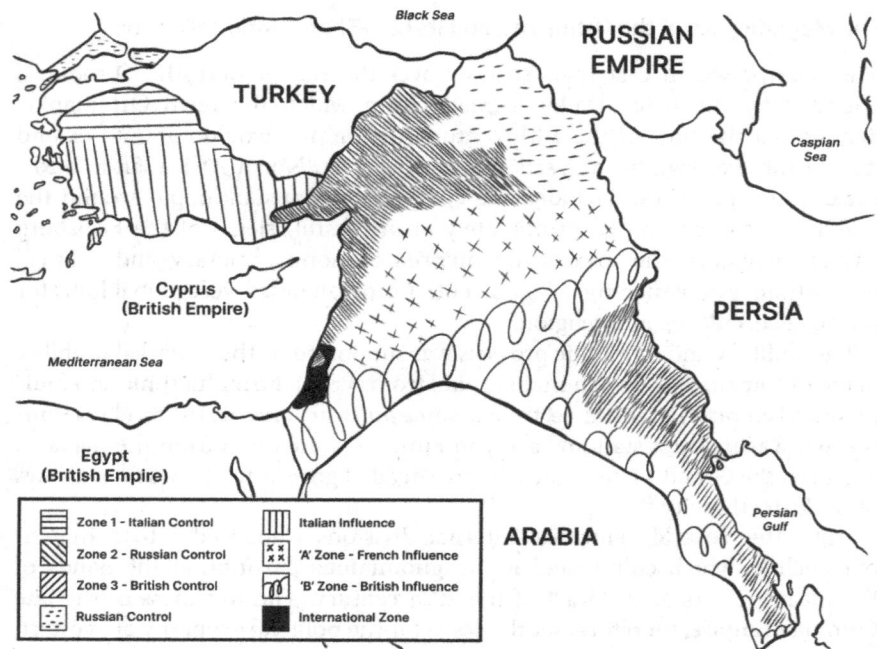

Figure 8.4 The Sykes-Picot Agreement was a key component in establishing the respective areas of influence for the British and French (and to a lesser extent, Italians and Russians) in the Middle East. These administrative divisions did not respect existing ethnocultural cleavages, and are one of the reasons for continued civil conflict in the region.

The Rise of the Petrostates

In 1908, the Anglo-Persian Oil Company (the progenitor of today's BP) struck oil at Masjed Soleyman, a field in the southwestern reaches of Iran. This was followed, three decades later, by the further identification of large, productive wells in Saudi Arabia by the Standard Oil company (what is today ExxonMobil).

These discoveries would drastically and irreversibly alter the political economy of Western Asia. Hydrocarbons ushered in an era of unprecedented prosperity for the winners. Economies located at the fringes of Western Asia—which had been hitherto more backward, and hence able to bear comparatively smaller populations—found themselves with access to riches that only had to be shared with a limited pool of stakeholders. In contrast, longstanding cores of Islamic civilization—Egypt, Iran, Turkey—found themselves confronting a shift in the center of economic gravity away from the core to the periphery.

By the middle of the 20th century, oil had become a mainstay in Western Asian economies, leading to the economic rise of Saudi Arabia and the United Arab Emirates (as of 2022, the region's largest and third-largest economies by GDP).

As energy exports increasingly defined the region's global footprint, so too did interest from the energy-hungry, industrialized West. Indeed, the region would come to be known to most as the Middle East, a reference to how it is situated to the *east* of the Occident.

Inspired by the pan-Arabism of then-Turkish president Kemal Atatürk, Middle Eastern economies pursued nationalist development strategies focused on import substitution. The Yom Kippur War, which broke out in 1973, further reinforced this approach. In retaliation for U.S. support for Israel during the war, Arab oil exporters chose to slash production while simultaneously imposing an embargo on the sale of oil there (as well as to other countries perceived to have supported Israel). The predictable outcome was a recession, both in the U.S. as well as many of the oil-importing nations in the West.

The world economy would receive a renewed shock in 1979, as the Iranian Revolution—which overthrew the then-ruling Shah and replaced the country's leader with the Ayatollah Khomeini—prompting another spike in global oil prices and triggering the most severe recession in the United States since World War II, as well as severe contractions across most of the industrialized world.

But oil prices collapsed in the middle of the 1980s, revealing the weaknesses of import substitution. Many economies of the region—especially among the oil-rich but labor-abundant countries that had squandered much of their resource revenue on unsustainable consumption subsidies and military adventurism— would experience twin fiscal and balance-of-payments crises. This prompted a reexamination of the model, which ultimately resulted in a shift toward export orientation as a means of riding out the economic storm.

The Modern Middle Eastern Economies

The Dominance of the Energy Cycle in Economic Fluctuations

Although not all the Middle East's economies have been endowed with hydrocarbon resources, the region's economic cycles are inextricably linked to fluctuations in the energy cycles. For oil- and gas-rich nations, the volatility stems from the unpredictable nature of energy prices, which give rise to dramatic shifts their terms of trade. For economies not endowed with hydrocarbon riches, their economic cycles are nevertheless affected by the cross-border remittance receipts, capital flows, foreign assistance, and external demand shocks that emanate from energy exporters (Figure 8.5).

Even a casual examination of the changes to economic activity in the region reveals the first-order importance of energy in shaping these economies' business cycles. Over the past half-century, the world has experienced five distinct energy-price shocks: the 1973 and 1979 jumps due to the Yom Kippur War

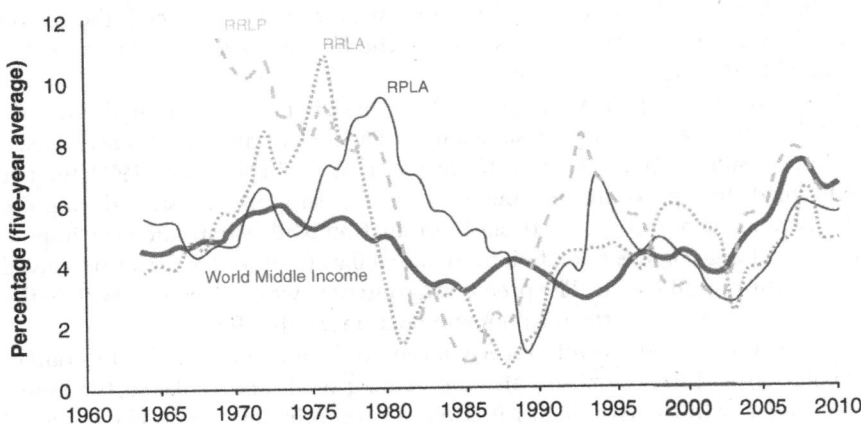

Figure 8.5 The business cycles of the economies of the Middle East tend to reflect the energy price cycle, even for countries that are resource-poor, due to the reliance on cross-border external demand and financial flows even for this group.

and Iranian Revolution, the 1990 spike that resulted from the Iraqi invasion of Kuwait, the 2008 commodity crisis that occurred in the aftermath of the global financial crisis, and finally, the pandemic-related surge in 2020.[23]

In each of these instances, the boom in output growth for the resource-rich economies is evident, as is the transmission of the shock to the resource-poor economies of the region, with a lag. Notably, these fluctuations are also more pronounced than is typical for global middle-income countries, a testament to the amplification effect that energy-related changes to terms of trade has on the Middle East.

This should came as no surprise, especially for energy exporters. Commodity prices appreciably alter each economy's ability to execute on fiscal policy, since revenue received from the sale of (usually) nationalized oil and gas companies goes toward funding myriad government programs. Similarly, the ability of the private sector to finance domestic investment activity, instead of relying on importing foreign savings in the form of FDI—is also affected by extant energy prices.

Taken together, these needs can be mapped into breakeven oil prices that would matter for each country, were they to target a zero fiscal or current account balance. Just as important, these breakevens tend to be significantly

---

23 Some observers term these broader movements as commodities supercycles, stemming from large, unanticipated, and persistent demand shocks, that are greeted by slow-moving supply responses.

higher than the costs of producing an additional barrel of oil in each country. For example, in Saudi Arabia and the UAE, onshore oil usually costs around $3 per barrel to produce (offshore oil is only fractionally more, about twice the price, owing to very shallow waters in the Gulf). In contrast, the fiscal breakevens for Saudi Arabia and the UAE are $84 and $53 per barrel, respectively, whereas external breakevens are $57 and $17. The difference between these costs and the various breakevens allude to the importance of commodity rents—the difference between costs and spending—for these economies, and point to the sort of constraints their government and businesses face in navigating energy prices (Figure 8.6).

Interestingly, the influence of the energy cycle is evident even when examining the overall level of prices (Figure 8.7). In contrast to the higher-frequency electronics manufacturing cycle—apparent in East Asia—or the even more unpredictable (and higher-volatility) food price cycle—which is the case in agriculturally-reliant South Asia—inflation in Western Asia marches to a very similar tune as output, more generally.

Part of the reason could be because the region remains less integrated—by way of production value chains—than others, and hence the transmission mechanism for the energy price cycle occurs primarily on the nominal side, through changes in prices (and attendant terms of trade).

Rolling Back the Public Sector in Saudi Arabia

The largest economy in Western Asia became that way only relatively recently, at least when considered over the long span of history. Fueled (literally and figuratively) by fabulous hydrocarbon export revenue,[24] the Saudis reinvested their petrodollars back into vast development projects across the once-desolate Kingdom. This is to the credit of the Kingdom's leadership, which did not squander this income solely on fleeting consumption, nor expend unnecessary resources contesting over the resulting rent (albeit keeping in mind that its population in 1970 only numbered about 6 million, which made generous redistribution of benefits very feasible).

The upshot of this redistributive action is that the share of government consumption in output is massive: for most years, these range from 20–30% (in the mid-1980s, this even went as high as 35%; the low over the past half-century—in 1974, as a result of the OPEC oil embargo—was 13%, although it also dipped to 18% in the aftermath of the 2008 global crisis). Regardless of how one slices it, this amount of public expenditure far outstrips the global average (of around 16%) (Figure 8.8).

---

24 Although much more widely known for oil—for which the country has the world's second-largest proven stock of reserves (after Venezuela)—it also has one of the world's larger natural gas reserves (after Russia, Iran, Qatar, the U.S., and Turkmenistan).

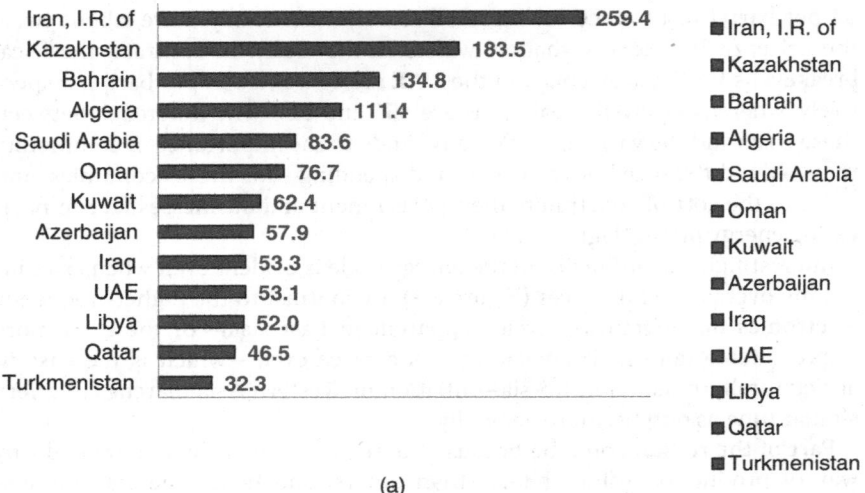

(a)

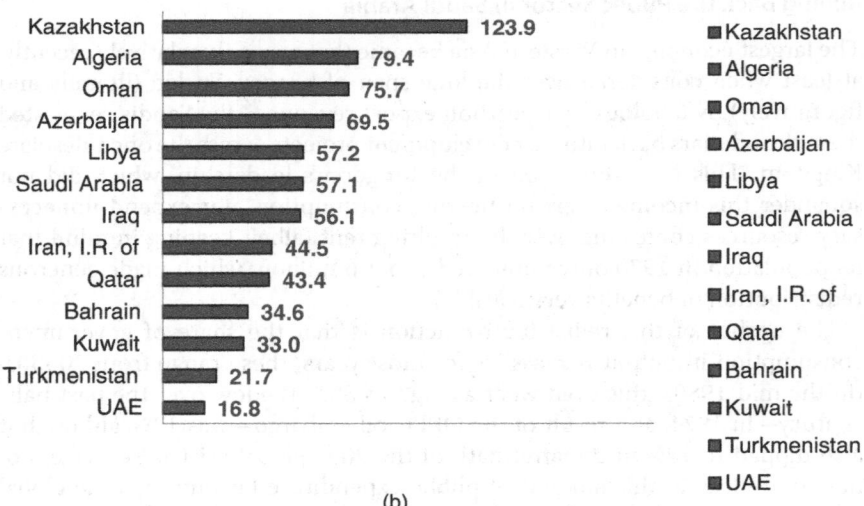

(b)

Figure 8.6 For oil-exporting countries, it is possible to map the price necessary to ensure that the (a) fiscal or (b) current account balance stays at zero. Such breakevens tend to be significantly higher than the actual marginal production cost of oil in each country.

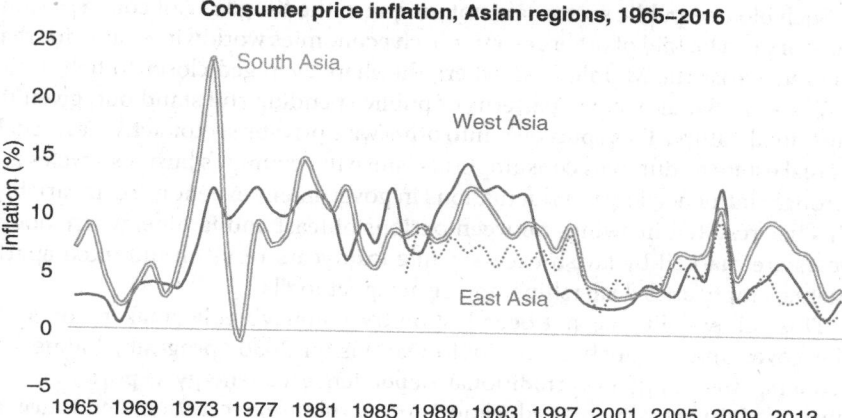

Figure 8.7 Inflation in the Middle East tends to be less volatile than in East Asia, where the high-frequency electronics cycle tends to dominate, and more muted than South Asia, where the higher volatility of food prices tends to amplify inflation in a region that is much more reliant on agricultural goods.

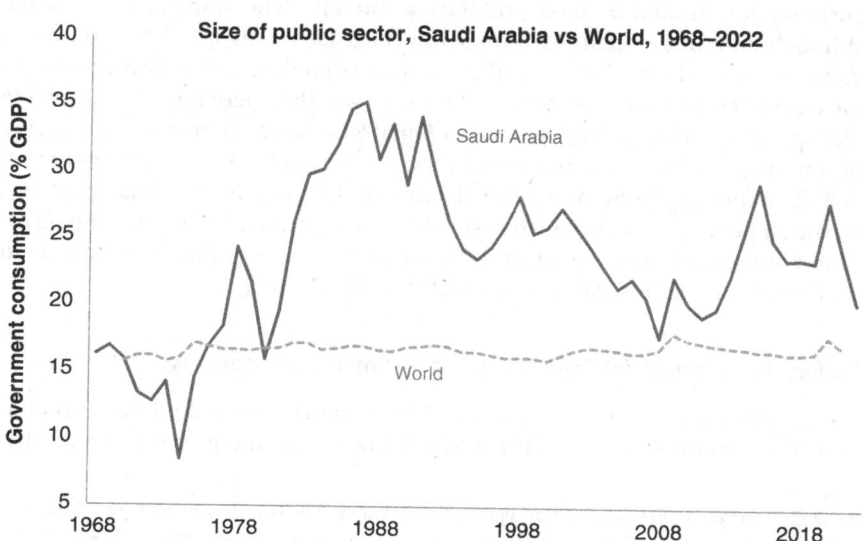

Figure 8.8 Public consumption in Saudi Arabia outstrips the global average, even in years of relatively lower public spending. This partly reflects redistribution, whether direct or indirect, of resource rents to the native population, but has resulted in significant volatility in the Kingdom's business cycles.

Such bloated public sectors are not unique to the Kingdom, of course; a similar story can be told of other resource-rich economies worldwide—and, for that matter, across the Middle East, where the share averaged closer to half in the 1970s—but Saudi Arabia's patterns of public spending still stand out, given its sustained nature. This spills over into otherwise private-sector activities—such as real estate or durables consumption—since the country's business cycles are strongly influenced by the fluctuations in government expenditure. Invariably, this has resulted in swings between periods of feast and famine, where boom years are marked by lavish excess, while lean years result in unrented apartments, empty auto dealerships, and eerily quiet malls.

This vulnerability has not been lost on the country's policymakers. In 2016, the government launched an ambitious "Vision 2030" program,[25] aimed at reducing the Kingdom's traditional dependence on energy exports, and to diversify into areas such as education, infrastructure, recreation, and tourism. The flagship project—a $0.5 trillion smart city dubbed NEOM, situated at the northern end of the Red Sea—will be financed by the Kingdom's Public Investment Fund. Importantly, the overall vision has modernization elements woven in, especially regarding women's participation in the labor force,[26] and rights more generally.

As a result of these reform efforts, FDI into Saudi Arabia—which was previously strictly limited by laws prohibiting foreign ownership—has increased, although amounts remain extremely low. Legislative changes have sought to improve the business climate, and there have been dramatic improvements in the ease of conducting business in the Kingdom. But there have been notable hiccups. The killing of Saudi journalist Jamal Khashoggi by government agents prompted global scrutiny and derailed planned investments in some quarters. Whether such problems affect the viability of the program depends, crucially, on the ability of policymakers to sustain the momentum of economic modernization and transformation, even if the current administration of Mohammad bin Salman should lose some of its zeal toward reforms.

Turkey as an Industrial Economy Built on Shaky Foundations

Along with Asian economies such as China, India, and Indonesia, Turkey is now often regarded as part of the next wave of major emerging economies that

---

25 Such strategic programs are not unique to Saudi Arabia. The UAE has an analogous Vision 2021 (albeit focused more on sustainable development and infrastructure), Egypt a Vision 2030 (aligned with the UN's Sustainable Development Goals), and Kuwait a Vision 2035 (focused on transforming the country into an international trade and financial hub).

26 These efforts are not always conventional. For example, due to the longstanding prohibition on driving by women—the ban was only lifted in mid-2018, and the issuance of driving licenses to women since has been painfully slow—one form of support for women to join the workforce has taken the form of transportation subsidies (which covers 80% of the cost of a taxicab fare).

would lead global economic growth.[27] This has certainly seemed to be the case since 2010, where the economy averaged an annual GDP growth rate of around 6% per annum. Solid growth has helped usher in an era of significant improvements in the welfare of the Turkish people; per capita incomes are estimated at around $41,400 (in PPP terms), within the neighborhood of peripheral European economies such as Greece and Portugal.

Yet the same incomes, in nominal terms, only come up to a little less than $12,000. While many emerging economies do exhibit some divergence between the two metrics, the huge gap for Turkey's case hints at a deeper challenge the country has faced, which is the weakness of the nation's currency. Between 2018 and 2022, the economy went through a wrenching economic crisis. The *lira* lost more than three-quarters of its value relative to the dollar, and inflation went from a high-but-acceptable 11% in 2017 to a hyperinflationary 72% in 2022 (Figure 8.9).

Much of the nation's recent travails are almost certainly attributable to the economic (mis)management of President Recep Tayyip Erdoğan, who has adopted an (to put it generously) unorthodox approach to macroeconomic

Figure 8.9 Turkey was in the throes of an economic crisis between 2018 and 2022, where the exchange rate lost three-quarters of its value and prices spiked to hyperinflationary levels.

---

27 Some have termed these emerging economies—Brazil, China, India, Indonesia, Mexico, Russia, and Turkey—the E7 (Emerging Seven), in reference to the G7 (Group of Seven) advanced economies comprising Canada, France, Germany, Italy, Japan, the United Kingdom, and the United States. See Hawksworth, J. and G. Cookson, *The World in 2050: Beyond the BRICs: A Broader Look at Emerging Market Growth Prospects* (London: PricewaterhouseCoopers, 2008).

policymaking. This has included a steadfast belief in suppressing interest rates in the face of rampant inflation, the imposition of price controls and fines for businesses that dated to raise prices, and controversial appointments to key posts (including running through a string of central bank governors at the rate of one a year, and installing his son-in-law as the country's finance minister).[28]

But the challenges faced by the economy predate its recent troubles. The *lira* has, after all, steadily depreciated since the global crisis in 2008. Persistent undersaving, especially in the private sector, has translated into chronic current account deficits—averaging –2.5% of GDP since the 1970s—and soaring foreign debt (amounting to more than 50% of income). And Turkey is no stranger to crises; it had previously endured a major financial crisis in 2001, as well as a debt crisis in 1977–79, and a currency crisis in 1994.

The macroeconomic dysfunction has unfolded over a backdrop of an otherwise sound economy: a diversified industrial base with manufacturing strengths in defense, electronics, textiles, and transportation, a mature banking system, relatively healthy public finances, and a generally entrepreneurial business climate. If there is one critical area of imbalance in the economy, it is in the construction and contracting industry, which has become bloated and often rife with corruption, resulting in low quality.[29] Yet the appetite for building remains unabated, owing in part to the stimulus effect deriving from construction projects (and, some would argue, Erdoğan's extensive business interests in the sector).

How Turkey subsequently develops might well hinge on the country's ability to rediscover some of the ingredients that made it successful in the first place. Following the dissolution of the Ottoman Empire, the nation pursued a secularization program, structured along Western lines. Kemal Atatürk, the founding father of the modern Turkish Republic, implemented progressive reforms that included expanding primary education, extending suffrage and civil rights to women, and enhancing industrial capacity.

Beyond modernization, Turkey had also made international economic relations a centerpiece of its development strategy. It intensified its relations with Europe, which exposed the economy to a large, valuable market.[30] But these early efforts stalled thereafter, and it took until 1995 before the country joined the European Customs Union. Current negotiations for accession into the EU have gone on for close to two decades, with little to show for it thus far.

---

28 Erdoğan has replaced finance ministers at a rate only slightly slower than central bank governors; since his administration began in 2014, there have been six different finance ministers.
29 The unfortunate consequence of this has been that earthquake-related casualties (the country is located almost entirely on faultlines, and faces thousands of earthquakes of various magnitude yearly) are higher than they otherwise would be.
30 Turkey was an early member of the Council of Europe—founded to promote human rights, democracy, and rule of law within the continent—and joined the European Economic Community in 1963.

Israel as an ICT Services Powerhouse

Together with Turkey, Israel is one of two advanced industrialized economies in the Middle East. The economy leans more heavily, however, on services, especially in advanced science and technology, where it rivals that of many Western nations. The country boasts more high-tech startups per capita than seasoned innovators such as Japan, Korea, and all of Europe, and has the world's largest venture capital sector (again on a per capita basis).

Some have suggested that the country's shortcomings may, ironically, have been a source of its dynamism.[31] Mandatory service in the Israeli Defense Forces has allowed young adults to foster their creativity in resolving security issues, build contacts, and acquire a sophisticated set of technical skills. Similarly, its reliance on immigrants to populate the country has allowed a risk-taking, hustle mindset to take hold.

But Israel was not always a free-market force. After the country's founding in 1948, policymakers adopted a developmental state, informed by social democratic ideals. Growth was brisk—routinely exceeding 10% annually—but the Yom Kippur War set off an inflation crisis, and government spending soared even as growth stagnated. Israel then embarked on market-oriented structural reforms in the 1970s—about a full decade before the global neoliberalist movement led by Reagan and Thatcher—which proved successful in stabilizing the economy, while also preparing it for the next two shocks: a wave of Jewish immigration after the breakup of the Soviet Union, and a major Palestinian uprising (known as the Second Intifada).

Despite these challenges, the economy was able to build up significant industrial capacity—especially in diamond polishing, electronics and military equipment, and industrial chemicals—alongside its strength in ICT services (Figure 8.10). The nation did briefly enjoy some energy independence (in terms of natural gas), but discoveries in the 2000s did not hold up, and reserves for a number of fields have mostly exhausted.

The UAE: A Tale of Two Cities

At the height of the global financial crisis of 2008, construction of what was then to be called the Burj Dubai—a 154-storey, 828-meter skyscraper—came to a virtual halt, plagued by financing issues associated with the crisis. The uncompleted tower became an awkward symbol of not only how Dubai's lofty ambitions were possibly misguided, but also a hint of how the emirate's growth-at-all-costs approach could instead be a mark of hubris. It came down to Abu Dhabi—Dubai's oil-rich neighboring emirate—to provide the $25 billion

---

31 Senor, D. and S. Singer, *Start-Up Nation: The Story of Israel's Economic Miracle* (New York: Grand Central Publishing, 2009).

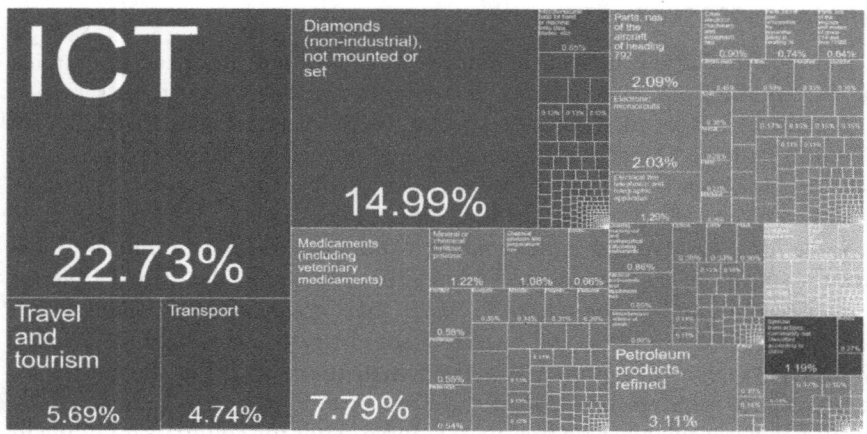

Figure 8.10 Modern Israel's export basket enjoys a substantial contribution from tradable services—especially information and communications technology (ICT)—but also has globally significant exports of polished diamonds, industrial chemicals, and electronics and military equipment.

in bailout funds necessary to keep the project afloat. When the tower was eventually completed in 2010, the building was renamed the Burj Khalifa, in honor of the then-ruler of Abu Dhabi.

Abu Dhabi was able to come to the rescue of Dubai in no small part because the price of oil remained buoyant throughout and after the crisis, peaking beyond $100 a barrel. But oil prices went into a precipitous decline thereafter, slumping to a low of $25 per barrel just a year-and-a-half later. This extended oil-price slump prompted much discussion of how rapid progress in green energy technologies could ultimately turn the emirate's vast oil reserves into "stranded assets," and many began to question whether Abu Dhabi's slow-and-steady approach was missing important opportunities that could quickly pass it by.

The two emirates'[32] contrasting development strategies underscore the tension underlying the Middle East's fourth-largest economy. While a third of the nation's output derives from oil revenues, this is unequally distributed. Consequently, Abu Dhabi contributes more than twice to the UAE's national income,

---

32 In addition to Abu Dhabi and Dubai, the other constituent emirates are Ajman, Fujairah, Ras Al Khaimah (RAK), Sharjah, Umm Al Quwain; all seven were all also part of the Trucial States (الإمارات المتصالحة, *Al-Imārāt al-Mutaṣāliḥa*), a confederation of tribes that had signed truces with Great Britain in the 19th century. The UAE was founded with six constituent emirates in September 1971. RAK was invited but only joined later, in February 1972, and while Bahrain and Qatar both participated in negotiations to establish a federation in the late 1960s, differences led to each declaring independence in 1971. See Smith, S., *Britain's Revival and Fall in the Gulf: Kuwait, Bahrain, Qatar, and the Trucial States, 1950–71* (London: Routledge Curzon, 2004).

compared to Dubai[33] Hence, while the economy as a whole has diversified immensely away from its traditional reliance on entrepôt trade and pearling, this owes much to the latter's forays into areas such as financial services, information technology, real estate, and tourism. In the former, oil remains singularly important, with the share of nonoil exports only a fraction of that of oil. Furthermore, nonoil economic activities remain very much dependent on spillovers from the energy sector (Table 8.2).[34]

There is clearly no single, unambiguous solution to the UAE's development challenge. The far more finite endowment of oil reserves—along with a historical tendency toward pursuing international trade opportunities—led Dubai to choose to heavily reinvest its limited oil revenues, resulting in the rapid transformation of the emirate into one of the few truly diversified economies in the Middle East over the span of two decades. In contrast, Abu Dhabi's tremendous oil wealth has lent itself to a more cautious but methodical approach, leveraging the comparative advantage in energy exports to gradually expand into nonoil sectors.

To be clear, there has also been a fair amount of emulation between the two. Following the success of Dubai's Emirates as an airline, Abu Dhabi launched its own flagship carrier, Etihad. While both have found some success,[35] it is a

Table 8.2 Foreign trade statistics for Abu Dhabi, 2021 and 2022

	2021		2022	
	Value	Volume	Value	Volume
Imports	25,180	28,106	27,463	28,712
Nonoil exports	20,001	10,491	21,494	11,230
Reexports	9,595	1,801	12,356	2,282

Source: Author's compilation, from Abu Dhabi Department of Finance (2022).
Notes: Values are in millions of USD, converted at contemporaneous year-end exchange rates. Volumes are in thousands of tons. Reexports are exports of foreign goods that are in the substantively same state as at the time of importation.

---

33 Data from 2017 indicate that Abu Dhabi's GDP was 832 million *dirhams*, versus 411 billion for Dubai. Together, the two emirates constitute 88% of the country's GDP. Reserves are also unequally distributed; the former owns more than 95% of the nation's reserves, and Dubai—having reduced its oil share of GDP from a quarter in 1990 to just 7% in 2004—no longer exports oil. See Sampler, S. and S. Eigner, *Sand to Silicon Going Global: Rapid Growth Lessons from Dubai* (Dubai: Motivate Publishing, 2008).
34 In an effort to credibly diversify its economy, Abu Dhabi launched an industrial strategy in 2022 that will invest $2.7 billion across a number of programs, aimed at increasing nonoil exports to a targeted $49 billion by 2031.
35 To date, both have been relatively successful as airlines, and are consistently ranked among the best globally. However, the business is by nature highly competitive and volatile, and Etihad, due to aggressive expansion plans in the latter half of the 2010s, reported significant losses for most of those years.

legitimate question to ask if the Gulf market (or beyond) is sufficiently large to support both. The same may be said about the relatively niche free port functions provided by the Dubai International Financial Center and Abu Dhabi Global Markets, as well as the many luxury hotels located within the country.

How the UAE economy will fare in the future will depend on which of these two models turns out to be more appropriate. While it is impossible to know for certain, it is more than likely that the optimal strategy will entail some balance between the two. After all, this was precisely the case when Dubai went through its travails in 2008, and yet also provided important ballast to the overall national economy when Abu Dhabi experienced its difficulties when oil prices collapsed after 2014. The trick is to minimize duplication from excessive, unproductive competition, and to coordinate decision-making over major strategic investments at the federal level.

Is the Egyptian Army Hijacking Its Economy?

Those who are less familiar with Egypt may be surprised to find out just how much the military—either directly or indirectly—controls the economy. The reach of the Egyptian Armed Forces is truly astounding. Beyond official defense expenditure—amounting to 7% of the total government budget over the past two decades (the global average is around 6%[36])—the military economy includes investments (both via shares and acquisitions) in civilian companies, involvement in infrastructure construction projects (from roads, bridges, and ports, to housing developments, to agricultural irrigation), to the supply of food and nonfood commodities, to the actual manufacture of civilian goods, such as household appliances, construction materials, transportation equipment, and even steel (Figure 8.11).[37]

The conditions that have allowed one entity to dominate so much of the economy have their roots in the import substitution development strategy, which was adopted by Egypt's most popular and consequential president in modern times, Gamal Nasser. This strategy was consistent with a centralized economy, and it was only in response to stagnating economic conditions and yawning fiscal deficits[38] that market-oriented reforms were finally acquiesced to. Military adventurism and internal conflicts throughout the 20th century

---

36 As a share of GDP over the equivalent period, this is closer to 2%, although this ratio has declined substantially. In the 1970s, the defense budget reached as high as 17%, before steadily falling over the course of the 1980s through today. However, this drop may well be artificial, and a function of shifting military spending to other areas, thereby keeping these costs off the official budget.

37 Sayigh, Y., *Owners of the Republic: An Anatomy of Egypt's Military Economy* (Washington, DC: Carnegie Endowment for International Peace, 2019).

38 At their nadir in 2013, the overall fiscal balance clocked in at a little more than −13% of GDP.

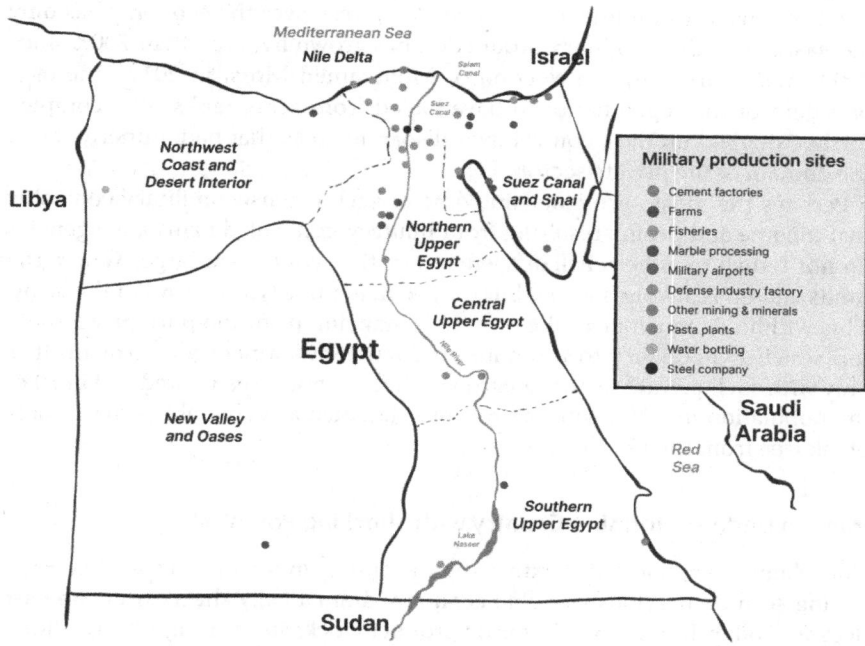

Figure 8.11 The reach of the Egyptian Armed Forces into disparate areas of the economy is truly astounding. In addition to official defense spending, the military lays claim to investments in civilian firms, public sector infrastructure projects, control over the supply of food and nonfood commodities, and even the direct manufacture of civilian goods.

provided further justification for military control, while simultaneously under-mining private sector development due to the economic burden of violence and instability.

When Egypt was a client state in the later stages of the Ottoman Empire—and at least a half-century thereafter through the 1930s—the country was essentially reliant on long-staple cotton (agricultural output, mainly in cereals, came a distant second). While an industrial sector (which includes automobile manu-facturing, consumer electronics, and home appliances, textiles, and construc-tion) does exist, it has often struggled to independently establish itself. This has translated into the overall poor performance of the Cairo and Alexandria stock exchanges—which has gone sideways for decades—despite the country's equity markets being among the oldest and deepest in the region.[39]

---

39 The Alexandria Exchange was founded in 1883, and the Cairo Exchange in 1903. Today, both operate under the aegis of the Egyptian Exchange, and are governed by the same board.

Yet the shadow of influence of the armed forces over the economy has only increased over time. Military production has grown by more than 700% since 2000. And spurred by the election of Mohammed Morsi in 2012—the only president of the republic not to have hailed from army ranks—the complex further stepped up their control over disparate areas that had, hitherto, been the domain of the private sector.

Perhaps the most pernicious outcome of such extensive military control is that income and profits resulting from military-controlled firms and agencies do not return to either civilian agencies, or the economy at large. Where the funds end up is anyone's guess, but they remain under the control of the army. This withholds much crucial credit and financing from the pure private sector, which is necessary to promote productive investment and growth. It is only with such private sector-led growth that the poor—estimated at 3 in 10 of the population in 2019, with many more classified as vulnerable—may finally break free from their cycle of poverty.

Iran: An Underperforming Country with Shocking Potential

The Islamic Republic is the sixth-largest economy in the modern Middle East, having seen its previously sizable economy dramatically shrink over the past decade. Today, Iran's gross domestic product clocks in at around $360 billion, about half that of its peak in 2012. While its output in terms of PPP stands much higher (around $1.5 trillion), crippling international sanctions have allowed previously smaller economies (like Egypt and the UAE) to catch up and overtake the former giant.

Although the country maintains a distinct religio-cultural heritage—unlike most of Western Asia, it practices the Shia brand of Islam, instead of Sunni—the country has always stamped its mark on the region. But by the beginning of the 20th century, Persia had—despite centuries of earlier economic, political, and military successes as empires under the Neo-Assyrians, Seleucids, Sasanians, Ilkhanate, Timurids, and Safavids (to name just some of the most established dynasties to have ruled)—retreated into a predominantly agrarian society.

Industrialization began in earnest post-World War II, under the final dynastic administration.[40] Tax collections were rationalized, which in turn financed both infrastructure development and public services in health and education. Production capacity diversified into both light and heavy manufacturing, and per capita incomes began to converge toward Western levels, reaching about two-thirds of European levels at the peak in 1976. A major impetus to encourage

---

40 The last royal dynasty, the House of Pahlavi, ruled from 1925 through 1979.

this transformation was the result of Iran's engagement with global markets, especially via the exchange of intermediate goods, knowledge, and technology.[41]

But following the 1979 revolution, the pace of modernization slowed significantly. Nationalization sparked capital flight, and investment collapsed. The economy became far more reliant on hydrocarbons, which became the mainstay of the economy; oil and gas proceeds now account for three-fifths of government revenue and four-fifths of export earnings. Hence, while the country's integration with the rest of the world has inspired a respectable rate of economic expansion since—GDP growth averaged around 3% per annum from the early 1980s—ironically, it has also hampered the ability of the economy to truly move beyond energy exports.

Iran has, consequently, fallen substantially behind when compared to its own pre-Revolution years (where growth averaged around 10% a year). This underperformance has, unfortunately, undermined what would have been singular achievements in terms of human capital gains: secondary enrollment rates that have tripled since 1970, and tertiary schooling that is a full order of magnitude higher (Figure 8.12).

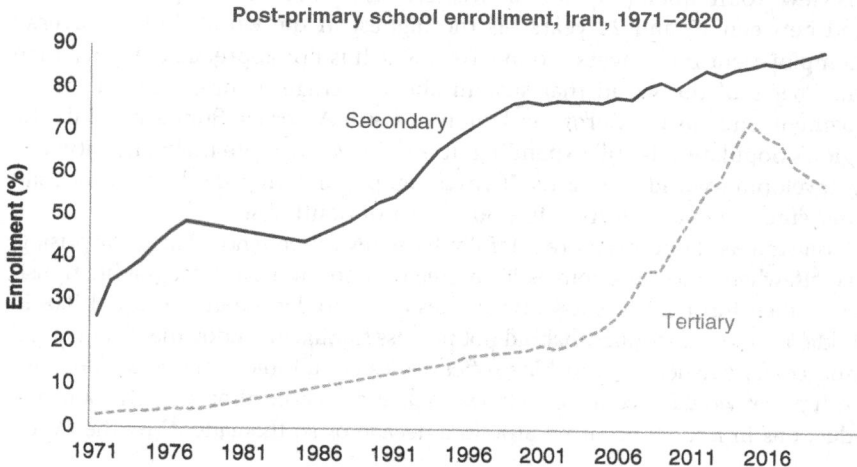

Figure 8.12 Iran has, since 1970, made incredible strides in expanding (a) secondary and (b) tertiary education, tripling enrollments in the former, and raising the latter by more than tenfold. But its signal accomplishments in schooling have been compromised by a mix of brain drain and international sanctions.

---

41 Esfahani, H.S. and M.H. Pesaran, "The Iranian Economy in the Twentieth Century: A Global Perspective," *Iranian Studies* 42(2) (2009): 177–211.

298 Western Asia: An Economic Arab Spring?

Where did these potential gains go? One factor has likely been a brain drain, which has been documented at least since the 1990s.[42] Another stems from the effects that on-and-off-again international sanctions have had in handicapping the economy.[43] The common element among these, of course, is that they are the result—both direct and indirect—of the country's external linkages. All that to show that, once again, the Iranian economy cannot extricate itself from its relationships with the rest of the world.

Western Asian Development in Comparative Perspective

Western Asia Began Its Demographic Transition in the 1960s and 1970s

There is a common perception—perhaps fed by television or movie images of crowded Middle Eastern cities—that the region is overpopulated yet underemployed, and has a bias against women in the workforce.

Like most nuggets of conventional wisdom, there is some grain of truth to this view. Youth unemployment in Western Asia—at around a quarter of those aged between 15 and 24 years—is the highest in the world. But the overall unemployment rate hovers around 10%, which is not appreciably higher than other parts of the world that sustain above-average natural rates of unemployment, such as the European Union or Latin America. Similarly, while the region's population is still expanding, it is doing so at a rate that is not atypical by developing-world standards. If anything, population growth is slower than other emerging parts of Asia, like Southeast or South Asia.

If one thinks about this more carefully, these revelations should be unsurprising. Like elsewhere, most economies in the region underwent a demographic transition as their income levels rose. Birth rates began to decline in the early 1960s in Middle Eastern economies that did not possess significant endowments of natural resources (and hence were unable to offer dedicated subsidies or other perks of citizenship that would encourage childbearing), and even in resource-rich countries, reductions in fertility occurred around a decade or so thereafter.[44] By the 1990s,

---

42 Carrington, W. and E. Detragiache, "How Extensive Is the Brain Drain?" *Finance and Development* 36(2) (1999): 46–49.
43 The most direct impact has been in the form of inflation, resulting from a weak rial that has given rise to ridiculous black-market exchange rates. Sanctions have also had real effects, as trade restrictions have led to chronic shortages of certain materials.
44 The delay was likely due to generous subsidies that supported family formation—such as free education and welfare payouts for nationals—that resource-rich economies were willing to provide. Even so, fertility rates have declined from highs of 7 to something closer to 3, even for the resource-rich group.

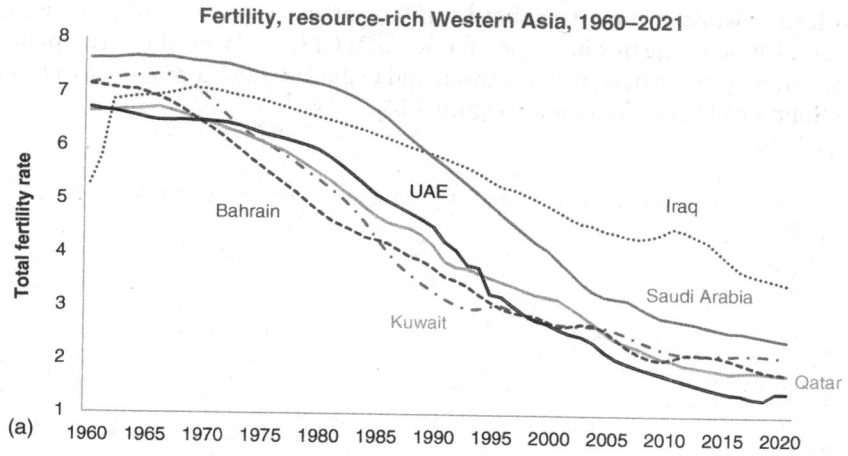

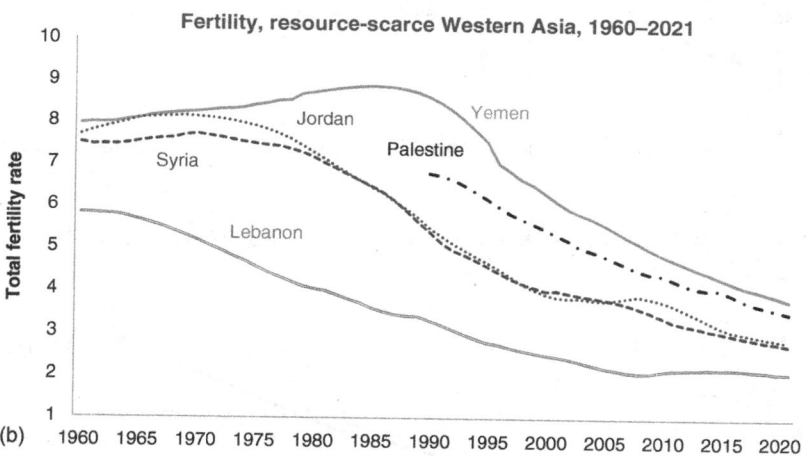

Figure 8.13 The demographic transition in the Middle East began first in (a) non-resource-rich countries, around the 1960s, but by the 1970s, these were followed by many economies in the region even if (b) they had greater endowments of resources. By the 1990s, fertility had come down to levels consistent with the global middle-income countries.

fertility rates had come down to a rate—of between two and three children per woman—common among middle-income economies (Figure 8.13).

Beliefs about systematic gender bias in labor force participation are, similarly, somewhat outdated. By the 1970s, non-resource-intensive countries in the region recognized that the contributions of women would be necessary to keep their economies afloat, and female labor force participation rose accordingly. For instance, only about 5% of women in Egypt and Jordan were involved in formal work in the 1960s, but by 1990, participation rates were closer to around 40%. While this may remain low by OECD standards, the participation rate in some countries, such as Kuwait and Qatar, are now comparable to those of Southern European nations (Figure 8.14).

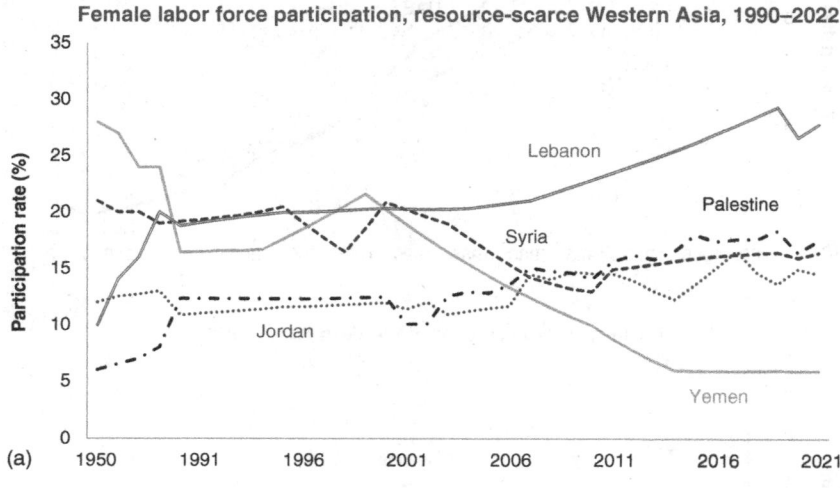

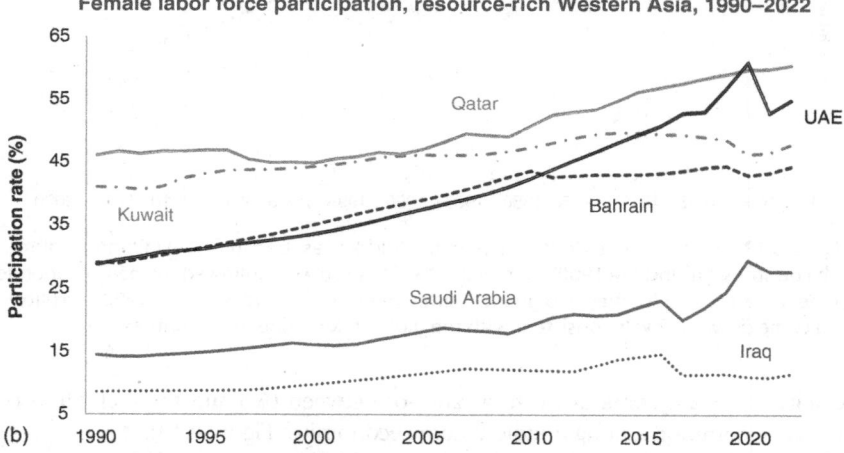

Figure 8.14 (a) Female labor force participation in the Middle East was often very poor—around the single digits—in the 1960s, but by the 1990s, most economies saw greater womens' representation in their national workforces. (b) In some resource-rich countries, such as Bahrain, the increase was incredibly sharp, despite (or perhaps because of) access to natural resource wealth.

This was the case even for certain resource-rich countries, and the shifts occurred surprisingly quickly in some cases. Bahrain, for example, had a miniscule participation rate of 2.4% in 1965, but just two decades later, this was closer to a fifth, and current estimates are almost at three-quarters. While one might wonder why this would be so since natural resource wealth may have been an offsetting force—due to the presence of financial support that would enable women to remain outside the workforce—the increase in girls' education was likely an instigator for women to seek employment.

The Conundrum of Human Capital Development

One of the paradoxes of the modern Middle East has to do with the manner of human capital development in the region. Many labor-abundant economies have done a decent job with training their workers, albeit not at the same speed as the high-performing East Asian NIEs (Figure 8.15). There have been some exceptions, such as Jordan, which have executed an incredible catch-up job. But Turkey's experience—a country that started off on the same trajectory as China, but fell behind in recent years—is more typical.

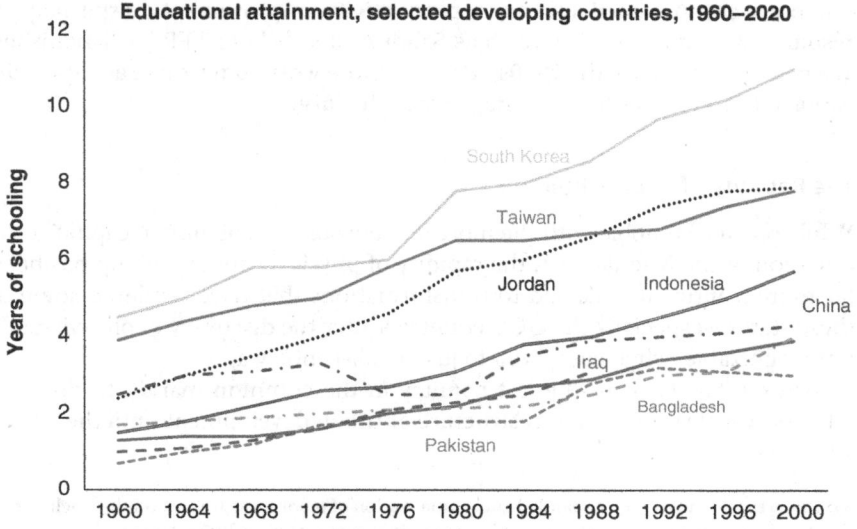

Figure 8.15 Schooling in the labor-abundant economies of the Middle East has been relatively rapid, although most have not kept up with the high-performing East Asian NIEs, and some have fallen behind despite having started off ahead. Similarly, resource-rich nations have managed to build up human capital fairly quickly, but the training received may be of more questionable quality.

Regardless, a scarcity of job opportunities within their home countries has resulted in relatively higher levels of unemployed and underemployed[45] skilled workers than in other parts of the world. Such individuals often resort to migration—usually within the region—to find work commensurate with their talent; the Jordanian engineer or Syrian doctor working in a Gulf country has become a common trope, but one that reveals a grain of truth. Unfortunately, this has resulted in a short-circuiting of the usual contribution of schooling to economic growth, leading to the infamous problem of brain drain in some of the labor-abundant economies, whether resource-rich or not.

The problem in resource-rich, labor-scarce economies has often been the opposite. Many have managed to build up their stock of human capital at a rapid clip. But the problem here is often the questionable quality of the training received. While Israel boasts several world-class universities (schools such as the Hebrew University, Weizmann Institute, or Technion), there are precious few Middle Eastern universities outside of that country in the global rankings. Otherwise highly-regarded institutions—such as Universitat Tel Aviv in Israel, King Abdulaziz University in Saudi Arabia, or Bilkent Üniversitesi in Turkey— often fail to break into the global top 100. Some may offer offbeat majors, such as home economics, which do not usually garner much demand in the market or contribute favorably to economic growth.

This disconnect may have contributed to how human capital formation has not been accompanied by major productivity improvements, especially in resource-reliant economies, such as Saudi Arabia (where TFP has languished at a negative rate since the 1990s). Perhaps more worrisome, there are few indications that TFP may be set to improve in the future.

The Rapidity of Capital Buildup

While one may quibble with the more languorous pace of human capital accumulation in the Middle East, the rapidity of physical capital buildup has been far more frantic, and has led to transformations that have rendered some of these states—especially the GCC countries after the discovery of oil—virtually unrecognizable, when compared to just a half-century ago.

For example, Oman—the last country in the common market to discover oil[46]—saw little by way of infrastructure or urban development until the 1970s,

---

45 Underemployment is an expanded conceptualization of labor force utilization that includes all who are working part-time but are able and willing to engage in additional work.

46 The date of the first oil well discoveries in each of the GCC countries (and the respective fields) was: Bahrain (1932, Jabal Dukhan field), Kuwait (1938, Burgan field), Saudi Arabia (1938, Dammam field), Qatar (1940, Dukhan field), the UAE (1953, Murban field), and Oman (1956, Marmul field).

(a)   (b)

Figure 8.16 (a) Oman was the final country among the GCC to have discovered oil, and until the 1970s, and had remained relatively underdeveloped until then. (b) It is even harder to conceive of how quickly Dubai's capital buildup has been, given how the downtown area was only comprised of a few buildings as recently as 1980.
Source: (a) Fabio Achilli / Flickr / CC BY 2.0, (b) Unknown / Wikimedia Commans / CC BY 3.0.

but Muscat now resembles a prosperous Southern European city, complete with an opera house and genteel cultural district. The modernization of Dubai has been even more dramatic (Figure 8.16). It is scarcely conceivable that a city selected for location filming for a *Star Trek* movie—owing to its futuristic setting—was, a mere four decades ago, a small cluster of buildings sitting at the edge of the desert. While the outrageous claim that the city was home to a quarter of the world's 125,000 tower cranes in the 2000s has turned out to be an urban legend,[47] the rate of increase in fixed capital formation across the region is virtually unprecedented worldwide.

This has meant drastic transformations in the economic structure of the region's economies since the 1960s. The 1970s and 1980s were characterized by very high levels of public investment. However, such spending was frequently inefficient.[48] By the 2000s, though, many countries saw private firms take the lead and move the economy toward greater private investment. While it remains true that investment rates in the region lag those of high-investment East Asian nations, capital accumulation has ramped up over time, averaging between 20% and 25% of GDP since 2000 (Figure 8.17).

---

47 The total in Dubai was likely closer to around 2,000, making the figure closer to 2%. This is still an order of magnitude greater than elsewhere in the world; in 2023, Toronto and Seattle—the two cities with the highest crane count in North America—had 238 and 51 cranes, respectively.
48 One crude approach to evaluating the efficiency of capital investment is to simply take the ratio of investment to GDP growth, a metric known as the incremental capital-output ratio (ICOR). Alternatively, the marginal product of capital—the change in output for a change in capital—is a more theoretically-informed metric, compared to ICOR.

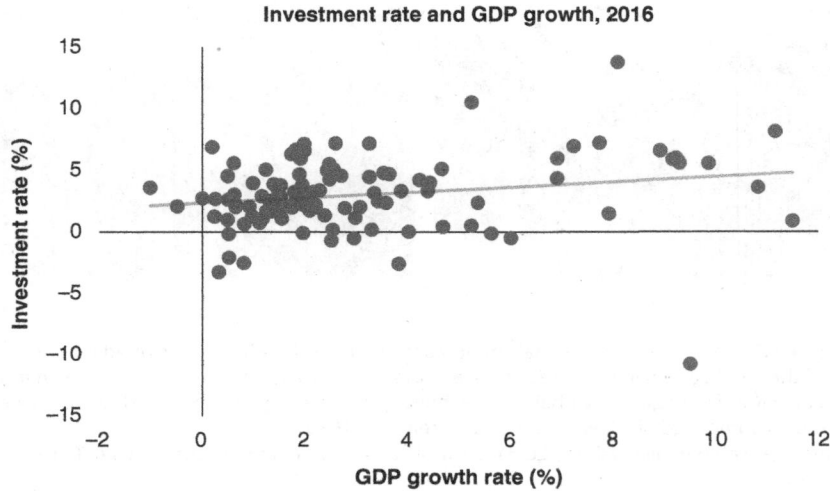

Figure 8.17 Investment in the Middle East has not always been the most productive, with low capital usage efficiency, perhaps due to excessive dependence on services-led growth alongside excess natural resource rents.

Another factor that may be responsible for the low TFP growth contribution is how many regional economies have already turned to services-led growth, even before their industrial sectors have fully matured. Some of this may be the result of deindustrialization—dating as far back to the late Ottoman period—but the harsh reality is that this legacy has stubbornly remained in place. Indeed, even after many Middle Eastern economies began to adopt free-market liberalization policies in the 1980s, industrial capacity remained relegated to light manufacturing (and even then, in only a number of economies, such as Lebanon and the UAE).

Further complicating the emergence of a more robust manufacturing sector has been the consistent absence of strong and fair competition in many countries in region.[49] The dominance of government-owned enterprises or state-sanctioned monopolies often snuffs out even promising SMEs, which are unable to compete against corporations that are assured a captive market, or which receive a steady diet of lucrative government contracts.

Where SOEs don't get in the way, crony capitalism does the rest. Many regional governments have also allowed politically-connected oligopolists to further consolidate their market standing. These range from influential families with close ties to political leaders, such as the Makhlouf family in Assad's

---

49 Arezki, R., A. Barone, K. Decker, D. Detter, R.Y. Fan, H. Nguyen, and G. Murciego, *Reaching New Heights: Promoting Fair Competition in the Middle East and North Africa* (Washington, DC: The World Bank, 2019).

Syria, or direct ownership by extended family members of the ruling house, such as the Al Maktoums or Al Nahyans in the UAE.

Institutional Governance Remains Deficient, Despite Modernization

As problematic as a lack of competition has been for the economic vitality of countries in the region, it merely points to a larger, underlying problem: that institutional quality is sorely lacking. Along the dimension of voice and accountability, specifically, most Middle Eastern economies remain heavily authoritarian—even after the Arab Spring. The score—which ranges from −10 (absolute autocracy) to +10 (full democracy)—is negative for virtually all nations, across the decades (Table 8.3).

The GCC economies have been (and remain) autocratic monarchies, even if almost all of them have created some form of legislative or consultative

Table 8.3 Decadal governance scores for Western Asian economies, 1960–2018

	1960–1969	1970–1979	1980–1989	1990–1999	2000–2009	2010–2018
Khaleej						
Bahrain		−9.3	−10.0	−9.3	−7.3	−9.2
Kuwait	−8.7	−8.9	−9.0	−7.2	−7.0	−7.0
Oman	−10.0	−10.0	−10.0	−9.1	−8.2	−8.0
Qatar		−10.0	−10.0	−10.0	−10.0	−10.0
Saudi Arabia	−10.0	−10.0	−10.0	−10.0	−10.0	−10.0
UAE		−8.0	−8.0	−8.0	−8.0	−8.0
Yemen				−1.4	−2.0	0.2
Levant						
Egypt	−7.0	−6.6	−6.0	−6.0	−4.5	−3.5
Israel	9.7	9.0	9.0	9.1	10.0	10.0
Jordan	−9.0	−9.6	−8.9	−2.4	−2.3	−3.0
Lebanon	1.0	1.5	0.0	–	6.0	6.0
Syria	−6.3	−9.0	−9.0	−9.0	−6.0	−8.3
Turkey	8.3	6.7	3.6	8.0	7.0	3.1
Mashriq						
Iran	−10.0	−9.6	−6.0	−3.3	−2.6	−7.0
Iraq	−5.4	−7.2	−9.0	−9.0	−9.0	4.7

Source: Author's compilation, from INSCR (2022).
Notes: Values are simple averages of Polity2 scores, which range from −10 (absolute autocracy) to +10 (full democracy), with anocracies/semi-democracies usually assigned a score of between −5 to +5. No data are available for Lebanon in the 1990–1999 period, as it was in an interregnum.

assembly.[50] Things are little better in the Levant, with only Israel having attained the status of a full democracy, while Lebanon—following an interregnum in the 1990s—transitioned to democratic norms only this millennium onward. Other countries have remained mostly mixed anocracies—semi-democracies that mix democratic practices amid strong autocratic control—with some even backsliding in recent years. Syria, for example, has regressed due to its civil war, and Turkey rolled back many liberal rights and secular practices over the past decade or so.

A similar retreat in democratic norms has occurred in Iran, although the fall of Saddam did usher in a fledgling electoral democracy in Iraq. The overall tendency of the region, however, has been a resistance to more decisive shifts toward democracy. This has been disappointing, of course, to activists and other boosters of citizen representation. But just as pertinent is how it has run in the face of the so-called modernization hypothesis[51]—where economies that experience increases in per capita incomes tend to embrace democratic norms—and is especially jarring given how other resource-rich comparators, such as Botswana, Indonesia, and Nigeria, have made greater progress on this front since the turn of the century.

It also raises the question of whether the absence of democracy could become a potential barrier to future economic performance, given how democratization can bring about higher growth.[52] One possible reason could be because so many economies in the Middle East have—and continue to be able to—finance public spending from natural resource rents (estimates indicate that rents could fund as much as three-quarters of total government expenditure, especially among the GCC countries). Since taxation has often been the genesis of representation, the diminished need to raise revenue from traditional tax levers has likely contributed to a weakened call for greater accountability. And even in states that aren't endowed with hydrocarbon resources, the ability of autocratic leaders to tap foreign aid flows generously released from their

---

50 Bahrain has a bicameral National Assembly (a lower house of elected representatives, and an upper house of royally-appointed members), Kuwait has a unicameral National Assembly (of elected members and ministers appointed by the Emir), Oman has a bicameral Council (an upper house appointed by the Sultan, and a lower house of elected members), Qatar has a unicameral Consultative Assembly (with elected members and members appointed by the Emir), and the UAE has a unicameral Federal National Council (comprising elected members and Sheikh-appointed members from each emirate). Saudi Arabia has an advisory consultative assembly appointed by the King, but no elections.

51 The modernization hypothesis is considered in detail in Acemoğlu, D., S. Johnson, and P. Yared, "Reevaluating the Modernization Hypothesis," *Journal of Monetary Economics* 56 (2009): 1043–1058.

52 The argument in favor of democracy as a causal driver of economic development is made forcefully in Acemoğlu, D., S. Naidu, P. Restrepo, and J. Robinson, "Democracy Does Cause Growth," *Journal of Political Economy* 127 (2019): 47–100, although the empirical evidence on this front is genuinely mixed.

nondemocratic resource-rich neighbors—Erdoğan's Turkey comes to mind—has kept these regimes in power.

The Middle East in the World Economy

Western Asia as the Least-Integrated Region in the World

Despite what might seem, *prima facie*, to be a strong interest in promoting trade relations—the preponderance of a globally-traded commodity in the economic output of the region, as well as its central location between other major economic powers—a long heritage of international exchange, and comprising a fairly homogenous set of constituents and economic structures, Western Asia is the least integrated region in the world.

The energy sector, for example, is inter*connected* between the different Middle Eastern economies, but the market is far from integrated (except for the GCC). Past pan-Arab integration efforts have often failed to gain the necessary buy-in from governments in the region, despite the potentially huge mutual gains that could be realized in areas such as electricity and water. Even other less-developed parts of the world, such as Africa, have raced ahead with large regional integration agreements, such as the 46-state African Continental Free Trade Area. The closest such agreement in Western Asia, the Greater Arab Free Trade Area, has mostly been erratic in its application and moribund in its operation, despite first being signed a quarter of a century ago.

Estimates of trade are even more discouraging; less than a tenth of imports and exports from West Asian economies is intra-regional in nature, compared to a quarter in ASEAN and close to a third in the EU. This is not entirely surprising, given the global nature of hydrocarbon exports. Still, the steady decline of trade since the peak (of more than 90% of GDP in 2008) has been far more severe in the Middle East—falling to below 60% presently—than even the deglobalization trend seen elsewhere (the global decline has been less than 10 percentage points).

Recycling Petrodollars into Sovereign Wealth Funds

Even though cross-border *trade* has lagged in the region, the flow of finance across the borders of Middle Eastern economies has been more fluid. Keeping in mind that financial flows tend, on net, to be lower than that of real goods and services, overall flows are nevertheless on the lower end, as compared to other regions. On balance, this has been both good and bad; on one hand, the global financial crisis of 2007/08 turned out to be mostly second-order for most Western Asian countries (the UAE, because of Dubai, was a notable exception, while Doha and Beirut also experienced some tremors, due to the size of their financial sector),[53] but on the other, some of the key benefits of free capital flows—improving international risk-sharing and efficiency resource allocation—were lost.

To the extent that such flows occur, the majority turns out to be intra-regional in nature,[54] which is less subject to capital flight, due to the increased familiarity with local macroeconomic conditions. Moreover, most take the form of foreign direct investment, which tends to be less flighty. And, finally, the overall stability of financing has also benefited from the presence of many sovereign wealth funds (SWFs) across the Middle East, which tend to be long-term investors (Table 8.4).

While each fund is undoubtedly unique, regional SWFs share a host of common features. Virtually all are financed from surpluses derived from the sale of oil and gas (in contrast to SWFs elsewhere, which may be financed through fiscal or current account surpluses).[55] Many are quite large, even from a global perspective, and hence play a role in shaping the contours of the global balance of payments. And most have a relatively long history, with the older ones evolving into sophisticated institutional investors in their own right.

To the extent that dissimilarities arise, they stem from variations in objective. Like many central banks. SAMA tends to invest conservatively in short-term, safe, and liquid instruments, owing to its reserve investment mandate. Institutions such as ADIA and the QIA are primarily savings vehicles, tasked with investing surpluses for the benefit of future generations, although they may also be called upon to provide stabilization functions when global energy markets become especially volatile (and hence typically maintain an emergency liquidity buffer). And outfits like the Palestine Investment Fund or the Saudi PIF stress development, providing cheap financing to bolster onshore investment opportunities, especially with regard to government policy priority areas.

Certain countries have chosen to maintain multiple SWFs. The best example of this is the UAE, where almost every emirate has a separate fund, along with purpose-specific funds in some cases. Within the emirate of Abu Dhabi, for example, Mubadala targets local firms in specific economic sectors, while ADIA focuses on deploying funds into non-regional assets. Duplication has led to some of these being merged; the former International Petroleum Investment Company (IPIC) was incorporated into Mubadala in 2017, and the same occurred with the Abu Dhabi Investment Council (ADIC) in 2019. Other states

53 Janus, T., J. Lim, and Y. Jia, "Recent Trends in Financial Flows to Arab Countries," *Development Prospects Group Policy Report* (Washington, DC: World Bank and Arab Monetary Fund, 2010).
54 Irving, J., T. Janus, J. Lim, and S. Kurlat, "Financial Flows to and among Arab Countries," *Development Prospects Group Policy Report* (Washington, DC: World Bank and Arab Monetary Fund, 2011).
55 That said, some SWFs that are predominantly funded by revenue from commodity surpluses—such as ADIA—do receive, for the purposes of management, excess fiscal surpluses in any given year.

Table 8.4 Sovereign wealth funds in the Middle East and rest of Asia, 2022

Country	Fund	Year	Type	Source	AUM ($bn)
Middle East					
Bahrain	Mumtakalat Holding Company	2006	Savings	Oil	19
	Bahrain Future Generations Fund	2006	Savings	Oil	0.6
Israel	Israel Citizens Fund	2022	Savings	Gas	1
Iran	National Development Fund	2011	Savings	Oil/gas	91
Kuwait	Kuwait Investment Authority	1953	Stabilization/ savings	Oil	738
Oman	Oman Investment Authority	1980	Stabilization	Oil/gas	42
	Oman Future Fund	2023	Development	Oil/gas	5
Palestine	Palestine Investment Fund	2003	Development	Fiscal	1
Qatar	Qatar Investment Authority	2005	Savings	Oil/gas	450
Saudi Arabia	Public Investment Fund	1971	Development	Oil	620
	SAMA Foreign Holdings	1952	Reserve investment	Oil	490
	Abu Dhabi Dev Holding Co.	2018	Development	Oil	159
UAE	Abu Dhabi Investment Authority	1976	Stabilization/ savings	Oil	853
	Mubadala Investment Company	1984	Development	Oil	284
	Investment Corporation of Dubai	2006	Savings	Oil	309
	Emirates Investment Authority	2007	Development	Oil	87
Rest of Asia					
Azerbaijan	State Oil Fund	1999	Stabilization/ savings	Oil	45
Brunei	Brunei Investment Authority	1983	Savings	Oil	170
China	China Investment Corporation	2007	Reserve investment	Trade	1,200
	State Administration of Forex	1978	Reserve investment	Trade	3,010
Egypt	Sovereign Fund	2018	Development	Fiscal	0.6

(Continued)

Table 8.4 (Continued)

Country	Fund	Year	Type	Source	AUM ($bn)
Hong Kong	Hong Kong Monetary Authority	1993	Reserve investment	Trade	430
Indonesia	Indonesia Investment Authority	2021	Development	Fiscal	25
Kazakhstan	Samruk-Kazyna	2008	Stabilization/savings	Oil/gas	94
	Kazakhstan National Fund	2000	Stabilization/savings	Oil/gas	61
Malaysia	Khazanah Nasional	1994	Savings	Fiscal	18
	Permodalan Nasional	1978	Savings	Fiscal	70
Singapore	Government Investment Corp	1981	Stabilization/savings	Trade	690
	Temasek Holdings	1974	Development	Fiscal	497
	Monetary Authority of Singapore	1971	Reserve investment	Fiscal	312
Turkey	Turkey Wealth Fund	2016	Development	Fiscal	33

Source: Author's compilation, from SWF Institute.
Notes: Current names reference the latest iteration of the investment vehicle, but founding years apply to the oldest known contributing fund(s), which may have a different name. Assets under management are valuations based on publicly available information/estimates, and may not have been disclosed by the funds themselves. For Singapore, source funding for GIC and MAS officially derives from fiscal surpluses, but these are collateralized by the national pension scheme. For the UAE, only the largest funds are listed.

appear to have followed this lead. Saudi Arabia, for example, repurposed the Public Investment Fund away from development objectives toward a savings diversification function, while retaining the traditional liquidity/reserve management role for SAMA.

Conclusion

Potential Growth for Western Asian Economies Is Clouded by Uncertainty

While the future of economies is typically murky, the uncertainty is especially acute for the economies of Western Asia. The commodity that has defined the region for close to a century—oil—is in the process of being steadily replaced all over the world, with nations introducing sustainability targets that often include the phasing out of internal combustion engine vehicles over the course of the next few decades. There is a very significant likelihood that these hydrocarbon assets will become stranded, as green technologies advance quickly and populations become more conscious of their environmental footprints.

This has sparked an urgency among policymakers in the region to ensure that their economies diversify into non-hydrocarbon sectors. But this has proven difficult, not least because a key instrument for change—accountability to local populations—tends to be weak, since many remain heavily authoritarian. Some countries will probably be more successful than others, owing to greater resource availability to devote toward expanding their production capabilities toward allied sectors; the comparative success of higher-income economies in already doing so attests to this likelihood.

The question remains as to how such diversification also ultimately translates into productivity. A simple illustration of this is to consider the future growth possibilities for Egypt and Saudi Arabia. Their divergent paths—where Egypt may be expected to outperform, by dint of better TFP growth contributions—not only hint at the importance of productivity, but also underscore how future growth potential may diverge from current observed outcomes (Figure 8.18).

Future Development Strategies Are Also Uncertain

Beyond the ability to elevate TFP, the development strategies that will be chosen for many of the economies of Western Asia remain similarly ambiguous. Many of the resource-rich sheikhdoms had previously intimated that diversification would be the order of the day. This was to occur in terms of both fiscal revenue sources—away from fossil fuels in favor of renewables, with an increased emphasis on relying on the diversified portfolios of their sovereign wealth funds as a source of government income—as well as their economies more generally.

But with so many regimes still operating under autocratic norms, future directions appear to be determined behind the closed doors of palace *majlises* and royal family-owned boardrooms. Construction of NEOM City—much like what occurred during the runup to Qatar's hosting of the 2022 FIFA Men's World Cup—has been wracked by controversy over working conditions, and both plans and progress appear to be shrouded in mystery.

This sense of uncertainty permeates even the more open regimes of the region. In 2020, subsidiaries of the International Holding Company (IHC) were first listed on the Abu Dhabi Securities Exchange. More were to follow, and by 2021, IHC had become the most valuable listed company in the Emirate, valued in excess of $650 billion, and comprising more than 400 subsidiaries.[56]

56 England, A., "The Sheikh's Empire Driving Abu Dhabi's Meteoric Stock Market Rise," *Financial Times*, February 5, 2023.

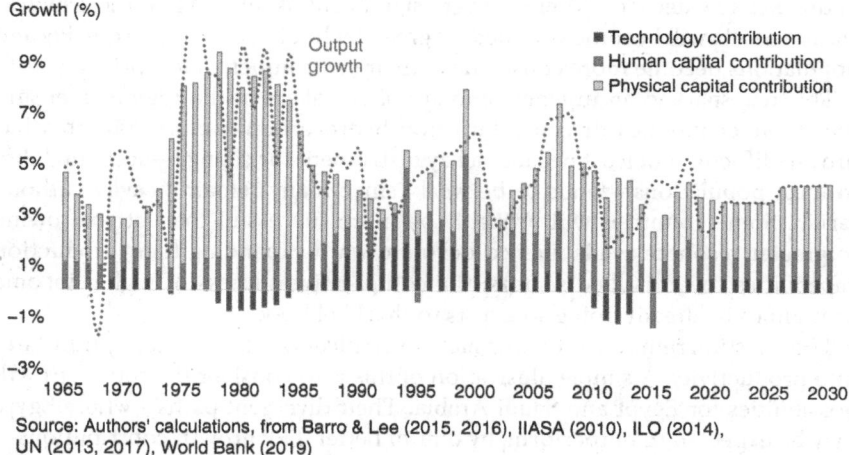

Source: Authors' calculations, from Barro & Lee (2015, 2016), IIASA (2010), ILO (2014), UN (2013, 2017), World Bank (2019)

(a)

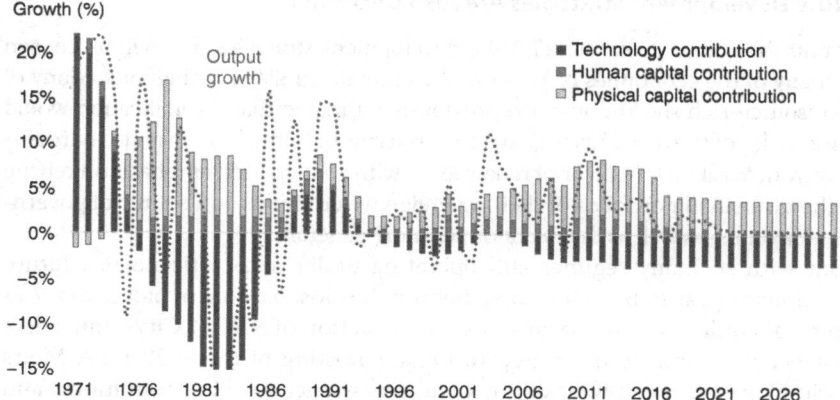

Source: Authors' calculations, from Barro & Lee (2015, 2016), IIASA (2010), ILO (2014), UN (2013, 2017), World Bank (2019)

(b)

Figure 8.18 The divergent growth possibilities for (a) Egypt and (b) Saudi Arabia hint at how high contemporary growth rates need not translate into sustained future growth potential, especially if TFP remains low.

Yet little is known about the conglomerate, or how it features in the nation's investment plans, especially relative to its established sovereign wealth funds.

Sources of Figures

Figure 0.1 "GDP Wealth 2018," by World Mapper is licensed under CC BY-SA 4.0 DEED. https://worldmapper.org/maps/gdp-2018

Figure 0.2 Author's compilation, from International Federation of Robotics (2023), *World Robotics Report*. https://www.robotics247.com/article/world_robotics_report_2023_shows_ongoing_global_growth_installations_finds_ifr

Figure 0.3 Author's calculations, from Barro, R. and J-W. Lee (2013), "A New Dataset of Educational Attainment in the World, 1950–2010," *Journal of Development Economics* 104: 184–198.

Figure 0.4 Author's calculations, from World Bank (2023), *World Development Indicators*. https://data.worldbank.org/indicator/sp.dyn.tfrt.in?contextual=default&locations=cn-hk-sg-kr-th

Figure 0.5 Author's calculations, from World Bank (2012), *World Development Indicators*. www.worldbank.org/en/news/press-release/2012/04

Figure 0.6 Author's calculations, from Maddison (2020), *Maddison Project Database*. www.rug.nl/ggdc/historicaldevelopment/maddison

Figure 0.7 Author's construction, from Quah, D. (2011), "The Global Economy's Shifting Center of Gravity," *Global Policy* 2(1): 3–9.

Figure 0.8 Author's compilation, from Asian Development Bank (2023), *Asian Economic Integration Report*, p. 25. https://aric.adb.org/pdf/aeir/aeir2023_complete.pdf

Figure 0.9 Author's compilation, from International Labour Organization (2013), *Estimates and Projections of the Economically Active Population: 1990–2030*, Geneva: ILO, and United Nations (2017), https://population.un.org/wpp, and World Bank (2022), *World Population Prospects*. https://data.worldbank.org/indicator/se.sec.enrr?locations=ir

Figure 1.1 Author's compilation, adapted from Naughton, B.J. (2018), *The Chinese Economy: Adaptation and Growth*, 2nd ed., Cambridge, MA: MIT Press, p. 31.

Figure 1.2 Author's compilation, adapted from BP (2023), *BP Energy Outlook*. https://www.bp.com/content/dam/bp/business-sites/en/global/corporate/pdfs/energy-economics/energy-outlook/bp-energy-outlook-2023.pdf

Figure 1.3 "A Chinese Chain Pump with Their Singular Method of Working It," illustration from Cooke, G. A. (1817), *Modern and Authentic System of Universal Geography* (First Edition), Evans and Bourne, illustration is marked with CC0.

Figure 1.4 "China—the Cake of Kings and. . . of Emperors," illustration from Meyer H. (1898) is licensed under CC0.

Figure 1.5 Author's construction, adapted from Sur, P.K. and M. Sasaki (2021), "The Persistent Effect of Famine on Present-Day China," *arXiv* 2104.00935.

Figure 1.6 Author's construction, adapted from Walder, A.G. (2014), "Rebellion and Repression in China, 1966–1971," *Social Science History* 38(3), 513–539.

Figure 1.7 Author's calculations, using World Bank (2022), *World Development Indicators*. https://data.worldbank.org/indicator

Figure 1.8 Author's calculations, from China/ONS Datastream (2023), https://www.ons.gov.uk/economy/nationalaccounts/balanceofpayments

Figure 1.9 Author's compilation, adapted from Huang, T. and N. Véron (2023), "China's Top Ranked Corporations are Not as Opaque as They May Seem," *Realtime Economics*, July 18, Washington, DC: Peterson Institute for International Economics.

Figure 1.10 Author's compilation, from World Bank (2023), *World Development Indicators*. https://data.worldbank.org/indicator/sp.dyn.tfrt.in?contextual=default&locations=cn-hk-sg-kr-th

Figure 1.11 Author's calculations, from Barro, R. and J-W. Lee (2013), "A New Dataset of Educational Attainment in the World, 1950–2010," *Journal of Development Economics* 104: 184–198; Barro, R. and J-W. Lee (2016), "Human Capital in the Long Run," *Journal of Development Economics* 122: 147–169; International Labour Organization (2013), *Estimates and Projections of the Economically Active Population: 1990–2030*, Geneva: ILO, and United Nations (2017), https://population.un.org/wpp, and World Bank, *World Population Prospects* (2022), https://data.worldbank.org/indicator/se.sec.enrr?locations=ir

Figure 1.12 Author's calculations, from Maddison (2003).

Figure 1.13 Author's compilation, from World Bank (2023). https://data.worldbank.org/indicator/sl.ind.empl.zs?locations=xt-cn

Figure 1.14 Author's compilation, adapted from CEIC and Chen et al. (2017).

Figure 1.15 Author's compilation, adapted from BIS (2023).

Figure 1.16 "Model of 15th century Ming Treasure Ship," by Mary Harrsch is licensed under CC BY-NC-SA 2.0.

Figure 1.17 "Shenzhen Sometime 1970s China" by Chris is licensed under CC BY-NC 2.0; "The West Panorama of Shenzhen," by Charlie Fong is licensed under CC BY-SA 4.0 DEED.

Figure 1.18 Author's compilation, adapted from Beaujard, P. (2019), "Were There World-Systems during the Bronze Age?" In *The Worlds of the Indian Ocean: A Global History*, Cambridge: Cambridge University Press, pp. 250–272.

Figure 2.1 Author's compilation, adapted from Fujita, M., T. Mori, J.V. Henderson, and Y. Kanemoto (2004), "Spatial Distribution of Economic Activities in Japan and China," in J.V. Henderson and J-F. Thisse (Eds.), *Handbook of Regional and Urban Economics* vol. 4, Amsterdam: Elsevier, pp. 2911–2977.

Figure 2.2 "Black Ship (*Kurofune*)," illustration from Bugei Kurabu (Literary Club), by Tomioka Eisen is marked with CC0 1.0.B.

Figure 2.3 米軍撮影 (1945), is marked with CC0.

Figure 2.4 Author's compilation, adapted from Flath, D. (2022), *The Japanese Economy*, 4th ed., Oxford: Oxford University Press, p. 122.

Figure 2.5 Author's calculations, using World Bank (2022), *World Development Indicators*. https://data.worldbank.org/indicator/sp.dyn.tfrt.in?contextual=default&locations=cn-hk-sg-kr-th

Figure 2.6 "Japanese Drink Vending Machines" by Jephso is licensed under CC BY 2.0.

Figure 2.7 Author's compilation, adapted from Gerlach, M. (1997), *Alliance Capitalism: The Social Organization of Japanese Business*, Berkeley, CA: University of California Press, p. 68.

Figure 2.8 Author's compilation, from Macrotrends (2023), Nikkei 225 Index, 67 Year Historical Data. https://www.macrotrends.net/2593/nikkei-225-index-historical-chart-data

Figure 2.9 Author's calculations, using World Bank (2022), *World Development Indicators*.

Figure 2.10 Author's calculations, from OECD (2023), *OECD Statistics*, https://stats.oecd.org and IMF (2023), *International Financial Statistics*. https://data.imf.org

Figure 2.11 "Bridge to Nowhere" in Fukui prefecture by Florian is used with permission from the photographer.

Figure 2.12 VentureINQ (2023), "3 Sets of Seal for Company Operation," permission granted by owner.

Figure 2.13 Author's calculations, using World Bank (2022), *World Development Indicators*. https://data.worldbank.org/indicator/sp.dyn.tfrt.in?contextual=default&locations=cn-hk-sg-kr-th

Figure 2.14 Author's compilation, adapted from fDI Markets (2018), https://www.ft.com/content/898fa38e-4882-11e8-cae73aab7ccb

Figure 2.15 Author's compilation, from Japan Ministry of Health, Labour and Welfare (2023). www.mhlw.go.jp/english

Figure 2.16 Author's calculations, using World Bank (2022), *World Development Indicators*. https://data.worldbank.org/indicator/sp.dyn.tfrt.in?contextual=default&locations=cn-hk-sg-kr-th

Figure 3.1 Author's compilation, adapted from descriptive statistics in the Annual Survey of Industries and National Sample Survey (2006).

Figure 3.2 "View from Nehru Centre," by zeeble is licensed under CC BY-SA 2.0.

Figure 3.3 Author's compilation, from World Bank (2011). https://data.worldbank.org/indicator/

Figure 3.4 "Taj Mahal, Agra, India," by Yann Forget is licensed under CC-BY-SA.

Figure 3.5 "Gandhi spinning Charkha," by TaleTown is licensed under CC0 1.0.

Figure 3.6 Author's calculations, using World Bank (2022), *World Development Indicators*. https://data.worldbank.org/indicator/sp.dyn.tfrt.in?contextual=default&locations=cn-hk-sg-kr-th

Figure 3.7 Author's compilation, using OECD (2023), *OECD Statistics*, https://stats.oecd.org and WHO (2023), *World Health Statistics*. https://www.who.int/data/gho/publications/world-health-statistics

Figure 3.8 Author's compilation, using the Prowess dataset (2023). https://prowessiq.cmie.com

Figure 3.9 Author's compilation, World Bank (2022), *World Development Indicators*. https://data.worldbank.org

Figure 3.10 Author's compilation, using ICE360 Survey (2021). https://www.nextias.com/ca/current-affairs/24-01-2022/ice360-survey-2021-price

Figure 3.11 Author's calculations, adapted from Mauro, P., R. Romeu, A. Blinder and A. Zaman (2015), "A Modern History of Fiscal Prudence and Profligacy," *Journal of Monetary Economics* 76: 55–70 and IMF (2023), *World Economic Outlook*. https://imf.org/en/publications/weo/weo-database/2023/april

Figure 3.12 Author's compilation, adapted from IMF (2018), *World Economic Outlook Database*. https://imf.org

Figure 3.13 Author's calculations, using World Bank (2022), *World Development Indicators*. https://data.worldbank.org

Figure 4.1 Author's compilation, adapted from Lewis, M.W. (2021), "Human Development Index Mapped for Greater South Asia and the Southern Himalayan Belt," *GeoCurrents*.

Figure 4.2 Author's compilation, adapted from Dalziel, N. (2006), *The Penguin Historical Atlas of the British Empire*, New York: Penguin Books.

Figure 4.3 Author's compilation, using World Bank (2023), *World Development Indicators*. https://data.worldbank.org/indicator/ny-gdp.mktp.kd.zg/1ff4a498/popular-indicators

Figure 4.4 Author's calculations, using World Bank (2023), *World Development Indicators*. https://data.worldbank.org

Figure 4.5 Author's compilation, using World Bank (2021), *World Development Indicators*. https://data.worldbank.org/opendata/new-world-bank-country-classifications-income-level-2022-2023

Figure 4.6 Author's compilation, using World Bank (2023), *World Development Indicators*. https://data.worldbank.org/indicator/bx.trf.pwkr.dt.gd.zs?locations=af-bd-bt-mv-lk-np-pk

Figure 5.1 Author's compilation, adapted from "The Four Asian Tiger States with Country Flags," by Furfur is licensed under CC BY-SA 4.0.

Figure 5.2 "Apartments, Nathan Road, Hong Kong," by stevecadman is licensed under CC BY-SA 2.0.

Figure 5.3 Author's compilation, using World Bank (2023), *World Development Indicators*. https://data.worldbank.org/indicator/ny.gdp.mktp.kd.zg/1ff4a498/popular-indicators

Figure 5.4 Author's compilation, from Quality of Government Institute (2023). www.gu.se/en/quality-government

Figure 5.5 "Korea at Night," by NASA Earth Observatory (2016) is licensed under CC0.

Figure 5.6 Author's compilation, adapted from Hong, Y., T. Kim, and J. Park (2015), *The Journal of Applied Business Research* 31(5): 1909–1926.

Figure 5.7 Author's compilation, adapted from Chen, L-C. (2015), "Building Extra-Regional Networks for Regional Innovation Systems: Taiwan's Machine Tool Industry in China," *Technological Forecasting and Social Change* 100: 107–117.

Figure 5.8 Author's calculations, using Barro, R. and J-W. Lee (2013), "A New Dataset of Educational Attainment in the World, 1950–2010," *Journal of Development Economics* 104: 184–198; Barro, R. and J-W. Lee (2016), "Human Capital in the Long Run," *Journal of Development Economics* 122: 147–169; International Labour Organization (2013), *Estimates and Projections of the Economically Active Population: 1990–2030*, Geneva: ILO, and United Nations (2017) https://population.un.org/wpp, and World Bank, *World Population Prospects* (2022), https://data.worldbank.org/indicator/se.sec.enrr?locations=ir

Figure 5.9 *Atlas of Economic Complexity* (2023). atlas.cid.harvard.edu

Figure 5.10 Author's calculations, using Barro, R. and J-W. Lee (2013), "A New Dataset of Educational Attainment in the World, 1950–2010," *Journal of Development Economics* 104: 184–198; Barro, R. and J-W. Lee (2016), "Human Capital in the Long Run," *Journal of Development Economics* 122: 147–169; International Labour Organization (2013), *Estimates and Projections of the Economically Active Population: 1990–2030*, Geneva: ILO, and United Nations (2017) https://population.un.org/wpp, and World Bank, *World Population Prospects* (2022), https://data.worldbank.org/indicator/se.sec.enrr?locations=ir

Figure 5.11 Atlas of Economic Complexity (2023). atlas.cid.harvard.edu

Figure 5.12 Author's compilation, from Bown, C. and Y. Wang (2023), "Taiwan's Outbound Foreign Investment, Particularly in Tech, Continues to Go to Mainland China Despite Strict Controls," *PIIE Charts*, February 27, Washington, DC: Peterson Institute for International Economics.

Figure 5.13 Author's calculations, using Barro, R. and J-W. Lee (2013), "A New Dataset of Educational Attainment in the World, 1950–2010," *Journal of Development Economics* 104: 184–198; Barro, R. and J-W. Lee (2016), "Human Capital in the Long Run," *Journal of Development Economics*

122: 147–169; International Labour Organization (2013), *Estimates and Projections of the Economically Active Population: 1990–2030*, Geneva: ILO, and United Nations (2017) https://population.un.org/wpp, and World Bank, *World Population Prospects* (2022), https://data.worldbank.org/indicator/se.sec.enrr?locations=ir

Figure 5.14 Author's compilation, using World Bank (2023), *World Development Indicators.* https://data.worldbank.org/indicator/ny-gdp.mktp.kd.zg/1ff4a498/popular-indicators

Figure 6.1 Author's construction.

Figure 6.2 Author's construction, adapted from "European Colonization of Southeast Asia," by Rumilo Santiago is licensed under CC BY-SA 4.0.

Figure 6.3 Author's photograph.

Figure 6.4 "Domino Theory," by Nyenyec is licensed under CC BY-SA 3.0.

Figure 6.5 Author's compilation, using World Bank (2023), *World Development Indicators.* https://data.worldbank.org/indicator/ny.gdp.pcap.cd

Figure 6.6 Author's compilation, using World Bank (2023), *World Development Indicators.* https://data.worldbank.org/indicator/sl.agr.empl.zs?/most-recent-year-desc=false

Figure 6.7 Author's compilation, using World Bank (2023), *World Development Indicators.* https://data.worldbank.org/indicator

Figure 6.8 Author's calculations, using Barro, R. and J-W. Lee (2013), "A New Dataset of Educational Attainment in the World, 1950–2010," *Journal of Development Economics* 104: 184–198; Barro, R. and J-W. Lee (2016), "Human Capital in the Long Run," *Journal of Development Economics* 122: 147–169; International Labour Organization (2013), *Estimates and Projections of the Economically Active Population: 1990–2030*, Geneva: ILO, and United Nations (2017) https://population.un.org/wpp, and World Bank, *World Population Prospects* (2022), https://data.worldbank.org/indicator/se.sec.enrr?locations=ir

Figure 6.9 Author's compilation, using World Bank (2023), *World Development Indicators.* https://data.worldbank.org

Figure 6.10 Author's compilation, using World Bank (2023), *Worldwide Governance Indicators.* https://info.worldbank.org.governance/wgi/home/reports

Figure 6.11 Author's compilation, using World Bank (2023). https://data.worldbank.org/fp/cpi.totl.zg?end=2022&locations=id-xn&start=1970

Figure 6.12 Author's calculations, using IMF (2023), *World Economic Outlook Database.* https://imf.org/en/publications/weo/weo-database/2023/april

Figure 6.13 Author's calculations, using World Bank (2023), *World Development Indicators.* https://data.worldbank.org

Figure 6.14 Author's calculations, using World Bank (2023), *World Development Indicators.* https://data.worldbank.org

Figure 6.15 Author's calculations, using World Bank (2023), *World Development Indicators.* https://data.worldbank.org

Figure 6.16 Atlas of Economic Complexity (2023). atlas.cid.harvard.edu

Figure 6.17 Author's compilations, using UNCTAD (2023). www.unctad.org

Figure 6.18 Author's compilations, from fDi Markets (2023).

Figure 6.19 Author's calculations, using Barro, R. and J-W. Lee (2013), "A New Dataset of Educational Attainment in the World, 1950–2010," *Journal of Development Economics* 104: 184–198; Barro, R. and J-W. Lee (2016), "Human Capital in the Long Run," *Journal of Development Economics* 122: 147–169; International Labour Organization (2013), *Estimates and Projections of the Economically Active Population: 1990–2030*, Geneva: ILO, and United Nations (2017) https://population.un.org/wpp, and World Bank, *World Population Prospects* (2022), https://data.worldbank.org/indicator/se.sec.enrr?locations=ir

Figure 7.1 Author's construction, adapted from ADB (2010), *Central Asia Atlas of Natural Resources*, Manila: Asian Development Bank.

Figure 7.2 "Coin of the Kushan King Kanishka Depicting Buddha," by Classical Numismatic Group is licensed under CC BY-SA 3.0 DEED.

Figure 7.3 Author's compilation, from World Bank (2023), *World Development Indicators*. https://data.worldbank.org/indicator/ny.gdp.pcap.pp.kd?locations=tm-tj-uz-kz-kg

Figure 7.4 Author's compilation, from World Bank (2023), *World Development Indicators*. https://data.worldbank.org/indicator/se.sec.enrr?end=2021&locations=tm-tj-uz-kz-kg&start=1989&view=chart

Figure 7.5 Author's compilation, adapted from UNESCO (2023), *UNESCO Science Report: Towards 2030*, p. 373. https://unesdoc.unesco.org/search/e6c39313-a68c-42aa-94cd-18318d7dd725

Figure 7.6 Author's compilation, using World Bank (2023), *World Development Indicators*. https://data.worldbank.org/indicator/se.sec.enrr?end=2021&locations=tm-tj-uz-kz-kg&start=1989&view=chart

Figure 7.7 Author's compilation, adapted from Batsaikhan, U. and M. Dabrowski (2017), "Central Asia—Twenty-Five Years After the Breakup of the USSR," *Russian Journal of Economics* 3(3): 296–320.

Figure 8.1 Author's compilation, adapted from U.S. Energy Information Administration, in turn based on Energy Intelligence Group (2023), *International Crude Oil Market Handbook*, Lytham St Anne's: Energy Intelligence Group.

Figure 8.2 Author's construction, adapted from Mazarei, A. (2019), "Oil Exporters in Middle East and North Africa Have Made Uneven Progress to Diversify Economies," *PIIE Charts*, April 22, Washington, DC: Peterson Institute for International Economics.

Figure 8.3 "Babylonian Cuneiform Tablet with a Map from Nippur 1500–1155 BCE," photographed at the *Indiana Jones and the Adventure of Archaeology* exhibit at the National Geographic Museum in Washington, D.C,, is licensed under CC BY 2.0; and "Clay Tablet, Beer for Workers, Late Uruk Period, 3000–3100 BCE," by Osama Shukir Muhammed Amin is licensed under CC BY-SA 4.0 DEED.

Figure 8.4 Author's construction, adapted from RadioFreeEurope (2016), *The Legacy of Sykes-Picot*. https:/www./rferl.org/a/the-legacy-of-sykespicot/ 27732567.html

Figure 8.5 Author's compilation, adapted from Cammett, M, I. Diwan, A. Richards, and J. Waterbury (2013), *A Political Economy of the Middle East*, 4th ed., Abingdon: Routledge, p. 70.

Figure 8.6 Author's compilation, using International Monetary Fund (2022), *Breakeven Oil Prices in MENAP and CCA Regions*. https://knoema.com/ IMFBEOP2021/breakeven-oil-prices-in-menap-and-cca-regions.

Figure 8.7 Author's calculations, using World Bank (2023), *World Development Indicators*. https://data.worldbank.org/indicator

Figure 8.8 Author's compilation, using World Bank (2023), *World Development Indicators*. https://data.worldbank.org/indicator/ne.con.govt.zs?locations= sa-1w

Figure 8.9 Author's compilation, using World Bank (2023), *World Development Indicators*. https://data.worldbank.org/indicator

Figure 8.10 Atlas of Economic Complexity (2023). atlas.cid.harvard.edu

Figure 8.11 Author's construction, adapted from Sayigh, Y. (2019), *Owners of the Republic: An Anatomy of Egypt's Military Economy*, Washington, DC: Carnegie Endowment for International Peace, p. 18.

Figure 8.12 Author's compilation, using World Bank (2023), *World Development Indicators*. https://data.worldbank.org/indicator/se.sec.entr/locations=ir

Figure 8.13 Author's compilation, using World Bank (2023), *World Development Indicators*. https://data.worldbank.org/indicator/sp.dyn.trft.in?locations=kw- qa-bh-iq-om-sa-ae

Figure 8.14 Author's compilation, using World Bank (2023), *World Development Indicators*. https://data.worldbank.org/indicators/s.tlf.totl.fe.zs?

Figure 8.15 Author's compilation, using World Bank (2023), *World Development Indicators*. https://data.worldbank.org/

Figure 8.16 "Wadi Bani Awf, Oman" by travelourplanet.com is licensed under CC BY 2.0 and "Sheikh Zayed Road in 1990" is licensed under CC BY 3.0.

Figure 8.17 Author's compilation, using World Bank (2023), *World Development Indicators*. https://data.worldbank.org/indicator/ny.gdp.kd.zg?locations= 1w8&most-recent_year_desc_false

Figure 8.18 Author's calculations, using Barro, R. and J-W. Lee (2013), "A New Dataset of Educational Attainment in the World, 1950–2010," *Journal of Development Economics* 104: 184–198; Barro, R. and J-W. Lee (2016), "Human Capital in the Long Run," *Journal of Development Economics* 122: 147–169; International Labour Organization (2013), *Estimates and Projections of the Economically Active Population: 1990–2030*, Geneva: ILO, and United Nations (2017) https://population.un.org/wpp, and World Bank, *World Population Prospects* (2022) https://data.worldbank.org/indicator/ se.sec.enrr?locations=ir

Index

Asian Economies: History, Institutions, and Structures, First Edition. Jamus Jerome Lim.
© 2024 John Wiley & Sons Ltd. Published 2024 by John Wiley & Sons Ltd.

fundamentals favoring growth   252, 254
growth in spite of governance
        challenges   234–5
Indonesia *see* Indonesia
leadership and development strategy   252
Malaysia *see* Malaysia
maritime vs mainland   215–18
modern economies   236–45
natural resources   13
open economy   220–1
Philippines *see* Philippines
physical and human capital accumulation,
        potential of   228–30, 231*f*
plutocrats and family business
        empires   223–5
post-independence policy choices   222–3
poverty   220, 230, 232–3, 236
structured transformation following
        standard development   226–7, 228*f*
Thailand *see* Thailand
trade policies and integration   247–50
Vietnam *see* Vietnam
and world economy   245–52
Southern Sakhalin, Southern Korea   90
sovereign wealth funds (SWFs)   12
recycling petrodollars into   307–8, 309–10*t*
special economic zones (SEZs)   43, 66
Sri Lanka   14, 158n7
    civil war   154
    coastal   155
    conflict   153
    corruption in   162
    economic crisis   170
    export orientation   166
    GDP   163n25, 167n32
    Hambantota, port of   70, 71*f*, 170
    healthcare   xii, 133
    highlands   155
    independence   159n15
    and India   157
    insurgency   160
    poverty   167
    Tamil Tigers   130n28, 160
State Bank of India   135
state capitalism   11, 49, 57, 223
state-owned assets   57
state-owned enterprises (SOEs)   4, 11, 18, 60,
        62, 135, 266, 304
    in China   43, 47, 48*f*, 51
    privatization   43, 45
Stolper-Samuelson theorem   72n75, 148n65
Sui dynasty, China   32

Sykes-Picot Agreement   281, 282*f*
Syria   274

Taiping Rebellion, China   35, 56
Taiwan   181–3
    as a dependency   90
    as a distinct economy   xiii
    importance in global electronics supply
        chain   198–9
    and Japan   90
    as an NIE   7
    SMEs in   10, 198, 199*f*, 209
Tajikistan   26
Taliban   22
Tamil Tigers   130n28, 160
Tang dynasty, China   26, 32, 34
Taoism   32
Tata Group, India   134
    Tata Consultancy Services   148
Tech Mahindra, India   148
TFP (total factor productivity) *see* total factor
        productivity (TFP)
Thailand   18, 22, 111, 174n4, 185n26, 214,
        215, 217–20, 223, 230, 232
    as Asian Tiger/Southeast Asian Tiger
        Cub   7
    compared with Singapore   224
    crisis recovery   252
    excess reliance on tourism, whether   240–
        1
    fishing industry   219
    industrialization   245, 246*f*
    rice production   218
    as Southeast Asian Tiger Cub   140
    tariff rates   249*t*
    workforce   245
Thucydides Trap   77
Tianjin, China   29
Timor Leste   214n2, 223, 225, 248, 248n43
Tokugawa Ieyasu (warlord)   85
Tokyo, Japan   84
    bombing of   90, 91*f*
    Tokyo-Yokohama, megalopolis of   82
"tortoise" economies   225
total factor productivity (TFP)   21, 92, 188
    in China   44, 45, 46, 59
    in Japan   92, 105
Toyota   98
trade unions, Sino-U.S. trade war   11–12
Trans-Pacific Partnership (TPP)   249
Trump, Donald   73, 249
Turkestan   26